UNDERSTANDING BUSINESS: ENVIRONMENTS

This book – *Understanding Business: Environments* – is one of a series of four readers which constitute the main teaching texts of the Open University course *Understanding Business Behaviour* (B200). The other titles are: *Understanding Business: Markets* edited by Vivek Suneja; *Understanding Business: Processes* edited by David Barnes; and *Understanding Business: Organisations* edited by Graeme Salaman.

This course is one of three core courses which are compulsory elements in the Open University's BA in Business Studies. In addition to the compulsory courses, students who are working toward this degree also study courses which include topics such as Economics, Organisational Change, Design and Innovation and Quantitative Methods.

The approach of *Understanding Business Behaviour* (B200) as an introductory course in Business Studies is innovative. The traditional approach employed by courses in this area is to offer introductions to the key social science disciplines: sociology, economics, law, etc. This course uses another approach: it focuses not on disciplines but on key elements of the business world: environments, markets, processes and organisations. This still allows for the discussion of relevant social science theory and research but organises this material not by the logic of academic structures and disciplines but by the logic of business applications and relevance.

As with all Open University courses, students are not only supplied with teaching texts; they also receive comprehensive guidance on how to study and work through these texts. In the case of B200, this guidance is contained in four Study Guides which are supplied to students separately. These guides explain the choice of readings, identify key points and guide the students' work and understanding. A core feature of the guides is an explicit focus on the identification, development, deployment and testing of a series of business graduate skills. These include study skills, cognitive skills of analysis and assessment, IT, and numeracy.

Each student is allocated a local tutor and is encouraged to participate in a strategically integrated set of tutorials which are held throughout the course.

Details of this and other Open University courses can be obtained from the Course Reservations Centre, PO Box 724, The Open University, Milton Keynes, MK7 6ZS, United Kingdom; tel: +44 (0) 1908 653231; e-mail: ces-gen@open.ac.uk

Alternatively, you may visit the Open University website at http://www.open.ac.uk where you can learn about the wide range of courses and packs offered at all levels by The Open University.

For information about the purchase of Open University course components, contact Open University Worldwide Ltd, The Berrill Building, Walton Hall, Milton Keynes, MK7 6AA, United Kingdom: tel.+44 (0) 1908 858785; fax: +44 (0) 1908 858787; e-mail: ouwenq@open.ac.uk; website: http://www.ouw.co.uk.

SERIES INTRODUCTION

It is hardly necessary to justify the study of business, or to over-emphasise the importance of a knowledge and understanding of business organisations and their functions, or of the environments of business. The world of business is the world in which we live and work, every aspect of which may well be on the verge of fundamental change as a result of the Internet and converging communications technologies. It affects us as consumers, workers, voters, citizens, whether of nations, unions of nations or of the world. We have to understand it. We have to understand how organisations work and their core processes. This involves an understanding of their impact on employees and consumers; how markets work (and don't work); the role and nature of business environments and how these impact on business organisations (or vice versa).

This book is one in a series of four readers which bring together classic and seminal materials, many of them summaries and reviews, which are designed to achieve the teaching objectives of the Open University course *Understanding Business Behaviour* (B200) – a core course in the Open University's BA in Business Studies. The volumes are organised in an innovative way around four key areas of the world of business: environments, markets, processes and organisations.

The volumes have been designed to supply a selection of key introductory materials in each of these areas of business applications and, with the use of appropriate study guidance, to allow the identification, development, deployment and practice of a range of skills required from Business Studies courses in general. Therefore, while they constitute the core teaching resources of this Open University course, they would also make admirable selections for any course concerned with these areas. They are not intended to be cutting edge or fashionable. They are designed as a resource for anyone seeking an understanding of the nature and development of the world of business.

Each of these volumes has been edited by an individual member of the course team. But in a very real sense they are collective products of the course team as a whole. That is why all the members of the course team deserve recognition and acknowledgement for their contribution to the course and to these collections. The course team consisted of:

David Barnes, Hannah Brunt, Rob Clifton, Mike Conboy, Martin Dowling, Gill Gowans, Carol Howells, Jacky Holloway, Bob Kelly, Mike Lucas, Alison Macmillan, Chris Marshall, Jane Matthews, Konrad Mau, Terry Morris, John O'Dwyer, John Olney, Anthea Rogers, Judy Rumbelow, Graeme Salaman, Dawn Storer, Jane Sturges, Vivek Suneja, Tricia Tierney, Richard Whipp.

Two other members of the team deserve special mention for their enormous contribution to the course as a whole and to the work of managing the course team and the processes involved in assembling and organising these collections: Chris Bollom and Georgina Marsh. To them, many thanks.

UNDERSTANDING BUSINESS: ENVIRONMENTS

Edited by
MICHAEL LUCAS
at The Open University

In association with

LONDON AND NEW YORK

First published 2000
by Routledge
11 New Fetter Lane, London EC4P 4EE

Simultaneously published in the USA and Canada
by Routledge
29 West 35th Street, New York, NY 10001
Routledge is an imprint of the Taylor & Francis Group

Typeset in Plantin and Rockwell by
Keystroke, Jacaranda Lodge, Wolverhampton
Printed and bound in Great Britain by
Bell & Bain Ltd, Glasgow

British Library Cataloguing in Publication Data
A catalogue record for this book is available from the British Library

Library of Congress Cataloging in Publication Data
Understanding business: environments / edited by Michael Lucas.
    p. cm.
    "One of a series of four readers which constitute the main teaching texts of the Open University course
    Understanding business behaviour (B200)" – Half t.p.
    Includes bibliographical references and index.
    1. Environmental economics – Great Britain. 2. Environmental economics. I. Title: Environments.
    II. Lucas, Michael, 1951–
    HC260.E5 U63 2000
    333.7'0941–dc21
                                                                 00–036592

ISBN 0–415–23859–5 (hbk)
ISBN 0–415–23860–9 (pbk)

CONTENTS

FIGURES AND DIAGRAMS

TABLES

ACKNOWLEDGEMENTS

The author and publishers would like to thank the following for granting permission to reproduce material in this work:

Blackwell Publishers Ltd, for excerpts from S. Wilks, 'Conservative Governments and the Economy' in *Political Studies*, XLV, 1997; R. J. Bennett, 'Business Routes of Influence in Brussels' in *Political Studies*, XLVII, 1999.

Jonathan Cape Ltd, for excerpts from Will Hutton, *The State We're In*. Published by Jonathan Cape, 1995.

Department for Education and Employment, for, *Pupils staying on at school for at least one extra year, and at least 2 extra years: by sex, England Wales and Scotland*; *Highest qualification level of population by age, 1985, Great Britain*; *Distribution of wealth, United Kingdom, Inland Revenue*. Crown copyright is reproduced with the permission of the Controller of Her Majesty's Stationery Office.

Harvard Business Review, for excerpts from *A Road Map for Natural Capitalism* by A.B. Lovins, L.H. Lovins and P. Hawken, May–June 1999. Copyright © 1999 by the President and Fellows of Harvard College; all rights reserved.

Professor Geert Hofstede for 'The position of 50 countries and three regions on the power-distance and uncertainty – avoidance dimensions' from G. Hofstede, *Cultures and Organisations: Intercultural Cooperation and Its Importance*. Published by McGraw Hill International (UK) Ltd, 1994.

International Thompson Publishing Services Ltd, for excerpts from Min Chen, *Asian Management Systems*, 1995.

Ivey Management Services, for excerpts from Dipak K. Rastogi, 'Living Without Borders' in *Business Quarterly*, Summer 1997, 1997. One time permission to reproduce granted by Ivey Management Services on 23 February 2000.

MCB University Press for excerpts from A.J.C. Manders and Y.S. Brenner, 'Globalisation, Production Concepts and Income Distribution' in *International Journal of Business Economics*, 1999.

National Association of Business Economics, for H. Hudson, 'Global Information Infrastructure: Eliminating the Distance Barrier' in *Business Economics*, April 1998.

Office for National Statistics, for excerpts from 'Trends in the Economy', Guy Routh, *Occupation and Pay in Great Britain*, Cambridge University Press, 1965; 'Women's Activity Rates', 'Employment in Manufacturing and Services 1971–1989', 'Sectoral Employment of Men and Women in 1989 including the Self-Employed', *Social Trends 21* © Crown copyright 1991; *Expenditure Survey* © Crown copyright; 'Trends in the Family' *British Labour Statistics Historical Abstract* © Crown copyright; 'Women's Activity Rates' data for 1997, *Labour Force Survey* © Crown copyright, 1997; A.H. Halsey, 'Social Trends Since World War II', *Social Trends 17* © Crown copyright, 1999.

The Open University, for 'Identifying Environmental Issues' and 'Cultural Differences in Attitudes and Values' from R. Armson, J. Martin, S. Carr, R. Spear and A. Walsh, *Interorganisational Relations*. Copyright © 1990 The Open University; D. Coates, 'The Management of the Economy', and 'A Marxist Reading of the UK Economy and its Management' in *Work, Markets and the Economy*. Copyright © 1993 The Open University; S. Hall, 'The Structure of Society' in *Social Structures and Divisions*. Copyright © The Open University; H. McKay, N. Heap and R. Thomas, 'Daniel Bell and the Information Society' in *Differing Perspectives* © 1997 The Open University.

Oxford University Press, for G. Lehmbruch, 'A Cumulative Scale of Corporatism' in J. Goldthorpe, *Order and Conflict in Contemporary Capitalism*. Published by Clarendon Press, 1984. Reprinted by permission of Oxford University Press.

Perseus Books Group, for table from D. Bell, *The Coming of Post Industrial Society*. Published by Basic Books, New York, 1973.

Polity Press, for excerpts from H. Bradley, 'Changing Social Divisions' in R. Bocock and K. Thompson, *Social and Cultural Forms of Modernity*, 1992; P. Braham , 'A New International Division of Labour', A. McGrew, 'Putting the Advanced Capitalist State in Perspective', A. McGrew, 'Globalisation and the Advanced Capitalist State' in J. Allen, P. Braham and P. Lewis, *Political Forms of Modernity*, 1992.

Prentice Hall Inc, for 'Mintzberg's Cast of Players: or framing organization physiognomy' from A. Mintzburg, *Power in and Around Organisations*, 1983.

Taylor & Francis Ltd, for excerpts from Sonja Boehmer-Christiansen, 'Reflections of the Politics Linking Science, Environment and Innovation' in *Innovation: The European Journal of Social Sciences* 8(3), 1995. Reproduced by permission of Taylor and Francis Ltd, PO Box 25, Abingdon, Oxfordshire, OX14 3UE; for figure illustrating structure of Welfare Capitalism from C. Offe and J. Keane, *Contradictions of the Welfare State*.

John Wiley & Sons Inc, for excerpts from R.L. Ackoff, *Creating the Corporate Future*, 1995. Adapted by permission of John Wiley & Sons Inc.

INTRODUCTION: THE CONCEPT OF THE BUSINESS ENVIRONMENT

The aim of this book is to provide a framework for understanding what business decision-makers, academics and educationalists have come to call the 'environment'. Everyday use of this word is loaded with images like the idyllic countryside, 'green' product labelling, 'eco-warriors' and many others linked to the ongoing debate about the treatment of our 'natural' environment. This book is not about that debate because in terms of the study of business 'environment' is a more all-embracing term. In a sense anything external to a business – in the 'outside' world – may be thought of as part of the environment. As a subject of study, business environment is a notoriously ill-defined and messy amalgam of topics and issues which normally forms part of the introductory element of a business studies course. It is essentially rooted in the study of the academic disciplines often referred to as the social sciences – namely economics, sociology, politics and law – without allowing students to delve into them in detail. More often than not it ends up as either an unconnected collection of theories from each of these disciplines or a current (or not so current!) affairs scrapbook. It is intended to provide a backdrop against which the 'real' subjects of business organisations and activities are taught. However, a thorough grounding in how to analyse the environment could offer great insights into other more developed areas of business studies, most notably decision-making, strategy and business ethics. This collection is my attempt to provide that grounding.

Very few of the writers whose work I have included here would consider themselves to have been writing *for* business. The bulk of them are dispassionate 'observers' – journalists, academics and educationalists – of their 'environments' with no particular interest in peddling management solutions or pet theories of management. Their interest stems from their role as a 'stakeholder' in an environment which they observe. What is common to them all is that they are writing *about* business. They all address, very often indirectly, the question of how businesses interact with their environments. Some may emphasise how businesses are influenced by their environment, while others examine how they shape the environment.

The collection is organised into five sections. The introductory section consists of three pieces about the meaning of the business environment. The other four sections deal with the four 'environments' commonly referred to in business – the economy, society, the state and the system. The material in each of these sections is principally an examination of the methods used by economists, sociologists, political scientists and technologists to analyse the role of businesses in each of these environments. In doing so it will also lead you to explore the foundations of the current debates about the phenomenon of globalisation and its relationship to business behaviour. From the outset, however, I am also going to encourage you to consider the importance of values in interpreting and analysing the business world. In each of the sections a number of articles illustrate differing perspectives on the same issues – economic performance, social inequality, the power of businesses in relation to nations, the physical environment and, of course, globalisation. These perspectives reflect differences in the values held by the writers in question. What I hope emerges is a broad template for making sense of the business–environment relationship, which any stakeholder may use or adapt.

It is important for business decision-makers not only to be aware of events in the outside world, but to adopt and use some techniques for organising their thoughts on the implications of these events for their business. They need to establish how to respond to events and how they might influence them. They need also to recognise that many events do not happen randomly. They may be connected to other events via broader phenomena such as that dealt with in our opening chapter by Giddens – what he terms 'globalisation'. We will return to this phenomenon at various points throughout the book to examine economic, political and technological perspectives on it. For now though Giddens offers us his definition of globalisation as an overwhelming cultural phenomenon which provides both driving force and direction to most of the changes we are observing in the contemporary world. The role of businesses in this theory is as a processor through which the dominant images of globalisation become reality in their products and practices. The point he is making indirectly is that a growing belief that globalisation is happening is making it happen via business responses to it in a sort of perpetual circle.

Accepting Giddens' theory without question leads us into two traps. The first is what we might call the 'inevitability' trap. This centres around the belief that it is all happening around us and all we can do is adapt to it. It may seem natural to do this, but in business terms it narrows the range of actions open to decision-makers. Rather than accepting his explanation we should perhaps be questioning it. The first stage of this questioning involves analysing the thing which is subject to this globalisation phenomenon, i.e. the world (or as we have called it, the environment); and also by analysing the phenomenon itself. This should allow us to see a broader range of options for our business. In chapter 2 by Armson *et al.*, the authors provide us with a starting point, by offering a range of models of the environment. These models are simply different interpretations of the same world. Some of them emphasise the flow of resources around the environment (like the transformation model), others emphasise the people in it (like Mintzberg's stakeholder model or 'physiognomy'), while still others see the environment as principally defined by its structure (like the STEP analysis model). The main point here is that different people view the world differently and business decision-makers need to maintain a breadth of vision.

The second trap we may refer to as the 'values' trap. Giddens' explanations are reasonable and might reflect aspects of what we ourselves experience or think about the world. As such they are very persuasive. He does admit, however, that there is another school of thought which disputes the whole phenomenon of globalisation – he refers to its members as the 'sceptics'. Here, however, he is over-simplifying the picture. There are many strands of thinking on the issue of globalisation reflecting a variety of different values amongst writers on the subject. The roots of this diversity are explained in chapter 3 by Coates. Coates outlines the dominant 'traditions of thought' which developed in the study of economy and society during the eighteenth, nineteenth and twentieth centuries. As Coates states, these traditions are evolving and undergoing considerable renegotiation and fragmentation, but again they offer us another starting point from which to identify values held by writers in the four main environments which we will now go on to examine.

To recap then, the three articles in this section offer some useful insights into business environments and their analysis. First, an environment basically consists of collections of events and phenomena which we observe. If we are to analyse these events or phenomena we need to have a clear idea of what they mean. Giddens' article is about the meaning of the phenomenon called 'globalisation'. Second, we could then construct models of the environment. These models, like the ones in the article by Armson *et al.*, give us some idea of the shape of the environment. We could then manipulate the models to look at how the environment is affected by events and phenomena. Third, we must recognise the values inherent in any piece of writing or information about an environment. What type of thinking is reflected in the writer's views and why are they writing it? Coates' article examines some of the established ways of thinking which have influenced people's values over a significant period of time. These tools of definition, modelling and evaluation of views may, I hope, prove useful to you in examining each of the environments in the later sections of this book and in all your studies of business and its behaviour.

1

GLOBALISATION

Anthony Giddens

A friend of mine studies village life in central Africa. A few years ago, she paid her first visit to a remote area where she was to carry out her fieldwork. The evening she got there, she was invited to a local home for an evening's entertainment. She expected to find out about the traditional pastimes of this isolated community. Instead, the evening turned out to be a viewing of *Basic Instinct* on video. The film at that point hadn't even reached the cinemas in London.

Such vignettes reveal something about our world. And what they reveal isn't trivial. It isn't just a matter of people adding modern paraphernalia – videos, TVs, personal computers and so forth – to their traditional ways of life. We live in a world of transformations, affecting almost every aspect of what we do. For better or worse, we are being propelled into a global order that no one fully understands, but which is making its effects felt upon all of us.

Globalisation is the main theme of this lecture,[1] and of the lectures as a whole. The term may not be – it isn't – a particularly attractive or elegant one. But absolutely no-one who wants to understand our prospects and possibilities at the century's end can ignore it. I travel a lot to speak abroad. I haven't been to a single country recently where globalisation isn't being intensively discussed. In France, the word is mondialisation. In Spain and Latin America, it is globalization. The Germans say globalisierung.

The global spread of the term is evidence of the very developments to which it refers. Every business guru talks about it. No political speech is complete without reference to it. Yet as little as 10 years ago the term was hardly used, either in the academic literature or in everyday language. It has come from nowhere to be almost everywhere. Given its sudden popularity, we shouldn't be surprised that the meaning of the notion isn't always clear, or that an intellectual reaction has set in against it. Globalisation has something to do with the thesis that we now all live in one world – but in what ways exactly, and is the idea really valid?

Different thinkers have taken almost completely opposite views about globalisation in debates that have sprung up over the past few years. Some dispute the whole thing. I'll call them the sceptics. According to the sceptics, all the talk about globalisation is only that – just talk. Whatever its benefits, its trials and tribulations, the global economy isn't especially different from that which existed at previous periods. The world carries on much the same as it has done for many years.

Most countries, the sceptics argue, only gain a small amount of their income from external trade. Moreover, a good deal of economic exchange is between regions, rather than being truly world-wide. The countries of the European Union, for example, mostly trade among themselves. The same is true of the other main trading blocs, such as those of the Asia Pacific or North America.

Others, however, take a very different position. I'll label them the radicals. The radicals argue that not only is globalisation very real, but that its consequences can be felt everywhere. The global marketplace, they say, is much more developed than even two or three decades ago, and is indifferent to national borders. Nations have lost most of the sovereignty they once had, and politicians have lost most of their capability to influence events. It isn't surprising that no one respects political leaders any more, or has much interest in what they have to say. The era of the nation state is over. Nations, as the Japanese business writer Keniche Ohmae puts it, have become mere 'fictions'. Authors like Ohmae see the economic difficulties of last year and this as demonstrating the reality of globalisation, albeit seen from its disruptive side.

The sceptics tend to be on the political left, especially the old left. For if all of this is essentially a myth, governments can still intervene in economic life and the welfare state remains intact. The notion of globalisation, according to the sceptics, is an ideology put about by free-marketeers who wish to dismantle welfare systems and cut back on state expenditures. What has happened is at most a reversion to how the world was a century ago. In the late 19th century there was already an open global economy, with a great deal of trade, including trade in currencies.

Well, who is right in this debate? I think it is the radicals. The level of world trade today is much higher than it ever was before, and involves a much wider range of goods and services. But the biggest difference is in the level of finance and capital flows. Geared as it is to electronic money – money that exists only as digits in computers – the current world economy has no parallels in earlier times. In the new global electronic economy, fund managers, banks, corporations, as well as millions of individual investors, can transfer vast amounts of capital from one side of the world to another at the click of a mouse. As they do so, they can destabilise what might have seemed rock-solid economies – as happened in East Asia.

The volume of world financial transactions is usually measured in US dollars. A million dollars is a lot of money for most people. Measured as a stack of thousand dollar notes, it would be eight inches high. A billion dollars – in other words, a million million – would be over 120 miles high, 20 times higher than Mount Everest.

Yet far more than a trillion dollars is now turned over each day on global currency markets, a massive increase from only 10 years ago, let alone the more distant past. The value of whatever money we may have in our pockets, or our bank accounts, shifts from moment to moment according to fluctuations in such markets. I would have no hesitation, therefore, in saying that globalisation, as we are experiencing it, is in many respects not only new, but revolutionary.

However, I don't believe either the sceptics or the radicals have properly understood either what it is or its implications for us. Both groups see the phenomenon almost solely in economic terms. This is a mistake. Globalisation is political, technological and cultural, as well as economic. It has been influenced above all by developments in systems of communication, dating back only to the late 1960s.

In the mid-19th century, a Massachusetts portrait painter, Samuel Morse, transmitted the first message, "What hath god wrought?", by electric telegraph. In so doing, he initiated a new phase in world history. Never before could a message be sent without someone going somewhere to carry it. Yet the advent of satellite communications marks every bit as dramatic a break with the past. The first communications satellite was launched only just over 30 years ago. Now there are more than 200 such satellites above the earth, each carrying a vast range of information. For the first time ever, instantaneous communication is possible from one side of the world to the other. Other types of electronic communication, more and more integrated with satellite transmission, have also accelerated over the past few years. No dedicated transatlantic or transpacific cables existed at all until the late 1950s. The first held less than 100 voice paths. Those of today carry more than a million.

On the first of February 1999, about 150 years after Morse invented his system of dots and dashes, Morse code finally disappeared from the world stage, discontinued as a means of communication for the sea. In its place has come a system using satellite technology, whereby any ship in distress can be pinpointed immediately. Most countries prepared for the transition some while before. The French, for example, stopped using Morse as a distress code in their local waters two years ago, signing off with a Gallic flourish: 'Calling all. This is our last cry before our external silence'.

Instantaneous electronic communication isn't just a way in which news or information is conveyed more quickly. Its existence alters the very texture of our lives, rich and poor alike. When the image of Nelson Mandela, may be, is more familiar to us than the face of our next door neighbour, something has changed in the nature of our everyday experience.

Nelson Mandela is a global celebrity, and celebrity itself is largely a product of new communications technology. The reach of media technologies is growing with each wave of innovation. It took 40 years for radio in the United States to gain an audience of 50 million. The same number were using personal computers only 15 years after the PC was introduced. It needed a mere four years, after it was made available for 50 million Americans to be regularly using the Internet.

It is wrong to think of globalisation as just concerning the big systems, like the world financial order. Globalisation isn't only about what is 'out there', remote and far away from the individual. It is an 'in here' phenomenon too, influencing intimate and personal aspects of our lives. The debate about family values, for example, that is going on in many countries, might seem far removed from globalising influences. It isn't. Traditional family systems are becoming transformed, or are under strain, in many parts of the world, particularly as women stake claim to greater equality. There has never before been a society, so far as we know from the historical record, in which women have been even approximately equal to men. This is a truly global revolution in everyday life, whose consequences are being felt around the world in spheres from work to politics.

Globalisation thus is a complex set of processes, not a single one. And these operate in a contradictory or oppositional fashion. Most people think of it as simply 'pulling away' power or influence from local communities and nations into the global arena. And indeed this is one of its consequences. Nations do lose some of the economic power they once had. However, it also has an opposite effect. Globalisation not only pulls upwards, it pushes downwards, creating new pressures for local autonomy. The American sociologist Daniel Bell expresses this very well when he says that the nation becomes too small to solve the big problems, but also too large to solve the small ones.

Globalisation is the reason for the revival of local cultural identities in different parts of the world. If one asks, for example, why the Scots want more independence in the UK, or why there is a strong separatist movement in Quebec, the answer is not to be found only in their cultural history. Local nationalisms spring up as a response to globalising tendencies, as the hold of older nation-states weakens.

Globalisation also squeezes sideways. It creates new economic and cultural zones within and across nations. Examples are the Hong Kong region, northern Italy, or Silicon Valley in California. The area around Barcelona in northern Spain extends over into France. Catalonia, where Barcelona is located, is closely integrated into the European Union. It is part of Spain, yet also looks outwards.

The changes are being propelled by a range of factors, some structural, others more specific and historical. Economic influences are certainly among the driving forces, especially the global financial system. Yet they aren't like forces of nature. They have been shaped by technology, and cultural diffusion, as well as by the decisions of governments to liberalise and deregulate their national economies.

The collapse of soviet communism has added further weight to such developments, since no significant group of countries any longer stands outside. That collapse wasn't just something that happened to occur. Globalisation explains both why and how Soviet communism met its end. The Soviet Union and the East European countries were comparable to the West in terms of growth rates until somewhere around the early 1970s. After that point, they fell rapidly behind. Soviet communism, with its emphasis upon state-run enterprise and heavy industry, could not compete in the global electronic economy. The ideological and cultural control upon which communist political authority was based similarly could not survive in an era of global media.

The Soviet and the East European regimes were unable to prevent the reception of western radio and TV broadcasts. Television played a direct role in the 1989 revolutions, which have rightly been called the first "television revolutions". Street protests taking place in one country were watched by the audiences in others, large numbers of whom then took to the streets themselves.

Globalisation, of course, isn't developing in an even-handed way, and is by no means wholly benign in its consequences. To many living outside Europe and North America, it looks uncomfortably like Westernisation – or, perhaps, Americanisation, since the US is now the sole superpower, with a dominant economic, cultural and military position in the global order. Many of the most visible cultural expressions of globalisation are American – Coca-Cola, McDonalds.

Most of giant multinational companies are based in the US too. Those that aren't all come from the rich countries, not the poorer areas of the world. A pessimistic view of globalisation would consider it largely an affair of the industrial North, in which the developing societies of the south play little or no active part. It would see it as destroying local cultures, widening world inequalities and worsening the lot of the impoverished. Globalisation, some argue, creates a world of winners and losers, a few on the fast track to prosperity, the majority condemned to a life of misery and despair.

And indeed the statistics are daunting. The share of the poorest fifth of the world's population in global income has dropped from 2.3% to 1.4% over the past 10 years. The proportion taken by the richest fifth, on the other hand, has risen from 70% to 85%. In Sub-Saharan Africa, 20 countries have lower incomes per head in real terms than they did two decades ago. In many less developed countries, safety and environmental regulations are low or virtually non-existent. Some trans-national companies sell goods there that are controlled or banned in the industrial countries – poor quality medical drugs, destructive pesticides or high tar and nicotine content cigarettes. As one writer put it recently, rather than a global village, this is more like global pillage.

Along with ecological risk, to which it is related, expanding inequality is the most serious problem facing world society. It will not do, however, merely to blame it on the wealthy. It is fundamental to my argument that globalisation today is only partly Westernisation. Of course the western nations, and more generally the industrial countries, still have far more influence over world affairs than do the poorer states. But globalisation is becoming increasingly de-centred – not under the control of any group of nations, and still less of the large corporations. Its effects are felt just as much in the western countries as elsewhere.

This is true of the global financial system, communications and media, and of changes affecting the nature of government itself. Examples of 'reverse colonisation' are becoming more and more common. Reverse colonisation means that non-western countries influence developments in the West. Examples abound – such as the Latinising of Los Angeles, the emergence of a globally-oriented high-tech sector in India, or the selling of Brazilian TV programmes to Portugal.

Is globalisation a force promoting the general good? The question can't be answered in a simple way, given the complexity of the phenomenon. People who ask it, and who blame globalisation for deepening world inequalities, usually have in mind economic globalisation, and within that, free trade. Now it is surely obvious that free trade is not an unalloyed benefit. This is especially so as concerns the less developed countries. Opening up a country, or regions within it, to free trade can undermine a local subsistence economy. An area that becomes dependent upon a few products sold on world markets is very vulnerable to shifts in prices as well as to technological change.

Trade always needs a framework of institutions, as do other forms of economic development. Markets cannot be created by purely economic means, and how far a given economy should be exposed to the world marketplace must depend upon a range of criteria. Yet to oppose economic globalisation, and to opt for economic protectionism, would be a misplaced tactic for rich and poor nations alike. Protectionism may be a necessary strategy at some times and in some countries. In my view, for example, Malaysia was correct to introduce controls in 1998, to stem the flood of capital from the country. But more permanent forms of protectionism will not help the development of the poor countries, and among the rich would lead to warring trade blocs.

The debates about globalisation I mentioned at the beginning have concentrated mainly upon its implications for the nation-state. Are nation-states, and hence national political leaders, still powerful, or are they becoming largely irrelevant to the forces shaping the world? Nation-states are indeed still powerful and political leaders have a large role to play in the world. Yet at the same time the nation-state is being reshaped before our eyes. National economic policy can't be as effective as it once was. More importantly, nations have to rethink their identities now the older forms of geopolitics are becoming obsolete. Although this is a contentious point, I would say that, following the dissolving of the cold war, nations no longer have enemies. Who are the enemies of Britain, or France, or Japan? Nations today face risks and dangers rather than enemies, a massive shift in their very nature.

It isn't only of the nation that such comments could be made. Everywhere we look, we see institutions that appear the same as they used to be from the outside, and carry the same names, but inside have become quite different. We continue to talk of the nation, the family, work, tradition, nature, as if they were all the same as in the past. They are not. The outer shell remains, but inside all is different – and this is happening not only in the US, Britain, or France, but almost everywhere. They are what I call shell institutions, and I shall talk about them quite a bit in the lectures to come. They are institutions that have become inadequate to the tasks they are called upon to perform.

As the changes I have described in this lecture gather weight, they are creating something that has never existed before, a global cosmopolitan society. We are the first generation to live in this society, whose contours we can as yet only dimly see. It is shaking up our existing ways of life, no matter where we happen to be. This is not – at least at the moment – a global order driven by collective human will. Instead, it is emerging in an anarchic, haphazard, fashion, carried along by a mixture of economic, technological and cultural imperatives.

It is not settled or secure, but fraught with anxieties, as well as scarred by deep divisions. Many of us feel in the grip of forces over which we have no control. Can we re-impose our will upon them? I believe we can. The powerlessness we experience is not a sign of personal failings, but reflects the incapacities of our institutions. We need to reconstruct those we have, or create new ones, in ways appropriate to the global age.

We should and we can look to achieve greater control over our runaway world. We shan't be able to do so if we shirk the challenges, or pretend that all can go on as before. For globalisation is not incidental to our lives today. It is a shift in our very life circumstances. It is the way we now live.

NOTE

* This chapter is a transcript of Professor Giddens' BBC Reith lecture, broadcast on 7 April 1999

2

IDENTIFYING ENVIRONMENTAL ISSUES*

Rosalind Armson, John Martin, Susan Carr, Roger Spear and Tony Walsh

ENVIRONMENTAL INTERACTIONS

If an organization or system were described as 'closed' it would mean that there were no interactions across its boundaries. It is not easy to think of an example of such an organization but by scratching my head very hard I came up with the idea of a group of people lost in space. Their well-equipped space station allows them to grow their own food, they recycle all their waste to produce the materials they need. They are out of contact with any civilization and too far from any star to draw energy from its light. They have their own on-board energy supply. No 'real' organization is truly closed. Sadly, the laws of thermodynamics mean their self-sufficient voyage is doomed; their energy source will eventually need renewal. For all intents and purposes, *virtually all organizations can be considered open*, with continual (and usually extensive) exchanges across their boundaries. Organizations exchange people, energy, information, expertise, equipment, money, goods and services with their environments. One can view an organization as a *transformation process*, transforming inputs into outputs. For example, a school can be viewed as an organization to take raw pupils and transform them into socialized, educated and useful members of society. One could formulate different views of the education process, such as a process to equip people to lead a fulfilling life, but the main point I want to make is that exchanges across an organization's boundary are essential for the organization to exist and achieve its purposes. In this section we look in more detail at how the environment influences an organization and its transformation process.

IDENTIFYING ENVIRONMENTAL ISSUES

Because the environment is so complex and is not 'contained' in organizational structures, it is very easy to oversimplify your perception of it, like a person in a forest who just sees 'lots of trees' and has no sense of its biological richness. This section offers several simple methods to open up your perception of a system's environment.

The STEP checklist

This uses the *STEP* (Social, Technological, Economic, Political) checklist shown in Table 2.1.

The advantage of the STEP framework is its simplicity and wide applicability. In this context, I am suggesting that you use it simply to think about current and continuing influences on the organization, though it is often used also for looking at future changes.

To use it, you work your way through the STEP list, brainstorming as many possible factors in each category as you can think of that might conceivably be relevant to the chosen system – every possible social factor, every possible political factor, etc.

Though you can attempt a limited brainstorming on your own (particularly if you come back to it again and again over a period of days) you will probably generate more ideas if you can do it with others.

When working in a group, you will probably get more ideas if you ask each person to first list all their ideas *privately*. When their private flow has more or less dried up, you then pool the ideas publicly, preferably by using a round robin in which you go round and round the group, asking each person to contribute one idea only in turn; someone lists each idea on a blackboard as it is offered so that everyone can see all the ideas proposed. Once most of the privately generated ideas are up, you can merge gradually into free-for-all brainstorming.

Table 2.1 The STEP checklist and an example

The STEP headings	Typical STEP sub-categories	Example for a corner grocery shop in a suburb of a medium-sized town
Social factors	Demographics, values, lifestyle, age structure of population, class and income-structure of local population	Catchment area, number and type of people living nearby, number of families, age groups, migration from and to the area, trends in buying patterns, car ownership, etc.
Technological factors	Equipment available, technologies, products	Availability of shop-display equipment, electronic communications possibilities for advertising, new check-out equipment, (e.g. bar-code systems and automated stock control), ordering and stock control systems/technologies.
Economic factors	Economic growth, inflation, market trends, local economic and market circumstances	Number of potential suppliers, their terms and prices, pricing strategies, advertising possibilities, purchasing quantities, information about customer demand, competitors, competitor strategies, 'out of town' shopping patterns, national economic environment etc.
Political factors	Legislation, regulations, policies, likely developments	Sunday-opening legislation, car boot sale legislation, regulations on opening hours, Shops and Offices Act, planning restrictions, etc.

The transformation model

The STEP list was a general-purpose one. A simple way to generate a checklist that is specific to your system is to use the idea (mentioned at the start of this chapter) that the organization is a *transformation process*.

First draw your system using an input–output diagram that shows your system as a set of *processes* that transform a range of *inputs* into a range of *outputs*. For instance, Figure 2.1.

Try to make the items on your diagram concrete enough to be informative; a diagram that includes the output: '300–400 tons per year of scrap steel' is likely to be more informative than one that just includes the output: 'waste metal'. A well-constructed input–output diagram should be a simple, compact and informative way of answering the question: 'what do we do?'.

If well constructed, such a diagram also offers you a checklist of keywords around which you can begin to brainstorm (exactly as you did for the STEP list) possible environmental factors that could affect these inputs, transformations and outputs. [. . .]

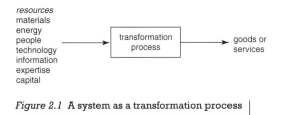

Figure 2.1 A system as a transformation process

Mintzberg's 'physiognomy'

Physiognomy is the art of judging someone's character from their face and palmistry is the art of reading the lines in your hand! I don't expect you to believe in either of these, but Figure 2.2 is Mintzberg's rather more serious attempt to produce a generalized picture of the 'cast of players' in and around any organization. The 'character' of the organization is very much determined by the varying natures of these various groups of players. Mintzberg's diagram shows a clown-like face that you can remember easily but it is really very much like a generalized systems map.

Mintzberg takes a power perspective, arguing that coalitions may be formed between external groups, and also between internal and external groups, so that when major decisions are being made, it is these coalitions that are likely to form the power groups representing different interests.

This 'cast list' and the possible coalitions that could arise can once again be used as a checklist around which you can enquire and brainstorm in order to enrich your perception of your environment. You could then use the results of this to draw an influence diagram, showing the cast members and the coalition links between them.

The players immediately outside the organization are the owners and employee associations. *Owners* may be closely involved with management, for example, if the organization is a family firm; or they may be rather distant, as in the case of most shareholders. Slightly more distant from the core are associates; suppliers, clients, partners and competitors. *Employee associations* are representative bodies. The most obvious employee associations are trades unions but professional associations are also important, along with occupational institutions, company unions, and staff associations. Such staff

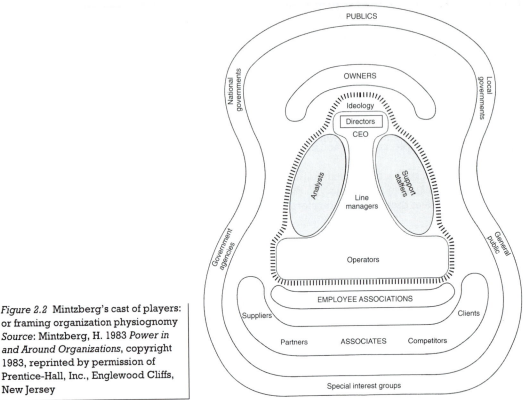

Figure 2.2 Mintzberg's cast of players:
or framing organization physiognomy
Source: Mintzberg, H. 1983 *Power in
and Around Organizations*, copyright
1983, reprinted by permission of
Prentice-Hall, Inc., Englewood Cliffs,
New Jersey

associations are usually within the organization although they may be allied to staff associations in related organizations.

Associates include groups which the organization depends on for resources or vice versa.
Their activities influence the strategy of the organization, and the scope for cooperation and
competition.

Finally, Mintzberg uses the term *publics* to refer to the State with its regulatory bodies;
special interest groups (e.g. environmental groups); community bodies and the general
public.

Economic sector analysis

A final approach to analysing the environment is to draw on economists' concepts of sectors
and markets. Economists group economic activity according to *sectors*. All the organizations
in a particular sector produce similar products or services, and tend to be affected by similar
influences. For instance the competitiveness within the sector, the rate it is growing, the
dominant effects of particular large companies, etc. will tend to affect all organizations in
the sector in much the same way, but may well have rather little effect on organizations in
another sector – cut-throat competition in the computer sector is unlikely have a big effect
on the clothing sector.

So another useful way to explore an organization's *environment* is to identify its sector,
identify some other organizations in the same sector, and try to see what is distinctive about
organizations in this sector and how they relate to one another.

Remember, of course, that phrases like 'rapid growth' or 'stable markets' applied to a sector are really shorthand for quite specific measures – e.g. 'rapid growth in production of products of type X', not 'rapid growth in everything'! Indeed you might find that while production capacity was rising, number of employees was stable, cost per unit was falling and level of borrowing was cyclical!

NOTE

*   This chapter has been adapted from, The Open University (1995) T245 *Managing in Organizations*, Block 4 *Interorganizational Relations*, Unit 13 'Environmental Influences', Milton Keynes, The Open University.

3

THE TRADITIONS OF THOUGHT IN THE STUDY OF ECONOMY AND SOCIETY[1]

David Coates

We are concerned here with four traditions of thought, each of which is built around a particular set of assumptions, concerns and categories, and each of which addresses a series of important social questions. The traditions chosen tap real divisions between social scientists both now and in the past. They constitute an important set of alternative frameworks with which to make sense of the contemporary world. They are not the only packages of ideas available to us. Much creative thought goes on outside the traditions as specified here, and the dividing lines between them are now under review. Traditions of thought need to be distinguished from the political ideologies that share their names. All traditions of thought are workings out of basic assumptions about human nature and human knowledge.

LIBERALISM

As a fully-fledged way of reading the nature of contemporary society, liberalism emerged out of the vast changes that occurred in Western Europe and North America in the three centuries before 1800. In the sphere of *economic* life, the rise of commerce and the spread of wage labour in the leading economies of Western Europe slowly replaced feudalism with first mercantile and agrarian, and later industrial capitalism. In the sphere of *politics*, the three centuries saw the consolidation of the European system of nation-states, with their recurrent internal battles between absolutist and representative systems of government. *Culturally*, the three centuries witnessed the erosion of the Catholic domination of late medieval Europe by intellectual forces released by the twin initiatives of *Renaissance* and *Reformation*. Liberalism indeed turned out to be among the most potent of those cultural challenges, fuelled as it was by its relevance to the political battles against absolutism and to the economic transformations associated with the rise of capitalism.

- Liberal thinkers made a sharp break with previous modes of thought by taking as their starting point the existence of self-interested individuals.

- Early liberal thinkers disagreed about the degree of human sociability, and about the role of intuition and reason in the formation of individual action: but they shared a common view of society as composed of individuals in the pursuit of their own ends.
- Liberal thought specified individuals as free and equal, and judged the acceptability of political systems by the degree to which states respected and enhanced individual liberty. Liberal thought divided the world into private and public spheres, and privileged the private, linking its understanding of freedom to that of privacy.
- Liberal commitments to representative government did not make early liberal thinkers democrats; and even today, some liberal thinkers are uneasy about the tendency of democratic government to 'over-govern'.
- Early liberal thought equated 'the individual' with 'the male', and either denied, ignored or played-down the rights and freedoms of women.

Economy and society

By the end of the eighteenth century, liberal thinkers were beginning to forge a powerful theory of economic behaviour which enabled them to explain and defend the developments of first mercantile and agrarian, and later industrial capitalism. Again the tight logic of liberal thought was well in evidence, as now economic life, rather than politics, was subjected to an analysis based on the premise of rational individuals in the pursuit of their self-interest. If all that we can know is ourselves as individuals, then what we have as individuals gathers particular significance. The amount of our property becomes a basic measure of how well we as individuals are achieving our individual goals. According to this view, mechanisms which facilitate the growth of our property become vital tools for the enhancement of liberty as a whole. By the time Adam Smith was formulating his arguments in *The Wealth of Nations*, liberal thinkers were confident that the *market* was such a mechanism: that the producing and selling of commodities through individual enterprise would enrich the society in total. Smith himself had an ambiguous attitude to the new society he saw emerging around him, being personally unenthusiastic about the manufacturing and merchant classes who would soon adopt a bowdlerized version of his theory as their own. Yet none the less it was his view that when, in a market economy, an individual seeks.

> his own advantage . . . and not that of the society . . . he is, in this as in many other cases, led by an invisible hand to promote an end which was no part of his intention. Nor is it always the worse for the society that it was not part of it. By pursuing his own interest he frequently promotes that of the society more effectively than when he really intends to promote it.
>
> (Smith, 1776, Book 4, Chapter 2)

Adam Smith was an early figure in liberal political economy. When he was writing in the 1770s, industrial development had hardly begun, the bulk of the population still worked in agriculture, and it was trade, rather than industry, that attracted much capitalist enterprise. But in the decades after 1780, as an industrial capitalist economy emerged, a whole body of what became known as political economy was developed to explain its inner workings. The economic world described by these nineteenth century economists was quintessentially liberal. It was made up of individuals acting rationally in the pursuit of their self-interest. It was a world of people making and selling things, and of people driven to do so only through their own ambition for personal success. It was a world whose perpetual motion required no central direction, since its dynamism derived from 'the spontaneity of the independent mind and the power of the liberated will' (Manning, 1976, p.16). To the liberal mind, the overriding strength and moral appeal of the emerging capitalist economy lay in just this spontaneity. Its market order was what a much more recent liberal (F.A. Hayek) was to call a *catallaxy* – 'a network of many economies, firms, households etc. . . . not a deliberately made organization but . . . a product of spontaneous growth' which 'because it has no common purpose of its own, enables great variety of individual purposes to be fulfilled' (Barry, 1979, p.45).

For liberal thought, the self-interest of these individual purposes was all to the good. It was to be encouraged. The only question was how all those personal ambitions were to be co-ordinated: and, more to the point, how were they to be co-ordinated in a way which would bring the maximum benefit to all. Preliberal thought might have given that task to the Church or the State. But for liberals neither was necessary for this purpose, and indeed each would only make matters worse. For they believed that the free and undisturbed play of market forces could normally act as *the invisible hand*, efficiently and effectively co-ordinating the activities of free individuals in ways which advanced the interests of all. The interplay of supply and demand, the uninterrupted movement of prices and goods, would – in this view – enhance the wealth of nations and underpin the freedom of the producing and consuming individuals of this new world of trade and industry. All that was left for the state to do was to hold the ring: provide external defence and internal order, and supplement private endeavours with certain public institutions that private profit alone could not sustain (the main example of this, for Adam Smith, was publicly-funded education). To do more would be to *interfere*: (and indeed this notion of state 'interference' shows how strongly liberal thought was prepared to privilege the individual and the private over the collective and the public). A 'free market' and a 'strong but restrained state' became liberalism's vision of an ideal economic and political world.

This view of market forces also gave liberal political economists a way of explaining world trade. According to **David Ricardo,**[2] economies specialize under the logic of market competition in that for which they are best equipped – in the production of those commodities for which they have a comparative advantage. By specializing in this way, they both enhance the productivity of their own economy and further the growth of wealth in the world economy as a whole. Individual economies, like individuals within economies, best guarantee the interests of everyone by simply looking after themselves. On a liberal view of the world, *competition* between nations, just like competition between individuals, is the key to prosperity for everyone.

Smith and Ricardo were highly representative figures of an entire school of liberal political economy which came to public prominence in the United Kingdom in the decades after 1800. Nineteenth century liberal economists saw a new world of trade and industry emerging, and were conscious of its immense potentiality. Their view of this world had a powerful optimism written into it: optimism about the rationality of individuals and their basic ability to get on with their own lives in ways which benefited everyone; optimism that history was the story of wealth creation and cultural progress if people were free to run their own lives; and optimism that markets were the great clearers and co-ordinators of economic life. By 1820 at the latest their moral vision of an ideal liberal universe was in place. In an ideal liberal world, individuals would be free – free from political constraint, free from monopolies, free to act alone, to produce independently and to trade without barriers, and free to enhance the common good by the unbridled pursuit of their own self-interest. By 1820 the notion of individual freedom and capitalist enterprise were fused in a liberal vision that reinforced the confidence of a rising industrial and commercial class. It was a vision, moreover, which rose to public prominence as that class rose to political power. As Keynes said, 'Ricardo's doctrine conquered England as completely as the Holy Inquisition conquered Spain' (Keynes, 1936, p.32); so that by the third quarter of the nineteenth century the tradition we have just examined was to all intents and purposes the 'conventional wisdom' of an entire society.

For this reason, even when challenged later, this tradition left behind powerful residues of its early dominance. Even today major intellectuals – of whom Hayek is one of the better known – continue to argue for the supremacy of markets as economic allocators and for the freedom of individuals to act in their own self-interest without state intervention. Indeed Hayek was instrumental in creating in 1948 the Mont Pélérin Society, certain of whose members – most notably Milton Friedman and Hayek himself – had a considerable influence on the economic and social policies of a number of leading western governments in the 1970s and 1980s. 'A strong attachment to liberalism unites the members of the Mont Pélérin Society', an attachment to 'the classical brand of liberalism . . . that wants the individual to be free from coercive interferences, especially from interventions by the state' (Machlup, 1977, p.xiv). This is just one indication of what is undoubtedly more generally the case: that the 'classical brand of liberalism' which we have described here needs to be understood not simply as one of the earliest coherent responses to the arrival of modern industrial society. It has also to be understood as one of the most pervasive, influential and tenacious.

Summary

- Liberal thought came to see 'the market' as an effective and impartial allocator of economic resources and an invaluable arbiter of conflicting interests.
- The overriding appeal of markets is that they work without human direction, as an 'invisible hand' enabling a multiplicity of purposes to be reconciled and attained.
- This defence of markets can be applied to international trade as well as to domestic economic activity; and continues to be a major theme in contemporary thinking on state and economy.

MARXISM

This is an appropriate moment in which to pause in our exposition of liberalism since we are beginning to touch on questions of its political impact. Our concerns in this section of the essay are with the *history* of ideas rather than with their *influence*; and we will return to our history of liberal thought when we discuss 'social reformism'. But before we do that – before we look at liberalism in its more troubled phase – we need to see the way in which liberalism, even at its moment of highest optimism in the years to 1870, was called into question as an interpretation of modern social life. For however much liberal political economists might assert the superiority and desirability of markets as economic allocators, not everyone was as contemptuous as they were of earlier ways of organizing economic life, nor as enthusiastic about the rise of industrialization. Instead, conservatives of many kinds, as we will see later, tried to stem the emerging social order and turn it back; and many kinds of socialists tried to circumvent the new capitalism – going beyond it, or outside it, to create equally new, but this time non-competitive and egalitarian, forms of social organization. From the explosion of socialist thought and experimentation which the arrival of industrial capitalism precipitated in the first half of the nineteenth century, marxism emerged as the most coherent and comprehensive critique of capitalism as a social system and of the liberalism that would justify it.

- **Karl Marx's**[3] own analysis of capitalism began from a quite different point than that commonly adopted by liberal thinkers. Marx rejected as an 'insipid illusion' their belief that social analysis should begin with the examination of the isolated individual. He argued that individuals did not exist in that isolated form, insisting instead on the primacy of social relationships.

- For Marx, individual action was socially conditioned and socially constrained. 'Men make their own history, but not just as they please . . . '.
- Since for Marx human labour is what distinguishes humans from animals, it is the social relationships which surround production which then shape society as a whole. Societies, that is, have an economic base and a social, political and cultural superstructure.

Economy and society

For Marx, epochs of human history were distinguishable one from the other by the way production was organized in each. Each epoch (and he tended to talk, for Europe, of the epochs of *Antiquity, Feudalism* and *Capitalism*) was defined by the way production was organized within it: on the basis of *slavery* in the ancient world, on *serfdom* in feudalism, and on *wage labour* under capitalism. Each mode of production, that is, differed from the one before it; and the key difference lay in the way that those who did the labouring, who actually produced the goods and services, relate to those who did not produce at all.

According to Marx, in each epoch to date, production has been organized in a socially divisive way. In each epoch production has been controlled by a tiny class of non-producers (slave owners, feudal lords and now capitalists) who, because they were effectively able to lay claim to the ownership and control of the means of production, could then live off the goods and services provided by and extracted from the vast majority of producers (the slaves, the serfs and the wage labourers) who were denied that ownership. Every mode of production, that is, has been dominated by a class division, by a separation into two main classes, those who own and control the means of production and those who do not. It was Marx's belief that capitalism would be the last mode of production to be divided in this way: that a socialist society would be free of this class division, because it would be free of the private ownership of the means of production which had hitherto set the class of producers and the class of non-producers into struggle against each other.

The existence of the private ownership of the means of production in all complex societies to date did a number of things to those societies, according to Marx. It gave individuals interests in common with others in a similar position in the property system. It turned liberalism's isolated individuals into members of whole social classes, whose individualism was drowned in a shared set of experiences and interests. And it set class against class – with the interests of the owners of property locked into mutual incompatibility with the interests of those denied property. Slave clashed with slave-owner, serf with feudal lord, worker with capitalist in class divisions so basic as to dominate all other forms of social division, self-definition and group struggle. Indeed it was because Marx argued for the centrality of this battle around production that he and **Engels**[4] were prepared to assert in *The Communist Manifesto* that 'the history of all hitherto existing society is the history of class struggles'.

So where liberal thought encouraged us to emphasize the market-based nature of contemporary social life, Marx emphasized instead the capitalist framework of property relationships within which markets were obliged to operate. For Marx, capitalism had two main differentiating features from its feudal predecessor. The first was that in capitalism productive activity was overwhelmingly geared to the sale of what was produced, rather than to the making of things to be directly consumed by the immediate producers. Under capitalism, what were produced were *commodities* – things to be bought and sold. So where Adam Smith emphasized the novelty and importance of the market as a mechanism of exchange, Marx emphasized instead the novelty of sending everything to market.

Capitalism's first distinguishing feature, for Marx, was the generalized commodity production going on within it.

Its second feature for Marx, and the source both of its dynamism and of its ultimate instability as a way of organizing economic life, was its reliance on *wage labour*. The producing classes were no longer tied to the land in various forms of serfdom. Instead they had been separated from any ownership of (or rights to) the land – had been dispossessed – and were now available as 'free wage labour'. That is, they were free to sell their labour power where they could – so they were free, untied labour – but equally they were obliged to do so, having no other means of subsistence – free to move between capitalists if they could, but never free of the need to find some capitalist to employ them. Indeed, Marx's central criticism of liberal political economy turned on this point, their misreading of the 'freedom' of the individual. Liberals focus on markets – and the marketplace for commodities is a sphere of individual freedom under capitalism. People buy and sell as they choose, in what Marx characterized as the 'noisy sphere of *exchange* . . . a paradise of the rights of man. Here liberty, equality, [and] property are supreme' (*Das Kapital*, Volume 1, p.167). But the commodities themselves emerge from a sphere of *production* in which people do not enjoy an equivalent equality: because there what one person is obliged to sell (his/her labour), another is free to buy. Beneath the individual freedom of the consumer lie the class inequalities of the social relations of production.

We should note that major classes, in Marx's way of thinking, normally come in twos. There were slave-owners and slaves in antiquity; there were lords and serfs in feudal Europe; and now, under capitalism, there are capitalists and workers (or bourgeoisies and proletarians – Marx used both sets of terms). Marx argued that as the European peasantry and independent artisans were proletarianized (were obliged to sell their labour power for money wages in order to survive) the ruling classes of pre-capitalist Europe had to come to terms with a new social force – a class of merchants, industrialists and financiers – who survived only by turning money into more money by the organization of the production and exchange of commodities. Capitalism, that is, brought into existence – according to Marx – a class with the accumulated wealth to organize production. By buying raw materials and machinery (means of production) and by purchasing and utilizing the labour power of the proletariat. Within this class, individuals then prospered only by successfully competing with other capitalists, each attempting to realize his/her profits by the successful sale in Adam Smith's market-place of the commodities produced by the labour power of those they employed.

Marx's attitude to this new system of production was, of course, quite different from Adam Smith's. But it was not entirely negative. Marx realized that the emergence of a class of capitalists competing with each other had developed the productive forces of the society as a whole in ways which the social relationships of production under feudalism had no potential to do. Competition was the great locomotive of economic growth under capitalism, as Smith had recognized. This is Marx, writing in *The Communist Manifesto*:

> The bourgeoisie cannot exist without constantly revolutionizing the instruments of production, and thereby the relations of production, and with them the whole relations of society. Conservation of the old modes of production in unaltered form was, on the contrary, the first condition of existence for all earlier industrial classes. Constant revolutionizing of production, uninterrupted disturbance of all social conditions, everlasting uncertainty and agitation distinguished the bourgeois epoch from all earlier ones. . . . The bourgeoisie, during its rule of scarce one hundred years, has created more massive and more colossal productive forces than have all the preceding generations together. Subjection of Nature's forces to man, machinery, application of chemistry to industry and agriculture, steam navigation, railways, electric telegraphs, clearing of whole continents

for cultivation, canalization of rivers, whole populations conjured out of the ground – what earlier century had even a presentiment that such productive forces slumbered in the lap of social labour.

To this degree at least, Marx was at one with the optimism of the early liberal thinkers. For him, as for them, history was the story of progress. It was just that for Marx the route to progress was far stormier and more contradictory than liberalism allowed. Capitalism's historic role, for Marx, was to create the material conditions for a society of abundance. Once this had been created, in the hothouse of capitalist inequalities, more egalitarian and less exploitative sets of social relationships (to wit, socialism) became possible for the first time. It was Marx's view that capitalism would progressively outlive its usefulness and, like all modes of production before it, give way to another in what he termed 'an epoch of social revolution'.

It was Marx's view that such an epoch of social revolution now loomed, put there by the contradictions of the capitalist mode of production itself, by the fact that capitalism had now done its job and needed to go. Indeed, the sharpest point of contrast between liberal and marxist readings of the new market-based industrial economies lay here – in their attitudes to its stability. Liberal thought emphasized the market's capacity to harmonize interests for the benefit of all. Marx emphasized instead the anarchy and crisis-ridden nature of market forces in an economy in capitalist hands. It was his view that economic crises were endemic to capitalism, and that they would intensify over time. They were endemic because capitalism would always be unable to pay its workers enough to buy all the goods that it produced. They were endemic because anarchic competition between capitalists inevitably put first one sector of production, and then another sector, out of proportion with the rest. And they would get worse because capitalist production relied on the generation of profits from the labour of the proletariat, and that rate of profit would fall as machinery replaced human labour in the productive systems of ever larger capitalist units.

A second generation of marxists then began to argue that international activity by capitalist concerns was temporarily alleviating this tendency to crisis, so moving the final resolution of capitalism's contradiction up on to the international stage. If cheap raw materials could be found abroad to lower production costs in capitalism's core areas, then the squeeze on profits could be thereby delayed. If new markets could be found for capitalist goods, then deficiencies in consumption could be held in check; and if new sources of investment could be located in areas of the world not yet totally under the sway of capitalist relations of production, then imbalances between sectors of the capitalist core economy could be assuaged. In other words, marxists in the 1890–1914 period were able to look at the intensification of international economic competition, the scramble for colonies, and the growing military tension between capitalist powers, and argue that this outburst of *imperialism* was a direct response to economic contradictions in core capitalist economies. Instead of foreign trade being to the advantage of all its participants, as Ricardo had argued, many marxists insisted that trade was increasingly structured by the profit requirements of large capitalist concerns, acting in concert with their own state machines to capture markets, outlets for capital, and sources of raw materials, from the capitalist concerns and state machines of other national bourgeoisies. By 1914, marxism offered students of international relations categories of 'inter-imperialist rivalry' and 'capitalist crisis' to explain the drift to war, and to reinforce their own argument that capitalism and world peace were no longer compatible.

Marxists were not arguing here that capitalism would inevitably be replaced by socialism as profit fell and war came: only that capitalism, in its crises, would create the social force which in the end would sweep it away. Its replacement was to be achieved, in Marx's view, by a proletariat radicalized by all this inequality, instability and crisis. In the broadest sense,

Marx anticipated that capitalism would simplify and polarize class relationships, and because of its instabilities would not manage ultimately to legitimate itself in the eyes of its proletarian majority. Instead, over time, the size of the capitalist class would diminish (as big capitalists swallowed small ones), so pushing the whole system towards monopoly (what Marx termed the centralization and concentration of capital). In the process, the size of the proletariat would grow (as small capitalists and independent artisans were forced down into its ranks); and its levels of subsistence would fall relatively, if not absolutely, in comparison to the immense wealth of the monopolistic few. This would then radicalize more and more of them over time, and open them to the appeal of revolutionary socialist ideas. Their capacity to implement those ideas would grow as workers were concentrated into larger and larger factories, and as the overwhelming impact of capitalism on daily life drowned out any non-proletarian divisions between workers. On a bad day, Marx was prepared to concede that the radicalization of workers would still be a problematic process, requiring astute political leadership. But on good days, his confidence in the fall of capitalism was quite overwhelming – and to later socialists, highly infectious. As he put it in *The Communist Manifesto*, 'what the bourgeoisie thereby produces, above all, is its own gravediggers. Its fall and the victory of the proletariat are equally inevitable'.

Summary

- Historically, societies have been divided between producers and non-producers – divided that is, into antagonistic social classes. Different social classes have developed and dominated in different periods. In capitalism the key social classes are the bourgeoisie and the proletariat.
- The contemporary economy is organized on capitalist lines. Capitalism, for Marx, is a system of generalized commodity production based on free wage labour.
- Capitalism is more dynamic than earlier ways of organizing economic life, but it is also crisis-ridden. The ultimate source of its instability is the proletariat it creates, which comes to have an interest in its replacement and the capacity to replace it.

SOCIAL REFORMISM

Liberal and marxist bodies of thought quickly became, and have remained, important points of reference in the persistent debate about the character of modern society. But as presented here – one unashamedly enthusiastic about capitalism, the other totally opposed to its continuation – it is hardly surprising that they did not exhaust the range of interpretations available to twentieth century social science. It would appear that for many social thinkers what liberalism and marxism gained in the tight internal coherence of their analyses they lost either in comprehensiveness or in subtlety. They shut out the argument of the 'middle ground' that capitalism was a society in need of (and open to) extensive *reform*.

- Social reformism is more diverse tradition than liberalism or marxism. It stands closer to liberalism than to marxism. It differs from liberalism in its sense of the inadequacy of unregulated markets and in its associated willingness to advocate state action to enhance individual liberty.
- Social reformism is united around a belief in the malleability of human nature, in the capacity of circumstances to shape character, and in the role of the state as a reformer of circumstances.

- Social reformism is united by its recognition of the importance for social life of the interplay of individual action and social structure.
- Social reformism carried the egalitarian logic of liberalism to its logical conclusion: arguing for a democratic franchise and equal rights for women.
- **John Stuart Mill**[5] recognized the positive impact on human capacities of participation in political life, and discounted earlier liberal fears of democracy as 'mob rule'.

Economy and society

The writings of John Stuart Mill opened the door through which the 'new liberalism' emerged. If moral self-development was vital to individual liberty, then it was *illiberal* to leave unreformed the social institutions and practices which blocked the moral self-development of the poor and disadvantaged. No longer could the definition of individual freedom be restricted to a *negative* one – as the freedom from state-levied restraints on the individual ability to act. Freedom now had to become a *positive* right, the actual ability to do things, with the freedom to participate and develop fully as an individual guaranteed by state action against private barriers to equality. So the state gathered a new role: 'to create those conditions in which self-fulfilment of individuals could occur' (Held, 1983, p.64); and in this way the 'new liberalism' embraced social reform, and reduced earlier liberal dependence on competition as the driving force of human progress.

It is this pursuit of social reform as the prerequisite for the full realization of individual potentiality that has inspired the British non-marxist Left in the twentieth century. Its first political flowering came in the reforming Liberal Government of 1906; and when the Liberal Party disintegrated after 1916, many of the new liberals found their way into senior positions in the British Labour Party. Indeed, social reform inspired by this revitalized liberal philosophy was thereafter largely the preserve of Labour. The Attlee Government's creation of the welfare state – on lines designed by leading New Liberals such as **Beveridge**[6] and **Keynes**[7] – is a living testimony to the impact of this way of thinking on twentieth century political and social life in the United Kingdom. It has been an impact which has emphasized the role of the state far more than early liberal thought allowed; and it is an impact which has challenged marxist assertions on the impossibility of capitalist reform.

The early liberal faith in the ability of markets to generate prosperity and social stability remained influential throughout the nineteenth century; and indeed (as we have already seen) remains so to this day. Certainly John Stuart Mill retained that optimism throughout his life. But in the United Kingdom in the years after his death (in 1873) early liberal optimism about the inevitability of progress through *laissez-faire* policies began to diminish, as the intensification of international competition from the now rapidly-industrializing German and American economies ended the monopoly of industrial production enjoyed by British manufacturers in mid-century. Later nineteenth century English liberal thinkers became increasingly aware too of the social cost of *laissez-faire* policies to the vast reservoirs of the Victorian poor, locked as they were in the most appalling conditions of industrial and social degradation. Many liberals came to see (and to fear) in that degradation the dangers of radicalization for which marxists were calling; and this same fear of a socialist proletariat stimulated equivalent responses in liberals elsewhere in Europe. Those fears were still very much in evidence in the years after World War I, years scarred by mass unemployment, the rise of fascism and the spread of support for the Soviet Union. By then, the 'middle ground' badly needed an economic theory that could chart its way between the defenders of an unregulated market order and the revolutionary socialist claim that there was no hope of generalized prosperity while private property remained. That is why Keynes is such an important figure in the history of social reformism. For by 1936, when he produced his

General Theory of Employment, Interest and Money, the 'middle way' had at last found the economic analysis it so desperately required.

Keynes was by then a critic of what he termed 'unregulated capitalism'. In direct opposition to inter-war economic orthodoxy, he argued that the unemployment of the 1930s could not be solved by cutting government spending and money wages, as the Treasury at the time appeared to think. Of course he was aware that cutting wages would enable employers to lower their prices, as his critics emphasized. But he realized that cutting wages had two effects, not one. It enabled employers to reduce their prices, retain more of their income as profits, and hopefully sell more of their now cheaper goods. But at the same time it reduced the purchasing power of the workers whose wages were cut, and left business confidence low, with employers able to sell less. In fact Keynes was not convinced that cutting money wages would actually reduce the real purchasing power of workers, since prices would also fall, to leave the situation unaltered, and the real value of company debts and taxation much increased. It was better, in his view, to tackle the Depression by expanding the economy, and allowing prices to rise; since this too would not only reduce real wages (so long as money wages remained unaltered) but would also ease the burden of corporate debt, so boosting business confidence and investment levels. Against the argument of generalized wage cutting, Keynes insisted that if full employment was to be achieved, it would come only as a consequence of firms somehow being able to produce and sell goods again in large quantities and so employ more people. The question was, how was that volume of output to be generated?

In the conditions of the 1930s, Keynes argued, what the system required was more demand and more spending, not less demand and more saving; and that could best be generated, he thought, both by redistributing income from the high savers (the rich) to the low savers (the poor), and by government spending more money itself, generating a multiplier effect through the whole economy by an expansion of its own labour force, by its own investment-spending and by its purchasing of the products of the private sector. The Keynesian specification for the role of the state that emerged in the 1930s was one which required the government to manage levels of demand in the economy as a whole (by its instructions to banks, and by its own spending), to keep demand at that level which could generate high levels of employment. It was a specification that gave social reformers for an entire generation after 1945 an answer both to liberal criticisms of state action and to marxist criticisms of capitalism.

We should remember too that, as it did so, it reinforced a characteristic social reformist view that both liberalism and marxism systematically underestimated the complexity of the social structure created by industrialism. Society was not reducible to a billard table on which rational isolated individuals bounced off one another in egotistical competition. Nor was it – to change the metaphor – a battlefield of polarized classes. There were class divisions, of course, and the reality of working-class life, at least in the *early* stages of capitalist development, was as oppressive as Marx had said. But in line with the thinking of John Stuart Mill, social reformists tended to see the *abatement* of class tension over time, to anticipate that class divisions would lose their ferocity and centrality as prosperity grew, and as the democratic process generated universal rights of *citizenship* (to vote, to unionize, to enjoy access to education, health care, pensions and so on) that cut across the experience of class-based inequalities of income and power.

Though John Stuart Mill was one source for such social reformist thinking on social divisions, by far the most important challenge to marxist views on social class came from the German 'new liberal' sociologist **Max Weber**.[8] Politically, Max Weber was heavily involved in German liberal politics, advocating the democratization of the German state and its active involvement in economic and social reform. Intellectually, he saw his own work as in part 'rounding out' marxism by supplementing its explanatory variables. Weber recognized the importance of class divisions in modern society, and the existence of the proletariat and the bourgeoisie. He was prepared to identify the origins of class division in the way the economy was organized, but he resisted Marx's attempts to tie class to property ownership. For Weber, class divisions reflected the relative strength of groups in the market, and was best captured by variations of income, not ownership. Such variations in their turn generated a hierarchy of classes, relating to each other in more complex ways than the simple polarity of incompatible interests emphasized by marxism. And class was not, for Weber, the only form or cause of social divisions. Divisions of *status* and divisions of *power* also set groups apart, and into hierarchical relationships the one with the other; and stratification by status and power was not reducible, as marxism would argue, even in the last instance to questions of property ownership.

Weber was able to argue this because of his sense – shared by others within this broad tradition of thought – of the multiplicity of causal forces at work in society at large. But he was also able to argue it because of his sense, more particular to himself, of capitalism as being merely one, admittedly vital, manifestation of a much broader process at work in modern western society. This was a process he referred to as *rationalization*. From his liberal roots, Weber took as central the notion of 'reason', and defined what he termed 'instrumental rationality' as the ability to achieve specified goals by technically efficient means. In his view (and here he stood full-square with both liberalism and marxism) – the rationality of western culture in this sense had grown significantly of late, as science had replaced religion as the dominant mode of understanding the natural world, and as the means of production available to successive generations had grown with rapid strides under the force of capitalist competition. Indeed, as we saw, liberal optimism in the future, and marxist certainty on the possibilities of a society of abundance, rested precisely on this view of the desirability of science and industry as 'rational'.

Weber was less sanguine about the potentialities of modern society than Smith and Marx. There was a streak of pessimism in the Weber soul, a sense of trouble that they both lacked. He sensed that western societies were not just more rational in their cultures. They were also more rational in their modes of organization. History was less to be characterized by the struggle between classes than by the growing *bureaucratization* of all forms of social life. The emergence of the modern bureaucracy, according to Weber, gave to contemporary societies the capacity to achieve social ends of unprecedented complexity. They could now run standardized health systems, mass armies, international economies, and so on. But as this technical capacity had grown, as scientific knowledge had developed, the moral certainties of earlier belief systems had slipped away; and life had become so complex as to be literally beyond the capacity of isolated individuals to grasp. Here for Weber was the modern paradox eating away at the optimism of early liberalism and at the certainties of marxism: that modern men and women possessed an enhanced technical capacity to achieve ends that were no longer clear to them, that they were armed with a knowledge-based culture in a world that was now too complex to know. The capitalist oppression of the working class would not forge in the collective mind of the proletariat a vision of an emancipated utopia. It would simply throw up another bureaucracy – that of the revolutionary socialist party – which, if successful, would rule in the proletariat's name. As Weber put it, with the rise of socialism, 'it is the dictatorship of the official, not that of the worker, which, for the present at any rate, is on the advance' (*Essay on Socialism*, 1918).

Summary

- Social reformers, as new liberals, saw liberty as having both a negative and a positive face; and accepted the need for social reform if people were actually to realize the formal rights accorded to them by earlier liberal thought.
- Keynes provided social reformism with its economic analysis, rejecting earlier claims that markets guarantee full employment, and advocating state action to stimulate adequate levels of consumer demand.
- Social reformism emphasizes the complexity of social structure. Max Weber is the key figure here, arguing for a multiplicity of sources of social division, and warning of the danger of the bureaucratization of modern social life.

CONSERVATISM

There is a fourth reaction to the arrival of industrial society which we need to observe, because it too released into academic scholarship a particular set of concerns and ways of analysing them. That is conservatism. We have held it back to the end not because it is unimportant, but because conservative thought has never generated the scale and detail of social analysis characteristic of the other three traditions, and because its central assertions have in modern times largely been formulated in response to the others – and particularly in reaction to liberalism. So the other traditions of thought need to be in place first if the full significance of the conservative reaction to them is to be grasped.

- Conservatives tend to be reluctant to theorize, reacting instead to the proselytizing of others. Conservatives are wary of excessive rationalism, and conscious of the dangers of radical social engineering.
- Conservatism is a philosophy of imperfection. It rejects liberal optimism in progress and human reason, emphasizing instead the limits on human capacities, the importance of the past, and the risks involved in rapid social change.
- Conservative thinkers tend to treat the family as a natural institution, and to leave unexamined the gender relationships within them.
- Conservative thinkers give an important role to the state as a guarantor of social order and of minimum standards. Conservatives attach central importance to the maintenance of political authority and to the rule of law. They do not look to the state for grandiose schemes of social improvement.

Economy and society

The attitude of conservative thinkers to economic life under capitalism has shown a characteristic development over time. Early conservative thought, in the hands of people like **Coleridge**,[9] **Carlyle**,[10] and **Southey**[11] was as hostile to industrialization as it was to revolutionary politics; so the emerging capitalist industrial order faced – in its early years – a challenging of a conservative as well as of a socialist kind.

Indeed much of the support for early factory legislation came from conservative circles horrified at the inhuman working conditions created by the new employing class, and disturbed by what they saw as factory work's adverse effects on family life and individual morality. 'Commerce', as Southey said after his visit to Birmingham 'sends in no returns of its killed and wounded'. Its 'watch chains, necklaces and bracelets, buttons, buckles and snuff boxes, are dearly purchased at the expense of health and morality' (Southey, 1807, p. 196). But as industrialization became established, conservative thought shifted eventually to its defence, as the focus of conservative arguments moved away from an attack on liberalism towards a critique of socialist movements. By the end of the nineteenth century, conservative thinkers had largely made their peace with industrialization and its dominant classes, and moved to defend their rights of property against threats posed by calls for public ownership and state planning. Indeed, except for a brief flirtation with social reformist theories of demand management in the 1950s and 1960s, conservative-inspired governments this century have normally been keen to defend the market, and to attack state planning as ineffective, inefficient, and destructive individual freedom. This openness of modern conservative thought to liberal (and to a lesser extent, social reformist) ideas has meant that there is now no distinctly conservative way of analysing economic life; and it has given a distinctly liberal feel to the economic policies of recent Conservative governments.

If there is a considerable fusion of thought between liberalism and conservatism in their approaches to the economy, no such fusion has characterized their wider analysis of society as a whole. There, in opposition to both liberals and marxists, conservative thinkers throughout the nineteenth century insisted that any society had to be understood as more than a collection of self-interested individuals or antagonistic classes. They saw it rather as an *organic* whole, a functionally integrated set of parts, each needing to be in harmony with the rest, and each in possession of a set of *mutual* responsibilities and duties. They saw in the patterned social inequalities of previous societies the manifestation of real differences between people's social capacities and intellectual skills, and proof that within an ordered society each individual had a particular, if unequal, place or *rank*.

This sense of society as a functionally-integrated organic whole has long been central to conservative thought. Through it, conservatives have come to see social inequality as both inevitable and necessary – indeed, even socially desirable, because it is functional to the health of the society in total. The focus of conservative concerns in social analysis has therefore been less with individuals or classes than with features of society as a whole: questions of social balance and order, social stability, the mechanisms of social integration and the maintenance of a sense of community. Conservative thought from Burke onwards has insisted that institutions and practices that have stood the test of time have a claim on our loyalty and respect for their longevity alone. The family, the monarchy, the church, private property and the nation have all attracted conservative support on this ground; and industrialization was initially resisted precisely because it threatened the sense of community inherited from the agrarian past. Coleridge's unease about industrialization, for example, rested in part in his fear that 'all traditional ties would be dissolved and . . . an impoverished mass . . . left at the mercy of the manufacturing and commercial class' (O'Sullivan, 1976, p.87). He looked to universal education and religion to reintegrate the new industrial society; and Carlyle, in similar fashion, advocated charismatic political leadership to create a new organic society in place of the one destroyed by industrial change.

Their particular solutions are now not very important – but the problem of social order and integration to which they were a response continues to preoccupy much conservative social analysis. For 'the conservative attitude demands the persistence of a civil order' (Scruton, 1980, p.27). It is not a civil order/society understood – as in liberal thought – as ultimately based on contractual relationships between autonomous and rational individuals. Society is not seen in that way by conservative thinkers. Instead, for a conservative like **Roger Scruton**[12] a society has to be understood as ultimately natural in origin, as a complex social phenomenon bound together by relationships of authority, by bonds of allegiance and, and by powerful tradition and customs. Since society exists 'objectively as it were, outside the sphere of individual choice', it – and not the individuals subject to it – becomes for conservatives the key object of study and the key concern of politics. To a man like Scruton, 'there is, to put it bluntly, something deeply self-deceiving in the [liberal] idea of a fulfilled human being whose style of life is entirely of his own devising' (Scruton, 1980, pp.37–8). Instead individuals are 'stamped permanently' by the society they inherit; and because they are, the 'customs, traditions and common culture' of that society 'become ruling conceptions' of thought and action (ibid, p.38).

Summary

- Conservative attitudes to industrialization changed over time: from initial hostility to eventual advocacy of market forces. Conservatism no longer possesses any developed and distinctive economic theory of its own.
- Conservatives recognize the inevitability of social inequality and the necessarily organic nature of all complex societies. They accordingly attach importance to leadership and to the maintenance of social order.

NOTES

1 This chapter is an abridged version of D. Coates' 'Traditions of thought and the rise of social science in the United Kingdom' in J. Anderson and M. Ricci (eds) *Society & Social Science: A Reader* (2nd ed.) (OU, 1994).

2 **David Ricardo**: 1772–1823. *Economist, and successful stockbroker. Friend of James Mill. Member of Parliament 1819. Author of* The Principles of Political Economy and Taxation (1817).

3 **Karl Marx**: 1818–1883. German philosopher and political economist. Spent the last 35 years of his life in London, and is buried in Highgate Cemetery. His writings include *The German Ideology* (1845–6), *The Communist Manifesto* (with Engels, 1848), *The Eighteenth Brumaire of Louis Bonaparte* (1852), the *Grundrisse* (1857–8) and *Das Kapital* (3 volumes, 1867, 1885 and 1894).

4 **Frederick Engels**: 1820–1895. Marx's colleague for over 40 years. His writings include *The Condition of the Working Class in England* (1844), and *The Origins of the Family, Private Property and the State* (1884).

5 **John Stuart Mill**: 1806–1873. Son of James Mill, economist and philosopher, active political reformer and Member of Parliament. His writings include *System of Logic* (1848), *Principle of Political Economy* (1849), *On Liberty* (1859), *Representative Government* (1861), *Utilitarianism* (1863) and *The Subjection of Women* (1869).

6 **William Beveridge**: 1879–1963. Major influence on the development of social policy in Britain, author of the Report on *Social Insurance and Allied Services* (1942) which had a formative effect on the design of the post-war welfare state.

7 **John Maynard Keynes**: 1883–1946. Economist, member of the Bloomsbury group, his writings include *The Economic Consequences of the Peace* (1919) and *A General Theory of Employment, Interest and Money* (1936).

8 **Max Weber**: 1864–1920. German sociologist. His writings available in English include *The Protestant Ethic and the Spirit of Capitalism* (1904–5), *The Methodology of the Social Sciences* (1903–17) and *Economy and Society*.

9 **Samuel Taylor Coleridge**: 1772–1834. Poet, critic of utilitarianism and philosopher of Romanticism. Co-author, with Wordsworth, of the *Lyrical Ballads* (1798). Wrote *On the Constitution of the Church and State* (1830).

10 **Thomas Carlyle**: 1795–1881. Scottish essayist and historian. Critic of what he termed 'The Condition of England'. His writings include *History of the French Revolution* (1837), *Chartism* (1839) and *Heroes, Hero-Worship and the Heroic in History* (1840).

11 **Robert Southey**: 1774–1843. One of the 'Lake poets', friend and brother-in-law to Coleridge. Author of *Letters from England* (1807) and of an immense quantity of predominantly narrative poetry. Initially sympathetic to Jacobinism, he had accommodated himself sufficiently to the existing social order by 1813 to be made poet laureate, but he remained throughout his life committed to government regulation and improvement of the social conditions created by industrialization.

12 **Roger Scruton**: b. 1944. Professor of Aesthetics at Birkbeck College, University of London. Editor of *The Salisbury Review* and author of, among other works, *Art and Imagination* (1974), *The Meaning of Conservatism* (1980), *From Descartes to Wittgenstein* (1981), *The Politics of Culture* (1981), *The Aesthetic Understanding* (1983), *Thinkers of the New Left* (1985), and *Sexual Desire* (1986).

REFERENCES

Barry, N.P. (1979) *Hayek's Social and Economic Philosophy*, London and Basingstoke, Macmillan.

Held, D. (1983) 'Central perspectives on the modern state', in D. Held *et al.* (eds) *States and Societies*, Oxford, Martin Robertson.

Keynes, J.M. (1936) *The General Theory of Employment, Interest and Money*, London and Basingstoke, Macmillan.

Machlup, F. (1977) *Essays on Hayek*, London, Routledge and Kegan Paul.

Manning, D.J. (1976) *Liberalism*, London, Dent.

O'Sullivan, N. (1976) *Conservatism*, London, Dent.

Scruton, R. (1980) *The Meaning of Conservatism*, Harmondsworth, Penguin.

Smith, A. (1776) *The Wealth of Nations* (reprinted by Penguin Books, 1970).

Southey, R. (1807) 'Birmingham' in *Letters from England* (published by The Cresset Press, 1951).

SECTION 1: THE ECONOMY

INTRODUCTION

The economy is arguably the dominant environment in terms of its influence on business behaviour. Businesses, particularly those in the private, profit-orientated sector, often pay more attention to the current state of the 'economy' and the direction of governments' economic policies, than to any other external events. The fairly obvious reason for this is the strong influence changes in these factors can have on their financial resources. Predicting the impact of such changes has taxed economists for many decades and continues to do so. Academic economists work on producing complex and often mathematically-based models of the relationships between government policy, economic performance and business responses, particularly in the financial sector. Professional economists interpret and adapt these to generate future forecasts. In chapter 4, Wilks, while not offering a typical example of the work of 'pure' academic economists, which would be much more mathematical, does give us a flavour of their concerns in his appraisal of government policy between 1979 and 1997. Most crucially it focuses on one major tenet of policy which he regards as having contributed to the UK's relative success in economic performance during that period – the deregulation of corporate decision-making. This has been a dominant theme – some would say the underlying orthodoxy – of much of the work of academic economists during the last three decades or more. Will Hutton in his roles as a leading economic journalist for the *Guardian/Observer* and popular writer, has been one of the most prominent critics of this orthodoxy. In chapter 5, his appraisal of the effects of deregulation of the financial sector, one of the major 'policy successes' of the period, is much more stark and pessimistic. Between them, Wilks and Hutton portray quite clearly the divide between liberal and social reformist perspectives on the economy.

Chapters 6 and 7, both by Coates, provide us with further insights into contemporary mainstream economics. Chapter 6 offers us an overview of the basic model of the economy, around which the vast majority of economic debate stems – the circular flow of income model. This is developed in diagrammatic form by Coates, who then goes on to describe the historical roots of UK economic policy making in the twentieth century. All of this provides some context to the earlier chapters by Wilks and Hutton respectively. Chapter 7, however, offers a very brief outline of a third approach to economic analysis, the marxist one. Here we see that not only are the fundamental values of marxist analysts different they also use different models of the economy, based on Marx's own ideas.

A point we have not addressed up to now is the fact that we assumed the 'economy' to mean the domestic or more specifically the UK economy. There is an understandable, historically-based interest amongst many economists and observers of the economy with their own immediate region or country. Increasingly, however, businesses themselves operate in several economies simultaneously. Hence the interests of economists have also begun to focus on the phenomenon of globalisation. In chapter 8, Rastogi outlines what this means from the point of view of the financial sector, and given the strong influence of this sector on economic policy makers, the world economy as a whole. In chapter 9 Junne provides some evidence that the development of a single 'global' economy is by no means an inevitability and that national and regional economies are still evolving with the active participation of the governments who attempt to manage them.

4

CONSERVATIVE GOVERNMENTS AND THE ECONOMY, 1979-97[†]

Stephen Wilks[*]

Over the past eighteen years Conservative economic policy makers have taken the British economy on a remarkable roller coaster ride which has seen two deep recessions, a triumphant boom and a mature recovery. In the process they have created the electoral paradox of winning in a recession (1992 – and virtually 1983) and losing during a recovery (1997). The shape of macro-economic policy has been transformed by the ending of the British establishment's love affair with Keynesianism[1] and by its flirtations with Europe, although there remains considerable institutional continuity. In contrast, in the realm of micro-economic policy, on the supply side of the economy, there have been a series of profound institutional changes. Privatization has eliminated the state-owned sector of industry; the labour market has been transformed by measures in industrial relations and education; and financial re-regulation has changed the face of the financial sector. Meanwhile supply side policy has gone through a cycle of disengagement, detachment and revival of interest in the idea of competitiveness.

This period of Conservative ascendancy has employed new ideas, new policies, and a new style of government to affirm an ancient doctrine: the doctrine of the market. It is hardly surprising that one of the main outcomes of eighteen years of a pro-capitalist government should be a reinforcement of capitalist property relations and the triumph of the master institution of contemporary capitalism – the business corporation. Labour is also now a party of the market. Clause IV has been rewritten, and terms such as co-operative capitalism and stakeholder capitalism have entered the New Labour discourse.[2] In the following discussion less attention is paid to macro-economic policy and the influence of the European Union. Important though these factors are, they have been generously discussed elsewhere. Instead more emphasis is given to the supply side, to institutions and to changes in the importance of business corporations.

THE POLICIES, THE GOALS, AND THE SUCCESSES

The traditional goals of economic policy were fourfold: low inflation, high growth, low unemployment, and a trade balance. Since 1979 the single target of macro-economic policy has become the minimization – or elimination – of inflation. The other three goals have been regarded as residuals whose achievement is contingent on a favourable inflation outcome, although Major gave more emphasis to growth from 1993. The emphasis on inflation was central to the New Right, it was the key to the 1979 election victory and its pursuit shifted the balance of economic power away from labour (favoured by Keynesian full employment policies) towards the financial markets. Indeed, the control of inflation gives pre-eminence to abstract market forces and perpetuates the Keynesian tendency for economic policy makers to ignore specifics of industrial performance. Inflation came under fragile control but that in itself is an empty achievement. More important is whether indicators of real efficiency and wealth responded positively and here we can look to measures of GDP, productivity and purchasing power, all in comparative context.

On GDP measures the UK performance from 1979 to 1996 is respectable. Since 1979 we have seen two recessions of great severity and two recoveries. The 1979–83 recession was simply catastrophic as illustrated in Table 4.1. It saw the biggest slump in output and rise in unemployment since the 1930s. It was exacerbated by a series of doctrinaire policy stances and restrictive budgets, causing Peter Riddell to remark that 'the Thatcher administration's record in its first term was worse than that of any previous post-war government in Britain'.[3] Yet five years later, in his 1988 budget speech, Nigel Lawson asserted that the 'country is now experiencing an economic miracle comparable to that enjoyed by West Germany and still enjoyed by Japan'.[4] Although such claims generated magisterial rebukes,[5] for a short euphoric period the Lawson boom generated serious academic discussion of a breakthrough in British economic performance.[6] Then came the 1990–94 recession with its bankruptcies and property slump, the misery of long term unemployment and the sense of betrayal across the small business sector. As Mrs Thatcher was ejected from office in November 1990 she was accompanied by an aura of economic failure. But by 1995 the triumphalist voices were again being raised. More cautiously, and with less impact, Britain's performance in the mid-1990s was once again beginning to outstrip her European competitors, and particularly Germany. Growth in British GDP passed that of the united Germany in 1992 and is forecast to maintain that lead up to the end of the decade. Table 4.1 indicates that the UK growth rate for the 19 year period 1979–97 is reasonable, compared to the rest of the G7, and for the four most recent years is actually the best. Even on standardized, un-massaged, statistics British unemployment is on a par with Germany and has been better than France since 1988. This can be translated into living standards by looking at GDP per head at purchasing power parities. In 1994 the UK's output per head was the 16th highest in the OECD but no EU country exceeded the UK figures by more than 15 per cent,[7] our European competitors are 'within reach' and the frustration of Conservative ministers in search of the 'feelgood factor' as they entered the 1997 election was palpable.

Very little of this periodic economic success appears to have been due to the operation of macro-economic policy. In the ludicrous monetarist experiments of the early 1980s, the arrogant boom of the late 1980s, and the grotesque rout from the ERM on Black

Table 4.1 Average annual growth rates of GDP: G7 countries, 1979–97

	UK	G7	US	Japan	Germany	France	Italy	Canada
1979–83	0.9	1.8	1.3	3.4	1.2	1.8	2.3	1.8
1984–88	4.0	3.8	4.0	4.3	2.5	2.5	3.0	4.7
1989–93	0.4	1.9	1.7	3.0	3.1	1.5	1.1	0.7
1994–97	3.0	2.3	2.5	1.7	2.0	2.2	1.8	2.8
1979–97	2.1	2.4	2.4	3.2	2.2	2.0	2.1	2.5

Source: derived from *OECD Economic Outlook*: Annex Table 1, Real GDP, includes projections for 1997 at December 1996.

Wednesday, 16 September 1992, British macroeconomic policy has deepened slumps, stoked up booms, and produced inept policy. Panic remarks that 'the extraordinary tale of UK monetary policy from 1979 to 1992 is likely to be recounted in economic textbooks . . . as a classic example of how not to pursue such a policy'.[8] Since 1992 macro-economic policy has been emptied of content. No targets, except the control of inflation; and no dominant theory of how the economy works; instead a rather welcome pragmatism that has aided British industry through a mild reflation and devaluation. In retrospect Black Wednesday appears rosy and the debate on EMU has taken centre stage.

In his spectacular assault on the Treasury, Sidney Pollard accused the economic policy establishment of a contempt for production manifested in a concentration on symbolic values (like prices and the balance of payments) to the exclusion of 'real' quantities (like goods and patents).[9] This tendency was accentuated by the Conservatives' obsession with sound money and by the discrediting and dismantling of the industrial policy machinery. In many respects, however, the great disjuncture in economic policy post-1979 is in micro-economic policy.

In the early days of the Conservative neo-liberal counter-revolution Sir Keith Joseph (as Secretary of State for Industry) engendered much amusement in his hand-wringing approval of vast tranches of aid for coal, steel and cars; in his patent unhappiness at the mere existence of the Department of Industry (merged into the DTI in 1983); and in his reading list which he solemnly circulated to senior officials.[10] But Sir Keith's preoccupations were neither transient nor unattainable and the second term of office allowed the Conservatives to impose a new supply side orthodoxy on the British economy which was as radical, and as ideologically deep-seated, as anything on the macro-economic side. Much of the Conservative supply side policy was constructed in opposition to the collectivist consensus that had dominated post-war politics. The New Right ideologues who captured the Party rejected an interventionist role for the state – so they rejected indicative planning, public ownership, incomes policy, controls, especially exchange controls, and sectoral intervention. In a slightly more puzzling vein, which owed more to Mrs Thatcher personally, they also rejected dialogue with industry, which was felt to be an expression of British-style corporatism. Now it is very doubtful that Britain was ever systematically 'corporatist' even at the high point of tripartism, and to refuse to talk to industrialists and the CBI leadership, as Mrs Thatcher did much of during the 1980s, was perverse and caused Hannah to label her (approvingly) as a 'capital basher'.[11]

The detailed implementation of the supply side policies was spasmodic, experimental, and dispersed among several government departments. This makes it difficult to regard them as coherent, or programmatic and, as many have observed, there was no Thatcherite blueprint for the reconstruction of the industrial economy. Implementation was, however, determined and consistent at least in the underlying ideas of individualism, self-interest, and market amorality, which contrasted starkly with the collectivist, public interest and consensus orientation of the preceeding decades. As Gamble emphasizes, the policies also rested on a commitment to the strong state which was necessary to create or impose market relations. But these principles were tempered by political calculation. The term 'statecraft' has been coined to describe the mix of political populism, opportunism, and astute manipulation of the machinery of policy making which allowed Mrs Thatcher to push through her policies in the face of official scepticism and the lack of a popular mandate.[12] The true measure of her success is seen in the policy platform of New Labour which has accepted the desirability of many of the supply side measures. To this extent the Conservative supply side policies constitute an hegemonic project. They have created a new conventional wisdom, a cultural transformation which could also be characterized as an institutional transformation. But what are these new policies? How new are they and how successful have they been?

The two most important have been privatization and labour market policy; also significant are policy towards small business, towards inward investment and, belatedly, towards education and training. There has been much talk of a general trend towards deregulation and the reassertion of managerial prerogatives but the reality is of re-regulation rather than de-regulation (both domestically and as part of the Single European Market)[13] and the 'right to manage' idea is hard to pin down (Chandler calls it 'new and corrupting').[14] Each of the first four policies are seen to have made significant contributions to industrial productivity.[15] The privatized utilities have achieved substantial improvements in labour productivity (especially remarkable are the electricity generators). Inward investment has brought some of the most productive companies in the world to Britain. A significant growth in the number of small businesses has provided new sources of innovation and flexibility; and the labour market has seen some startling improvements in efficiency. More recently commentators have begun to stress the improvements in human capital and the growth of participation in, and qualification from, further and higher education. All these have contributed to the main and most important indicator of economic policy success: the growth in industrial productivity since 1981.

For labour productivity the UK's record for 1979–94 is surpassed only by Japan – a rate of 3.9 per cent per annum (output per hour in manufacturing); the figures for gross output are less flattering but Oulton also records good productivity growth for service industries and for total factor productivity, causing him to conclude that 'the period of relative economic decline has ended'.[16] This is, he accepts, an optimistic assessment, but the facts of internationally competitive productivity rates are conceded even by the government's sternest critics.[17] This is a remarkable success for a set of ideas rather than a coherent package of policies. The Conservatives had no industrial policy: both the concept and the term were anathema under Mrs Thatcher, and it followed that there was no programme for industrial recovery. At the high point of monetarist insouciance, when the manufacturing trade balance went into deficit in 1983 (where it has remained ever since). Nigel Lawson reproached the House of Lords Select Committee on Overseas Trade for its complaints about the manufacturing deficit. He told them that their bias against services was distasteful and declared that 'there is no adamantine law that says we have to produce as much in the way of manufactures as we consume. If it does turn out that we are relatively more efficient in world terms at providing services than at producing goods, then our national interest lies in a surplus on services and a deficit on goods.'[18] By 1990 John Major was backtracking on this piece of economic hubris so that the 1992 Conservative Manifesto declared that 'a vigorous manufacturing sector is essential to a healthy British economy'.[19] This is just a small example of contradiction in a supply side reconstruction replete with abandoned policies, empty exhortation, and acute inconsistency. One can only feel sympathy for the officials of the DTI who cohabited with no less than eleven Secretaries of State in seventeen years, where such ideologues as Joseph, Parkinson, Tebbit, Ridley and Lilley outnumbered pragmatists such as Jenkin, Channon and Heseltine. Thus successful policies like privatization and inward investment have co-existed with disappointing policies such as skills training and technological innovation. The whole picture was not evaluated in any coherent way until Michael Heseltine became President of the Board of Trade in 1992 (an appointment inconceivable under Mrs Thatcher) whereupon he discarded the candyfloss enterprise jargon of Lord Young in favour of a return to dialogue, engagement, assistance, sponsorship and co-ordination in the form of the Competitiveness Reports which have become an annual DTI programme.[20]

Under the Heseltine reconfiguration of supply-side policy the emphasis was put strongly on competitiveness. The term itself is controversial. American economists have argued that nations do not compete. Krugman maintains that competitiveness is an irrelevant or even dangerous concept at the national level. Reich believes that national boundaries have broken down in the employment relationship: and Porter argues that companies rather than nations compete.[21] Porter had a considerable impact on the British debate. His work was cited in official publications and even incorporated into the Monopolies and Mergers Commission guidance on how to assess the competitive effects of mergers. Porter's analysis affirms the importance of markets but has been used to shift the emphasis from the anarchic individualism of the Thatcher years to the structured individualism of the Major/Heseltine era. Since structure is being provided by companies working within market rules, this shift can be presented as a move from collectivism to capitalism via individualism; or as a shift from an interventionist stage to a regulatory state.

Thus the level of state intervention in the economy is still high. In a modern, technologically sophisticated state, government cannot avoid regular and intense engagement with industry. But the institutional structures for engaging with industry have changed from interventionist or planning bodies such as the National Enterprise Board (abolished in 1981) and the National Economic Development Office (eventually abolished in 1992) to regulatory bodies such as OFFER (Office of Electricity Regulation) or SIB (Securities and Investments Board). Hence the level of co-ordination and political oversight has been reduced and the emphasis has moved to creating markets and establishing rules rather than on the detail of industrial performance. The DTI Competitiveness White Papers are revealing here. They present the mass of supply side measures as a coherent package under the wing of the Ministry but in fact they make clear that the coherence of policy is provided by its company focus, not by administrative programmes. John Major has been happy to talk of a 'new partnership' with industry and Michael Heseltine defined his mission, and the mission of the DTI, as 'helping British companies to win'. By 1996 this had metamorphosed into the aim 'to make this country the unrivalled Enterprise Centre of Europe, with an open, flexible and dynamic economy, able to win in world markets'.[22] The DTI official is now expected to view his or her task through the prism of company priorities rather than in a framework of government policy or the national interest. Put another way, the national interest is now that companies based in Britain succeed commercially: the equivalent of the inflation obsession in macro-economic policy has become the company obsession in micro-economic policy.

None of this should be regarded as new or surprising. It represents a transmigration of the traditional economic liberalism of the nineteenth century, and of a tolerance of private action which was widely emphasized as one of the deep seated cultural traits which undermined the industrial policy interventionism of the 1970s. In a trailblazing study of industrial policy Stephen Young emphasized the priority given – instinctively and automatically in Britain – to the autonomy of the firm and an arms-length relationship between government and industry.[23] The autonomy of the company has been expanded continuously since 1979. From the abolition of exchange controls through labour market reforms to privatization, the big winners have been companies and their senior management. Even though deregulation has been followed by re-regulation the new regulatory frameworks in utilities, financial services, health care or competitive tendering have been designed to create markets within which companies can make profits. This renaissance of British capitalism was boosted by the historic collapse of state socialism in eastern Europe which shifted the terms of debate. In the 1990s the central question in political economy is not – is capitalism better than the alternative? but, what *sort* of capitalism is best? This is a question which is generating a fertile debate on comparative capitalism.[24]

Although the debates have become increasingly sophisticated, and moved well beyond the stage of caricature, Albert's polemic on *Capitalism Against Capitalism* still captures the flavour of the contrasts. He compares the socially responsible, solidaristic, nationalistic, and long-term orientated nature of 'Rhineland' capitalism with the selfish, individualistic, globalized, and short-term neo-American or stockmarket capitalism growing in Britain.

In comparing capitalisms he emphasizes the historical legacies which have created different conceptions of the market, different ethical standards and different institutional structures between the major capitalist economies.[25] While Albert has emphasized the differences in moral and distributional outcomes of variations in the institutions of capitalism, others have emphasized the competitive implications of the institutional legacy. The Nobel prize winning economic historian Douglas North asserts 'a much more fundamental role for institutions in societies: they are the underlying determinant of the long run performance of economies'.[26] This is now widely accepted in British government and is a view which informs the Competitiveness White Papers. It suggests that nations do compete, but they compete in providing the appropriate institutional environment in which firms can succeed, rather than competing as an identifiable participant in the market. We go on to ask whether the changes in British economic institutions produced by Conservative governments, seem to have made Britain a more effective competitor on world markets.

ECONOMIC POLICY AND INSTITUTIONAL TRANSFORMATION

The conventional context for evaluating economic policy is Britain's relative economic decline. The history of relative decline is extensive going back, on some accounts, to the 1860s, but it is an appropriate framework for evaluating the Conservative record partly because an eighteen-year period provides the sort of timescale over which remedial action could be taken, partly because the 1979 Conservative manifesto famously declared that 'our country's relative decline is not inevitable, we in the Conservative Party think we can reverse it'. As noted above, some economists are now of the view that relative economic decline has been halted, but to confirm that view we need more substantial evidence than a few percentage points in superior labour productivity.

Britain's relative economic decline has been so persistent that it must be attributed to very deep-seated features of the British political economy. Explanations have accordingly embraced virtually every feature of contemporary British life from the allegedly anti-industrial culture to craft-based unions, amateur management and the electoral system with its bias to 'adversary politics'. At its broadest there is agreement that there is something wrong with Britain's institutional inheritance. In Oulton's words, 'it is now generally accepted that the explanation for differences between countries in long run growth rates should be sought in institutions'.[27] The institutional approach has become fashionable in political science although it comprises several different tendencies and is difficult to apply.[28] Institutional analysis has great strengths, not least its openness to multi-disciplinary analysis which can embrace law and sociology as well as economics. One of the most influential political economy approaches is associated with North who provides a fruitful analytical approach to the relationship between economic policy, institutions, and long term growth.

North's treatment is expansive. He argues that 'institutions include any form of constraint that human beings devise to shape human interaction'; so that they are much wider than organizations, include formal and informal (cultural) constraints, and have a cognitive dimension. Institutions shape the perceptions and attitudes of actors, they present an interpretive and moral schema, and provide a repertoire of procedures and choices to guide action. North sustains the economist's paradigm of rational choice but presents it as a form of procedural rationality structured by institutions. It follows from North's argument that economic and political models are institution-specific and therefore nation-specific; they may be efficient or inefficient but inefficient institutions will not necessarily be eliminated. Institutional arrangements are very hard to change and institutions such as the City of London induce 'path dependency'. Institutional efficiency derives from the way in which institutions structure incentives and allocate property rights. Benign institutional arrangements will deliver massive benefits by generating increased returns to institutions (falling unit costs, co-ordination, learning, compliance and positive expectations); and by reducing transaction costs in imperfect markets (by familiarity, trust, and legitimacy).[29] Space prohibits a full elaboration of a North-type analysis but it does focus our inquiry. The important questions are, therefore: have Conservative Governments redesigned institutions over the past 18 years, and are the new institutions more or less likely to create long-term competitive growth?

The answer to the first question is of course affirmative. Not only have institutions been redesigned but Conservative Governments have explicitly redesigned them in order to increase international competitiveness. Defining institutions in a North-type usage gives a large number of areas where aspects of economic activity are structured by a combination of traditions, ideas, organizations, government involvement, and tacit norms. Candidates for study include the following dozen:

- privatized industries and their regulation;
- the labour market;
- inward investment;
- the financial markets;
- education and training;
- technology and innovation;
- macro-economic policy;
- the European single market;
- the European monetary union;
- the tax system;
- competition policy;
- corporate governance.

The European influence has become central and is helping to set the agenda but, with the possible exceptions of competition policy and macro-economic policy, 'Europe' has not established an institutional identity. If Britain were to join EMU the institutional picture would be revolutionized. Policy would take on a new pan-European character and there would no longer be an indigenous British macro-economic policy. The economic columns of the newspapers would fill with analysis of the German economy and the domestic emphasis would shift decisively to the supply side. Britain would compete on the basis of efficiency and productivity. But Britain's eventual membership of the EMU is uncertain. It is not a Conservative policy commitment and its institutional impact remains latent.

In each of the dozen areas enumerated above there have been new ideas, new policies, new legislation and, as a result, changed configurations of property rights, transaction costs and incentive structures. We have seen that some of these areas have been widely regarded as successful – and including privatization, labour market policy, and inward investment; others have been regarded as failures, especially technology and innovation,[30] education and training,[31] and competition policy.[32] This prompts the second question: are these new institutions likely to promote long term growth?

Of course this question is unanswerable in any unambiguous sense, at least for the next ten years, but there are certain institutional consistencies which might aid prediction. The deliberate withdrawal of the state from supply side institutions had an ambiguous character. The state is no longer a direct participant – it does not own industry, negotiate incomes policy or undertake training – but it does establish a framework of regulations which ensures that the same functions will be provided by private actors operating within a market. In creating markets the state has also created or changed property rights throughout the economy. The most dramatic examples are in the privatized industries where millions of new shareholders have been created and privatized utilities now account for about 17 per cent of stock market capitalization; a process which Coakley and Harris call 'financialization' – the creation of new financial assets (it applies also to former mutual building societies).[33] But in other areas too, property rights have been created or changed, for instance by labour market legislation, the establishment of TECs, the commitments made to inward investors, and the creation of assets such as personal pensions and health-care schemes. Analysis of property rights is at the core of North's institutional approach. 'Property rights', he argues, 'are the rights individuals appropriate over their own labour and the goods and services they possess. Appropriation is a function of legal rules, organizational form, enforcement and norms of behaviour – that is, institutional frameworks.'[34] Analysis of property rights has provoked some stimulating work on the implications of ownership and has been used to identify the efficiency gains generated by particular institutional configurations in successful capitalist economies such as Japan and Germany.[35] These economies enjoy a distribution of property rights and attendant incentives which generate co-operation, trust, shared effort, long term commitment, and a willingness to make sacrifices for solidaristic ends which create efficiencies through reductions in transaction costs.[36]

This brief rendering of a rapidly evolving literature leads to the conclusion that changes in British property rights have potentially dangerous consequences. The shift to expanded property rights extends the scope for possessive individualism, extends the extent of market vulnerability and the liquidity of rights which are traded in a context of information scarcity. The danger is that this marketization will increase transaction costs and shift incentive structures to short term, instrumental calculation. Wealth maximizing actors unconstrained by other considerations are unlikely to create efficient institutions, which brings us back to the corporation.

COMPANY AUTONOMY AS AN INSTITUTION

The master institution that integrates these supply-side complexes and which has emerged as a major winner in the reforms of the last eighteen years is the business corporation. As noted above, the corporation has been liberated by regulatory changes that have removed some constraints (such as exchange controls) whilst restraining opposition (as with labour market controls). Although new obligations have been imposed, in areas like environmental protection or product specification, the new emphasis on compliance costs in the design of new regulations is a telling indicator of the order of priorities. The company has been exhorted and cosseted by ministers, it has enjoyed the most favourable tax regime in Europe, its reach has extended into the privatized sector and into the public sector through service delivery and competitive tendering, and business people increasingly take leadership roles as advisers, temporary civil servants, and quango appointees. Business leaders are the most prominent group among the 'new magistracy'. As the balance of power has shifted Perkin has re-emphasized the pre-eminence of the professionalized corporate élites who control companies without owning them.[37] In some ways Perkin's analysis is reminiscent of Galbraith's analysis of the technostructure in the *New Industrial State*[38] and, similarly, the Conservatives are faced with the challenge of the corporation just as Labour was faced by the same challenge in the mid-1970s. The Labour response was to attempt to control the corporation through industrial planning and planning agreements, an experiment that failed and lived on in only shadowy form in Labour's Industrial Strategy from 1976 to 1979.

The Conservative response to the challenge of the corporation has been to celebrate rather than to control. Ministers maintain that corporations will be controlled through the natural operation of the market, guaranteed by the competition policy regime, by natural monopoly regulation of the utilities, and by self-regulation where necessary. For free market purists Milton Friedman's rationale prevails which, as he provocatively put it, maintains that 'few trends could so thoroughly undermine the very foundations of our free society as the acceptance by corporate officials of a social responsibility other than to make as much money for their shareholders as possible'.[39] To construct any other framework would be economically inefficient. Hence pressures for reform of corporate governance have come up against a brick wall of ideology. Conservative ministers have continued to conceive of the corporation in a nineteenth century liberal light as an autonomous legal person, owned by shareholders, to be allowed complete freedom to operate and contract in the interests of those shareholders. In this sense the atavistic nature of Thatcherism is at its most damaging. Supply side policy has certainly changed, but in the area of corporate governance it has regressed. It is not surprising that Conservative ministers should reject the calls from social democrats to model corporate law reform on the Japanese developmental state or the German social market;[40] but it is genuinely surprising that ministers should not recognize that 'it is absurd that a law [the Companies Act] designed for a family business a century ago should continue to apply without substantial change to the whole of industry today, regardless of the size and purpose of the Company. This represents the abdication of the state from its responsibility to create responsible institutions'.[41]

Although most of the issues germane to the corporate governance debate have been the subject of discussion for many years the debate has only begun to cohere in the 1990s. It draws on an immense literature dealing with corporate concentration, the separation of ownership and control, the rise of managerial capitalism, the theory of the firm, the role of stock markets and banks, and the comparative experience of competitor economies (especially Germany and Japan). Political science has devoted relatively little attention to corporate governance which is regrettable since the company is the central institution of the market economy in Britain as elsewhere.[42] If the economy is performing badly it is logical to give attention to that central institution. By the same coin the improvement in the British economy and the increased salience of companies under the Conservatives are surely not unrelated.

Company autonomy in Britain exhibits the essential characteristics of North's institutions. It developed in the nineteenth century under the influence of the independent entrepreneurs who initiated the market-led English industrial revolution, but it metamorphosed into a shareholder dominated, centralized system centred on the City of London and linked to (eventually dominated by) by commercial capital. Company autonomy has meant that government – national or regional – has been kept at arm's length, but also that the collective organization and representation of capital is weak. Grant emphasizes this and terms Britain a 'company state'[43] in which companies are 'hostile brothers'.[44] British companies are also, in Rowthorne's memorable phrase, 'de-nationalized', by which he means that they have few patriotic norms, profits taking precedence over national interests. British companies have always been among the most internationalized and, for the most part, the British state has resisted mercantilist impulses and strongly encouraged inward investment. Foreign companies now account for two fifths of manufactured exports and increased their share of UK manufacturing output from 18 per cent in 1986 to 24 per cent in 1992.[45] They have been hailed as a significant addition to employment, technology and productivity and the British government's stance is the most welcoming among the G7 group of large industrial nations.

Company directors, shareholders and business organizations who defend corporate autonomy are able to rely on the company law which defines companies as legal persons and director's duties in terms of the shareholders alone.[46] It is a commonplace that the division of ownership and control has allowed directors and senior executives almost untrammelled independence, with effective control over the property rights created by the company, whilst denying the property rights of other stakeholders – such as employees. This distribution of property rights, it is argued, generates incentives which contribute to highly inefficient behaviour on the part of company management. Shareholders are instrumental, managers emphasize short term profit maximization, are unwilling to invest – in capital, technology, research, or training – and the system destroys trust. The UK system of corporate governance is peculiar in refusing to recognize the rights of other 'stakeholders' and wider societal interests. These features have been accentuated by eighteen years of Conservative rule which has taken the British corporate system steadily closer to the US model. But the United States has recognized and lived with rampant corporate power for 100 years. It has evolved techniques of control including extensive anti-trust, well developed regulatory mechanisms, countervailing powers through pressure groups, a corporate élite often integrated into government and an ethic of corporate social responsibility. In the UK these safeguards are much weaker and the British institution of company autonomy appears overdeveloped.

Yet government has continued to defend company autonomy, not least from Brussels. It has opted out of the social chapter and the directive on worker representation. It has resisted a European company statute and instead put its faith in traditional models of self-regulation through stock exchange regulation and voluntary codes of conduct such as the Cadbury and Greenbury codes – more honoured in the breach. The corporate governance movement was originally crass, concerned with exerting greater shareholder control, but has recently become much more sophisticated and inventive. The 'stakeholder' concept of companies being required to give attention to all groups who are involved in their activities is interesting. It has long been debated in business schools and 'there is political (and corporate) consensus that the involvement of key stakeholders is vital to corporate success':[47] a marriage of equity and efficiency that has been exploited by the two prophets of stakeholder capitalism John Kay and Will Hutton.[48] The stakeholder idea has been seized upon by New Labour and, while the Kay/Hutton model has been challenged and there are several different variants, it is likely that a Labour Government would put corporate governance and company law reform high on its agenda.

Variations in corporate governance provide a defining institutional feature of different models of capitalism. These models have different implications for equity, public services, and economic competitiveness. The choice of a neoAmerican model of stock-market capitalism based on company autonomy was in some ways natural. It accords with British traditions and appears suitable for a rapidly changing, flexible and innovative global economy. But this choice raises serious philosophical questions of whether it can be sustained or whether it is based on a depleting moral legacy; practical questions of whether it can be reconciled within a European Union with models based on very different traditions and principles;[49] and moral issues of whether the human cost in growing inequality is a cost worth paying.[50]

CONCLUSION

The British economy has performed well enough over the past eighteen years to justify realistic discussion of the end of relative economic decline. But this is a conclusion that could only be reached at the very end of the period, the last five years that have made all the difference. A similar conclusion could not have been reached in 1992 and improvements may yet be found to be a reflection of the stop–go cycle from which Britain seems unable to escape. If a supply side miracle has taken place it has taken a long time to work and has come to fruition under the more pragmatic macro- and micro-economic policies practised by the Major Governments.

The structure of the economy has changed in important ways which cannot be reviewed in the space available. Manufacturing has declined in favour of business services; information-based industries have blossomed; the direction of British trade has shifted dramatically towards Europe; the mix of the workforce (more part-time, self-employed and female) has changed. Other important aspects such as the good fortune of North Sea Oil, the effects of the 'peace dividend' on defence spending, the apparent failure of the Single European Market to deliver significant efficiency savings, and the impact of environment awareness on business strategy all deserve attention.

The British economy remains peculiar in international comparison and continues to present a paradoxical picture. It is extraordinary that the principles of economic activity should have become so much more neo-American while the country was integrating economically with Europe. It is ironic that an era of *de*-regulation and celebration of the spontaneous market should necessitate extensive *re*-regulation to create and police markets. It is perverse that governments so rhetorically committed to the concept of competition should be persistently unwilling to modernize and strengthen competition policy. It is worrying that the measurable improvement in industrial productivity should be coming from the manufacturing sector which has continued to shrink, raising the continuing spectre of deindustrialization and trade deficits. Finally, it is regrettable, but not unexpected, that the Treasury policy establishment has retained its stranglehold on macro-economic policy making.

Assessments of the record need to emphasize the implications of Britain becoming the 'Enterprise Centre of Europe'; implications which are at least as profound as EMU. As noted above, this policy stance requires the adoption of a particular model of Anglo-American capitalism which is based on internationalized capital, entrepreneurial freedom, non-intrusive regulation, a commodified workforce (and possibly a low-wage workforce), low social overheads, and free trade. It is a model that explicitly rejects the developmental state or Rhenish capitalism and it is embodied, or so my argument goes, in the institution of company autonomy.

This model has been coruscatingly criticized[51] but dazzling rhetoric avails little against the entrenched institutional pattern observed above. An equally important source of change is dissatisfaction from those who have been excluded from the development of 'enterprise' in Britain. This presents a challenge to the next government, but also a challenge for the companies that have become more nearly governing institutions over the past eighteen years.

NOTES

† This chapter has been adapted from, S. Wilks, 'Conservative Governments and the Economy, 1979–97', *Political Studies*, XLV (1997), 689–703.

* The author gratefully acknowledges the support of the ESRC through a Senior Research Fellowship, and the comments of Andrew Hindmoor.

1 D. Winch, 'Keynes, Keynesianism and State Intervention', in P. Hall (ed.), *The Political Power of Economic Ideas* (Princeton, NJ, Princeton University Press, 1989), pp. 107–27.

2 W. Hutton, *The State We're In* (London, Vintage, rev. edn, 1996).

3 P. Riddell, *The Thatcher Government* (Oxford, Martin Robertson, 1983), p. 76.

4 Cited in R. Martin, 'Has the British Economy been Transformed? Critical Reflections on the Policies of the Thatcher Era', in P. Cloke (ed.), *Policy and Change in Thatcher's Britain* (Oxford, Pergamon, 1992), p. 136.

5 See, for instance, K. Coutts and W. Godley, 'The British economy under Mrs Thatcher', *Political Quarterly*, 60 (1989), 137–51, who call the claims 'preposterous', p. 150.

6 For instance, L. Hannah, 'Mrs Thatcher, Capital Basher?', in D. Kavanagh and A. Seldon, (eds), *The Thatcher Effect* (Oxford, Clarendon, 1989), pp. 38–48.

7 See W. Eltis and D. Higham, 'Closing the UK competitiveness gap', *National Institute Economic Review*, 154 (1995), p. 72.

8 M. Panic, 'Comment: UK Monetary Policy in the 1980s', in J. Mitchie (ed.), *The Economic Legacy 1979–1992* (London, Academic, 1992), p. 59.

9 S. Pollard, *The Wasting of the British Economy* (London, Croom Helm, 2nd edn, 1984), p. 72.

10 See S. Wilks, 'Conservative Industrial Policy 1979–83', in P. Jackson (ed.), *Implementing Government Policy Initiatives: The Thatcher Administration 1979–1983* (London, Royal Institute of Public Administration, 1985), pp. 123–43.

11 Hannah, 'Mrs Thatcher, Capital Basher?', p. 38.

12 See J. Bulpitt, 'The discipline of the new democracy: Mrs Thatcher's statecraft', *Political Studies*, 34 (1986), 19–39; A. Gamble, *The Free Economy and the Strong State: the Politics of Thatcherism* (London, Macmillan, 2nd edn, 1994), p. 139.

13 See S. Vogel, *Freer Markets, More Rules: Regulatory Reform in Advanced Industrial Countries* (Ithaca, Cornell University Press, 1996); S. Wilks, 'Regulatory compliance and capitalist diversity in Europe', *Journal of European Public Policy*, 3 (1996), 536–59.

14 G. Chandler, 'The Political Handicap', in T. Buxton, P. Chapman and P. Temple (eds), *Britain's Economic Performance* (London, Routledge, 1994), p. 13.

15 N. Oulton, 'Supply side reform and UK economic growth: what happened to the miracle?', *National Institute Economic Review*, 154 (1995), 53–70.

16 Oulton, 'Supply side reform and UK economic growth', pp. 54, 58.

17 See, for instance, A. Glyn, 'The "Productivity Miracle", Profits and Investment', in Mitchie, *The Economic Legacy*, p. 77.

18 Cited in S. Wilks, 'From industrial policy to enterprise policy in Britain', *Journal of General Management*, 12 (1987), 5–20, p. 10.

19 See S. Wilks, 'Economic Policy', in P. Dunleavy, A. Gamble, I. Holliday and G. Peele (eds), *Developments in British Politics 4* (London, Macmillan, 1993), p. 244; on manufacturing see also S. Lee, 'Manufacturing' in D. Coates (ed.), *Industrial Policy in Britain* (London, Macmillan, 1996), pp. 33–61; and D. Mayes and S. Soteri, 'Does Manufacturing Matter?' in T. Buxton *et al.*, *Britain's Economic Performance*, pp. 373–96.

20 Cm 2563, *Competitiveness: Helping Business to Win* (London, HMSO, 1994); and Cm 3300, *Competitiveness: Creating the Enterprise Centre of Europe* (London, HMSO, 1996).

21 P. Krugman, 'Competitiveness: a dangerous obsession', *Foreign Affairs*, 73 (1994), 28–44; R. Reich, *The Work of Nations: Preparing Ourselves for C21st Capitalism* (New York, Vintage, 1992); M. Porter, *The Competitive Advantage of Nations* (London, Macmillan, 1990).

22 John Major, 'Foreword', in Cm 3300, *Competitiveness: Creating the Enterprise Centre of Europe*.

23 S. Young with A. Lowe, *Intervention in the Mixed Economy* (London, Croom Helm, 1974), ch. 16; his insights were pursued during the 1980s, see A. Cawson, K. Morgan, D. Webber, P. Holmes, and A. Stevens, *Hostile Brothers: Competition and Closure in the European Electronics Industry* (Oxford, Clarendon, 1990); and P. Reynolds and D. Coates, 'Conclusions' in Coates, *Industrial Policy in Britain*, pp. 241–68.

24 See, for instance, C. Crouch and W. Streeck (eds), *Modern Capitalism or Modern Capitalisms?* (London, Francis Pinter, 1996).

25 M. Albert, *Capitalism Against Capitalism* (London, Whurr, 1993); see also M. Albert and R. Gonenc, 'The future of Rhenish capitalism', *Political Quarterly*, 67 (1996), 184–93.

26 D. North, *Institutions, Institutional Change and Economic Performance* (Cambridge, Cambridge University Press, 1990), p. 107.

27 Oulton, 'Supply side reform and UK economic growth', p. 53.

28 The literature is rapidly expanding, see J. March and J. Olsen, 'Institutional perspectives on political institutions', *Governance*, 9 (1996), 247–64; P. Hall and R. Taylor, 'Political science and the three new institutionalisms', *Political Studies*, 44 (1996), 936–57: R. Goodin (ed.), *The Theory of Institutional Design* (Cambridge, Cambridge University Press, 1996).

29 North, *Institutions, Institutional Change and Economic Performance*, pp. 4, 110, 94–5.

30 M. Sharp and W. Walker, 'Thatcherism and Technical Advance – Reform Without Progress?', in Buxton *et al.*, *Britain's Economic Performance*, pp. 397–429.

31 Criticism has recently given way to tentative approval of recent policy changes although there is still much scepticism about quality; see 'Education and Training in the UK', ch. 3 in *OECD Economic Surveys: United Kingdom, 1995* (Paris, OECD, 1995), pp. 46–84; and R. Bennett, 'Training and Enterprise Councils: are they cost-efficient?', *Policy Studies*, 15 (1994), 42–55.

32 S. Wilks, 'The Prolonged Reform of United Kingdom Competition Policy', in B. Doern and S. Wilks (eds), *Comparative Competition Policy: National Institutions in a Global Market* (Oxford, Clarendon, 1996).

33 J. Coakley and L. Harris, 'Financial Globalisation and Deregulation', in Mitchie, *The Economic Legacy*, p. 49.

34 North, *Institutions, Institutional Change and Economic Performance*, p. 33.

35 In the abstract see Y. Barzel, *Economic Analysis of Property Rights* (Cambridge, Cambridge University Press, 1989); on ownership see A. Gamble and G. Kelly, 'The new politics of ownership', *New Left Review*, 220 (1996), p. 71; on efficient companies see M. Aoki, B. Gustafsson and O. Williamson, *The Firm as a Nexus of Treaties* (London, Sage, 1990).

36 On this theme Fukuyama is stimulating, F. Fukuyama, *Trust: The Social Virtues and the Creation of Prosperity* (London, Hamish Hamilton, 1995).

37 H. Perkin, 'The third revolution and stakeholder capitalism: convergence or collapse?'. *Political Quarterly*, 67 (1996), pp. 198–208.

38 J. K. Galbraith, *The New Industrial State* (Harmondsworth, Penguin, 1969).

39 M. Friedman, *Capitalism and Freedom* (University of Chicago Press, 1982 [1962]), p. 133.

40 See e.g., D. Marquand, *The Unprincipled Society* (London, Fontana, 1988). Neither is it clear that Tony Blair would respond. He has presented a 'pro-business, pro-enterprise' theme, see *Financial Times*, 'Interview', 16 January 1997, p. 27.

41 From G. Goyder, *The Just Enterprise*, cited in S. Sheikh and W. Rees, 'Introduction' in S. Sheikh and W. Rees (eds), *Corporate Governance and Corporate Control* (London, Cavendish, 1995), p. x.

42 But see Gamble and Kelly, 'The new politics of ownership'. For political science and the corporation see D. Held, *Models of Democracy* (Oxford, Polity, 1987), ch. 6: and R. Sally. 'Multinational enterprises, political economy, and institutional theory: domestic embeddedness in the context of internationalisation', *Review of International Political Economy*, 1 (1994), 161–92.

43 W. Grant, *Business and Politics in Britain* (London, Macmillan, 2nd edn, 1993), pp. 14, 18.

44 Cawson *et al.*, *Hostile Brothers: Competition and Closure in the European Electronics Industry*.

45 OECD, *OECD Economic Surveys: United Kingdom, 1996* (Paris, OECD, 1996), p. 55.

46 J. Parkinson, *Corporate Power and Responsibility: Issues in the Theory of Company Law* (Oxford, Clarendon, 1993).

47 Gamble and Kelly, 'The new politics of ownership', p. 92.

48 J. Kay and A. Silberston, 'Corporate Governance'. *National Institute Economic Review* 153 (1995); Hutton, *The State We're In*.

49 See, Wilks, 'Regulatory compliance and capitalist diversity in Europe'.

50 For a review of growing disparities see P. Johnson, 'The assessment: inequality', *Oxford Review of Economic Policy: Inequality*, 12 (1996), 1–14.

51 As in the studies by Albert, Perkin and Hutton cited above.

5

FINANCE UNBOUND*

Will Hutton

THERE IS NO ALTERNATIVE!

The Conservative government decided early on that its overriding priority was low inflation – and the means to that end was control of the money supply by limiting government borrowing and setting appropriate interest and exchange rates. The precise weight applied to the chosen policy levers changed as the years and the theory wore on, but the consistency of intent was remarkable.

Although inflation picked up from around 4 per cent in the mid 1980s to over 10 per cent in 1990, the average inflation rate over the ten years from 1983 to 1993 was just over 5 per cent – a significant improvement on the previous twenty-five years during which it had averaged 9 per cent, and much closer to the average of the industrialised countries. Single-mindedness of purpose was beginning to yield results.

Low inflation was seen as the 'supply-side' reform to cap them all. Apart from improving the functioning of the market economy (by making price signals less distorted by volatile and unpredictable changes in overall price level) low inflation was important because it would stop savers being robbed of their efforts. Indeed, some of the messianic fervour that consecutive chancellors brought to their task was the sense that inflation was the ultimate sign of economic degeneracy; the battle was less an economic than a moral one. A famous *Times* leader of the early 1980s linked Keynesian economics, homosexuality and treachery to one's country as part of the same pattern. A revitalised British capitalism, having thrown off the dead-weight of socialism, should simply never inflate the value of its money.

But behind that conviction lay the long-standing dominance of the values of finance – of *rentiers* who live off the income others produce – over the values of production. The concern was less to promote the interests of production, which would flourish if the promised land of low inflation and low interest rates could be reached, than to set the framework that would – in the words of endless Treasury statements – 'bear down upon inflation'. All the majesty of Conservative hegemony in the unreformed state was deployed to increase the role of markets, disengage the state and fight for price stability. It was the apotheosis of rentierdom.

The genuine gains of low inflation were bought at terrible cost, from the growing dilapidation of the public infrastructure to the erosion of the country's productive base. The attempt to contain monetary and credit growth in a deregulated banking system without exchange controls led to a decade of high real interest rates and a level for sterling in relation to other currencies that fluctuated from fantastically excessive levels in the early 1980s to never less than significant overvaluation for the rest of the decade – at least if the levels of the 1960s and 1970s are used as a benchmark. Before this onslaught, investment in productive industry wilted while credit-driven consumer spending climbed to ever higher levels, bringing in its wake a flurry of investment in consumer services and property, all dependent upon spending that could never be sustained. Britain had become the laboratory for an extraordinary experiment in economic theory – and with a dominant party running a centralised state, there was no escape.

The period began with declarations of slavish belief in the notion that there was a systematic relationship between the rate of growth of some measure of the money supply and the subsequent inflation rate. This identity could only hold if a number of impossible assumptions were made about the nature of a market economy, in particular that it actually stood at or was tending to a perfect state of economic grace – but such belief was the badge of the New Right. Economists call this a competitive equilibrium – a condition where every market in the economy has simultaneously arrived at a point of balance: it depends on the idea that as producers and consumers in a free market will undertake no act against their economic self-interest, so the market must always tend to an unimprovable equilibrium. Because the economy is in this state of grace, all the government can do by permitting the money supply to expand above some target consistent with that state, is to push up prices. On this piece of theology a great nation's economic policy was based.

So how was the money supply to be controlled? The ultimate responsibility for money, reasoned the theorists, lies with the state – because money is legal tender. And what dictates above all else the amount of legal tender the state issues is the level of its borrowing. As long as it sticks to borrowing from the nation's pool of savings by offering savers its longterm debt there would be no need to print money; but if it strays from that sacred injunction and issues legal tender to finance its deficit (in other words printed money) the money supply would grow and inflation would result.[1] Thus the first task was to eliminate government borrowing; and while that was going on, to set increase rates at a level that could attract sufficient savings to finance the deficit. The process would necessarily be gradual – but eventually inflation would be eliminated.

This 'monetarist' philosophy neatly dovetailed with the long-standing prejudices of the Conservative right, because it provided a heaven-sent justification for the crusade against collectivism in all its forms. The best way to lower public borrowing, of course, was to reduce public expenditure rather than raise taxes, which were felt already to be too high; and reducing public expenditure would entail shedding the responsibilities that the state had undertaken in the fruitless attempt to make Keynesianism work, along with endlessly expensive social contracts with trade unions. Low inflation and the attack against the red menace became intertwined.

So in the spring of 1980 the Medium Term Financial Strategy (MTFS) was unveiled – the concrete policy targets that put numbers on the strategy. Public spending as a proportion of national output was to fall progressively in the years ahead, thus lowering public borrowing; and as borrowing fell the growth of a particular measure of money supply, M3 (the total lendable deposits of the banking system, but excluding building societies), was to fall in tandem – and with it the projected inflation rate. The performance of the economy was to be improved by tackling its other 'supply-side' deficiencies. Overmighty trade unions were to be cut down to size and managers encouraged by lower taxes to work harder. Competition and market forces would energise the economy as the government grimly struggled to meet the terms of the MTFS.

The intellectual deficiencies of this approach were numerous. The alleged linkage between public spending, public borrowing, money supply, interest rates and inflation was tenuous to say the least, with all kinds of qualifications required at each link in the chain; and the basic assumption that private sector activity in an unregulated market would tend to improve the economy was unreal. Indeed, throughout the decade interest rates remained high in real terms, and money supply broached the government's targets without any predictable effect on inflation, and government borrowing fell. It became ever more clear how idealistic the theory and policy were.

Already Britain's place in the international monetary order was driving the pound too high; the impact of domestic monetarism encouraged it to rise still further. The government felt it had to do more than just set interest rates to finance its deficit; it had to pitch them high enough to deter borrowers from demanding bank loans, and so inflating the money supply. In the autumn of 1979 bank base rates soared. International speculators not only diversified into a widely traded petro-currency; they could get 17 per cent interest as well.

The results were catastrophic. Facing super-competitive imports and priced out of export markets by a fantastically expensive pound, manufacturing production fell by 14 per cent in 1980 and 1981 and profits dropped by a third. National output (GDP) fell cumulatively by nearly 5 per cent and by 1983 there were 2 million fewer people with jobs than in 1979.

But although interest rates were to come down, the concern to hold back credit demand and make sure government borrowing was financed wholly from the nation's savings kept them well above inflation – so that in real terms they remained much higher than at any time since the war. The 1981 budget raised taxes by some 2 per cent of GDP in an attempt to control borrowing (and thus the growth of the money supply) in the middle of a recession, signalling decisively the change in economic priorities; but the growth of the money supply stubbornly failed to slow down as the monetarists had expected. On the other hand, the recession did not become more prolonged, as the Keynesians warned. In fact the economy picked up and the inflation rate remained relatively subdued despite the excessive growth of money supply – confounding everybody.

What was happening was, in truth, very simple. The high exchange rate and the associated growth in unemployment were together depressing inflation through their twin impact on import prices and wage increases – even though the money supply was growing rapidly. For at the same time financial deregulation was propelling a dramatic increase in credit-financed consumer spending. In the previous three decades, governments had aimed to manage the level of demand in the economy through changes in taxes, public spending and borrowing – the policy that the Thatcherites deplored, arguing that it produced ever higher inflation and unemployment because it enlarged the power of the state. Although such management of demand by the government was now officially eschewed, financial deregulation was producing the same result. In the old days governments had incurred public debt to finance their stimulation of the economy; now, private consumers and businesses were doing the same with private debt. In effect the government, by deregulating finance, had privatised an enormous reflation.

Over the 1980s private debt levels doubled, so that by 1990 households held £114 of debt, up from £57 in 1980, for every £100 of disposable income; both the fastest growth rate and highest absolute level of debt of any western industrialised country. Most of the lending was for buying houses and flats, and the stock of mortgage debt increased sixfold from £52 billion in 1980 to £294 billion in 1990. House prices more than doubled over the same period.[2]

Banks and building societies were inadvertently taking over the role of managing demand. Lending against house purchases seemed a cast-iron risk, and together with the sale of insurance policies – notably endowment policies to finance mortgage repayments – the business quickly earned a reputation as an apparently bottomless source of commission income, fees and bank charges. From 1979 to 1990 there was no year when bank and building society lending did not grow by at least 15 per cent, reaching a peak of 24 per cent in 1988.

This could not have happened without the banks campaigning for further deregulation to exploit the fact that the monetary corset and reserve requirements had gone. Hire purchase controls on consumer credit were scrapped. Banks were allowed to enter the mortgage market in 1981; building societies were allowed to compete for longer-term deposits in the London money markets; neither were asked to check how their borrowers used mortgage loans, so that increasingly the loans allegedly for home purchase were used for consumption purposes. This was the phenomenon of 'equity withdrawal' – in effect, people were eating their own seed-corn. And as property prices rose, lenders became more and more confident in their lending – advancing ever higher proportions of the value of homes at ever greater multiples of the borrowers' income.

Borrowers for their part became more confident about taking on such debt. Wages for those in work outpaced the rise in prices, which were depressed by the same high pound that was making British producers' trading prospects so difficult. With real incomes rising, borrowing followed suit and gradually house prices began to increase. Occupants of houses felt wealthy, able to borrow and spend in their own right. And around the whole activity a mini-industry of financial services was being constructed, which took on workers and allowed the number employed to start rising as early as 1983.

There was a self-reinforcing circle – well described by Professor Duncan Maclennan in his report for the Joseph Rowntree Foundation. As employment rose, there was more spending and borrowing power – and consumers began to learn that the Conservatives meant business when they talked about tax reductions. This created yet more false confidence about taking on extra debts, and gave yet another impetus to the rise in house prices.

The growth in consumer spending was slow at first, rising by about 1 per cent in 1982, but its growth averaged 3.3 per cent in the next three years to climax at 6.3 per cent in each of the three years straddling the 1987 election.[3] Yet the growth within that total was heavily skewed towards consumer services – everything from dry cleaning to private schools – where growth averaged 6.4 per cent a year over the 1980s. And on the back of this growth new firms and industries – from luxury chocolate importers to designer lingerie – prospered.

That all of this had its origins in the abolition of exchange and banking controls in 1979 and 1980, which in turn had been triggered by Britain's particular role in the international financial system, was beside the point. For entrepreneurs in the bustle of the marketplace the experience was that people were spending; and they invested in the expectation that they would go on doing so.

As the upturn swept to its climax, some two million houses were bought and sold in 1988 – each requiring new kitchens, bathrooms, curtains and carpets; each transaction required estate agents, banks, building societies, insurance companies, lawyers and architects, thus generating a new round of income, employment and spending. The boom was feeding on itself.

The government boasted that private business investment was reaching new peaks, and so it was; but it was only in 1988 that manufacturing investment recovered to its 1979 level. While manufacturing investment represented some 5 per cent of GDP at the peak of the boom, investment in services and construction climbed to 12 per cent of GDP – predicated upon levels of consumption growth and property price inflation that could not continue. Rising house prices and rising spending had defied the fact of high interest rates for a decade; and the correction when it came would surely be painful.

The government itself was wrestling with the inconsistencies of its theory. Its aim was to produce low inflation by controlling the money supply, but inflation between 1983 and 1988 averaged 4.7 per cent while the growth of broad money supply averaged 14.7 per cent. If the theory had been true, inflation should have been in double figures: instead it seemed low and stable.

For a non-monetarist it was no mystery at all. The economy had never been in the state of grace represented by competitive equilibrium, so no systematic relationship between money growth and inflation was ever likely to be provable. The chief influences keeping inflation down were unemployment and the high exchange rate. But this meant that the balance of payments became a kind of disinflationary safety-valve, with demand leaking abroad to buy cheap imports, which doubled over the decade. At the same time exports increased by 40 per cent – less than half the rate of imports – so that the visible trade deficit mushroomed.

The first grim milestone was passed in 1983 when Britain became a net importer of manufactured goods for the first time since the Industrial Revolution, but the process continued remorselessly so that in 1989 the visible trade deficit – excluding oil – climbed to £26 billion, close to 5 per cent of GDP. Yet as the evidence mounted that success in lowering inflation had little to do with monetary targets the government persisted in believing that the cause of low inflation was monetary stability. In fact, the chain of causation runs from economic strength to low inflation to price stability – but the government, fixated on financial variables and free market economics, believed that the chain ran the opposite way.

The world beyond the UK was increasingly unbelieving, and so in an attempt to give its ideas more intellectual credibility the government switched horses in the second half of the decade, moving away from trying to control the money supply to fixing targets for the exchange rate. If the money supply seemed a poor anchor for monetary policy, then at least the exchange rate was more explicit. Other European countries had tied their exchange rate to the mark in the European exchange rate mechanism, and if they were to hold the rate then their inflation could be no higher than Germany's – famous for its commitment to price stability. France was in the process of dramatically lowering its inflation rate, and the Thatcherites sat up and noticed. Chancellor Lawson may have been rebuffed by Mrs Thatcher in his attempt to join the system in 1985 but for five years he and his successor, John Major, either explicitly or tacitly used a strong exchange rate as a yardstick for how tight or loose monetary conditions were – and to 'bear down upon inflation'.

As we have seen, by trying to control the exchange rate the government necessarily (given that anyone could move capital into or out of the UK at will) surrendered control of interest rates. In the first phase of shadowing the mark at DM3, interest rates were driven down too low to stop the pound from rising above its 'shadow rate', helping the boom to reach its climax – and the famous fall-out between the Chancellor and the Prime Minister over the merits of 'trying to buck the market' was to lead to Lawson's resignation.

Interest rates were then ratcheted higher as the government at last recognised that it was presiding over a credit boom.

Sterling, which had been allowed to depreciate from the absurd levels it had reached in 1980 to a still overvalued but lower level in 1986, began to strengthen again under the new policy direction. The squeeze on manufacturing was relentless. Although profits as a share of national output rose remarkably, the distribution of profitability was skewed, as John Muellbauer and Anthony Murphy have shown; the more a sector was exposed to international competition, the less profitable it was – and the lower its rate of investment. The capital stock of manufacturing as a whole barely rose across the decade, outstripped by the rise in the capital stock of financial services, dwellings and hotels. Britain finished the 1980s with shopping malls, banks and houses aplenty but its manufacturing base static.

A decade of attempts to control the money supply and produce monetary stability was in danger of collapsing in near farce – and the Treasury saw ERM membership as the best solution. When Britain finally joined in the autumn of 1990, in a last attempt to find a credible monetary anchor, control of interest rates was lost completely. Real interest rates (as measured by mortgage rate less retail price inflation) climbed to nearly 10 per cent, as German interest rates rose to contain the inflationary consequences of reunion. The great surge in lending and borrowing that had characterised the 1980s came juddering to a halt – and a second severe recession began.

The processes that had fuelled the nine-year boom were thrown into reverse. Burdened by debt and shaken by unemployment and wage cuts in the new deregulated labour market, buyers withdrew from the property market. Lenders took fright. Property prices fell, exposing banks and building societies to unprecedented levels of bad debt – and they drew in their horns. Turnover in the housing market halved and equity withdrawal collapsed. Consumption stagnated.

The financial and consumer services industries had swollen too much and now retrenched, adding further to the downward spiral as they laid off workers. The government's tax revenues fell and its spending on income support to offset the recession ballooned; the public sector, in surplus in 1990, went into the biggest underlying deficit in peacetime history. And all the while real interest rates, with Britain's exchange rate pegged to the mark inside the ERM, remained at a stifling 5 to 6 per cent.

Finally a wave of speculation sprang the trap, and Britain was forced out of the ERM. The devaluation and lower interest rates that the economic establishment had confidently predicted would provoke a fresh round of inflation instead proved the trigger of recovery, while inflation remained low. Purely by chance and against all its instincts and efforts, the government found itself presiding over a successful devaluation – at the bottom of a recession and compelled by its own finances to increase taxes.

For the Conservative government re-elected in 1992 found that the mushrooming budget deficit required drastic attention. Stripping out all capital expenditure and receipts, the public sector's current deficit had plunged into the red to the tune of 6 per cent of GDP. Chancellors Lamont and Clarke together imposed £17 billion of tax increases in the two budgets of 1993 (to be phased in over three years), which were regarded as the minimum necessary to rectify the situation. Public spending was cut dramatically, involving a further 17 per cent drop in public capital investment that was already the lowest as a proportion of GDP since the war.

Burdened by tax increases, and with the debts of the 1980s still hanging over their heads, it is obvious that consumers cannot drive the recovery onward. Indeed, with consumption at a post-war high and its counterpart, savings, at the lowest level in the international league table, consumers are not in any position to do so. Britain has to look to production, investment and exports to capitalise upon the gains from devaluation – the sectors that have been left so weak by the fifteen-year experiment.

THE RECKONING

Among the industrialised countries only the growth of manufacturing output in France, Greece and Norway was worse than Britain's during the 1980s. At the peak of the 1980s boom, in 1989, manufacturing output had grown no more than 1.2 per cent per year from the peak of the previous cycle. Manufacturing investment as a proportion of national output had continually *fallen* over the decade – intensifying a trend discernible since 1960. Since then Britain has suffered the largest fall of manufacturing employment of any industrialised country, and the switchback ride of the 1980s intensified the rate of job loss. Yet as the defenders of the Thatcher and Major years argue, manufacturing productivity in Britain has risen significantly faster than in the years beforehand.[4] But this rise did not translate into investment and output growth. Why?

The answer lies in the dominance of financial values over British corporate life and economic policy. The overvalued exchange rate damaged industrial competitiveness, but in the Treasury/Bank of England scheme of things that took second place to the contribution a high exchange rate could make towards price stability. High real interest rates, designed to contain the avalanche of credit unleashed by financial deregulation, were always judged in terms of their impact upon inflation and never upon the internal rates of return that firms set for their investment projects. The policy priorities were always firmly financial; there were targets for the money supply, for the exchange rate, for the reduction of public borrowing, for the percentage share of public spending of national output and latterly for the inflation rate. These were the ancient totems of the British state speaking in the new economic language of monetarist economics. Targets for employment or for growth were never mentioned. They were to be left to the market.

But if manufacturing output growth was depressed, it was argued that Britain's export performance had improved. The British share of the industrialised countries' manufactured exports was stabilising and even rising; something was improving.

However, as Kirsty Hughes and others have shown, the improvement has to be seen in a world context. If the newly industrialised Asian and Latin American countries' exports are included in the computation, then Britain's performance was as indifferent as its position in the manufacturing output league table suggests. What was happening was that the UK was specialising in fewer sectors – such as chemicals and aerospace – while giving up ground in others like textiles and mechanical engineering. In high-growth sectors there was virtually no British representation, while in areas like consumer electronics and cars the turnaround was wholly due to inward direct investment, notably from Japan, which itself implied rising imports of Japanese-made parts. Although exports were rising, imports were rising even faster. Between 1979 and 1989 exports rose by 18.7 per cent, Kirsty Hughes calculates; but imports rose by 56.5 per cent. And while total production in the economy fell by 3.8 per cent over this period, British producers' production fell even further – by 9.6 per cent. The 1980s were not a success story for indigenous British producers.[5]

As a result, the country is in an unsustainable position. It is running a chronic trade deficit, financed increasingly by bank lending. Between 1990 and 1993 the cumulative current account deficit was just under £50 billion, yet at the same time inward direct investment flows were more than offset by British companies investing overseas. British pension funds and insurance companies have invested £87 billion abroad. The balance has been made up by British banks cumulatively borrowing over £90 billion.[6] Britain may have assets overseas amounting to some 30 per cent of GDP, but it also has short-term liabilities to foreigners equivalent to 30 per cent of GDP – the highest in its peace-time history.[7]

This cannot continue – and in any case makes the UK highly sensitive to changes in interest rates abroad and the willingness of foreign institutions to continue to build up short-term deposits in Britain. The larger their holding of British debt becomes, the more powerful their veto over the autonomy of British economic policy. If they were all to withdraw their money simultaneously the exchange rate would fall and interest rates rise sharply, generating unwanted inflation and a slow-down in economic activity. The country therefore needs to move towards balance on its trading account.

This places a particularly heavy responsibility on the already weakened manufacturing sector. As the Select Committee on Trade and Industry reported, every 1 per cent fall in manufacturing exports must be compensated for by more than a 2.5 per cent rise in exports of services. Although Britain's service sector is held up as the industry of the future, world trade is still predominantly in manufactures. To achieve balance on the UK's international accounts by the year 2000, while economic growth averaged 2.5 per cent a year, would require Britain's financial sector to absorb the entire current international financial activity of New York and Tokyo.[7] Since this is plainly impossible, manufacturing exports simply have to play an enlarged role.

As a result the economy and state now face a series of strategic dilemmas. There has to be economic growth to lower unemployment and improve the government's fiscal position but, if the current relationships hold, any significant economic growth would suck in imports so greedily that the balance of payments deficit would explode superimposed upon Britain's already heavy short-term borrowings. Because this is unsustainable, the financial markets would demand a policy change and interest rates would rise and the exchange rate would fall. Consumers would be squeezed savagely as their wages bought less, for the scale of the necessary adjustment is staggering.

If economic growth were to average just 3 per cent over the next five years, the government's budget deficit would fall towards near balance by 1998 or 1999, as long as public spending grew at less than half the rate of the economy as the government currently projects. But the growth of consumption, on current form, would imply such high import growth that the total balance of payments current account deficit – visible and invisible trade – would climb to between 4 and 5 per cent of GDP even after allowing for the improvements in 1994 following devaluation in 1992.[8] The difficulty is compounded because the City has reclaimed its ancient freedom to invest overseas which, as we have seen, has meant a cumulative outflow of £87 billion between 1990 and 1993. The consequence of such growth in these conditions would be unfinanceable, and long before the deficit climbed so high the exchange rate would have fallen and the growth in the economy checked by a tightening of economic policy.

To put it another way, if Britain's shrunken manufacturing base were able to support export growth of 5.5 per cent, this would prevent the current account deficit from becoming unsustainably large, but the most the wider economy can grow is by 1.5 to 2 per cent.[9] This would imply unemployment staying above 2.5 million, with the economy unable to offer any prospects for the one-in-four adult men who are economically inactive. But it would also imply, as social security expenditure rises to relieve poverty, that the government's current budget deficit would stay at around 4.5 per cent of GDP. There would have to be tax increases to correct the imbalances, which would slow growth down even further.

The terrible paradox is that modest growth is almost too much for Britain to bear. The economy is trapped by its own weaknesses. As Tony Thirlwall and many others have observed, economies that experience strong GDP growth depend upon a strong growth in their manufacturing output and exports – otherwise they find themselves in Britain's present situation. The position is worsened by the use of international borrowing to finance consumption and not investment, so that the adjustment, when it comes, will be more severe. The City's power to set policy is matched by its capacity to borrow to hide the consequences – but that cannot continue for ever.

Manufacturing output cannot rise without investment, R&D and innovation. One of the key free-market propositions is that growth and investment are determined 'naturally' by technical change and population growth, and that the best governments can do is not 'artificially' interfere with these processes. To lift investment above its 'natural' rate by government action is to reduplicate existing factories, offices and machines, lower the profit rate and overheat the economy. The best policy is just to improve 'natural' market efficiency. But, as John Wells argues, this neglects the statistical fact that across countries and time the higher the growth rate, the higher the investment rate, especially in plant and equipment. Moreover, government action from raising skill levels to redesigning systems of finance has succeeded in raising investment levels and the rate of growth of productivity – as the experience of Japan and East Asia highlights dramatically. It is possible, via government institution-building, to improve the trajectory of growth, investment and export performance – whatever the free-market purists claim.

Over the 1980s and 1990s this insight has been neglected. British investments in human capital, in the physical infrastructure and in industries which can trade internationally has languished, focusing instead on the service sector. Business R&D is the lowest of the major industralised countries while the registration of new patents has continued to fall.[10] The country's competitive sinews have wasted even as the strategic options facing the nation have become more challenging.

What is now required is a national effort to organise a sustained increase in investment, but the economic institutions and state structures are no more ready to respond to such a call than they ever were. The dominance of financial values and targets, the tolerance of ever rising consumption as a proportion of GDP, and the indifference to investment and employment are deep-seated. The Conservative Party simply gave the old beast its head – with familiar results.

But even as it caved in to the City's age-old lobby for financial freedom, it had to listen to another lobby from industry that wanted to regain the right to manage – or more plainly to break the power of the trade unions. Monetary discipline would produce price stability and financial freedom would ensure the productive use of savings, the third prong of the free-market attack was to secure freedom from the unions in order to secure higher productivity. To achieve this the awesome power of the state was brought to bear, just as it had been used to free the City. But as the consequences of *laissez-faire* in finance had been perverse, so the deregulation of the British labour market brought precious little benefit and an awful lot of pain.

NOTES

*   This chapter has been adapted from, W. Hutton, *The State We're In*, Jonathan Cape, 1995, Ch. 3, pp. 56–81.

1   In today's capital markets the equivalent to printing money is to issue Treasury Bills, short-term IOUs, which are bought by the banking system. The banks part with cash which the government can spend, and now hold an asset – a Treasury Bill – which counts as cash as far as banks are concerned. They can use the bills to settle accounts with each other, and they are always realisable for a predictable amount of cash in the London money markets. In effect the government has printed money.

2   'Good Housekeeping', Will Hutton, IPPR, 1991.

3   Christopher Johnson, *The Economy under Mrs Thatcher*, Penguin, 1991.

4   Nic Crafts, 'Can Deindustrialisation Seriously Damage your Wealth?' IEA Hobart Paper 120, London 1993.

5   *The Future of UK Competitiveness and the Role of Industrial Policy*, edited by Kirsty Hughes.

6   Author's calculations.

7   Goldman Sachs calculations for the IFS 'Green Budget', 12 October 1994.

8   Evidence by the Cambridge-Harvard Research Group to the Trade and Industry Select Committee, p. 22.

9   Figures supplied by Bill Martin, chief economist of UBS, in advice to the Treasury and Civil Service Select Committee, November 1993.

10   Trade and Industry Select Committee, op. cit.

REFERENCES

Christopher Johnson, *The Economy under Mrs Thatcher*, Penguin, 1991

Bill Martin, Evidence to the Treasury and Civil Service Select Committee, January 1994. Also 'Invisible, visible, risible', UBS Economic Commentary March 1994 and 'Debt by Misadventure', UBS Economic Commentary, March 1994

6

THE MANAGEMENT OF THE UK ECONOMY*

David Coates

MODELS AS AN AID TO UNDERSTANDING

I want us now to turn to address the question of how to make sense of the complicated pattern of government policy and economic performance. With so much going on, how can we explain it all? How indeed can we even begin to put such an explanation together?

I think that we can best begin the pursuit of that explanation by recognizing our limitations, by being quite clear that we just can't hope to make sense of all this complex detail at one go. But there is nothing unusual about this. On the contrary, social scientists often face such a problem: the danger of being 'swamped' by too much information, too many variables, too complicated a set of interconnections. And a characteristic and very valuable response is to stand back from the complexity for a while, choosing instead simply to abstract from that complexity just part of what's going on, for examination first. Inevitably that means that analysis begins (though it will not end) in a very simplified way. There is great virtue – in social analysis – in starting with the simple and moving to the complex, and that is what I would like to do here.

So one way of reaching an understanding of all that complexity is to start with a simple model that captures some key elements of the overall picture. Then, later, we can work our way back towards the complexity from which we began, but only once the simplified picture has been grasped and understood [. . .] A number of such models are available to us. The one that we will use treats the economy as a series of flows of resources and expenditures. Let's see what use we can make of it in the pursuit of our understanding of the pattern and impact of government attempts to manage the post-war UK economy.

Building a model of the economy

At its most elementary, it helps to think of the economy as a series of exchanges between two key economic institutions: between households (which among their other functions, provide labour power and consume products) and firms (who employ labour, and make products). The households supply workers to the firms and the firms supply goods and services to the households. We can draw that set of exchanges as Diagram 6.1. The shaded

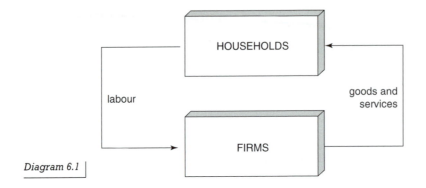

Diagram 6.1

square denotes the area of the economy. The boxes denote the key economic institutions, the arrows the exchange between them.

At the same time, spending flows round the circuit in the opposite direction. The firms pay the households wages for the labour they supply, and the households pay the firms for the goods they obtain from them. We can draw that as Diagram 6.2, with the flows of expenditure shown as broken lines.

But life of course is not so simple. Banks and other financial institutions get into the act, as households deposit money with them, and as they lend money to firms, and to other households. The firms then use that money (and some of their income from the sale of goods and services to households) to buy machinery and raw materials from other firms – firms who don't themselves sell anything directly to households. We can draw that too (see Diagram 6.3).

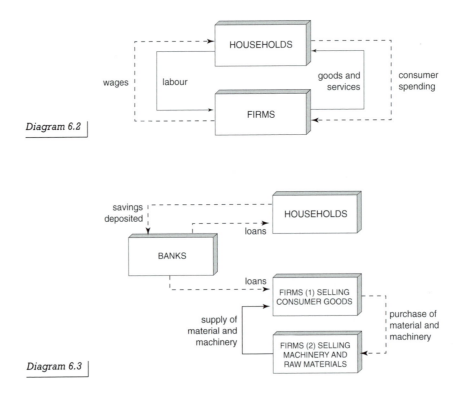

Diagram 6.2

Diagram 6.3

The government is in there as well, taxing some households and paying benefits to others, and taxing some firms and spending money with others (see Diagram 6.4).

Perhaps you are beginning to see that we could easily make each of these flow diagrams a lot more complicated. We could add a flow of taxes from firms to government in Diagram 6.4, for example, or firms' deposits with banks in Diagram 6.3. But our simplified diagrams are capturing some of the important exchange flows at work in the contemporary UK economy; and if we overburden them with detail they will begin to lose their clarity. That is a common trade-off in modelling: the loss of complexity in the pursuit of clarity. So let us keep it simple for a moment, and add some of the flows associated with foreign trade. We will draw it with households doing all the buying of imported goods, and firms all the exporting – just to keep it simple. In truth, of course, both firms and households engage in foreign trade – buying foreign goods and (in the case of firms at least) selling things to foreign consumers. In each case money goes in one direction, goods and services in the other – to give us a picture of the kind shown in Diagram 6.5.

You should notice here that, for the moment, we have left 'foreign buyers and sellers' totally unconnected with the banks and firms of the UK economy. In Diagram 6.5 the complex interconnections between the local UK economy and the global one hardly surface at all. The linkages between UK firms and multinationals, the international linkages of the money markets, the close relations between governments – all that is for the moment left to one side. We will look at Diagram 6.5 in considerable detail – and make it more complex – towards the end of the chapter, when we have used the simpler version to clarify government economic policy within the UK itself.

Armed with these diagrams, let's go back to the government's economic policy objectives. The four policy commitments adopted after the Second World War [. . .] were as follows:

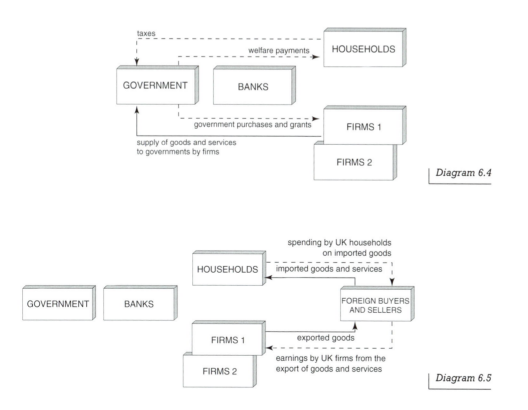

Diagram 6.4

Diagram 6.5

- high and stable employment;
- rising living standards;
- price stability; and
- a healthy balance of payments.

Let's fit each of these to the exchange flows we have isolated so far (see Diagram 6.6).

- *High and stable employment* requires that the flow of labour called to the firms is large enough (and remains large enough) to absorb as many as possible of those who want to leave the household to obtain paid employment. That flow of labour can be seen at point 'A' in Diagram 6.6.
- *Rising living standards* require that the flow of goods from the firms to the households steadily increases over time (that flow, of course, can include imports). The flow is marked at point 'B' in Diagram 6.6.
- *Price stability* is more difficult to capture in Diagram 6.6, because the diagram shows movements in resources rather than changes in price. But for the moment it is enough to note on our diagram the point at which any price inflation will first manifest itself. That is at point 'C'. Price stability requires that the price of goods and services leaving the firms remains as unchanged as possible.
- And *the balance of payments* requires that spending on imports does not outstrip earnings from exports (point 'D' in Diagram 6.6).

So when the government manages the economy with those four policy goals in mind, it has to influence the full set of money and resource flows to obtain a satisfactory result at points 'A', 'B', 'C' and 'D' in Diagram 6.6. The question, of course, is how.

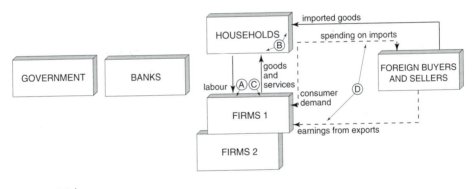

Diagram 6.6

THE MANAGEMENT OF THE ECONOMY

The answer to the question, 'how should the UK economy be run?', has varied over time, as bodies of economic theory have risen and fallen in popularity in government circles. Fashions here have been dictated partly by which issues were uppermost in the minds of politicians and the electorate. In the 1940s and 1950s, with memories of inter-war unemployment still firmly in mind, the prime concern of policy was full employment. In the 1960s and 1970s, as international competition intensified, attention shifted to the balance of payments and economic growth. In the 1980s, attention moved to inflation, and the commitment to full employment took more of a back seat. The benchmark of government economic success in the 1950s was the level of unemployment. By the 1970s, it was the rate of economic growth. A decade later, it was the rate of growth of the price index; and that shift of benchmark coincided with a shift too in the focus of policy itself. In the 1950s governments concentrated on the management of levels of *demand* in the economy. By the 1980s, politicians had come to see how important it was too to influence levels of *supply*. We can trace that shift of emphasis by looking at the rise and fall of particular bodies of economic theory.

THE MANAGEMENT OF DEMAND

The most influential set of answers available to policy makers in the first twenty-five years after the Second World War derived from the writings of John Maynard Keynes. His general position is discussed in [chapter 3 of this book] on traditions of thought.

The orthodox view of how to solve unemployment in the 1930s was to leave it to market forces. Markets will in the end 'clear' if the prices of the goods handled within them respond to the demand and supply conditions evident in the market place. But such a view – of long term solutions to unemployment that involve reducing wage levels in the labour market – did not satisfy Keynes. He wasn't convinced that wage cutting and reductions in government spending would bring the economy out of depression. Instead, he believed that what the economy required – in conditions of mass unemployment at least – was an increase in *Aggregate Demand*, not a reduction.

Let's pause for a moment to clarify this notion of 'Aggregate Demand'. If you look back to our earlier diagrams, you will see that we have already introduced some of the component elements of total/aggregate demand in the economy.

1 In Diagram 6.2, we introduced spending by households on goods and services (a flow often known as consumer demand or 'c').
2 In Diagram 6.3, we introduced spending by firms on machinery and raw materials (often known as investment demand or 'i').
3 In Diagram 6.4, we introduced spending by governments ('g'); and
4 In Diagram 6.5, we introduced the amount earned from exports ('x') less that spent on imports ('m').

These are the component elements of demand in the economy; and often appear in economics textbooks as:

Aggregate Demand = $c + i + g + x - m$

Keynes argued strongly that the task of increasing Aggregate Demand fell to government. If governments wanted firms to flourish, jobs to expand and living standards to rise, then they had to *increase* the flows of demand in the economic system. Look at the position of the firms in our diagrams, and at the flows reaching them. If they are to employ more people, they will need more income coming into their coffers, with which to pay the extra workers. The diagrams suggest a number of sources of income for the firms.

No doubt as the economy expands, all of these sources of income for the firms will grow; but the expansion has to start somewhere, and the question is where. Keynes's answer was broadly as follows (see Diagram 6.7). That the expansion would *not* begin with:

- *exports* (flow 1). It is obviously desirable to sell more abroad; but it is very hard to guarantee such a growth in exports from within the UK itself. Governments can encourage industrial efficiency in UK-based firms, but even so levels of demand abroad depend on many factors over which UK governments have no direct control. Nor would it begin with:

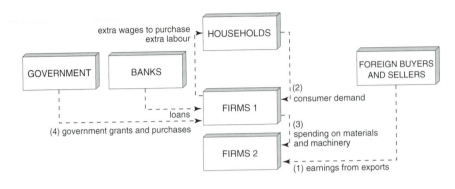

Diagram 6.7

- *consumer demand* (flow 2). This was exactly what Keynes wanted to increase. If it went up, firms would sell more, employ more people, pay out more wages, and so expand further. But there was, and is, a real chicken and egg problem here. More wages won't be paid out until consumer demand has already gone up (or until some aspect of the total demand experienced by firms has risen). The process of expansion cannot therefore start here. As Keynes said in 1930, 'you cannot start the ball rolling in this way' (Clarke, 1988, p.115). Nor can it start with:

- *investment goods* (flow 3). This too was something that Keynes wanted to see expand. But he realized that firms would only buy new machinery if they had confidence in the future profitability of their operations. That confidence could be improved if the cost of borrowing was low – which was why Keynes favoured a policy of low interest rates. But he also realized that banks wouldn't lend to firms who couldn't sell their extra output; and that firms wouldn't seek extra funds until they too could be sure of new markets. So business had to be stimulated by the creation of an environment of economic expansion; and for that stimulation Keynes looked to the government.

- *government spending* (flow 4). This was the key entry point for Keynes and for other Keynesian-inspired economists: for the State to use its own spending to generate new demand in the economy, and to alter tax rates to free the private spending of others. We had to spend our way out of recession, and use the revenues generated by that expansion to pay off the government spending which had precipitated it. Such government spending would have a *multiplier effect* throughout the whole economy, as the expenditure and income initially released passed from hand to hand, generating income on each occasion, so overall providing an increase in the volume of total demand far in excess of the original government injection – and stimulating new investment and production in the process.

AN ILLUSTRATION OF THE MULTIPLIER

This notion of the 'multiplier' is easiest to grasp in a simple game. Gather five friends and one pound in cash (in the form of five 20p pieces). You be the government, injecting a pound into this economy, and let your friends save 20p whenever the money reaches them. Now inject your pound by spending it with your first friend. Her income will go up by £1. She will then spend 80p of that pound with the next friend. That friend will have an extra income of 80p. That friend will then spend 60p with friend No. 3. Friend No. 3 will spend 40p with friend No. 4, who will in turn spend 20p with friend No. 5. Your original pound will have generated a total income of £1 (friend 1) plus 80p (friend 2) plus 60p (friend 3) plus 40p (friend 4) plus 20p (for friend 5). That is £3.00 in total. Not bad for one pound injected. That is the multiplier!

KEYNESIANISM IN PRACTICE

British governments in the post-war years were economically active in ways which seemed to meet well the role anticipated for them in Keynes's *General Theory*. From 1944, as we have seen, they accepted a commitment to full employment, and from even earlier (it is conventional to cite the 1941 budget as the first occasion) politicians in power used both fiscal and monetary techniques to keep economic activity as near to full employment as they could manage. As we saw in the summary of policy earlier, they used fiscal techniques (alterations in taxes) to influence purchasing power. They also influenced money flows through the banks by the scale and character of their own borrowing, and by altering the terms on which private credit could be obtained. Overall, governments superintended a quite unprecedented peace-time growth in the scale of their own spending, and in the provision of bank credit to private borrowers; and as the years passed government activity in the economy became increasingly vital to the processes of private investment there. When state activity was greatest – in 1975 – 57.9 per cent of the Gross National Product passed through its hands. Of that 57.9 per cent, 28.3 per cent was only transfers by state agencies (such as the social security system) from one person to another, but the rest (26.9 per cent of GNP) was resources actually directly consumed by public bodies such as hospitals, schools, the police and the army. For in the years after 1945, governments became major employers in their own right. In 1975, 7.2 million people worked for central and local government, the nationalized industries and the armed forces; and many more, in private industry, were dependent on the government for the purchase of what they produced, for the regulation of the conditions under which they worked, and even for the investment on which their jobs depended (Coates, 1984, pp. 219–20).

Academics still disagree about whether all this did, or did not, constitute a genuinely Keynesian revolution in economic policy after the war. But at least there can be no doubt that the politicians responsible for these policy changes invariably thought of themselves as Keynesians. And well they might. For they were prepared to stimulate private investment as Keynes had suggested they should, and, with very few exceptions, they all seemed to have absorbed the very Keynesian assumption that it was the government's responsibility to manage the economy in the pursuit of full employment. Governments of all political persuasion in Britain in the 1950s and 1960s seem to have recognized that the total level of demand in the economy could be too low to persuade firms to employ everyone who wanted a job, and that it was the government's responsibility to alter the level of total demand in order to keep employment levels high.

So the impact of Keynesian ideas on government policy in the first twenty-five years after the war is clear. It is also clear, however; that the impact of those ideas diminished over time: and that the 1970s and early 1980s witnessed something of a counter-revolution in economic theory and policy against what had become by then the ruling Keynesian orthodoxies. That revolution was fuelled by the emergence of two difficulties for Keynesian-inspired policy makers, difficulties which for a while eroded both public and professional support for Keynesianism.

The first of those difficulties arose out of the *local–global* tension in economic policy. The second arose out of the altered relationships between the *public and private* in the modern economy associated with the implementation of Keynesian policies. Let's take each difficulty in turn.

Difficulty number one

Ask yourself what happens after the government has injected spending into the economy, if local industry is less efficient than its foreign rivals?

The answer to that question points to a major long-term weakness in Keynesian solutions to unemployment. Keynesianism has no monopoly of this weakness, as we will see later. The difficulties created by the lack of international competitiveness of UK-based industry were evident from the 1880s, and remained into the 1980s, long after Keynesianism had been formally abandoned as the source of economic policy. But the lack of competitiveness of UK-based manufacturing firms first re-surfaced as a problem after the war in the era of Keynesian dominance, and indeed helped to bring that dominance to an end. So its impact needs to be understood first as a source of difficulty for Keynesianism.

For if locally-produced goods are more expensive, or of poorer quality, than similar goods produced abroad, then it is not unreasonable to suppose that export earnings will fall (as foreign consumers buy fewer UK-made goods) and that the amount spent on imports will rise (as home consumers buy better foreign-made products). Then if the government allows levels of internal demand to rise, instead of local jobs being created, foreign ones will be created (as much of the extra income will literally 'leak out' of the system as spending on imports). Governments in such situations will therefore not just face problems of local unemployment. They will also face a *balance of payments* problem.

This certainly happened in the UK in the 1950s and 1960s. Governments tried to implement Keynesian policies of demand management; and as they did so, they increasingly ran into balance of payments difficulties. Indeed this recurring balance of payments problem was *the* way in which successive British governments in those years – and their Keynesian-inspired economic advisers – became aware of the diminishing competitiveness of UK-based industry. They kept running into balance of payments deficits – in 1955, 1960, 1964, 1965 and 1968 – deficits which were small by comparison to those of the late 1980s, but which at the time were deemed large enough to require a governmental reaction.

Governments reacted initially by concentrating on the immediate payments crisis. Only later did they begin to probe seriously for underlying causes. As they did so, economists and politicians of a broadly Keynesian persuasion put together what we might term a Keynesian explanation of the competitive decline of UK-based industry. Their understanding of this issue developed through a number of stages.

1 Their first characteristic reaction to the balance of payments crises, as we have said, was to *slow down demand* (in policies known at the time as 'stop–go'). They increased taxation and reduced their own spending.

2 Then they began to see the problem as one, not of demand alone, but of the *trade union power* which seemed partly to generate it. They began to see that twenty-five years of full employment gave workers and unions the confidence to negotiate high wage and income settlements: and that these high wages added to industrial costs and inflated levels of consumer demand. In such a situation, all Keynesian-inspired governments could do, whilst struggling to maintain full employment, was to seek wage restraint – either voluntarily through agreement, or statutorily by imposition – in effect throwing a barrier across the inflated wage flow (at the line 'X–Y' in Diagram 6.8). We can illustrate that on our flow diagram. Follow the sequence of points 1, 2, 3, 4 and 5.

3 Here indeed was one major reason for the supplementation of demand management by direct negotiations with trade unions in the 1960s and 1970s. While employment was high and trade unions strong, governments needed voluntary agreements with union leaders and members to restrain money wages and to keep costs down, if they were to avoid the build up of inflationary pressures: and for this reason stop–go policies were supplemented with incomes policies, one after another between 1961 and 1979.

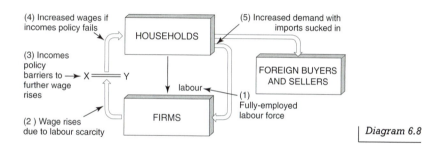

Diagram 6.8

4 The realization grew too that 'stop–go' was itself a problem – that this *persistent blocking of demand* was a serious disincentive to investment. Many Keynesian economists saw low levels of investment in manufacturing plant and equipment as the key to the UK's relative economic decline, and explained that as a consequence of a general lack of reliable and expanding levels of demand in the economy. Such a view encouraged many of them to urge a rapid expansion of the economy, in the hope that investment would surge in volume in response to easier selling conditions. It also encouraged Keynesian-inspired economists of a more left-wing predisposition to advocate direct government action to stimulate investment even when market incentives were low: action in the form of indicative planning in the National Economic Development Council, or (more radical still) direct government investment in industry and infrastructure. They began, that is, to suggest government action on the *supply* side of the economy, as well as the *demand* side.

Let's pause for a moment to clarify this notion of the 'supply side' of the economy; since the term is often used these days by politicians and political commentators. Run your eye back over Diagrams 6.1–6.5. Can you see any flows of resources supplied into the economy by firms or households? I can see four:

1 the supply of labour from households to firms;
2 the supply of goods and services from firms to households and government;
3 the supply of machinery and raw materials from firm to firm; and
4 the supply of exports from UK-based firms.

These flows make up the *supply side* of the economy. When politicians talk of 'supply side problems' they mean problems in the quantity, quality and price of labour, and in the price and availability of the goods and of services produced by that labour. They also mean, of course, the conditions of production that create such problems of supply in the economy: the quality of its technology, its working practices and its ability to produce efficiently goods and services that are in demand.

---

5 Keynesian-inspired analysts also increasingly recognized that the quality of 'demand management' here couldn't constitute the entire explanation of any inadequacies on the supply side of the UK economy. After all, virtually every government in the leading capitalist economies was using similar policies, and they weren't presiding over increasingly uncompetitive manufacturing sectors. So why 'we' were doing so badly then came to be explained by the interplay of a series of ultimately *non-economic* factors: things

such as poor education, inadequate management, entrenched class divisions, unregulated industrial relations, and an amateur civil service. This list in its turn inspired many of the reforms of education, industrial relations, the civil service, and the training system pursued by governments in the 1970s.

Difficulty number two

This inability of Keynesian-inspired governments to improve the UK's economic performance might have been enough to undermine the general credibility of Keynesian ideas in political circles in the 1970s. There certainly was a moment in the late 1960s when Keynesianism seemed available as an explanation of *unemployment* but not of *relative economic decline*. What finally undermined the dominance of Keynesianism however in the 1970s was the sudden reappearance of mass unemployment as well.

This second face of the crisis of Keynesianism can easily be grasped if we go back to our flow diagrams again, and re-examine what we have established so far. If there is unemployment, what does Keynesianism suggest that governments should do?

The obvious answer is to 'increase demand', 'most easily by increasing government spending'. Now what happens if you increase demand too far – that is, if you put into the system more income than can easily be satisfied by the purchase of UK-produced goods and services? What happens if all UK workers are employed, and there is still excess demand in the system?

This is more difficult. As we have seen, imports will be sucked in, with balance of payments consequences; but in addition the general price of all goods will probably rise. You will get *price* inflation.

It should be said that Keynes himself was well aware that inflationary pressures could grow as full employment was reached, and that he was quite cautious in his own estimates in the 1930s of the level of unemployment at which governments should *stop* increasing demand. Many of his followers however eventually shed that caution, and felt the economy could be run at very nearly full employment before inflation would occur. For them, there was no conflict between inflation and unemployment. One would arrive only as the other departed. But by the late 1950s even they had come to see that inflationary pressures could build up before full employment levels had been attained – that in fact what they faced was a trade-off between unemployment and inflation in which the control of inflation required them to run the economy at less than full employment. That was in itself something of an intellectual retreat by Keynesians; but at least through the 1950s and 1960s Keynesian economists and the governments they advised experienced that trade-off as one between *low* levels of unemployment and *low* levels of inflation. As we saw in our earlier graph, prices rose at most by 5 per cent a year in the 1950s and 1960s, and normally by much less; and unemployment averaged just 2 per cent in the First World as a whole. Governments in Britain experimented with incomes policies, and with 'stop–go' cycles of economic expansion and contraction, to keep unemployment and inflation in balance and at a low level.

The age of Keynes can be said to have ended abruptly in the 1970s when economic crisis (in the form of a dramatic increase in the level of unemployment) returned; and to have ended with Keynesianism itself in crisis because suddenly rapid inflation and high levels of unemployment were occurring *together*. Some commentators dubbed this 'stagflation' (a mixture of *stag*nation and in*flation*). Stagflation was not supposed to happen in a world of Keynesian economics; and initially Keynesianism had no effective policies to deal with one of its faces that would not, at the same time, accentuate the other.

Not surprisingly, this impasse precipitated a very serious crisis in Keynesian economics. Keynesian suggestions just didn't seem to work any more. At least, they didn't seem to work with the degree of success they had enjoyed in the 1950s and 1960s. This was the second face of the crisis of Keynesianism. The first face (the difficulty of solving the UK's relative economic decline) weakened the credibility of Keynesianism here. But this second face (the re-appearance of mass unemployment and inflation in all the major western economies) produced a more generalized retreat from Keynesianism among economists and state planners everywhere.

THE MANAGEMENT OF SUPPLY

The strengths and weaknesses of Keynesianism remain a major issue in contemporary economic theory, and are indeed one of the reasons why contemporary economics is such an exciting area in which to work – big theoretical debates have re-appeared to break the consensus on Keynesian policies that characterized much of the discipline in the 1950s and 1960s. These days economic texts often start with lists of some of the available 'schools of thought'. The one in front of me (Roger Backhouse's *Macroeconomics and the British Economy*) starts, as we will do here, with the clash between Keynesianism and Monetarism, though it is quick to stress that in reality 'there is a much greater diversity of thought than is suggested by this division . . . for there are many economists who fit into neither category' (Backhouse, 1983, p.2). Eclecticism is now very much the order of the day among many professional economists. They borrow bits and pieces from a number of 'schools of economic thought', to come to their own particular position on questions of economic policy.

I emphasize that because we lack the space here to follow the detailed contours of this debate between schools of thought. All that I can do here is to suggest to you that, although the detail of contemporary debate in this area ebbs and flows between a number of eclectically-constructed positions, the centre of gravity of the anti-Keynesian position was originally – and largely remains – a monetarist one. There are few 'pure' Keynesians left in the trade these days; and not many 'pure' monetarists. But debate still oscillates in large part between these 'pure' positions; and it is hard to grasp the contemporary debate without some grounding in them. So to round out our understanding of contemporary economic policy choices, let me lay out for you a broadly *monetarist* explanation of the problems facing those who would manage the UK economy back to competitive health and full employment.

The 'liberal' legacy to modern day anti-Keynesian economists is at least twofold: a faith in the capacity of markets to act as economic allocators, and a belief in the capacity of individuals to act rationally – within markets – to maximize their own self-interest. Liberal economists tend to believe that markets will pull the supply and demand for goods and services into harmony (into equilibrium, as economists would say) if prices are allowed to rise and fall undisturbed by government regulation; and that individuals are capable of adjusting their behaviour in a rational way in the light of all the information that is available to them. From this viewpoint, Keynesian management of the economy – far from being a good thing – is an 'interference'. It both disturbs the market's capacity to generate an optimal equilibrium of demand and supply, and sets up new pressures on individuals rationally pursuing their own self-interest. These are disturbances and pressures which will produce, not economic growth and full employment, but ultimately economic stagnation and price inflation. The legacy of Keynesian demand-management, on this view, is a diminution in the *supply* of goods and services generated by UK-based firms and entrepreneurs.

The broadly 'monetarist' critique of Keynesian economics goes as follows:

• The only secure guarantee of long-term full employment lies in the existence of efficient and competitive firms. So if governments concentrate on managing the level of demand in the economy, and ignore difficulties of supplying goods to meet that demand, their attempt to produce full employment will fail. All that will happen is that a gap will emerge between demand and supply, so creating inflation.

- The risk of such an inflationary gap is particularly great if governments try to push unemployment down below its 'natural level'. Monetarists believe there is a necessary residuum of unemployment whose level is determined, not by levels of demand, but by local standards of training, degrees of job mobility, levels of trade unionism and other 'blockages' on the free movement of labour. If governments use increases in demand to push unemployment below that level, labour will become scarce, wage rates will rise, and the general level of prices in the economy will be forced up. If politicians really want to get the residuum of unemployment reduced, they ought to direct policies instead at the supply-blockages – at trade union power, barriers to job mobility and so on.

- When price levels are rising rapidly, and particularly when they are rising more rapidly here than in competitor economies, business confidence in the viability of investment projects will weaken, because the market-strength of local business will be undermined and because trade unions will begin to demand wage settlements which *anticipate* future price inflation. The resulting diminution in business confidence and industrial competitiveness will then produce unemployment. So getting rid of inflation is the real key to job protection, and demand management of the Keynesian kind is not.

- Indeed Keynesianism actually makes things worse, and has become a major cause of unemployment in its own right. For Keynesianism means big and active government. It means high taxes, lots of regulations, plenty of welfare provision, and generous subsidies to firms. All this is a serious disincentive, so the monetarist argument runs, to efficiency and private initiative, and hence to the creation of an adequate supply of goods and services. Welfare provisions, if too generous, stop labour coming forward at a proper price. Subsidies to firms encourage industrial inefficiency. What Keynesianism does, according to monetarists, is to encourage government to 'over govern'; and by getting in the way, governments actually block the supply of goods from the private sector on which in the end non-inflationary economic growth depends. Far from being a solution to unemployment and economic recession, Keynesianism, according to monetarists, has become part of the problem.

- The solution to inflation (and through it to high levels of employment) is therefore for the government to refrain from detailed economic management. Governments cannot – on this argument – create 'real' jobs. Private firms do that. All governments can do is to *create the conditions* in which firms can expand: and it is on that task, and on that task alone, that they ought to concentrate.

Monetarism as a school of economic thought gathered its name from its belief that the prime task of government was to *control the supply of money*. Initially many monetarists argued for a close and relatively quick relationship between money supply and inflation. Cut one and the other would fall. However, that didn't happen in the 1980s, and economists sympathetic to monetarism became more aware than once they had been that the link between money and inflation was much weaker, and less reliable, than they had originally thought. So these days monetarists come in many shades and colours, and at one border of the 'school' slide away into positions close to Keynesianism. But the stronger the monetarist they are, the more they remain preoccupied with the control of the money supply as the key to price stability, economic growth and full employment. Monetarist-inspired economists remain wedded too to what we can call a general *liberal* stance on the use of market forces to improve the supply of goods and services in the economy. It is a stance that prefers private economic activity to public regulation. It is a stance that wants labour markets to operate without political interference or trade union monopoly power. It is a stance which is unhappy with government initiatives in the areas of welfare or industrial aid, initiatives that soften the impact of market forces on individual companies and individual workers. It is a stance, that is, which believes that governments govern best that govern least.

Overall therefore we can say that the reappearance of a broadly monetarist presence in contemporary economic debate in the 1970s and 1980s marked the return of liberal views to a political agenda otherwise dominated since 1945 by social reformist ways of thinking and acting. It is monetarism's roots in a liberal preference for markets over governments which help to explain why the 'rolling back of the state' became *the* watchword of monetarist thought in the 1970s, and its ultimate solution to the unemployment and inflation that was initially so perplexing to economists of a more Keynesian hue.

This re-assertion of a liberal commitment to self-regulating markets, and its associated critique of social reformist 'interference' in market processes, then prepared the way for a monetarist explanation of why the manufacturing sections of the UK economy had become progressively less competitive over time. They had suffered, we were told, more than comparable economies elsewhere, from an excess of economic management. They had experienced too much Keynesianism.

1 Monetarists pointed to this 'excess' as a general tendency of all Keynesian-inspired democratic politics. There were votes to be won by short-term economic tinkering. Politicians promised jobs, but produced inflation. They overheated the economy, and so reinforced the capacity of strong trade unions to extract high wage settlements. They also spent too much as governments, and in this way fuelled inflation directly. In other words, what was missing – according to monetarists – from the original flow diagrams with which we explained Keynesianism was the 'political weight' provided to the households as voters by the experience of full employment and rising living standards, to supplement the 'industrial muscle' given to trade unions by the same. If we now bring back our flow diagram from the section on Keynes, we can amend it in the following way.

2 Not all countries however were equally susceptible to this political consequence of Keynesianism. Their 'vulnerability' varied with the strength of their labour movements, the electoral success of Labour parties, and the particular legal codes surrounding trade unionism. From a monetarist perspective, UK-based manufacturing firms have been particularly prone to dwindling competitiveness because the particular strength here of these pro-Keynesian forces, as enshrined in the post-war settlement which obliged governments to maintain full employment at all costs.

3 The political dominance of Keynesianism in the UK then triggered dwindling competitiveness; because

- UK-based firms faced by strong trade unions inside their factories and high demand in the economy around them, couldn't easily alter their labour practices and so modernize their productive systems to meet that demand. Instead an inflationary gap opened up, greater than that experienced by their international competitors.
- Capital was exported out of the UK, and not invested here, because rates of return were higher abroad, in economies where labour was cheaper and industrial modernization easier to implement; and this set up a 'vicious circle' of economic decline, where low investment in the UK left productivity and profits low here by international standards, and so deterred local investment still further.
- Excess demand in the UK economy was quickly mopped up by imports from more efficient foreign producers, whose better quality and lower-priced goods destroyed local firms (and hence local jobs) and created balance of payments problems. If governments then held interest rates high here, to attract in foreign funds to cover the resulting balance of payments deficit, that just made life even tougher for local firms, who invested less and became weaker still in international terms.

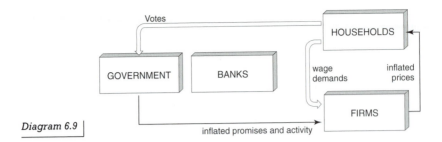

Diagram 6.9

On this argument, the continual decline in the competitiveness of UK-based industry could not be avoided without dramatic changes in policy and a painful period of re-adjustment. Monetarism, like Keynesianism before it, then suggested a political programme. In principle there is no reason why economists convinced of the importance of the supply of money in the creation of inflation should all subscribe to the 'package' which follows. But many influential monetarist economists did (and still do); and the logic of their argument, and its roots in a liberal tradition of thought, explains why. They favour reductions in government activity in the economy, and a strengthening of markets (by the denationalization of publicly-owned concerns and reductions in trade union legal rights). They are prone to advocate tax reductions and the removal of regulations on working conditions or wages – which they see as a barrier to work, saving, enterprise and efficiency; and they want industries to rationalize and modernize under the stimulus of competition.

CONTEMPORARY POLICY OPTIONS

If we now go back to our flow diagrams once more, they will help us to place much of the current controversy in economic management. As we have already seen, Keynesian economists in the 1950s and 1960s advocated the stimulation of demand by the government as the key to economic growth and full employment. We can mark that on the flow diagram at point 'A' on Diagram 6.10. Later Keynesian positions, as we have also seen, emphasized the importance of incomes policies as a way of heading off wage-led inflation. That we can mark at point 'B'. The thrust of monetarism, on the other hand, was to curb government spending (at 'A') and to cut taxes (at 'C'), to free greater supply of labour to (and commodities from) a revitalized private set of firms. These tax cuts (though falling on households) were seen by monetarists as inspiring a more bountiful supply of labour

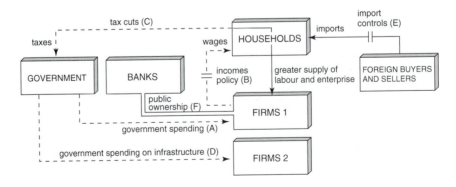

Diagram 6.10

and enterprise, which in their turn were supposed to generate a greater quality and volume of output from firms.

But when Conservative Governments in the early 1980s implemented policies of an apparently monetarist hue, they still ran into balance of payments problems, and seemed incapable of squeezing inflation out of the system. The money supply proved hard to define and even harder to control, so that 'by 1985–6 effective monetary targeting was virtually abandoned' (Maynard, 1988, p.131). Attempts to stimulate the supply of goods and services by cutting taxes also inflated levels of consumer demand; and the decision in 1979 to remove barriers to the free export of capital initially produced just that – an outpouring of capital from the UK. This exported capital then earned lots of interest payments in foreign currency, but still made no direct contribution to the stimulation of output and employment at home; and, indeed, by 1990 the Conservative Government was having to run a policy of high interest rates – to attract foreign investors back into the UK and to dampen down levels of consumer demand (particularly for imports). Yet these same high interest rates also made investment by UK firms more expensive to finance and meant that only projects yielding a very high rate of return were worth undertaking; so that, as in previous decades, the protection of the balance of payments seemed to be in tension with the expansion of the manufacturing base.

In consequence, by 1990 a supposedly monetarist-inspired government was open to the charge that it had returned to old-fashioned Keynesian-style demand management, and had still not presided over a supply-side miracle capable of guaranteeing long-term employment and prosperity for all. In their defence, ministers often pointed to the unbroken sequence of economic growth which followed the slump of 1979–81; but they were still vulnerable to two kinds of criticism:

- that they had not been monetarist enough; or
- that what was required now was a 'supply-side Keynesianism'.

The first of these criticisms should be intelligible to us. The call went out for yet greater retrenchment of government policy at points 'A' and 'C' on the flow diagram. 'Supply-side Keynesianism' however may be less clear. It derived its force from the assertion that during the:

> Thatcher era a great deal of productive capacity had been scrapped and there had been relatively little investment in new plant and equipment. As a result manufacturing industry was now operating fairly close to full capacity such that, without renewed investment, there was only limited potential for a rapid Keynesian style of reflation.
>
> (Rowthorn and Wells, 1987, p.315)

So this time the call for an increase in demand in the UK economy was focused – not on tax cuts to boost consumption – but on heavy government investment in industry and in industrial infrastructure. This would involve government action at point 'D' in the diagram. Supply-side Keynesianism was (and is) often accompanied by a number of other proposals: namely to re-introduce incomes policy (at point 'B') to stop wage-led inflation; or (in more radical versions) to use import controls (at point 'E') to prevent adverse affects on the balance of payments; or even (in more radical versions still) to extend public ownership to the banks and big corporations to ensure compliance with such expansionist policies (at point 'F').

In effect we now face a spectrum of proposals for the management of the UK economy that we might label as:

| pure monetarism | mild monetarism | orthodox Keynesianism | supply-side Keynesianism |

These of course coincide with a political spectrum that runs from the right wing of the Conservative Party through the Centre parties and out to the Labour Left.

NOTE

* This chapter has been adapted from, The Open University (1991, 1995) D103 *Society and Social Science*, Block 3 *Work, Markets and the Economy*, Unit 12 'The management of the UK economy', Milton Keynes, The Open University.

REFERENCES

Clarke, P. (1988) *The Keynesian Revolution in the making*, Oxford, Clarendon Press.

Coates, D. (1984) *The Context of British Policies*, London, Hutchinson.

Maynard, G. (1988) *The Economy under Mrs. Thatcher*, Oxford, Basil Blackwell.

Rowthorn, R.E. and Wells, J.R. (1987) *De-industrialization and Foreign Trade*, Cambridge, Cambridge University Press.

7

A MARXIST READING OF THE UK ECONOMY AND ITS MANAGEMENT*

David Coates

So far we have stayed, in our theorizing on economic performance and decline, within the confines of mainstream economics – operating within an intellectual universe bounded by *liberalism* and *social reformism*. Now it is time to step outside; to examine a marxist reading of the same thing.

Can you see now that marxists expect capitalist economies to be in perpetual difficulties: competing with each other, constantly changing their production systems, forever displacing workers, creating unemployment and poverty of a relative, if not always of an absolute kind? What marxists are not so good at explaining is why, for twenty-five years after the war, mass unemployment did not occur. If monetarists have a sort of answer to the question of why Keynesianism ran into difficulties in the 1970s, marxists need one for why those difficulties took so long to appear. And marxist economists, like everyone else in this debate, also need to explain why, in the struggle between competing capitalist economies, it is the manufacturing section of the UK economy which has progressively lost out in that competition.

To get to grips with all that, we require a different model. The flow diagrams used in the unit so far create a picture of an economy in which already-produced commodities and money are exchanged between households, firms, banks and governments. By their very constitution and use, the flow diagrams suggest that the difficulties faced by state economic managers ultimately rest in these processes of *exchange*. We have already seen that many Keynesian and liberal economists have now gone beyond this focus on exchange and demand, to look at questions of supply. What we need to emphasize now is that, in addition, our model's preoccupation with processes of exchange does not sit easily with many marxist approaches to contemporary economics. Many marxist economists are willing to concede that economic difficulties manifest themselves in the sphere of exchange, but they insist that their origins lie elsewhere, in the processes of *production* from which commodities emerge – in the social processes, that is, which take place before exchange can begin.

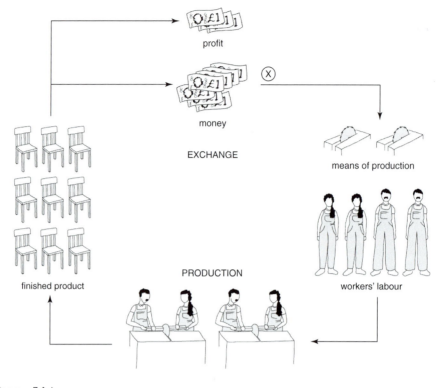

profit

money

EXCHANGE

means of production

workers' labour

finished product

PRODUCTION

Diagram 7.1

Our flow diagrams do not include that production process, and in that way help to shut out a consideration of marxist positions. To grasp these, we will therefore need a different model, one that can grasp production as well as exchange; and we will also need some sense of the relationship between this new model and the flow diagrams we have used so far. One way of visualizing that relationship is to think of the flow diagrams as resting – as perhaps they actually are as you read this – flat on the top of the desk/table at which you are working. Marxists suggest that, beneath the table, social processes of production go on, processes which eventually throw up onto the table's surface commodities to be bought and wage-earners to buy them. Underneath the table (underneath the flow of exchange relationships) a circuit of production goes on, one that can be illustrated in a different diagram (see Diagram 7.1).

According to marxists, the circuit of production in a capitalist economy starts at point 'X', with capitalists spending their money on the purchase of machinery, raw materials and labour power. That labour power is then set to work on the materials and machinery to make commodities – in this instance, chairs – which are then sold. So long as the sale of those chairs realizes more money than the original sum released, the capitalists make a profit, and the circuit of production can begin again.

As each circuit of production follows from the one before, marxist economists expect that the volume of machinery being used to produce chairs will actually grow (as individual capitalists, obliged to survive by out-competing each other, do so not simply by working their own labour force harder and longer, but also by giving them better and better equipment as well). So over time, on this argument, the proportion of labour to machinery in the circuits of capitalist production necessarily shifts towards machinery. This is what produces economic growth, by adding to the stock of capital locked up in production. But at the same time this expansion of the capital stock threatens the rate of profit on which the continuation of economic growth depends. For with more and more capital tied up in production, capitalists need more and more profits to make the whole exercise worthwhile. It was Marx's view that the generation of more and more profits could not be sustained indefinitely as the balance between labour and machinery shifted in the economy as a whole. It was his belief that, over time, employers would find it harder and harder to squeeze the necessary volume of profits out of their diminishing work forces; and that in consequence crises would occur because of a tendency for the rate of profit to fall.

Such crises in the cycle of production occur, according to marxist economists, when the whole cycle fails to produce enough profits to fuel the next cycle. That is, *crises occur when profits collapse*. Now profits can collapse within the cycle at two points. Marxists argue that capitalists meet problems at times in *selling* what they produce. They do so because the workers lack the purchasing power to buy all the commodities that their labour produces; and lack this purchasing power necessarily because capitalists cannot pay workers enough. They have to hold back some money as profits. Each individual capitalist has both to keep wage costs down, and to keep prices as high as can be managed. Capitalists can therefore make goods but cannot always sell them. They cannot 'realize' their profits. When working-class purchasing power is too weak, capitalism experiences a *crisis of realization*. It is to this kind of crisis that Keynes was reacting in the 1930s. Such a crisis manifests itself at point 'A' on the circuit of production in Diagram 7.2.

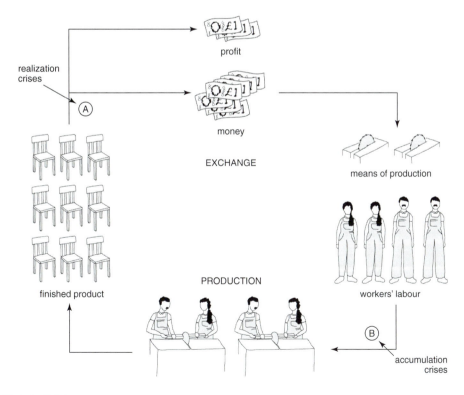

Diagram 7.2

Profits collapse too when workers are strong. But then the problems arise at the point at which commodities are *made*, rather than at which they are sold. Capitalists cannot then work their labour force hard enough to extract a sufficient surplus from them, nor pay them low enough wages to leave a satisfactory margin of profits. The ratio between what capitalists pay their workers and the value of what they produce is too low to generate profits on a scale sufficient to fuel another round of investment and production. In these circumstances capital does not 'accumulate'. The system has a *crisis of accumulation*. This occurs when the working class is too strong. It manifests itself at point 'B' on the cycle of production. One such crisis occurred in the 1970s.

Marxists believe that this tension will never go away until capitalism does. If attacks on trade unions and working-class living standards go too far, local firms will find it difficult to sell their goods. That is why even monetarist-inspired governments have in the end to expand local demand. But when they do, they run the risk of strengthening local working-class industrial power, with all the consequences that has for local competitiveness. So the management of the economy never finally 'succeeds'. Governments just ride the tiger, and will carry on doing so through the 1990s.

So marxists are sceptical of the long-term effectiveness of the policy measures that we have discussed in [chapter 6]. They believe that the deep-rooted differences of interest between capitalists and workers will not go away; and that because they will not, governments will always find themselves trying to balance unemployment and inflation, profits and wages.

Yet it is clear that such a balancing act is easier to perform successfully in some periods than in others (after all, in retrospect, even in the UK the long post-war boom between 1948 and 1973 was a period of sustained growth, high employment, and only slowly rising prices). And it is equally clear that such a balancing act has been easier in the post-war period for some countries than for others. The Japanese economy in the post-war years has experienced spectacular rates of economic growth. So too has the West German economy; and neither has seemed as beset as the UK with problems of unemployment, inflation and balance of payments deficits. Let us see how marxist economists explain all that.

They do so by deploying their understanding of capitalism not as a system of markets, as liberal thought would have it, but as a system dominated by a competitive struggle between individual capitalists, and as a system driven by fundamental cleavage of interest between capitalists and workers. In other words, they handle the question of the performance of this economy against that of another by talking about 'social classes'. They concentrate on *the balance and character of class forces* in particular societies, examining the way in which, in each society, capitalists compete with one another and with their work force. The critical feature of the UK economy to which marxist economists have recently drawn attention, as indeed have many of their non-marxist colleagues, is the competitive weakness of local manufacturing firms. They have also been disputing among themselves as to whether to root that weakness in features of the capitalist class in the UK, or in features of the relationship between capital and labour. There is an on-going debate within marxist economics and economic history about whether the weakness of UK-based manufacturing capital has been caused primarily by the strength of other sections of the capitalist class (in this instance finance capital, the City) or by the strength of non-capitalist classes (in this instance the working class, organized in trade unions). In other words, marxist economists have argued that UK industry has declined relative to its competitors in the post-war years either because the City has been too strong or because the trade unions have.

NOTE

* This chapter has been adapted from, The Open University (1991, 1995) D103 *Society and Social Science*, Block 3 *Work, Markets and the Economy*, Unit 12 'The management of the UK economy', Milton Keynes, The Open University.

8

LIVING WITHOUT BORDERS†

Dipak K. Rastogi*

Deregulation, technological advances and financial management innovations have caused a truly global market to form. But, we are just beginning to see the changes and opportunities.

We are moving toward a world in which capital knows no borders and does not necessarily respect the traditional value chain in financial intermediation; a world in which financial instruments are no longer bound by their traditional form. In this new world, financial services companies will face strategic inflection points that lead either to significant opportunities or to the seeds of decline. Governments will continue to lose control over many of their traditional policy levers, such as exchange rates and interest rates, as these will find real values in free markets. These changes will bring us a world in which the opportunity for exponential increases in wealth accrue to individuals in all countries that participate freely.

Three major forces at work in financial markets have caused a truly global market to form. First, the past three decades have seen a significant shift toward deregulation of trade and financial markets around the world, resulting in increased international capital flows. Second, explosive advances in computing and communication technology have provided the platform for tremendous growth in the scale and complexity of financial markets, thereby meeting the need for international flows. Third, significant innovations in financial management have produced an unprecedented number of innovations in securitization and derivatives.

Many developments – such as the formation of trade zones, the fall of communism, the movement to floating exchange rates and significant pension reforms have led to increased internationalization of capital markets and made capital efficiency more important. These changes have created the need to mobilize financial assets and unlock their hidden values. Simultaneously, financial-market volatility and uncertainty have created the need to transfer, reduce or modify risk.

Developments in technology and communications have paralleled the growth in financial markets. From the 1970s' invention of the microchip to the 1990s' explosive Internet growth and deregulation of the developed world's telecom industries, we have seen an unprecedented increase in our ability to communicate and transact globally. From a financial-markets perspective, these inventions have resulted in the development of a large-scale, transaction-processing infrastructure, cost-effective access to timely information, the introduction of personalized automated transaction systems, and the ability to structure and deliver highly complex financial solutions to users and providers of capital.

The tools of technology have fed financial innovation and simplified the processes of mobilizing assets and managing risks. New products and structures have produced a wide array of investment options and increased use of tradable, highly liquid securities. Mutual fund assets have grown as commercial banks continue to be disintermediated. Total mutual funds assets in the US increased from US$185 billion in 1980 to $2.2 trillion in 1996. In 1996 alone, an average of $22 billion per month flowed into equity funds. New, customized, knowledge-based tools, such as derivatives and asset securitization, continue to be developed.

We believe that the trends to deregulate and open economies, the growth in technology and the innovation in financial markets will continue to build on each other and drive further growth. These forces are highly interlinked. Advancement in technology leads to enhanced productivity and explosion of information, which in turn leads to demand for higher living standards and to pressure being placed on governments to deregulate and open the economy, which in turn causes further global economic integration. The demand for international capital rises and new risks and opportunities are created, which leads to demand for financial innovation.

As this interaction gains momentum, each cycle continues to grow larger at each pass. The cycle is evident today; as financial barriers continue to fall, global markets continue to grow. The foreign exchange market, for example, is now truly global and trades more than $1 trillion per day. Derivatives, created to solve global risk-management issues, represent another huge global market – over-the-counter derivatives alone currently trade more than $25 billion per day.

THE PLAYERS

These trends are affecting the financial markets' players (savers, investing institutions, users and broker-dealer intermediaries) in different ways:

- *Savers*: Savers, who are the providers of funds, are saving for their retirement or for the benefit of succeeding generations. Their primary goal is to maximize risk-adjusted return while preserving their capital. Over the past decade, they have gained significantly more access to country, company, industry and market information as a direct result of technological advances. Pension reform has given savers more control over their assets and investments. For example, retirement savings can now be managed by Canadians in self-administered RRSPs. Some governments are currently examining plans to allow individuals to manage their own social security investments. The increasing number of investment vehicles and new types of investment accounts are allowing savers to select, for a particular risk preference, a customized investment portfolio. As a result, individuals are participating in a broader array of financial instruments and vehicles. Their involvement has been furthered by the introduction of low-cost discount brokers. Thus, the individual saver increasingly bears investment risk that, traditionally, has been borne by other institutions. Investment returns are correspondingly more attractive.
- *Investing Institutions*: Investors, such as banks, funds managers, insurance companies and money managers, pool assets to manage investment risk for savers. For this they earn a fee. Their objective is to maximize risk-adjusted returns for the savers who use their services, based on a stated investment objective. The range and sophistication of investors continually broaden as they seek to gain a competitive edge by achieving greater capital efficiency. Today, there is an investor for virtually every slice on the risk spectrum, each fiercely competing to outperform their peers. They tend to move toward cross-border

investments because these offer an opportunity to achieve higher returns and greater diversification for a given set of risks.

- *Users of Funds*: Corporations, governments and individuals use funds to finance real investment and current consumption. Their objective is to minimize their cost of capital within acceptable risk parameters. Using their access to investors with varied risk and return requirements, and using derivative instruments, users can optimize their financial liabilities. The broad availability of capital and financial tools enhances their ability to efficiently deploy productive assets and resources by optimizing the cash-flow dynamics of these resources. These gains have come with a corresponding obligation for fiscal and monetary prudence. For example, the global capital market evaluates a country relative to such measures as its budget deficit, total indebtedness, level of reserves and productivity. In evaluating these factors, the markets are uncompromising. Therefore, governments must demonstrate proper fiscal and monetary behaviours to maintain investor confidence.
- *Broker/Dealer Intermediaries*: For a fee, intermediaries, such as Wood Gundy and Gordon Capital, facilitate the market flow of funds between investing institutions, savers and users. The increasing complexity of the financial markets has made their role more important. With today's array of financial instruments and tools, the intermediary is a guide through the jungle of potential options in the global arena. They play an increasing role as the market becomes more dominated by tradable securities. Intermediaries have responded to this challenge through product innovation and development of global networks. However, competition has been increasing as well.

THE FORCES AT WORK TODAY

The aging of the developed world's population, the growth of the middle class in emerging economies and the expansion of pension reform are producing an increasing supply of and demand for capital. Consequently, the competitive dynamics in the financial markets are continuing to intensify and will drive an unprecedented growth in assets around the world.

As the baby boom generation matures, they continue to be net savers. The world stock of financial assets is growing faster than the underlying GDPs. This is also true of many emerging economies. The demand for capital efficiency has increased the proportion of securities in the mix of global financial assets. In 1980, bonds and equity securities represented a little more than half the world's total financial assets. By the year 2000, it is expected to grow to more than 75%. At the same time, assets allocated to investments in emerging economies are increasing to satisfy investor demand for higher total returns.

Technology will continue to advance exponentially, allowing individual savers to find information, make investment decisions and execute transactions online. The basics of this capability already exist; you can now execute securities transactions on the World Wide Web, and electronic funds transfer is already provided through private networks, such as Citibank's, and is under development for the Internet.

A word of caution is warranted here. Further advancement of such capabilities depends on:

1 Making the necessary investment in the communications infrastructure to create the bandwidth needed to support electronic commerce. This would include fibre-optic cable and switching networks.
2 Resolving the problems surrounding security.
3 The regulatory agencies working with the financial and technology industries to establish an acceptable framework to protect investors and develop confidence in open, real-time transactions systems.

Another force shaping today's markets is the increasing deregulation and opening of economies. The opening of the world economies has resulted in more international trade and increased capital flows among countries. These in turn have resulted in improved fiscal performance. One consequence of opening a country to international trade is that the exchange rate becomes a critical competitive factor. As the exchange rate for a country increases, its goods and services become less competitive. A lower exchange rate, on the other hand, may imply a lower standard of living. Similarly, as a country opens its financial markets, its credit rating becomes more important. A lower credit rating implies a higher cost of capital for participants in the economy and for the government.

The competitiveness of an economy requires optimizing several variables. Strong, growing economies that compete internationally must do so based on price and cost in order to maximize their citizens' well-being. Therefore, governments will have to behave more like corporations in managing their fiscal and monetary performance. To a large extent, this phenomenon is already occurring. Inflation and fiscal performance have improved steadily in the developed countries. The trend has been even more dramatic in the developing world where economies have recently been opened. Here inflation has fallen from 36% in 1992 to a projected 11% in 1997, and fiscal deficits have declined from 3.4% of GDP in 1992 to a forecast of 1.8% in 1997.

In short, we are moving toward a world where, from a financial perspective, there are no borders. We can envision a global interactive financial-market network that will link individual savers with users of capital in a virtual marketplace. Transactions will occur directly between savers and users on products, such as standardized equity and debt instruments. The openness and interdependence of world economies coupled with these technological capabilities will reduce the importance of geopolitical borders. The increasing sophistication of investors coupled with wider access to tools like derivatives will result in the blurring of financial instruments. This means that the form of the investment will become less important because the saver will have the necessary tools to construct an optimal portfolio suited specifically to his or her needs based on their requirements. This optimal portfolio construction will be accomplished by using analytical software tools and accessing real-time information and research.

IMPLICATIONS OF A BORDERLESS WORLD

These changes will provide significant social and economic value to the global village. Risks will be transferred to where they are most suited. In some cases, risks may be completely and optimally offset. Funds will flow where they can provide the best uses for the global economy. Individual savers will reap most of the benefits. They will take direct control over their savings. Their returns will be greater due to better risk/reward matching, and their costs will be cut due to reduced or eliminated management expenses and lower transaction costs. Users of funds will benefit as well, as they will be able to reduce their financing costs through increased customization and access to a broader set of investors. Governments will have to be more responsible in their fiscal and monetary policies or suffer the severe consequences of capital restrictions as, for example, was the case with Mexico a few years ago.

In a borderless world of financial services, the roles of investing institutions and inter-mediaries will further converge. Illustrations abound today – ManuLife and Altimara in Canada, and Morgan Stanley and Dean Witter in the US. Savers and users will have the capability to exert pressure on both investing institutions and intermediaries. Savers may not be as dependent on mutual funds and insurance companies to manage their money. As the public educates itself in investment techniques and gains more money management tools from software companies, they will be less reliant on professional money management. This will lead to fee compression for investing institutions. Such institutions will seek to differentiate themselves by tracking specific geographies and industries or by providing specialized techniques, such as arbitrage, leverage and synthetic investments.

Similarly, intermediaries will have to find ways of differentiating themselves in an environment where savers can execute their trades and gain information electronically. Pressure will also come from users who will self-register with regulatory agencies, work through low-cost distributors and access savers directly through financial markets. I am not saying that intermediaries or investing institutions will disappear – not all distribution will be conducted through financial networks. Traditional methods will survive, but both groups will be under more pressure by the market to add more value. This pressure to find value and to differentiate will result in more consolidation in the financial services industry. Investing institutions will need to acquire the structuring skills of intermediaries, and intermediaries will need to find vehicles, such as pooled funds, to use as building blocks to structured solutions.

As the virtual marketplace evolves, distribution of financial products will go through a massive change. There will be new substitutive competition as software firms develop, refine and connect the pieces of the investment puzzle of individuals. They will do this by providing integrated interfaces with standardized sockets connecting the desktop to financial service providers of choice, research and news services and ultimately to the users of capital.

This software interface will include the kind of standard financial management software available today and will provide sophisticated portfolio management and analysis tools. What does this mean for the financial service industry? It reinforces the concepts of value and differentiation. Financial services providers will have to provide value-added specialization and highly reliable, timely and cost-effective products and services. We envision a sort of market-certification process that these products and services will have to go through to be made available through popular financial software.

What do we mean by specialized products? New financial tools and techniques will continue to develop allowing for significant changes in the way financial products are packaged. Traditional financial instruments are standardized and inflexible. However, structuring tools, such as derivatives and securitization techniques, can overcome these limitations to tailor risks and match investment profiles to investor or user needs. Investors can make better asset-allocation decisions and take incremental risk in markets of their choice without liquidating their current investments. These tools enable the investors and users to assume desirable risk profiles as their needs and market views change and to transfer unwanted risk away. The key feature these tools provide is the flexibility for investors and users to undo previously done decisions with ease and at low cost. These tools will in fact be the linchpin of the financial services industry of the future. Customized investment solutions arising from the use of these tools will then be made available to savers via the distribution channels I referred to earlier. Over time, this pool of customized solutions will become commoditized and will need to be continually replenished with additional ideas and structures.

Successful participants in the financial markets will have to adapt and add much more value in a borderless world. Global reach or presence will be a strategic asset that will help overcome lingering information, regulatory and settlement barriers. Responsiveness and quality in successfully satisfying customers' needs will differentiate the winners.

BARRIERS

A final word of caution: in the financial markets, there are still several barriers to a borderless world to overcome including regulatory, legal, and accounting and tax differences among different countries. In addition, not all national governments will have or will immediately embrace free-market reforms completely. These barriers may slow the globalization of

Table 8.1 Forces at work

	1980	*1992*	*2000*
100% =	*$11 trillion*	*$35 trillion*	*$83 trillion*
Global Portfolio by Asset Class			
Cash	45%	32%	22%
Bonds	29%	39%	50%
Equity	26%	29%	28%
Global Portfolio by Geography			
Developed countries	100%	98%	93%
Developing countries		2%	7%

Source: McKinsey & Co. (amounts in US dollars)

financial markets, but the phenomenon is unstoppable in the long run. It is important to note that convergence of regulatory and legal systems is already occurring in response to global capital living without borders.

NOTES

† This chapter has been adapted from, 'Living Without Borders', Dipak K. Rastagi, *Business Quarterly* (1997), summer, p. 48.

* As the Executive Vice President of Finance for Citibank NA, Dipak K. Rastogi is responsible for capital markets, corporate finance and trading activities for all emerging-market countries. This article is based on his speech as the James C. Taylor Distinguished Lecturer in Finance at the Ivey Business School.

9

GLOBAL COOPERATION OR RIVAL TRADE BLOCS?*

Gerd Junne

This chapter examines the question of whether the world will continue to move towards a liberal, multilateral world trade system or whether it will fall apart into rival trade blocs. It starts with a short comparison of different scenarios for the development of the world economy. It then tries to illustrate the importance of developments inside the major trade blocs for the relationship between these blocs, taking as an example (a) the impact of German unification, (b) the impact of a possible break-up of China, and (c) the impact of domestic polarization within the United States.

It then discusses how different research avenues give rise to different expectations with regard to cooperation versus rivalry. For instance, from a long wave perspective increasing rivalry can be expected. However, an analysis of strategic alliances points in the direction of more cooperation and collective management of international economic relations. And finally, analyses which give more attention to the internal restructuring of companies lead to the hypothesis that new societal demands for a more active state will be articulated, implying more frictions at the international level. An analysis in terms of "concepts of control" points in the same direction. The tentative conclusion of this paper, meanwhile, is that "managed rivalry" will characterize future relations between the main trading blocs.

GLOBALIZATION VERSUS REGIONALIZATION: DIFFERENT SCENARIOS

We are unable to predict the future of international relations with any certainty (e.g. Van Ginneken 1993). This is not because the discipline is still underdeveloped. It is rather because

- the topic of research does not develop independently from how people think of it,
- the future is the outcome of social struggle, which is still contingent, and
- social forces interact in a dialectic way: the more the pendulum sways in one specific direction, the stronger the countervailing forces become.

Instead of trying to forecast the most probable future development, it makes more sense to elaborate a number of scenarios which cover a broader range of possible alternative developments, and then analyze the social forces that work in favour or against each of the different scenarios.

The CPB scenarios

The present enquiry into whether the world is heading towards more globalization or more regionalization can build upon earlier work by many others. An interesting effort was made two years ago by the Dutch Central Planning Bureau (CPB) in its book "Scanning the Future," in which it describes four scenarios for the development of the world economy. The four scenarios were dubbed (1) "Global Shift", (2) "European Renaissance", (3) "Global Crisis", and (4) "Balanced Growth" (CPB 1992a: 22–26, 182–207).

1 In "Global Shift", Japan and the "Dynamic Asian Economies" (DAE's) get strongly attached to a free-market orientation. Under heavy competitive pressure, growth impeding factors in the United States (such as the low quality of basic education) are tackled by private enterprise. The resulting recovery of productivity within the United States generates the financial means by which the government deficit can be reduced. While the US economy thrives again, economic reforms in Europe remain half-hearted. The European bias in favor of security, stability, and risk-aversive behavior prevails once again. Economic growth slows, and important industrial sectors quickly lose ground. Social and political tensions, which have already risen sharply as a result of the recession, are further inflamed by large migratory movements to Western Europe.
2 In "European Renaissance", global competition increasingly leads to the emergence of world-wide oligopolies and strategic alliances, supported by governments. In a climate in which "coordination" rather than the free-market plays a dominant role in the regulation of the economy, European integration advances quickly, creating favorable conditions for European business. US business, on the contrary, remains unable to change the success formulas of the past. Increasing US trade deficits strengthen protectionist moods. Japan and the DAEs reorient their interests towards Europe and each other.
3 In "Global Crisis," neither the US nor European economies prosper. The economic rise of the Far East and the impotence of Europe and America ensure a deepening of tensions on trade issues; the major regions of the world gradually degenerate into antagonistic protectionist blocs. Unable to earn their living by producing for the world market, the demographic trap in many developing countries closes, and a world-wide crisis of food supply occurs.
4 For "Balanced Growth," an ever stronger drive towards sustainable economic development and continuously strong technological dynamism constitute the dominating forces. Reforms practically everywhere lead to renewed economic growth, which facilitates an open and cooperative attitude in international trade negotiations. Both the free-market and the coordination element play an important role at the domestic level, as well as in the international economy.

In a follow-up study on perspectives for the Dutch economy (CPB 1992b:18), only three scenarios were kept. "Global Crisis" was skipped, because the situation for Europe and the Netherlands in "Global Crisis" was roughly the same as in "Global Shift". Furthermore, it is generally not advisable to work with more than three scenarios, because it becomes too difficult to compare a larger number (Schwartz 1991:29).

A number of comments can be made on the scenarios produced by the CPB. In "Global Shift," the US economy is booming, while the European economy busts. In "European Renaissance," it is the other way round. This implies that the interdependence of the world economy is still limited: the economy in one major region can prosper for longer periods, while the economy in other major regions is in a deep recession. Is this plausible?

It seems to me that the economies of North America and Western Europe have become mere communicating vessels. Though differences persist, the application of new technologies will not take place at a dramatically different pace: this will differ more from company to company rather than from country to country. Strong links between companies on both sides of the Atlantic (often belonging to the same concerns) mean that demand in one region stimulates demand in the other. Protectionist measures taken by one side would also provoke protectionist measures by the other. It seems more appropriate, then, to conceive a scenario in which the major industrial centers prosper more or less together and keep a rather liberal trade system, and another one in which regional rivalry dominates.

The BRIE scenarios

This has been done in a recent project of the Berkeley Round Table on the International Economy (BRIE). The authors put forward three different scenarios, which are described as "managed multilateralism," "benign regionalism" and "regional rivalry" (Sandholtz *et al.* 1992).

Managed multilateralism "amounts to an extension of the post-war American system into a new era in which power is more evenly distributed" (Sandholtz *et al.* 1992: 173). Though trade will not become totally liberalized, governments will be able to agree on the rules that will govern the international trade system and these rules will be relatively liberal, leaving the market to determine the outcomes.

Regional rivalry describes a kind of "twenty-first century mercantilistic regionalism" (Sandholtz *et al.* 1992: 174–5). Governments will worry more about relative positions, rather than about absolute welfare gains. Relative shifts in positions will become security concerns for the great powers, thereby greatly diminishing the chances for collective coordination and leadership amongst these powers.

Benign regionalism (or "defensive protectionism"), finally, depicts a situation in which different world regions live rather independently from each other, "with low levels of sensitivity to each other's choices and low levels of vulnerability to each other's actions" (Sandholtz *et al.* 1992: 174). This last scenario seems to be the least likely. It does not take into account that international interdependence has reached such an intensity that this scenario can be discarded even in the case that world trade becomes concentrated largely on intra-regional trade. Even then, two important levels of interdependence would remain.

Interdependence via international financial markets

International financial and currency markets actually link economic developments in all parts of the world. Any kind of government policy which implies deficit spending and increases inflationary pressures, will immediately face reactions which will put that country's currency under pressure and affect domestic interest rates.

Interdependence via the international ecological system

Economic policies also affect each other even if no international transactions in the classical sense take place. Almost all economic activity, for instance, leads to the emission of polluting substances and gases which may destroy the ozone layer or contribute to global warming through the greenhouse effect. In this way, societies have become much more vulnerable to each other's choices (Cf. MacNeill, Winsemius, and Yakushiji 1991).

As a result, the "benign regionalism" scenario will be dropped. Instead, we will look for a scenario that takes the increased importance of the environmental dimension into account.

The Amsterdam scenarios

Schwartz has suggested that scenario writers should avoid depicting an optimistic scenario (like "free trade"), a pessimistic scenario (like "rivalry") and a "middle of the road" scenario, because this last scenario would probably be accepted by most readers as the most probable one, and the whole exercise of scenario writing would be devalued. He suggested that a third scenario, instead, should bring in another important factor (e.g. a fundamental social change, like a shift in basic values) which the other scenarios do not yet sufficiently take into account. The increasing importance of environmental imperatives is a case in point.

Imagine that imperatives of sustainable development get more attention around the world. This could lead to very different trade structures, and certainly to new types of trade conflicts (see Van der Wurff and Kolk 1993). We have therefore decided in favor of a third scenario in which priority is given to environmentally-friendly production and trade structures. This probably would be done in different ways in North America, Japan and Western Europe, implying new frictions between the trade blocs.

In sum, the three scenarios taken as a point of departure for future analysis are:

1 Managed multilateralism, in which the vision of a "global village" – if only for the northern half of the globe – is approached, the fast introduction of new technologies leads to another period of worldwide economic growth, and the leading trading nations are able to agree on increasingly liberal rules for world trade and production;
2 Regional rivalry, in which slow economic growth combines with highly conflictual relations among the major trading blocs; and
3 Greening of business, in which a high priority is given to the imperatives of worldwide sustainable development, and economies are restructured in order to become less environmentally-harmful. This last scenario will not be extensively explored in the present chapter, but will be considered in future research.

Before we look at the relations between the blocs, however, it is useful to look at developments within the three blocs, because these developments can have important consequences for intercontinental relations.

INTRA-BLOC DEVELOPMENTS AS A DETERMINANT OF INTER-BLOC RELATIONS

What happens with regards to relations between the blocs depends to a large extent upon developments within the three blocs. The more united and cohesive the blocs become, the higher the chances are for inter-bloc conflicts. Conversely, the less united the blocs are internally, the less intense conflicts between the blocs tend to be.

This hypothesis will be illustrated by discussing one specific aspect of cohesiveness for each of the three blocs.

The cohesiveness of Europe

A great deal has been published on whether the Common Market project ("1992") will lead to a "Fortress Europe" or not. Seen from within the European Union (EU), the Community seems much less of a Union than is often envisaged from the outside. Already the Union can hardly agree on anything, not even on the number of votes necessary for majority decisions of the European Council of Ministers, its main decision-making body. And, with every enlargement, its cohesiveness may decline even further.

It is particularly important to note that, in many instances, the United Kingdom still plays an independent role within the EU. The dominant value system within Britain often corresponds more to that put into practice in the United States than to that on the European continent (cf. Albert 1991). To some extent, General De Gaulle proved to be right when he expressed the fear that Great Britain would act as a kind of "Trojan Horse" in the European Community.

What are the preconditions for European unity? There are basically three situations which could lead to a united European stance. One is outside pressure, which has been the strongest uniting force in the past. The second could be internal dominance by either one member state (with a united Germany being the most obvious candidate), or a coalition of core states (a Paris/Bonn axis, for instance). The third possibility would result from a complicated bargaining process among the governments of the member countries. Where the latter is the case the results tend to be relatively inflexible, which can put some strain on inter-bloc bargaining because it impedes the usual process of give and take in international negotiations.

I will not discuss the first possibility, that of outside pressure leading to European unity, because I instead want to concentrate on internal developments within this bloc. I therefore single out the chances of future dominance of a united Germany for further discussion. The most important question thus becomes: what has been and will be the impact of German reunification on European integration?

Many observers expected (and some still expect) a stronger and even dominant role of Germany in the EU as the result of German reunification. During the first years since unification, however, this has clearly not been the case. On the contrary, optimistic expectations that the introduction of a market economy would lead to an explosion of productivity in the former GDR, and that its population would quickly reach the income level of their Western compatriots, turned out to be wishful thinking. Instead, Germany got its own "Mezzogiorno:" a large area that depends for its living standards on massive state intervention. It is this shift towards massive state intervention which might be most relevant for future inter-bloc relations.

The intensity of state intervention is one of the most contentious elements in the relations between the United States, Western Europe and Japan. The US government remains the strongest advocate of further deregulation and liberalization, while Japan has adopted a cautious stance regarding these issues. European governments, meanwhile, tend to fall somewhere in between on the question of state intervention in economic matters.

Before unification the European Community maintained a delicate balance between governments that were free-market oriented and in favor of far-reaching deregulation (mainly Great Britain and the Benelux countries), and governments with a much stronger tradition of state intervention (such as the southern European states and France). Germany used to hold a position in between, and acted as a kind of balancer. As a result of unification, however, Germany may lean towards more intensive state intervention for two reasons: (a) it suffers from structural internal imbalances which cannot be solved by market forces alone, but which demand state intervention to prevent these imbalances from becoming increasingly extreme, and (b) with unification the German electoral system has expanded to incorporate millions of voters who were socialized in the context of a strong state which regularly intervened in all areas of daily life. For many of these people, it is completely self-evident that the state should intervene heavily in the economy; they cannot in fact imagine otherwise. With a changing balance between the forces in favor of more rather than less state intervention in Germany, the balance of these forces in Europe in general has changed. As a result, the EU itself may become more inclined towards state intervention, with clear-cut repercussions for its future relationship with the United States.

German unification had also other, more short-term ramifications with consequences for inter-bloc relations: it delayed European recovery in the early 1990s and undermined European competitiveness. It delayed recovery because of the immense transfer payments to East Germany (of annually about 100 billion US$). These payments (mainly for social security) helped stabilize the social and political situation in the Eastern part of the country, but at the same time constituted a large-scale shift from investment to consumption. In order to limit the impact of the financial transfers on inflation, the Bundesbank had to continue a tough monetary policy, hindering economic recovery not only in Germany, but in Europe as a whole. This is one of the reasons why Europe is emerging from the recession much more slowly than is the United States.

Furthermore, the enormous shift from investment to transfer payments can undermine Germany's (and Europe's) long term competitiveness on the world market, thus laying the basis for further conflict between Europe on the one hand, and the United States and Japan on the other. This is because, sooner or later, a decline in competitiveness will be translated into protectionist measures against other trading blocs.

The impact of German unification on European integration and the relationship between Europe and the outside world is interesting in itself, but it is even more interesting as it provides some ideas about what the future enlargement of the European Union might imply, as Central European countries (Hungary, Poland, Chechia and Slovakia) join in the first two decades of the 21st century.

An East Asian trade bloc?

In any analysis of present international trade conflicts, the role of Japan is crucial. However, if we try to develop scenarios for the development of trade patterns over the next 25 years, the position of China seems at least as relevant. This idea does not imply that the role of Japan will diminish; it only reflects the assumption that changes in Japan's international position will be much more incremental in the future. Japan's position in international trade will probably normalize somewhat with increasing domestic consumption, changes in work ethics, less pronounced productivity advantages, and less disinclination to buy foreign products.

Destabilizing effects for the world trade system might instead come from China, for it is not the intensity of competition nor the volume of trade which leads to trade conflicts, but the rapidness of change and the resulting imbalances. Slow changes can normally be easily accommodated. Quick changes, however, leave little time to adapt and easily cause political clashes. It seems that China's trade will actually increase by large percentages for a while. While Japan has reached a wage level where rises in the value of the yen can easily nullify competitive advantages, the wage gap between China and the highly industrialized countries is such that the competitive advantage will not easily be destroyed.

If the assumption is correct that China will become one of the big players in world trade, this would imply a new generation of trade conflicts. It is highly probable that China will continue to have strong state intervention in its economy, even if it is no longer ruled by a communist regime. It will continue to show strong state intervention because of its relative level of development (compared to the highly-industrialized countries), and because high levels of internal inequalities demand a strong state.

However, it is not clear whether this important player in future world trade will be a state with the present borders of the People's Republic of China (including Hong Kong and Taiwan). Indeed, at the present the central state of the PRC no longer has effective control over some of its provinces. During the next 25 years, furthermore, the very success of certain regions within China in expanding industrial production will exacerbate internal tensions. Such increased tensions will emerge between the coastal provinces, where most capital accumulation takes place, and other provinces which are exposed to the negative consequences of this accumulation process (such as higher prices, a drain on qualified personnel, and large scale corruption). The inhabitants of China's less-successful provinces may also suffer from the attempts by their own polities to catch up with the coastal provinces (e.g. by imposing higher taxes to offer a better infrastructure, and by conferring other advantages to companies which are prepared to shift production there). There have always been tensions between the more urban coastal provinces and the rural provinces of the Chinese "hinterland", where many of the more revolutionary movements find their roots. Indeed, peasant revolts have already occurred in Eastern China, perhaps foreshadowing more serious conflicts in the future.

Additionally, thriving small-scale rural industries in disadvantaged provinces will be increasingly threatened by competition from large-scale industries, which produce primarily for the world market but are coming to serve the domestic market as well. Pressures will therefore build to protect local economies against outside competition. If local authorities cannot exert enough influence at the level of the central state, or if the central government cannot or will not respond to such demands, the disadvantaged regions may break away. An ideological umbrella which would justify such a move can always easily be found.

One may even say that the break-up of China is a precondition for the integration of large parts of the Far Eastern region into the world market, because neither China nor the world market could withstand the integration of all of China at the same time.

If the factual, if not formal break-up of China is a precondition for the rapid integration of parts of this region into the world economy, much will depend on the concrete modalities of this break-up. If this turns out to be a violent process, which draws neighboring states into the conflict, the entire region may be paralyzed for a considerable period of time. This would slow down the development of the region itself, and the world economy as a whole, and could perhaps contribute to a worldwide recession and increasing trade conflicts as well. If, on the contrary, the internal changes take place in a comparatively smooth way, this could open the door to another period of rapid economic growth in certain parts of China which would mean stiffer international competition for foreign producers in the most affected economic sectors.

The break-up of China would add to other major recent changes in the international state system, the most important of which has been the break-up of the Soviet Union. If we are to learn something from the far-reaching and largely unforeseen changes in the last five years, it is to not take the existing state structure for granted when we speculate on future international developments. Not only may China follow the example of the Soviet Union, but other countries show similar tendencies as well. An obvious candidate is India, where the (albeit cautious) opening of the domestic market is strengthening tendencies towards unequal development, which in turn may exacerbate ever-present centrifugal tendencies in this multi-lingual, multi-religious, multi-ethnic society.

Developments in North America

Compared to the other two continents, the situation in North America seems much less complicated. There are few manifest conflicts between Canada, the United States and Mexico. What could have important repercussions for intercontinental relations, in this case, are not so much the international relations between the three countries, but internal developments within the United States, where polarization may become exacerbated by the Free Trade Agreement with Mexico.

With about 30 per cent of the US population living below the poverty line, and about as many being illiterate, the North–South divide does not so much separate Mexico and the United States – it rather goes right through the United States itself. It may periodically lead to social eruptions, as in the case of the recent events in Los Angeles (cf. Davis 1993). These will remain temporary eruptions, however, because there is no ideology around which the disadvantaged groups of US society can rally. Nevertheless, these eruptions will force the US government to pay more attention to social problems at home.

Such a reorientation would not necessarily imply a more isolationist policy for the United States. During the last decades, declarations of a "war against poverty" often went hand in hand with an internationalist policy, as shown by the Kennedy, Johnson and Carter administrations. The indirect implications of domestic policy, however, might lead to new intercontinental conflicts. Increased government expenditures will, if not accompanied by tax increases (more and more difficult to accomplish in a highly internationalized world), lead to higher budget deficits, more international borrowing, a higher value of the dollar on international currency markets, and a decline in international competitiveness of the American economy – with all kinds of protectionist measures that this may entail.

With NAFTA, North America has internalized the periphery even more than before, to the extent that social stability has become increasingly questionable. Any move to improve this situation may cause additional international conflicts. In addition, the internalization of the periphery has other important side effects. It aggravates social cleavages within the United States, and it helps to reproduce a specific set of values and attitudes, like strong individualism at the expense of solidarity, which lays the basis for different policy orientations in the United States and European countries.

As has been illustrated by the above examples, internal developments in all three trade blocs have tremendous consequences for relations between the blocs. They may lead to a stronger position of the state in Europe, and to centrifugal tendencies within China and the United States. Finally, all these developments may increase the intensity of conflicts among the trade blocs, and contribute to more regionalization rather than globalization of the economy.

NOTE

* This chapter has been adapted from, Junne, G. 1995. "Global Cooperation or Rival Trade Blocs," *Journal of World Systems Research*, Volume 1, Number 9.

REFERENCES

Albert, Michel. 1991. *Capitalisme contre capitalisme*. Paris: Editions du Seuil.

CPB (Central Planning Bureau), 1992a. *Scanning the Future. A Long-Term Scenario Study of the World Economy, 1990–2015*. The Hague: Sdu Publishers.

CPB (Central Planning Bureau), 1992b. *Nederland in drievoud. Een scenariostudie van de Nederlandse economie, 1990–2015*. Den Haag: Sdu Uitgeverij Plantijnstraat.

Davis, Mike. 1993. "Who Killed Los Angeles? Part Two: The Verdict is Given," *New Left Review*, Number 199, May–June, 29–54.

MacNeill, J., Winsemius, P. and Yakushiji, T. 1991. *Beyond Interdependence: The Meshing of the World's Economy and the Earth's Ecology*, New York: Oxford University Press.

Sandholtz, Wayne *et al.* 1992. *The Highest Stakes: The Economic Foundations of the Next Security System*. New York: Oxford University Press.

Schwartz, Peter. 1991. *The Art of the Long View: Planning for the Future in an Uncertain World*. New York: Doubleday.

Van der Wurff, Richard and Ans Kolk. 1993. *Wereldhandel en Milieu: Vier scenario's voor 2018, Deelstudie uitgevoerd in het het kader van het onderzoeksproject "Structuurveranderingen in Wereldhandelsstromen" in opdracht van het Ministerie van Verkeer en Waterstaat en de Stichting Coordinatie Maritiem Onderzoek*. Amsterdam: University of Amsterdam.

Van Ginneken, Jaap. 1993. *Rages and Crashes. Over de onvoorspelbaarheid van de economie*. Bloomendaal: Aramith Uitgevers.

SECTION 2: SOCIETY

INTRODUCTION

Although economic events and phenomena will inevitably always be in the foreground of the environment for business decision-makers in the short-term, recent years have seen a re-focusing of their priorities on longer-term social developments. The growth in plans for and programmes of 'corporate (social) responsibility' appears to provide evidence of this. There has been furious debate over the social responsibility question in business for at least a century. Free market economist Milton Friedman considered the sole social responsibility of private business organisations to be the generation of profits with which to satisfy their shareholders, whereas writers such as the economist Thorsten Veblen and the popular business writer and columnist Peter Drucker viewed businesses as meeting the needs of a range of 'stakeholders' including both the consumer and the employee as key groups. The fundamental issue here is what do they mean by 'social'?

Here we draw on the work of sociologists, neatly summarised in chapter 10 by Stuart Hall. In his piece, Hall traces the roots of sociology as the study of society. He outlines the three major concepts which form the basis for sociological analysis – social relations, social processes and social divisions – arguing that it is these which give society its 'distinctive shape' or structure. For businesses, however, this is not a usual starting point. These are rather abstract concepts, with which most businesses do not consciously concern themselves. Very often their view of the social environment begins with an examination of 'social trends', statistics describing the changing picture of demography and social attitudes over a period of time. In chapter 11, Halsey gives us an analysis of this type of information, while at the same time evaluating one of its chief sources – the UK government publication aptly titled, *Social Trends*. This shows us how this information can be examined in more depth using the concepts offered to us by sociology. In particular Halsey uses the concept of the 'division of labour' to explain the nature of post-war social change in Britain. In principle he means the divisions which can be observed in employment patterns, in terms of female participation in paid employment (gender) and occupational mobility (class). This is clearly derived from and linked to the social divisions which Hall describes. The conclusion we may draw from this is that businesses' behaviour towards their employees, is intrinsically linked to the structure or shape of society.

In chapter 12, Bradley takes this analysis of the role of employment in shaping society much further. She examines the evolution of the social divisions and the developing subdivisions within them over the last three decades. Her conclusions are basically that even despite the widening diversity and fragmentation within society, the basic social divisions still remain, reinforced by businesses' employment and management practices. The more obvious, economic manifestations of these social divisions are dealt with by Hutton in chapter 13. He points out the vicious circle of social inequality in which businesses play a part, and produces a strong critique based on the notion that it hampers economic development. In chapter 14 by Braham, the argument is extended into the international economy where global and multinational businesses use the same employment criteria of a cheap and flexible workforce to perpetuate world socio-economic inequalities.

In chapter 15, Armson *et al.* examine perhaps the most important development in the study of the social environment in recent decades – cultural analysis. The work of Hofstede, which is reviewed in this chapter, provided a departure from the concerns of the structuralist sociological approaches. Hofstede attempted to provide a framework for companies and their managers to understand the cultural traits of various societies. Although strongly criticised in recent years, not least for the 'nationalistic' basis of his model, Hofstede at least gives us a flavour of how post-modernist social commentators view global society and its diversity. It has led to a new emphasis on 'cultural diversity' as a watchword for global business practice.

THE STRUCTURE OF SOCIETY*

Stuart Hall

We can now look at the structure of [. . .] 'society' and at what gives it its distinctive shape [. . .].

SOCIAL RELATIONS

One point which gives society its distinctive structure is the fact that it is made up of specific *social relations*. We should think of these as *relations* in their own right. The important thing about them is *not* the individuals who are placed and positioned within them, but the way the relations themselves constrain individuals and groups to behave in certain ways, whatever their individual feelings and inclinations. According to this way of looking at things, the obedient and the rebellious slave are both *slaves*. The paternalistic and the oppressive slave-owner are both *slave-owners*. Both are positioned by a particular system or structure of relations that exists independently of them. The slave society depended on these relations being in place, no matter which particular individuals actually performed the specific roles of 'slave' and 'slave-owner' in it.

SOCIAL PROCESSES

A second factor is that a society needs activities which reproduce it over time and keep it going. We call these *social processes*. All societies, of whatever type, have strong, persistent, regular sets of activities of this kind, and these processes must be sustained, in a regular way, across time. Particular societies (be it eighteenth-century England or twentieth-century England) could not exist without an economic process which produces and distributes goods, and reproduces the material basis of life; or a reproduction process which produces and socializes the next generation; or a legal process which punishes those who deviate too far from what is considered the norm, and so on.

Contemporary western societies are, of course, advanced, industrial capitalist economies, not early mercantile capitalist ones. People are hired to work for a wage; their labour is not forced, as it was under the colonial slave system. Our legal systems of property ownership and inheritance are different too. We are not allowed to 'own' people, though we do hire their labour. Married women are no longer debarred from owning property and a person's estate is no longer necessarily inherited by the eldest son. In a more secular world, fewer people might be inclined to regard a shipwreck as, by definition, a sign of God's providence. Contemporary society is multi-racial. And so on.

The first point we can draw from this comparison, then, is the point about historical specificity. Social processes in general may be 'the same' (every society has an economy), but in each society in different historical periods they are structured and organized differently (a slave economy differs from an advanced industrial capitalist one).

SOCIAL DIVISIONS

Another thing to notice is that, though individuals must relate and associate together in order to keep a social process going, the positions they occupy within that process are *different*. [. . .] The Caribbean plantation economy created one economic 'system', but the groups and individuals had very different positions within that system. Each had different degrees of power. The slave-owner's power was absolute. He exercised powers of life and death over his slaves. Technically, the slave had no power at all and was subject to the master's will and whim. The plantation-owner took all the profits made from his estate after the costs were paid. The slave received enough food and shelter to keep him or her alive and working, but had no share in the rewards of his/her labour. We call these differences between them *social divisions*, and can see now that these divisions form an essential part of the basic *structure* of slave society.

We have now identified three fundamental dimensions of 'society' – *social relations, social processes* and *social divisions*. Along these three dimensions we can begin to make sense of society (or perhaps, since we are giving particular attention now to differences – between one type of society and another, we had better start saying it in the plural – 'societies'). Of course, social processes take place somewhere. Social processes are sustained within different institutions which keep the processes going. Institutions connect the different parts of a process together and regulate the behaviour of individuals and groups within it. In the economy we can identify institutions like factories which produce goods, markets and shops where goods are bought and sold, industrial enterprises or multinational corporations which own and coordinate the different activities that make up the economy, banks and other institutions which accumulate capital and invest, and so on.

Another fundamental aspect of all societies is power, how it operates and how it is distributed. Power is also exercised within social relations, and through very different institutions, in our society. The state, for example, has considerable power in the political process. Those who own a great deal of wealth wield economic power: they can command a larger share of the resources and goods in society deriving from the economic process. The law exerts a different kind of power - legal power, the power to require the citizen to obey the law and to deprive a person of his/her liberty if the law is infringed. To exert that particular kind of power, a number of different legal institutions are linked within the legal processes: the legislature, which frames the laws; the police, who apply them on the ground; the courts, which decide whether or not an individual has broken the law; the judges, who have the power to impose a sentence; and the penal system, which supervises confinement. Each of these particular institutions functions differently. It is the connections between them that sustain what we call 'the legal process'. It is this process which not only decides, on the basis of the law, who is guilty and innocent, but also delivers, in practice, different legal outcomes for different social groups – the poor and the rich, men and women, black and white. One of the key points where power operates in society is across such social divisions – not only in law but between employers and employees, the well and the poorly educated, the governors and the governed and so on.

If we were trying to build a model of society, then in terms of what gives it its shape and structure, and reproduces its pattern over time and space, the following would be our key building blocks: *relations, processes, divisions*.

THE SOCIAL DIVISIONS OF AGE, CLASS, 'RACE'/ETHNICITY AND GENDER

We now look specifically at the third dimension of social structure: social divisions.

One such division is age. Age is a significant line of division in modern societies. The old have very different social experiences from the young, as well as different – and sometimes conflicting – interests. Misunderstanding between the generations has frequently been a source of social tension. If we divided the population of the UK into age groups of about ten or fifteen years each, and counted the numbers in each group, it would give us a broad picture of the 'age structure' of the society. This has real social consequences for society. A society with large numbers in the younger age groups has a 'youthful' population, but it will have to provide schools for them. A society with a larger percentage of its population in the older age groups has an 'ageing' population, and therefore needs to provide forms of care for the aged. The latter is now the case in Britain: the proportion of people in the over-65 age group rose from 5 per cent in 1901 to 16 per cent by the end of the 1980s.

You might be aware, from newspaper articles or comment in the media, of the growing importance of the older sections of society. As they have increased in relative size in the population, they have become more organized as a group and have attracted more attention as a target audience for advertisers and a focus for policy-makers.

However, the kinds of social division that have preoccupied social scientists are those where power and inequality are very strongly linked. The social divisions which social scientists believe exert the greatest influence and carry the most explanatory power are those associated with *class, gender* and *'race'/ethnicity*. Inequalities of class arise from the differential access of different groups to economic goods, resources and opportunities. Inequalities of gender are associated with the differential position of and opportunities for women and men to participate in social life and the differences of power and influence between them in shaping the world. Inequalities associated with 'race' or ethnicity are where one group is disadvantaged *vis-à-vis* another because of its 'racial' or ethnic characteristics.

You should bear in mind that, for the moment, we are not making a very sharp distinction between power and inequality: we are using them more or less interchangeably as a way of defining social divisions. The different social classes, the different gender groups (men and women) and the different 'racial' groups (black and white) all have different degrees of *power*, influence and authority in the society. They also have unequal access to wealth, goods and material resources – and consequently there are significant degrees of *inequalities* between them. Both power and material goods are unequally distributed throughout the society and there is a pattern to this structure of inequalities. There are certainly debates as to how and why these two things – power and inequality – are linked, but we do not need to go into those here. For our purposes, I am accepting the well-documented fact that they do appear to be closely associated. The powerful are able to amass wealth, have higher incomes, own a greater share of the property and can purchase more of the available goods and resources than those with less power. By the same token, those who come low in the 'equality' stakes also tend to wield less power, authority and influence.

The social divisions based on class, 'race' and gender have a wide-reaching impact on society. Class divisions, especially, figure in the analysis and explanation of a very wide range of social phenomena. Until recently, class was the privileged explanation in social science – the one which, most social scientists believed, explained, or was in some way essential for explaining, all aspects of society. You can see this 'privileging' of class explanations even in so simple a thing as the way social statistics are organized. Most of the official statistics issued by government and research agencies automatically and routinely classify their data by social class. Agencies like the UK Tobacco Research Council . . . now regularly classify their data by both class and gender. However, this was not always the case. It is only relatively recently that social scientists have come to understand the significance of gender divisions in society and to give them comparable weight in the way they organize and present their information.

It is doubtful whether, even today, you could find much data on smoking organized according to 'racial' or ethnic groups, since 'race' is a form of social division that is still not taken with equal seriousness either by those who gather and arrange data or by social scientists who are trying to explain social behaviour. So the social divisions we have been discussing do not have 'equal weight' in the work and thinking of social scientists. In the past, class was widely considered the 'master category' – the one that affects everything else and influences all the other divisions and relations, and thus the one which best explained the patterning of social phenomena. You may appreciate the irony of calling this category of explanation, which has so often failed to include issues of gender or 'race', the 'master' category, with all the connotations of masculine authority and colonial dominance that the word 'master' carries. Try, for example, describing 'class' as the 'mistress' category! This example reminds us that the way meanings are constructed through language in our culture has always been influenced by gender and ethnic divisions.

It may be of no surprise to you to learn, then, that the privileged position of 'class-based' explanations has come under increasing challenge in social science, as people have become more aware of the growing importance in our society of gender and 'race'/ethnicity and as the new social movements have begun, once again, to organize. The 'privileging' of (i.e. the granting of special explanatory importance to) class has been effectively contested; many social scientists have moved towards a more 'interactive' model of social divisions where each is considered to have an impact on the other [. . .] In general terms, however, these critical questions of theory and research in social science remain ultimately unresolved. [. . .] As you will have seen from the previous discussion, these divisions shape the societies in which we live, determine how wealth, opportunities, resources (material and cultural) and 'life-chances' are distributed, unevenly, between different groups in society and position or place individuals within the social structure.[. . .]

Of course, even the interaction of these different social divisions has itself to be 'theorized' – theoretically analysed and explained. Is the impact of these divisions on individuals, groups, society as a whole, *autonomous*? That is to say, does each of these factors have its own, separate way of working, its own dynamic, its own causes, requiring its own explanatory theories? Or is this taking the reaction against the 'privileging' of class explanations too far? Are each of these divisions of equal weight in explaining the patterns of inequality and disadvantage we find in society? Are there over-arching theoretical concepts, models and explanations – like patriarchy or 'race' or marxism or liberalism, for example – which can account for *all* the divisions, without reducing one to, or explaining it in terms of, another? Or is there something still to be said for thinking that, despite the danger of reductionism, one of these divisions – say, gender – really *is* the one which can explain or encompass all the others, and which therefore deserves a privileged position in social science explanations? [. . .]

IS 'STRUCTURE' THE RIGHT WORD?

The word 'structure' is [. . .] an essential concept in filling out and giving 'body' to this idea of 'the social'. The relations, processes and divisions we have been looking at are not a random assortment of activities. They occur in the central areas of life. They give regularity to what happens and help us to predict the ways in which people are likely to behave. They constrain the activities of large numbers of people. They create patterns in the distribution of resources, cultural and material, which remain remarkably stable across time. Regularity and predictability are key features of a 'structure'. Another key feature is continuity through time. The processes and divisions of society are the means by which a society reproduces itself across historical time. The concept of 'process' is important, because it calls to mind the notion of an activity that is continuous and sustained over long periods. Processes and divisions are also organized spatially . . . This spatial network of processes and institutions and the cleavages or lines of division that they produce are yet another dimension along which a society acquires a structure.

However, one problem with the concept of 'structure' is that it can also sound very static. Where have these processes, relations and divisions come from? In one sense they are nothing but the organized activities of men and women living, producing and associating together. The metaphor of a 'structure' makes a lot of sense when thought of in terms of a building. But what it sometimes leaves out is the activity of construction itself: people doing things, activity, practice. Relations, processes and structures don't seem to have an active subject. They just exist. They confront us with their brute existence. We forget who built them, who keeps them going. We can't use these concepts in an active way – it's difficult, for example, to say that a social process or a structure 'does something'! Like Topsy, they seem to 'just grow' and work by themselves.

This is one aspect of the problem which social scientists sometimes call 'agency versus structure'. This refers to the argument between those who stress how individuals and groups produce society, and those who put greater stress on how they are shaped and 'produced' by society. The great advantage of taking a more individualist perspective is that it helps you to see agency, activity, people wanting things, doing things. There is a sort of parallel between those who take a more individualistic view of society and those who emphasize the agency or 'active' side of social processes – men and women actively making the social world what it is. On the other hand, there is a similar parallel between those who emphasize structures and those who view society more in terms of how structures limit and constrain the group's or individual's freedom of action, from the outside. However, it is dangerous to push these parallels too far: groups (classes, gender or ethnic or age groups) can be seen as active agents too – collective social actors.

There is no immediate solution in sight to this 'agency versus structure' dilemma. It would be nice to be able to square the circle and to have both agency and structure. And it may be that both things are operative at the same time. Men and women do actively construct the world, but they do so under conditions and constraints, built into the structures they inhabit, which limit their freedom to act. Moreover, the processes and institutions they actively construct are 'experienced' by the next generation, not as a set of active relationships, but as a set of already fixed relations, within whose limits they, in their turn, must act. We were making a very similar point earlier when we said that relationships (active), when sustained over long periods, come to be experienced and function as relations (passive). The argument is also similar to that advanced by the contemporary social theorist, Anthony Giddens, with his idea of 'structuration'. It is worth bearing it in mind, as a sort of corrective against a too-structural view of what society is:

Social structures are made up of human actions and relationships: what gives these their patterning is their repetition across periods of time and distances of space. Thus the ideas of social reproduction and social structure are very closely related to one another . . . The actions of all of us are influenced by the structural characteristics of the societies in which we are brought up and live; at the same time, we recreate (and to some extent alter) those structural characteristics in our actions.

(Giddens, 1989, p.19)

NOTE

* This chapter has been adapted from, The Open University (1991, 1993) D103 *Society and Social Science*, Block 2 *Social Structures and Divisions*, Unit 6 'The idea of the "social" in social science', Milton Keynes, The Open University.

REFERENCE

Giddens, A. (1989) *Sociology*, Cambridge, Polity Press.

11

SOCIAL TRENDS SINCE WORLD WAR II*

A.H. Halsey[1]

Social Trends was introduced in 1970 by the Head of the Government Statistical Services.[2] From the outset it included trend statistics from official sources reaching back to the 1951 census and even further back towards the beginning of the century on some demographic topics.[3] The publication also included some attempt to compare Britain with other countries, especially the 'first world' states with membership of the Organization for Economic Cooperation and Development (OECD). By 1987, therefore, an arithmetic post-war history of a large number of facets of British social structure had been compiled with at least some comparative international reference.

So the purpose of this article could be to elaborate its title. But that simple definition is impracticable: a focus, even an arbitrary one, is necessary if only for reasons of space. And even so there could be no unique and objective recipe for choosing particular social trends. Selection is inevitable, stemming from an implicit or explicit interpretation as to what social processes have been significant. More fundamentally there is always an underlying theory of social structure and social change. [. . .]

Moreover it must be remarked in caution that the very concept of a trend may generate unintended distortion. Trends are absurdly easy to find. If between two points of time a series of observations yields neither random fluctuation nor absolute stability there must be a trend. But so what? Even stability may be significant; for example a zero rate of population growth would have momentous social implications in most countries in our time. There is no escape from interpreting the significance of a phenomenon, whether rising, falling or trendless. Moreover bias may come in subtle forms from contentious, unproven, or false theories of history. There are no established laws of historical development or decline. Thus modern scepticism towards the view that social institutions evolved and culminated in Victorian liberal society – the so-called Whig version of British history – could be said to be an extravagant preference for graphs moving upwards to the right. The underlying theory is a belief in progress and in the superiority of European civilization, especially the activities of British men. Similarly the Marxist theory of history, at least for 'capitalist' societies, looks for downward trends, for example in the rate of profit or the income of proletarians, towards a revolutionary crisis.

These cautions notwithstanding, the trends identified as significant by one observer can at least serve to invite other readers to specify or sharpen their own interpretations of [social changes]. I have chosen from a thousand possibilities to consider how the evidence from official statistics bears on two widely accepted generalizations in the contemporary social sciences. The first is that Britain has experienced a comprehensive renegotiation of the division of labour over the past forty years. The second is that a post-war period can be identified as having come to an end in the mid-1970s, followed by a decade exhibiting a new form of polarization in British society.

THE CONTEXT

Britain's position in the world is the anxious subject of popular debate at the present time. The United Kingdom is still a major figure in the world as a whole. It has a gross domestic product (GDP) of over £300 billion (about 6⅓ per cent of the GDP of the OECD countries). However, its relative economic position has been weakening for many years. In the decade 1975 to 1984 the GDP of the OECD block grew by 12 per cent more than in the United Kingdom. On the other hand the first quarter century of the reign of Elizabeth II was one of mounting prosperity. Between 1951 and 1976 real disposable income per capita at 1980 prices rose from £1,375 to £2,536. The average real weekly earnings of male manual workers aged 21 or over rose from £60 in April 1951 to £109 and further to £111 in April 1983.[4] Basic paid holidays for manual workers increased from one and three quarter weeks to three and a half weeks; ownership of cars rose from about 14 per cent of households to 56 per cent (62 per cent in 1985) and, in general, post-war Britain has been an increasingly prosperous society.[5]

In April 1986 the newspapers were carrying comment on the possibility of new rules concerning the retirement of women from employment and their entitlement to pensions. This single news item is sufficient to dramatize how much British society has changed in the period since the end of the Second World War. Today the underlying assumptions are that men and women should be treated equally with respect to employment and that laws with respect to gender and employment relations could originate in Europe and have a claim to adherence in Britain. Both assumptions would have seemed weird to British citizens under an Attlee government. Women at that time were thought of as belonging primarily and essentially to the domestic economy, social equality was thought to be about class rather than gender, and the idea of any kind of primacy for European over British law would have been swamped by the shared conception of Britain as an imperial world power, of London as the centre of the world through which the Greenwich meridian appropriately ran, and by awareness that a quarter of the world's population as well as a quarter of the land surface were under British control. . . .

In 1945 the island society, on this perspective, comprised the upper echelons of a worldwide commonwealth. In the 40 subsequent years the size of the UK population, though 16 per cent up in absolute numbers, has declined from constituting one fiftieth to contributing a mere one hundredth to the population of the world as a whole. For better or worse, the first industrial and the greatest imperial nation has been displaced within the memory of those aged 50 or more from the centre of the economic, military and political stage, if not to a marginal offshore station of Western Europe, at least to a relatively minor position among the world's major powers.

So much then for context and as a safeguard against the interpretation of British statistics as representing the inevitable historical pathway of all industrial societies. Every country has its peculiar genius. Britain's post-war record is not a reliable proxy for the recent history of Western, European, industrial, capitalist, 'first world', 'post-industrial', democratic, or any other postulated type of society. It is within the context of British experience that our two theses concerning the renegotiation of the division of labour and the passing of the post-war period into a new phase of polarization may be discussed.

THE DIVISION OF LABOUR

Behind its virtue and its victory Britain emerged from the Second World War as a classical industrial economy, a centralized democratic polity, and a familistic social structure. It was a society with historical roots in a social order in which there had been minimal government, and in which welfare had been dominated by the relation between the family and the workplace through the market for labour. The institutional division of labour of prototypic industrialism was an essential triangle joining the family, the economy, and the state. Families had raised children, men had worked, women had run households. The economy produced, the family reproduced and consumed, and the state protected and redistributed.

All this was to change. In political terms there was a national consensus built during the war on the need for a welfare state which, in an earlier political language, constituted 'interference' in the exchanges between the family and the economy. The rise of the welfare state required an elaboration of the collection of taxes (partly from households, partly from enterprises, and partly from the labour market transactions between them) to be used as redistributive resources for the education of children, the relief of men temporarily out of work, the maintenance of women without men to connect them to the economy, the sustenance of the old, and the protection of the health and safety of the population as a whole.

In the following generation a different and more elaborate pattern of relationships was developed. Thus the family produces as well as consumes. People take recreation, or 'live', as well as work in factories and work as well as live in houses. The family has fewer children and breaks up as well as re-forms more frequently. Women have become more incorporated into the formal economy and men have been drawn back more into the household and the informal economy. Adults as well as children learn. More children than in the past labour competitively for qualifications during their compulsory years at school. The state, especially in the early part of the period, was drawn more into the productive system, partly through the taxation and regulation of firms but also in the direct production of goods and of an increasingly complicated array of social services. In short, all of the words used to describe the classical triangle now have modified meanings because each of the major institutions has invaded or absorbed the traditional functions of the other two. Leisure in the family includes do-it-yourself activities, business enterprises and trade unions have taken on some of the regulatory functions of government, and the state, through its employment of policemen, doctors, nurses, teachers, and social workers, has comprehensively invaded the traditional role of the parent. All of these shifts, institutional and individual, together add up to a renegotiated division of labour in the Britain of the 1980s compared with that of the 1940s.

Accordingly, it should be possible to identify statistical trends reflecting, manifesting, or exemplifying the movements in the division of labour which I have sketched. Comparing the beginning and the end of the period we should find that the following changes have occurred.

In the family (see Table 11.1)
1 more women, especially married women, in employment
2 less childbirth, but more illegitimate childbirth
3 more divorce and remarriage and more one-person households
4 more men economically inactive whether as unemployed, retired, or drawn into the domestic economy

Table 11.1 Trends in the family, United Kingdom

	1931	1951	1961	1966	1971	1976	1981	1985
1 Percentage of all women aged 16 or over economically active[1]	34[6]	35[7]	37[7]	42[7]	43[7]	47	48	49
Percentage of married women aged 16 or over economically active[1]	10[6]	22[7]	30[7]	38[7]	42[7]	49	49	52
2 Total period fertility rate[1,2]		2.16	2.78	2.78	2.40	1.72	1.79	1.78
Illegitimate births as a percentage of all births	5	5	6	8	8	9	13	19
Persons divorcing per 1000 married population[3]		3	2	3	6	10	12	13
3 Remarriages as a percentage of all marriages	11[1]	18[1]	15[1]	16[1]	20	31	34	35
One-person households as a percentage of all households[1]	7	11	12	15	18	21	22	24
4 Percentage of all men 16 or over economically active[1]	91[6]	88[7]	86[7]	84[7]	81[7]	79	76	74
5 Thousands of students[4]								
In part-time higher education:[5] Men			107	115	142	168	207	212
Women			6	8	23	50	87	107
Aged 21 or over in								
Non advanced further education						2260[8]	1986[9]	2200
of which adult education					1987		1169[9]	1349
Part-time higher education[5]						201[8]	236	269
Full-time higher education[5]					216	266[8]	235	252
6 Children in extended schooling			See Figure 11.1					
7 Formal qualifications			See Figure 11.2					

1 Great Britain only.
2 The average number of children which would be born per woman if women experienced the age specific fertility rates of the period in question throughout their child-bearing life-span.
3 England and Wales only.
4 Data are for academic years ending in the year shown.
5 Includes Universities, Open University, and advanced courses in major establishments of further education.
6 Aged 14 or over.   7 Aged 15 or over.   8 1976/77.   9 1981/82.

Source: British Labour Statistics Historical Abstract: Population Trends, Office of Population Censuses and Surveys; Department of Education and Science; Central Statistical Office

5 more men and women in adult education
6 more children in extended schooling
7 a population with higher formal qualifications

Statistics taken from the various editions of *Social Trends* confirm these expectations. Between the end of the war and the mid-1980s the proportion of economically active women has risen from just over a third to nearly half, and the proportion of economically active married women, albeit mainly in part-time jobs, has more than doubled. In the same period fertility, though peaking in 1964, has fallen below replacement levels and there has been a multiplication of nearly four in the proportion of illegitimate to total births. Moreover, not only has reproduction made this marginal but significant movement out of the framework of the traditional family, but the family itself is less stable in the sense that there was a more than fivefold increase in the divorce rate between 1961 and 1985 and remarriages now account for over a third of all marriages. The fragility of the family is also represented in a different way by the rise of the one-person household from less than a tenth of all households before the Second World War to a quarter of them now. Some of this trend is, of course, attributable to the ageing of the population.

The reciprocal movement of men into domesticity is also revealed by the evidence in Table 11.1. But again the reduction in the percentage of men who are economically active is mainly caused by the retirement of increasing numbers of men over 65.

Figures for enrolments of adults aged 21 or over on both leisure and vocational courses illustrate the rising tendency for adults to learn, while Figure 11.1 shows the trend towards extended schooling among children. The tendency to voluntary extension has continued into the recent difficult years on top of the raising of the school leaving age from 15 to 16 in 1972.

And Figure 11.2 illustrates the marked rise in the level of qualifications held in the population during the past 30 years. This particular form of illustration also brings out how trends of this kind form, so to speak, geological strata of age cohorts in the population at a given point of time. In this case, in 1985, 72 per cent of the population in the 25 to 29 age group held an educational qualification, whereas only 40 per cent of those aged 50 to 59 did so.

In the economy (see Table 11.2)
The expected correlative changes in the economy include:
  8 a higher GDP per capita
  9 a less manual workforce
10 shorter hours of work
11 longer holidays

These changes are illustrated in Table 11.2. The national income continued to rise. At 1980 prices GDP grew from 1961 (£148 billion) to 1973 (£215 billion) at about 3 per cent per year. Growth from 1973 to 1980 slowed to about 1 per cent per year. Between 1973 and 1984 the increase in GDP per capita was 1 per cent compared with 1½ per cent for all the OECD countries.

The proportion of both men and women in manual occupations declined. This gradual transformation of what was, at the beginning of the century, the most proletarianized country in the world (i.e. composed mainly of the industrial working class), appears in a different guise in Table 11.3. In 1984, 29 per cent of a national sample of adults thought of themselves as having moved into a higher social class and only 9 per cent thought of themselves as having come down in the world compared with their parents. Between the two generations, hours of work were reduced and holidays enlarged. Whereas at the end of the war no manual workers were entitled, now virtually all have the right to four weeks paid holiday.

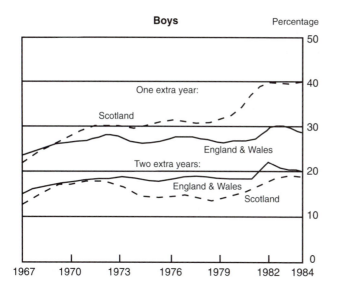

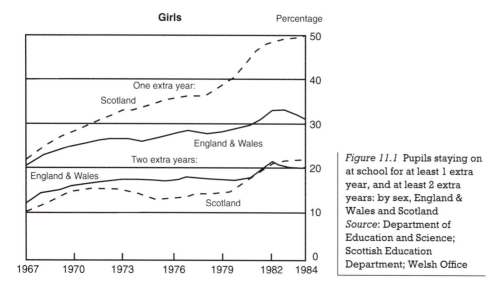

Figure 11.1 Pupils staying on at school for at least 1 extra year, and at least 2 extra years: by sex, England & Wales and Scotland
Source: Department of Education and Science; Scottish Education Department; Welsh Office

In the state (see Table 11.4)
With respect to statistics concerning government we would expect to find:

12 higher expenditure on education
13 increased numbers of parent surrogates in the employment of the state (police, teachers, doctors, social workers, etc)
14 increased nursery provision for the under fives
15 a higher proportion of the GDP spent by the state

These invasions of the traditional realm of the family are illustrated in Table 11.4. Expenditure and manpower in education, health, and the social services are higher today

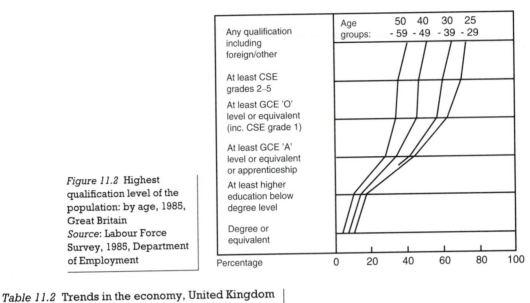

Figure 11.2 Highest qualification level of the population: by age, 1985, Great Britain
Source: Labour Force Survey, 1985, Department of Employment

Table 11.2 Trends in the economy, United Kingdom

	1931	1951	1961	1966	1971	1976	1981	1985
8 Gross domestic product at market prices								
1980 prices (£s billion)		112	148	171	195	220	228	253
Index (1980 = 100)		49	64	74	85	96	99	110
Per head (£s)		2226	2811	3138	3495	3918	4037	4465
9 *Percentage of men in manual occupations*[1]	77	72			62		58	
Percentage of women in manual occupations[1]	76	64			53		44	
Percentage of total in manual occupations[1]	77	70			59		52	
10 Average weekly hours of work,[1,2] for full-time male manual employees	48[4]	48	48	46	46	45	44[2]	44
11 *Percentage of manual employees*[3] *with basic holiday entitlement of over 3 weeks*	–	–	–	4	81	98	100	

1 Great Britain only.
2 At April. Prior to 1983 data cover males aged 21 or over; since then they cover males on adult rates.
3 Employees covered by national collective agreements or Wages Council Orders.
4 October 1938.

Source: Guy Routh, *Occupation and Pay in Great Britain*, Cambridge University Press, 1965; British Labour Statistics Historical Abstract; Central Statistical Office; *Social Trends*

than they were at the end of the 1940s. The state spends more than it did then out of a much bigger national purse. There are in fact more policemen, doctors, nurses, and social workers and there are more children in school or otherwise in the care of the public authorities. [. . .] Between 1976 and 1983 the total of those employed in the health and personal social services increased by nearly 13 per cent. It is true that the numbers working in the NHS in England fell by about 2 per cent between 31 March 1983 and 31 March 1985.[6] But this is an element in the second of our theses to which we can now turn having given the first a reasonable foundation in the statistical record.

Table 11.3 Self-rated social class, 1986, Great Britain

| | *Percentages and numbers* | |
	Self	*Parents*
Social Class (*percentages*)		
Upper middle	*1*	*2*
Middle	*24*	*17*
Upper working	*21*	*12*
Working	*48*	*59*
Poor	*3*	*8*
Don't know/no response	*3*	*2*
Sample size (= 100%) (numbers)	3066	3066

Source: British Social Attitudes Survey, 1986, Social and Community Planning Research

Table 11.4 Trends in the state, United Kingdom

| | | | | | Percentages and thousands | | | |
	1931	*1951*	*1961*	*1966*	*1971*	*1976*	*1981*	*1985*
12 *Government expenditure on education as a percentage of gross domestic product*[1]						*5.2*	*6.3*	*5.5*	*5.1*
13 Manpower in social services[2] (thousands)	769	1188	1725	2088	1978[5]			
Regional and District Health Authorities Staff (thousands)						926	1026	*1023*[7]
Family practitioner professionals (thousands)						49	54	*58*[7]
Personal social services (thousands)						228	251	*273*[7]
14 *Under fives in education as a percentage of all 3 and 4 year olds*				*15*	*20*	*34*	*44*	*47*
Day care places for under fives (thousands)[3] at end March		51[4]	54[4]	128[4]	409	511	540	609
15 *General government expenditure as a percentage of gross domestic product*			*35*	*38*	*41*	*46*	*46*	*45*

1 Financial years ending in the year shown.
2 Education, health, welfare, and social security. Includes part-time.
3 England and Wales only.
4 At end December.
5 Estimated full-time equivalent total for 1970.
6 1972.
7 1984.

Source: *Social Trends* (various), Central Statistical Office.

ECONOMIC TRANSFORMATION AND SOCIAL POLARIZATION

It is now generally recognized that the post-war period for Britain and for other 'first world' countries came to an end with the oil crisis of 1973–74. The preceding 30 years had been a period of economic boom in the form of high rates of economic growth and full employment with burgeoning public sector activity. The more recent period has been one of declining employment, shifting economic activity out of classical towards 'high tech' or service industry, struggles with inflation, determination to move decision-making out of

Westminster and Whitehall into the market and the locality, and politics designed to move activity from the public to the private sector. The question is not so much as to whether this historical watershed is a reality; that is not in serious dispute. It is rather to ask how it is reflected in the statistics pertaining to the process of renegotiating the division of labour. Clearly the post-war boom and the current period of transition are fairly sharply distinguished by their rates of unemployment and their shifts out of manufacturing industry, into the service sector.[7] Meanwhile the arrest of upward trends if not the 'rolling back of the frontiers of the state' is indicated by expressing total government expenditure as a percentage of GDP (though the latter does *not* include transfer payments such as social security). It was 35.5 per cent in 1961, peaked at 48.6 per cent in 1975, and was 45.2 per cent in 1985. But most of the trends in the reorganization of family and economic life are the result of forces other than those which operate as relations between government and the governed. The changing structure of relations between classes, sexes, and age groups may or may not be modified by political activity but, at least in the case of Britain since the Second World War, have not been fundamentally changed in the direction of their development.

There remains, however, the question of whether the distribution of life chances – and the modern national state is, after all, the principal redistributive agent in society – has been crucially altered since the mid-1970s and particularly since the new administration which came in in 1979. This brings us to the hypothesized new trend towards polarization – a widening gap between two components of the population as a whole.

A hundred years ago, discussion of Disraeli's 'two nations' was the stock-in-trade of political arithmeticians. In the 1880s most social observers in Britain agreed that the Marxist polarization thesis of the 1840s, with its prophecy of mass pauperization, of exploited labour and the accumulation of surplus value into fewer and fewer capitalist hands, had been tested and found wanting in the natural laboratory of Victorian history. By and large, the social trends ran in the opposite direction and, however slowly and haltingly, continued to do so through the first three quarters of the twentieth century. But now the question is raised as to whether a new version of the two nations has appeared in the last decade in the form of a widening division between a prosperous majority in secure and increasingly well remunerated employment by contrast with a depressed minority of the unemployed, the sick, the old, and the unsuccessful ethnic minorities.

Evidence on three aspects of this thesis can be examined. First there are the trends recorded in *Social Trends* on the distribution of income and wealth between the better and the worse off families, shown here as Table 11.5. Between 1976 and 1984, the movement of original or market incomes was towards greater inequality. The bottom fifth of households dropped their share from 0.8 to 0.3 per cent and the top fifth moved up from 44.4 to 48.6 per cent. The redistributive activity of the state modified this inequality but did not change the direction of movement. The bottom group had final household incomes amounting to 7.4 per cent of the whole in 1976 reduced to 7.1 per cent in 1984, while the top fifth raised their share from 37.9 to 39.0 per cent.

On the side of wealth the story shown in Table 11.6 is less clear. In 1984, the richest 1 per cent and 10 per cent of the adult population owned 21 and 52 per cent respectively of marketable wealth. With the addition of pension rights (both occupational and state) these shares declined to 12 and 35 per cent. In the early 1970s the share of marketable wealth owned by the richest groups was reduced by a marked fall in the prices of stocks and shares. The late 1970s and early 1980s brought very little change in the pattern of ownership.

With respect to social mobility John Goldthorpe and Clive Payne have concluded unequivocally from their analysis of the 1983 General Election study that 'the stability of relative rates or chances of inter-generational class mobility, which our analyses of the 1972

Table 11.5 Distribution of original, disposable, and final household income, United Kingdom

Percentages

	Quintile groups of households					
	Bottom fifth	Next fifth	Middle fifth	Next fifth	Top fifth	Total
Original income[1]						
1976	0.8	9.4	18.8	26.6	44.4	100.0
1981	0.6	8.1	18.0	26.9	46.4	100.0
1983	0.3	6.7	17.7	27.2	48.0	100.0
1984	0.3	6.1	17.5	27.5	48.6	100.0
Disposable income[2]						
1976	7.0	12.6	18.2	24.1	38.1	100.0
1981	6.7	12.1	17.7	24.1	39.4	100.0
1983	6.9	11.9	17.6	24.0	39.6	100.0
1984	6.7	11.7	17.5	24.4	39.7	100.0
Final income[3]						
1976	7.4	12.7	18.0	24.0	37.9	100.0
1981	7.1	12.4	17.9	24.0	38.6	100.0
1983	6.9	12.2	17.6	24.0	39.3	100.0
1984	7.1	12.1	17.5	24.3	39.0	100.0

1 Households ranked by original income.
2 Households ranked by disposable income.
3 Households ranked by final income.

Source: Central Statistical Office, from Family Expenditure Survey

data suggested went back to the 1920s, has *not* been disturbed to any appreciable degree in the first decade after the ending of the post-war era'.[8] But these authors then go on to examine whether absolute rates have been affected by the new period of transition and particularly whether there has been a freezing of mobility and especially the upward mobility of working class and lower-middle class sons into the middle-class professions, salariat, or 'service class'. The evidence is that absolute rates of upward and of total mobility have continued to rise. A comparison of the 1972 and 1983 samples of these national enquiries is given in Table 11.7. In 1972, 16.0 per cent of the men of working-class origin had found their way into the middle class; by 1983 the percentage had risen to 23.6. Again, in 1972, 61.2 per cent of those of working-class parentage were themselves in working-class jobs; by 1983 the percentage had fallen to 52.6. Thus there is considerable support for the optimistic liberal theory of a technologically led expansion of middle-class opportunities. But the picture has then to be modified by considering unemployment.

In 1972, the unemployment rate was virtually negligible. In 1983 it was in double figures at over 12 per cent, and more than a million had been out of work for at least a year. The unemployed could reasonably be viewed as an additional depressed class which has objectively to be analysed as a 'destination status' in mobility tables. So, while the expansion of the professional and technical middle class remains a feature of late twentieth century Britain, as it was in the long boom from mid century, unemployment has also emerged as a structure of negative opportunity which tends to polarize mobility chances, especially of those who begin in the working class.

Table 11.6 Distribution of wealth, United Kingdom

		Percentages and £s billion		
	1971	*1976*	*1981*	*1984*
Marketable wealth				
Percentage of wealth owned by:				
Most wealthy 1%[1]	*31*	*24* ³	*21*	*21*
Most wealthy 5%[1]	*52*	*45*	*40*	*39*
Most wealthy 10%[1]	*65*	*60*	*54*	*52*
Most wealthy 25%[1]	*86*	*84*	*77*	*75*
Most wealthy 50%[1]	*97*	*95*	*94*	*93*
Total marketable wealth (£s billion)	140	263	546	762
Marketable wealth plus occupational and state pension rights				
Percentage of wealth owned by:				
Most wealthy 1%[1]	*21*	*14*	*12*	*12*
Most wealthy 5%[1]	*37*	*27*	*24*	*25*
Most wealthy 10%[1]	*49*	*37*	*34*	*35*
Most wealthy 25%[1,2]	*69–72*	*58–61*	*55–58*	*56–59*
Most wealthy 50%[1,2]	*85–89*	*80–85*	*78–82*	*79–83*

1 Of population aged 18 or over.
2 Estimates vary with assumptions.
3 Between 1979 and 1980 there was a change in methodology as described in *Inland Revenue Statistics 1986.*

Source: Inland Revenue

Table 11.7 Class distribution: by class of father, 1972 and 1983, England and Wales

				Percentages
	Respondent's class			
	Middle	*Lower-middle*	*Working*	*All*
Father's class				
1972				
Middle	*57.7*	*23.2*	*19.1*	*100.0*
Lower-middle	*31.2*	*31.9*	*37.0*	*100.0*
Working	*16.0*	*22.7*	*61.2*	*100.0*
1983				
Middle	*62.0*	*22.2*	*15.8*	*100.0*
Lower-middle	*34.2*	*34.3*	*31.5*	*100.0*
Working	*23.6*	*23.8*	*52.6*	*100.0*

Source: Trends in Intergenerational Class Mobility in England and Wales 1972–83, John Goldthorpe and Clive Payne, *Sociology*, Vol. 20

Table 11.8 Inner city polarization: by type of area, 1971 and 1981

Numbers and percentages

	Advantage and deprivation index 1981[1]	Population change (%) 1971 to 1981
Metropolitan inner cities		
Inner Birmingham	− 2.37	− 19.3
Inner Manchester	− 1.77	− 25.5
Peripheral council estates		
Knowsley	− 1.36	− 15.3
Other old city centres		
Inner Derby	− 1.97	− 20.1
Other old industrial urban areas		
Outer Derby	0.58	+ 7.4
Rest of Greater Manchester	0.67	+ 0.4
Rest of Outer London	1.42	− 9.0
Fringe areas		
West Midlands south fringe	1.43	+ 16.6
Mersey north fringe	1.22	+ 17.1
Manchester south fringe	1.29	+ 5.3
London south fringe	2.32	− 3.8

Source: Faith in the City, Report of the Archbishop of Canterbury's Commission on Urban Priority Areas

A similar process of social division has also been observed in housing. The dominant trend in the twentieth century has been towards owner occupation and much encouraged in recent years. From this study of trends in housing tenure, Hamnett[9] concludes that, as between owner occupation and local authority renting, there has been 'an increasing degree of social polarization'.

Finally, we may consider the evidence of spatial polarization assembled in the Archbishop of Canterbury's report on Urban Priority Areas, *Faith in the City* (1985).[10]

Using the most recent studies of the Economic and Social Research Council,[11] the Archbishop's Commission assembled a comparison of types of deprivation.[12] The measures include such indicators as the proportion of people unemployed (negative), in professional jobs (positive), the infant mortality rate, the proportions of owner occupiers and of car owners, and many other manifestations of prosperity or poverty. Column 1 of Table 11.8 shows that there is a gradient of advantage ascending from the inner city districts and the peripheral council estates to the fringe areas outside classical industrial Britain. The second column of Table 11.8 shows the shifts in population between 1971 and 1981. Column 1 shows the clear gradient of multiple inequality from the urban priority areas to the fringe areas. Column 2 shows that the urban priority areas are losing population. The process is one of deprived people being left in the urban priority areas as the successful move out to middle Britain.

Of course, the poor are not confined to the urban priority areas. As the Archbishop's Commissioners put it: 'The city remains part magnet to the disadvantaged newcomer, part prison to the unskilled, the disabled, and the dispirited, part springboard for the ambitious and vigorous who find escape to suburbia, and part protection for enclaves of affluence.'[13]

SUMMARY CONCLUSION

The search for trends necessarily involves selection and interpretation. It is moreover a procedure which intrinsically emphasizes change rather than continuity. The perspective adoped here focuses on changes in the relations between family, economy, and government – what I have called the institutional division of labour – and shows a process of renegotiation of function between them. Government has taken on more familial and more economic functions; industry has absorbed more regulatory duties; the family has weakened in the stability of its marriages and its fertility. The traditional meanings and loci of masculinity, femininity, adulthood, childhood, work, leisure, and learning have all changed as the division of labour has shifted.

The post-war period to the mid-1970s was one of economic growth, full employment, and prosperity against an international background of rapid dismantling of imperial power and relative decline of economic productivity. The managerial, professional, and technical classes waxed and the industrial working class waned. Women, particularly married women, moved increasingly into paid employment.

Then, after the oil crisis of the mid-1970s, a new phase of economic and social transformation appeared. The shift away from nineteenth century urban industrial manufacturing was accelerated, unemployment rose, and population movement away from the inner cities towards suburbia, the South East, and new towns was discernable. And, in the process, a pattern has emerged of a more unequal society as between a majority in secure attachment to a still prosperous country and a minority in marginal economic and social conditions, the former moving into the suburban locations of the newer economy of a 'green and pleasant land', the latter tending to be trapped into the old provincial industrial cities and their displaced fragments of peripheral council housing estates. In short a still recognizable Britain is facing new challenges in the late twentieth century as it carries on its ancient struggle to combine freedom and equality in a United Kingdom.

NOTES

* This chapter has been adapted from, A. H. Halsey, 'Social Trends since World War II', *Social Trends 17*, HMSO, 1987.

1 Professor Halsey is Director of the Department of Social and Administrative Studies at the University of Oxford. The views expressed in this article are those of the author.

2 Now Sir Claus Moser, Warden of Wadham College, Oxford.

3 Independently my colleagues and I had attempted to trace the main trends from the beginning of the century. See A. H. Halsey (ed.) *Trends in British Society Since 1900*, Macmillan, 1972. [Revised edition published as *British Social Trends 1900–1986*, Macmillan, 1988.]

4 *British Labour Statistics Historical Abstract*, Tables 42, 90, and 94, and various editions of the *Employment Gazette*.

5 c.f. Daniel Bell, 'Report on England: the Future that Never Was', *The Public Interest*, No. 51, 1978, pp. 35–73. For statistics on basic holiday entitlement see Table 11.2. The figures for car ownership are rough estimates for 1951 and from the General Household Survey for 1976 and 1985.

6 *Social Trends 16*, p. 130.

7 The number of employees in manufacturing industry reached its highest point in 1956 (see *British Labour Statistics Historical Abstract*, Table 135).

8 John Goldthorpe and Clive Payne, 'Trends in Intergenerational Class Mobility in England and Wales 1972–83', *Sociology*, Vol. 20, No. 1, 1986, p. 9.

9 C. Hamnett, 'Housing the Two Nations: Socio-Tenurial Polarisation in England and Wales 1961–81', *Urban Studies*, Vol. 43, 1984, pp. 384–405.

10 *Faith in the City: a call for action by Church and Nation*, Church House Publishing, 1985.

11 See especially Victor A. Hausner (ed.) *Critical Issues in Urban Economic Development*, Vol. 1, Oxford University Press, 1987.

12 The analysis was supplied by David Eversley and Ian Begg. Essentially the method was to collect data at ward level of over 70 indicators of advantage and disadvantage and to standardize them as Z scores. By this means an average Z score was produced for every territorial grouping over a range of favourable and adverse social indicators. It is a robust and stable score which provides a refined map of inequality. See Eversley & Begg, 'Deprivation in the Inner City: Social Indicators from the 1981 Census; in Victor A. Hausner (ed.) *op. cit.*

13 *Faith in the City*, 1985, p. 25.

12

CHANGING SOCIAL DIVISIONS: CLASS, GENDER AND RACE*

Harriet Bradley

CLASS AND CHANGE

Theorizing class: Marxist and Weberian approaches

Most social scientists accept that changes in the economy since 1945 have affected class relations: but there is considerable debate on how to interpret these effects. These debates must be viewed in the context of the theoretical disagreements between neo-Marxists and neo-Weberians, who have provided the two dominant perspectives in the analysis of the British class structure.

Marx analysed class in terms of the relations of production [. . .] with the mechanism of exploitation at the core of the capitalist class structure. Although he recognized divisions within the working class ('the competition between the workers themselves' to quote from the *Communist Manifesto*), he believed that the unifying potential of the experience of exploitation and alienation would transcend them, and while he recognized the emergence of various 'fractions' of the middle class, he saw these groups as of marginal importance in comparison to the central antagonism between the bourgeoisie and the proletariat. By contrast, Weber saw divisions, within both the propertied and propertyless classes, as generated by the workings of the market; he emphasized that the fragmenting effects of these divisions would be supplemented by the overlapping of class with status and party-political groupings; he paid especial attention to the growth of the middle classes brought about by the spread of bureaucratic organization: and he believed that conflict would take diverse forms within and between all the different social groupings. It should be emphasized that both models of class can be used with considerable flexibility, a fact which is not sufficiently acknowledged. Nor are these two models as irreconcilable as some textbooks suggest, the differences being ones of final orientation. We can say overall, however, that the logic of the Weberian model is to suggest the existence of a plurality of class groupings, while the logic of the Marxist model leads us inexorably to focus on the confrontation between the capitalist class and the working class.

Neo-Weberians have suggested that Marxist theory cannot successfully account for the complexity of contemporary class relations. In their view, the class structure has been subjected to increasing fragmentation so that class conflict as envisaged by Marx is no longer a feasible outcome. Weberians also criticize Marx's assertion that a collective consciousness of oppression will arise from work relationships and lead to class-based action, an argument described by David Lockwood (1981) as 'the weakest link in the chain' of Marx's logic. Lockwood's own work has emphasized that consciousness has many sources, arising from particular 'social milieux' or environments. Some environments have tended to foster individualized and privatized orientations to society, which militate against collective action by working people.

One of the most powerful proponents of the neo-Weberian critique of Marx has been Ralf Dahrendorf (1959), who argues that although Marx's analysis was apposite in the nineteenth century it has become outdated in the context of what he terms 'post-capitalist' society. The bourgeoisie and the proletariat have both fragmented, the former because of the separation of the ownership of capital (by shareholders) from its control (by managers), the latter because technological advance has not, as Marx predicted, led to homogenization of factory work, but has deepened divisions between the skilled, semi-skilled and unskilled labourers. The middle class has grown in size and in social significance. These developments, along with other important changes, such as increased social mobility and the consolidation of a democratic political system, have resulted in an increasingly fragmented and complex class structure and brought a diminution in hostility between the classes.

Marxists have responded to these criticisms by asserting that the changes can be accommodated within an elaborated version of the basic Marxist framework, which still retains the analysis of conflict and exploitation. Marx's term 'fraction' can be employed to cover splits within classes. A fraction is a sub-group within a class distinguished by its distinct economic situation (a difference in skill, for example, or in type of property owned) but which still shares the basic relation to the means of production of the class as a whole. Marxists argue that the competitive drive at the core of the capitalist dynamic fosters such splits in both the capitalist and the working class, and often deliberately exploits them in order to 'divide and rule'. The concept of 'fraction' has also been used as a way to incorporate the analysis of gender and race into class theory.

Neo-Marxists have given special attention to the problem of explaining the class position of the middle classes. Attempts to do so often utilize one of two strategies. Either the middle class is divided into groupings which are essentially part of either the bourgeoisie or the proletariat (managers and professionals linked to the former, clerks and low-level service workers to the latter); or it is suggested that relations of production place the middle groupings in a curious position in which they fulfil some of the productive functions of the proletariat (helping produce and realize surplus value) and some of the functions of the bourgeoisie (co-ordinating production and controlling the workers). This is the notion of 'structural ambiguity' or 'contradictory locations'.

The stress in neo-Marxism on fractions within classes may suggest, as in the Weberian model, that conflict is as likely within classes as between them. However, neo-Marxists wish to cling to the idea of a central and potentially transformative class struggle, while conceding that it is offset by many other factors, particularly the ideological control over society exercised by the dominant class. The means of information (especially the mass media) and the education system can be used to spread ideas which favour the status quo. This notion of the 'dominant ideology' has been used by Marxists to explain why the working classes have failed to develop a critical class consciousness.

Try to bear in mind the main points of these two perspectives (summarized in Table 12.1) as we look in detail at post-war changes in class relations.

Table 12.1 Neo-Marxist and neo-Weberian positions

Neo-Marxist	Neo-Weberian
Class divisions generated by relations of production especially by the mechanism of exploitation	Class divisions generated by the operation of the market
Unifying effect of exploitation emphasized	Classes seen as subject to growing processes of fragmentation
The existence of 'fractions' and conflicts within classes acknowledged but seen as less important than the conflicts between classes especially the central conflict between proletariat and bourgeoisie	Divisions and conflicts within classes seen as just as significant as conflicts between classes
Middle classes seen as linked to one of the two major classes or as 'structurally ambiguous'	Middle classes seen as an autonomous grouping and considered as socially significant as the propertied and working classes
Consciousness arises from relations of production	Consciousness has many different sources
Dominant ideology accounts for the failure of the working class to develop a critical class consciousness	Fragmentation, social mobility and growth of democratic political structures inhibit the growth of class consciousness
Revolutionary potential of the working class remains	Class revolution is improbable

The upper class

The very term 'upper class' shows the problems of defining classes accurately, as it is often used to connote the aristocracy. It would be more helpful to employ Weber's term, the propertied class. This consists of some elements from the old landed aristocracy and gentry and some elements from the bourgeoisie. A social fusion of these two social groupings was achieved in the course of the nineteenth century, with the new class of manufacturers aspiring to the lifestyle and status of the older privileged class: the public schools had an important role in bringing together these two groups and merging them into a new elite.

The major change in the composition of this class pre-dates the post-war developments listed earlier. Towards the end of the nineteenth century, capitalist enterprises were subject to a process of concentration and reorganization which has continued ever since. Privately owned family firms were displaced as the major capital form by joint-stock public companies. Small businesses were swallowed by large companies and conglomerates with multiple interests across the economy. Since the Second World War, this shift in ownership has been extended on an international as well as a national basis, with the multinational corporations dominating economic development and co-ordinating it across the globe. For Dahrendorf, these charges implied a *decomposition of capital*. Rather than a single capitalist group who owned and controlled industrial production, the class had split into two: on the one hand shareholders who owned but did not control companies and, on the other managers who did not own them: (in Dahrendorf's terms 'capitalists without function' and 'functionaries without capital').

It can be argued that the last couple of decades have witnessed a further fragmentation of capital, because of the diffusion of property ownership through the populace, encouraged in the 1980s, [and 1990s] by the policies of [consecutive] Conservative governments. This diffusion has involved:

- an increase in home ownership so that approximately two thirds of households own their home.
- a further dispersal of share ownership across the nation [. . .]
- a major rise in the percentage of shares owned by insurance companies, pension funds and unit trusts, and a consequent massive increase in the numbers of wage-earners with stakes in these types of schemes.

(Central Statistical Office (1990) *Social Trends*, no.20)

These trends have led one author of a textbook on class to declare that the capitalist class has almost disappeared as a distinct stratum: 'Where is the capitalist class today? It has fragmented into millions of tiny pieces. To see these pieces, look around you' (Saunders, 1990, p.91).

This is a dramatic image! But most sociologists would reject this claim. One difficulty is that the upper class is hard to observe. It is not easy to discover who actually controls companies: moreover, top people are not keen to allow sociological researchers to sit in on their decision-making processes. The fragmentation process outlined above has contributed to making this class somewhat invisible. However, John Scott has carried out a series of studies of the propertied class and concluded that it definitely does still exist and 'derives its advantages from ownership of company shares *and* participation in strategic control. The "impersonal" structure of possession has not resulted in a loss of power by wealthy people . . . Wealthy families hold shares in a large number of companies and they form a group from which corporate managers are recruited' (Scott, 1979, p.175). He discerns three elements within the class: entrepreneurial capitalists, with large holdings in particular companies; internal capitalists, top executives who have risen to power within companies; and finance capitalists with interests across a range of companies. We could conceptualize these as either fragments or fractions of the capitalist class. He concludes, however, that 'the core of the class consists of those who are actively involved in the strategic control of the major units of capital of which the modern economy is formed' (Scott, 1982, p.114).

While it is true that many working- and middle-class people have, especially in the 1980s, acquired a few shares and have invested in a private pension scheme, this form of ownership is not just quantitively but qualitatively different from major capital ownership. Investment in shares may be the equivalent of a flutter on horses, a pension scheme an insurance against poverty-stricken old age. Possession of them makes little difference to people's working lives or lifestyles. Nor do they have any real say in the strategic decisions mentioned by Scott. By contrast ten per cent of the population still hold fifty per cent of the marketable wealth of the nation, if pension schemes are excepted.

Scott argues that this smallish upper class of wealthy families is linked together in a tight social network, which is strengthened by the 'Old Boy' network (based on attendance at public school and elite universities), and which also serves to deter women from participation in top political and economic decision making (Rogers, 1988). Male domination is marked within this class. Economic cohesion is also ensured by the system of interlocking directorships, whereby prominent members of the class have seats on the boards of a number of top companies. Although this elite is not closed (internal capitalists may have risen into it through company career line) it is extremely exclusive. The greatest threat to it comes from the internationalization of capitalist production, which makes it harder for any national economy and its 'captains' to direct internal investment in the way they would prefer.

We can, of course, identify individual members of this class who are prominent in the public eye. However, Scott suggests the class is better conceptualized as a structure, rather than as an identifiable group of people. The power of capital has taken a more impersonal form, embedded in a set of organizations and institutional practices. Neo-Marxists share this view, arguing that this class must be identified through its collective carrying out of the functions of capital (exploitation, accumulation and realization of profits, control of labour and production).

These developments have important consequences for the relationship of the propertied class with the working class. Victorian factory workers knew their bosses personally and could identify them as the 'exploiters'. This is not the case today, where many workers will know only their immediate superiors, not those on the directing boards. Moreover, many workers are now with companies where ultimate control is exercised from America, Germany and Japan. What we might call the 'depersonalization' of the capitalist class acts against workers developing the class awareness envisaged by Marx; indeed, those who work for the multinationals may be discouraged from industrial militancy by the knowledge that the company can close down production in their plant and move it to one of its sites in other countries. Rather than the disappearance of the capitalist class as suggested by Saunders, some would argue that the post-war period has seen the consolidation of a smaller, more integrated and internationalized capitalist class with heightened power. Others would argue that any such tendency is weakened by internal divisions such as the continuing rivalry between finance and manufacturing capital interests, and indeed by the fight for survival and growth inherent in the competitive process on a global scale.

The working class

The working class has been the focus of particular attention, largely because of its role in Marx's class model as the 'historic class'; you will recall that in the *Communist Manifesto* he argued that it was the only class capable of the overthrow of the capitalist system. Weberians challenge this argument and furthermore point to tremendous charges affecting the working class in the post-war period.

One major issue is the effect of increased affluence on working-class culture and values. In the 1960s, sociologists developed the concept of *embourgeoisement,* the idea that the boundary between the working and middle classes was breaking down altogether. This was partly due to increased social mobility. Also, rising incomes enabled manual workers to adopt middle-class values and lifestyles, and encouraged a change in political allegiance from Labour to Conservative. The embourgeoisement thesis was effectively demolished by the *Affluent Worker* studies (Goldthorpe *et al.*, 1969). The research team concluded that their sample of well-paid manual workers in Luton had not adopted middle-class values nor was there any special mixing between them and white-collar workers, Rather, the researchers concluded that this must be seen as a 'new working class' with a new lifestyle different from that traditionally associated with the working class.

Lockwood (1966) had previously identified two types of 'traditional worker' and a newer 'privatized' working class segment. Traditional proletarian attitudes were associated with the old tightly integrated communities, based round industries like mining and shipbuilding, which fostered a collective 'them and us' spirit. The other type of traditional worker, associated with agricultural work, domestic service and small businesses such as shops, had a deferential attitude to society, accepting an inferior station as justified; close personal links with employers encouraged a forelock-tugging attitude. [. . .] Both groups were in decline with the disappearance of traditional industries. In contrast, the growing number of workers in the new consumer industries had developed a much more individualistic consumerist outlook; detached from the old communities, they invested emotional energy in a family-based 'privatized' lifestyle. Economic self-interest promoted an 'instrumental' approach to politics and they joined trade unions for individualistic reasons, not because of class loyalties.

Lockwood's study, although written twenty-five years ago, remains the definitive study of working-class fragmentation. But a recent survey of class attitudes carried out by a team of researchers from Essex University makes the important point that the trends towards the private, and towards instrumentalism and self-interest among the working-classes are nothing new, but have been strands in working-class behaviour since industrialization. The Essex team suggests, moreover, that these tendencies may coexist with other contradictory tendencies to collectivism, solidarity and class identification. The specific economic and political context will affect the balance between these contradictory tendencies (Marshall *et al.*, 1988).

During the 1970s the focus in debates about the working class shifted from affluence to unemployment. The contraction of the manufacturing sector and the restructuring of the economy threatened traditional working-class jobs. Sociologists were drawn to the theories of post-industrialism and deindustrialization. Post-industrial theorists predict major upheavals in the class structure, affecting the working class in particular.

For example, André Gorz, in the dramatically titled *Farewell to the Working Class* (Gorz, 1982), suggested that new computer technology was, literally, making manual work redundant. So great was its productive potential that society would no longer need all its citizens to produce the necessary goods and services. Only a small technically advanced segment of the industrial proletariat would be needed to carry on production; the displaced industrial workers would become what Gorz called a 'neo-proletariat' consisting of the permanently unemployed, the semi-employed and casualized low-paid workers, effectively marginalized and with no stake in the economy. These developments would undermine the historic role of the working class. The employed minority would cooperate with capital interests because of fear of losing jobs. The neo-proletariat would be too distanced from work to be interested in the transformation of work relationships. Indeed, in strict Marxist terms this group is not a class at all as it has no relationship (other than exclusion) to the relations of production.

Gorz can be criticized for his assumption that unemployment rates would remain at the high levels of the early 1980s and for playing down the possibility that new types of jobs might evolve to replace those lost by automation; but other interpretations offered by sociologists also suggest that long-term unemployment will continue. Dahrendorf utilizes the concept of the *underclass*, a term developed in America in reference to the ghettoized black minorities. It refers to a group at the bottom of the class hierarchy, permanently trapped and unable to move upward because it faces multiple disadvantages.

Dahrendorf (1987) suggests that an underclass has emerged in Britain consisting of the unemployed and others who depend on benefits, such as one-parent families, and the sick, disabled and elderly. He argues that a culture of poverty develops among this group, making them fatalistic and apathetic, or else pushing them into crime or illegal participation in the 'black economy'. In this way the unemployed become unemployable. He also is concerned about the marginalization of this group suggesting that they are politically ignored and in danger of losing their citizen rights, as the state takes control of their life in return for benefits.

Critics of the underclass theory suggest that it overstates the extent to which this group is 'permanently trapped' by unemployment. A boom in the economy has often had the effect of drastically reducing the number of the supposed 'unemployable'. Unemployment and dependency on benefits can be seen as *cyclical* phenomena in two senses: first, they are linked to the fluctuations of the business cycle; secondly, people are more vulnerable to them at certain stages in the life-cycle, such as when they have small children, or in old age. Both Gorz and Dahrendorf might be criticized for extrapolating too much from short-term trends. By contrast many neo-Marxists view the future of the working class more flexibly. They suggest that processes of economic restructuring in Britain, along with a renegotiation of the international division of labour, have indeed brought increased unemployment, swelling the ranks of the 'reserve army of labour' or 'surplus population' which Marx saw as an integral part of the capitalist system. These changes imply not a disappearance but a *recomposition* of the working class. Capitalism is highly dynamic, ever engendering new markets, new processes and products, and its labour requirements also change. Wage labour in the coming decades may take the form of work in the newer service industries, for example leisure and retailing, which boomed in the later 1980s; or, if the international economy shifts again, there may be new forms of either 'high-tech' production work or low-wage assembly work provided by multinationals who decide it is profitable to invest in Britain.

Not all recent thinking puts unemployment and recession to the fore. A more optimistic version of post-industrial theory suggests that society is moving into a new phase based on information technology as the core of the production process, with a continued shift from manufacturing to service industries. Despite the short-term instability associated with the changes, the long-term outcome will be a more prosperous society, with increased leisure and greater democracy at work. Daniel Bell (1974), who exemplifies the optimistic strand in post-industrial theory, suggests an upgrading of the class structure and harmony between the classes as the end result: in effect, this amounts to a reassertion of the 'embourgeoisement' thesis.

We have, then, a number of possible interpretations of the future of the working class:

- increased affluence and upward mobility into the middle classes as a result of post-industrial change;
- further decline of the traditional core of the industrial working class and development of a casualized 'neo-proletariat' as a result of automation;
- recomposition of the working class into new forms dependent on the growth of the world economy;
- the development of a marginalized 'underclass' underneath a relatively privileged working class which enjoys increased affluence.

The middle classes

'Between capital and labour' lies the middle class. Sociologists tend now to speak of 'the new middle classes', both to indicate the heterogeneity of this grouping and to distinguish it from the 'old' middle class, the Victorian bourgeoisie itself. The new middle classes include all the service groups thrown up by the spread of bureaucracy, the growth of the welfare state and recent rapid growth of service industries. This is now the largest class. Table 12.2 shows the rise in service employment and the decline in manufacturing in the past two decades.

Sociologists have emphasized the diversity of the occupational groupings within the middle class. For example, we may distinguish a 'service class' (a high-level salaried group of managers, administrators and professionals who approach the privileged lifestyle of the

Table 12.2 Employment in manufacturing and services 1971 to 1989, in thousands

	1971	1979	1981	1989
Manufacturing	8,065	7,253	6,222	5,234
Services	11,627	13,580	13,468	15,688

Source: Central Statistical Office (1991), *Social Trends*, no.21, Table 4.11, p.71

propertied class) from the 'intermediate groupings' (a mass of lower-paid service workers, especially clerical workers, many with manual working-class backgrounds and connections). Another distinct and growing group are the self-employed, the petite bourgeoisie. Conservative ideology has supported the growth of small business [. . .].

The intermediate group have been the focus of a major debate between Marxists and Weberians. Neo-Marxists argue that clerical workers have been *proletarianized*, that is pulled down into the working class: like factory workers they are essentially powerless wage labourers. Although clerks have traditionally been seen by Marxists as not directly involved in producing surplus value since they do not produce goods, some neo-Marxists suggest that both groups could be conceived as part of the *collective worker*, that is the whole group involved in the cycle of surplus and profit: making goods, processing them, ensuring the goods can be sold and the profits realized.

In a classic study, the neo-Weberian Lockwood (1958) rejected the idea of proletarianization. Lockwood distinguished three dimensions of class: market situation (rewards, promotion chances, etc.), work situation (conditions, relations of control and workplace interaction) and status situation. He argued that clerks, despite declines in their pay, fared better than manual workers on each dimension.

Since Lockwood conducted his study, office life has been considerably altered by the implementation of computer technology. Braverman (1974), in a reassertion of the proletarianization thesis, argued that technology has been used to further erode the position of office workers. Braverman believed that there was a tendency towards task degradation (popularly known as 'deskilling') within capitalist industry which affected clerks as much as manual workers [. . .]. Braverman's account of the class position of American office workers makes a strong contrast to Lockwood.

Braverman also raised the issue of the feminization of clerical work, a factor ignored by Lockwood, who only studied male clerks. This is a major weakness in Lockwood's work: in Britain, too, clerical work has become a largely female occupation, as is shown in Table 12.3.

Crompton and Jones (1984) considered the gender issue more fully, arguing that clerical workers should be seen as a 'stratified hierarchy'. Although male clerks have managed to retain some of their old privileges (such as promotion chances), they have done so at the expense of women. Jobs which have been degraded by new technology have been assigned to women. Rather than seeing women clerks as being proletarianized, however, the authors suggested that women were originally brought into clerical work under different conditions to men, forming a kind of proletarian layer in an occupational grouping regarded as having higher status than manual work. Status considerations may continue to prevent clerical workers, despite some growth in trade union membership, from developing an identification with manual workers.

It has been suggested that new technology could also be used to degrade the jobs of higher-level service workers, such as professionals and managers. Although these groups can use their expertise, prestige and professional organizational bodies as a defence, the potential of computers in terms of information-processing and monitoring may make some high-level skills redundant and lead to diminished autonomy for some occupational groups.

Table 12.3 Percentage of women in the clerical workforce in England and Wales

1901	1911	1921	1931	1951	1961	1971	1981
11	18	46	45	60	64	72	78

Source: Lewis, 1988, p.34

However, the post-industrial framework suggests an alternative vision of the future of the middle classes. Bell envisages further expansion of all three main groupings (self-employed, service class and intermediate service workers), with jobs being upgraded rather than deskilled, and more and more people sharing the privileged employment conditions and lifestyles of the middle class.

Assessing the viability of these different accounts is complicated by the rapid pace of contemporary economic and technological change. These changes however, do seem likely to promote further class fragmentation, keeping the class structure in a state of flux. But it is worth re-emphasizing the need to take account of how gender interacts with class. As updated Figure 12.1a and 12.1b show, in 1998, 69 per cent of women workers were in non-manual jobs as opposed to 52 per cent of men. This casts doubt on the idea that a move into service jobs is necessarily a class upgrading; nor do we yet fully understand the effects of gender in terms of how people develop a class identification.

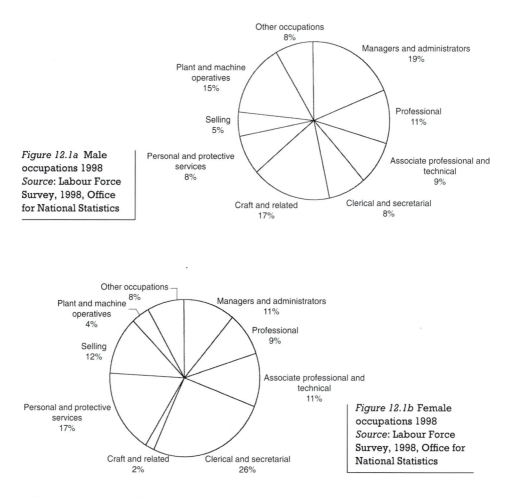

Figure 12.1a **Male occupations 1998** *Source*: **Labour Force Survey, 1998, Office for National Statistics**

Figure 12.1b **Female occupations 1998** *Source*: **Labour Force Survey, 1998, Office for National Statistics**

To summarize our discussion on the post-war growth of the middle classes:

- Weberians consider that the middle class groupings are becoming both numerically and socially more significant and that they are quite distinct from the working class.

- Marxists suggest that sections of the middle classes have been subject to processes of proletarianization; this applies in particular to the lower status service sector occupational groupings.
- Both Marxists and Weberians see the middle classes as fragmented internally into a number of subgroups, although they conceptualize these divisions in different ways.
- Post-industrial theory suggests a continued expansion of the middle classes, embourgeoisement of the working classes and upgrading of jobs.
- Finally, no perspective has satisfactorily grappled with the conceptual difficulties associated with the fact that women predominate in many service-sector jobs.

GENDER AND CHANGE

Theorizing gender

Our study of class has led us to the study of gender. It has been argued that patriarchy did not disappear after industrialization but took new forms: Victorian society saw the elaboration of a new ideology of gender which promoted the idea of separate spheres and this was reflected in the employment sphere where the sexual division of labour became more rigid. [. . .] Has segregation now begun to disappear?

Since the Second World War there have been major changes in women's social roles. Women have pushed their way into many occupations from which they were excluded, and the proportion of women in the labour force has steadily increased, as shown in Table 12.4 [updated]. The increase has been especially marked among married women, as the idea of mothers returning to employment has gained social acceptability.

Families have become more egalitarian with most of the legal backing for patriarchal domination now removed. Partly because of contraceptive improvements, women now have probably more sexual freedom than at any period in British history. These changes led in the 1950s and early 1960s to a widespread assumption that sex equality had been achieved in Britain. But the regenerated feminist movement of the late 1960s and 1970s challenged this assumption, demonstrating that gender inequalities were still marked in all spheres of life.

The theorists of this 'second wave' of feminism started to develop the concept of patriarchy as a way to understand gender relations. However, this key concept has been the subject of critical controversy. For example, Rowbotham (1981) argues that it is an imprecise and a historical term. Its use may encourage the unacceptable assumption that male dominance is universal, ruling out the possibility of the existence of societies characterized by sex equality or of matriarchal societies. Moreover, the term may imply a static view, whereas gender relations vary greatly between different historical periods and different societies. It has been suggested that a neutral term such as 'sex-gender system' or simply 'the sexual division of labour' would provide a more flexible analytic tool. More recently black feminists have criticized the use of the term. They argue it assumes a commonality between all women in their experience of male domination, which is not in fact the case. However, many feminist theorists have clung to the concept, perhaps because

Table 12.4 [updated] Women as a percentage of all employees

1931	1951	1961	1971	1981	1991	1998
30	31	n.a.	38	43	46	46

Source: Derived from census data [updated]

of the prominence it has come to enjoy within feminist literature. To overcome its shortcomings, they have attempted to define the term more precisely, to focus on the differential power positions of different groups and to develop historical typologies of its changing manifestations. We will turn shortly to Sylvia Walby's attempt to do this.

However, the analysis of patriarchy is not the only approach to understanding gender inequality. Many have tried to use the existing categories of class analysis to incorporate women into a class model. Neo-Marxists have suggested that women could be seen as a distinct fraction within each class or that their labour market role could be explained by the concept of the reserve army of labour. Neo-Weberians have considered women as a negatively-privileged status group and tried to explain their inferior work situation through the analysis of segmented labour markets. Such approaches, while not entirely satisfactory, are an improvement on the position taken by some mainstream stratification theorists. They argue that women are largely irrelevant to class analysis as they derive their class position from that of their father or husband, a claim tantamount to saying that sociology's most important category of analysis cannot be applied to half the population!

The major problem with adapting existing economic concepts to the analysis of gender is that gender is almost always reduced to a side effect of class. Such approaches imply that gender inequality is a direct product of the economic system in the same way as class differences. However, the insight of second-wave feminist theory was that gender divisions were rooted in every aspect of social life, including, in particular, the family, private life and sexuality. A convincing account of gender relations, therefore, has to be much more broadly based and comprehensive than any theory of class.

Traditional Marxism tended to link gender differentiation to class as an aspect of property relations, with the implication that when socialism brought an end to private property, gender divisions, like class divisions, would disappear. However, historical evidence shows quite clearly that gender divisions predate capitalism and persist after its overthrow. Thus, Marxist-feminist theorists came to accept the need for a separate theory of gender to be combined with Marxist class theory. Usually this has taken the form of an analysis of patriarchy. Some theorists have wished to conceptualize capitalism and patriarchy evolving jointly as a unified system, while others have suggested that they have to be seen as two analytically discrete systems. Two notable proponents of the latter *dual systems theory* have been Heidi Hartmann and Sylvia Walby.

Both have provided us with more precise definitions of patriarchy, either of which might serve as a useful 'working definition'. For Hartmann, patriarchy is 'a set of social relationships between men which have a material base, and which, though hierarchical, establish or create interdependence and solidarity among men that enable them to dominate women . . . The material base upon which patriarchy rests lies most fundamentally in men's control over women's labour power' (Hartmann, 1981, pp.14–15). This definition enables us to link the two sites, the home and the workplace, where men can profit from women's contribution of labour provided either free or for an inferior economic reward. Thus it connects wage labour and domestic labour as a dual base for male exploitation of women. However, in its focus on *labour power* as the base of gender difference it reflects Hartmann's own adherence to Marxism. Indeed, Young (1981) argues that the notion of 'control of labour power' is so central to Marxist analysis that it would be more useful to redefine the concept of relations of production, working towards a unified theory of class and gender, rather than conceiving patriarchy as a separate system.

For other feminists, the ideas of both Hartmann and Young are too narrow and economistic. By contrast, Walby's approach appears to pull together a Marxist focus on production with strands from radical feminist thought which give primacy to personal relationships, sexuality, and power in a more general sense. For Walby, patriarchy is 'a system of interrelated structures through which men exploit women . . . The key sets of patriarchal relations are to be found in domestic work, paid work, the state, male violence and sexuality; while other practices in civil society have a limited significance' (Walby, 1986, p.51). This definition is, admittedly, not as sharp as Hartmann's, but it has the merit of breadth, rightly suggesting that gender disparities are found in every sphere of social life and that these are mutually reinforcing. Moreover, Walby's schema can allow for the way that the particular focus of patriarchy can shift from one set of relationships to another at different times, so that, in the post-war period, paid work and the state have particular significance as the sites of patriarchy, with the family declining somewhat in importance. Walby conceptualizes this as a shift from private to public patriarchy: women are no longer subject to the same degree of domination by individual patriarchs as they were in pre-industrial or Victorian families. Instead, male control has become built into the structures of society, particularly the rules and procedures which regulate the public spheres of work and politics.

Not all Marxist feminists, however, are happy with the idea of patriarchy as a framework for analysing gender. Some wish to stay more firmly within the traditional Marxist framework. One possibility is to extend the idea of the production to include *reproduction*, that is the process whereby the human species reproduces itself. This concept can be used to cover all the activities such as childcare and housework that take place within the home and in which women's labour is central. Some, like Delphy (1977), see reproduction as a separate mode of production existing jointly with the capitalist wage labour system and having its own distinct relations of production whereby men exploit women's labour. A recent text by Glucksmann (1990) has suggested that it is better to see domestic labour and wage labour as two poles within one unified system, both being part of capitalist relations of production. Women's key role in the domestic relations of production means that they enter into wage labour relations of production at a particular disadvantage. This important idea of reproduction will be explored more fully in the next chapter.

Finally, in the last few years many feminists have been drawn to the theoretical framework of post-modernism, which challenges the validity of analysis of social systems and questions the value of overarching concepts such as capitalism and patriarchy. Post-modern feminists reject any idea of a universal pattern of male domination and female oppression and seek instead to trace out the many different variants of relations between the sexes. There is, they claim, no necessary logic of male domination: power relations between the sexes are flexible and often counter-balanced. Post-modern theory, however, is not very helpful in understanding patterns of inequality which have persisted over time, because its framework precludes the formulation of general statements or models of social structure. It is more useful as a critique of other approaches than as a way of understanding how societies work.

However, post-modernist feminism has one very useful insight in pointing to the differing experiences of women of different classes and ethnic groups. It is argued that, rather than making general statements which assume a common identity and experience among women, we must seek to unpack or 'deconstruct' the category of women. This involves exploring the specific situation of, for example, black women or homosexual women. The key concept here is *difference*. Michele Barrett (1987) has argued that this term is used in many diverse and rather confusing ways by post-modern theorists; but the sense in which it can help us towards an improved understanding of gender inequalities is that of 'experiential diversity', in Barrett's phrase. Black feminists have rightly criticized white feminists for assuming that the experience of white women was the norm.

As stated earlier, gender divisions permeate all social institutions from work to leisure, from the family to political organizations. Indeed, feminists argue that the very structure of language is itself 'man-made' (Spender, 1980) and reflects male control of cultural institutions and practices. This is crucial since it is only through language that we grasp the meanings of our social world and we are thus forced to apprehend it through categories derived from male experience. Within cultural discourses, male experiences are taken as the norm and women presented as 'the Other'. Women's experiences are unreported or marginalized and women's needs or desires obscured. The contemporary feminist project, then, must involve the re-examination of every aspect of social reality to uncover the experience of gender. This chapter, however, looks at just one aspect of the sexual division of labour, concentrating on [. . .] employment. [. . .]

Gender divisions at work

Since the war women have entered paid employment in increasing numbers. Table 12.5 shows the increasing proportion economically active since 1971. Note that the increase is particularly marked among women aged 25–44, the major childbearing group. The period which women spend out of the labour force for childrearing has become steadily shorter; not only are women having fewer children, they are also returning to work earlier.

However, much of this increase has been in part-time work. In [1998 over 6 million] worked part-time, as opposed to 900,000 men; this represents over 40 per cent of all women in paid employment. Married women with small children are particularly likely to work part-time.

Although part-time work may suit women with domestic responsibilities and be less exhausting than a full-time job, it has second-rate status. Generally part-time workers are lower paid, have few promotion chances and virtually no entitlement to paid holidays, redundancy pay or pension and maternity rights. Walby has argued that part-time work can be seen as a new increasingly significant form of gender segregation.

The more established form of gender segregation, however, persists as strongly as ever. In an influential paper, Hakim (1979) studied the pattern of segregation since 1900. She concluded that there had been no significant breakdown of segregation up to the late 1970s, although there was evidence of some improvement in the 1980s within the professional and managerial sectors. The majority of women and men are still likely to work only with their own sex. The clustering of men and women within different occupations is referred to as 'horizontal' segregation, in contrast to 'vertical' segregation which refers to differences within occupations.

[. . .]

Table 12.5 [updated] Women's activity rates 1971 to 1997

Age:	16–19	20–24	25–44	45–54	55–59	60+	All age groups
1971	65.0	60.2	52.4	62.0	50.9	12.4	43.9
1976	68.2	64.8	60.0	66.5	54.3	10.3	46.8
1979	72.0	67.7	61.7	67.0	53.8	7.4	47.4
1981	70.4	68.8	61.7	68.0	53.4	8.3	47.6
1983	66.8	68.2	62.2	68.1	50.8	7.5	47.0
1984	69.4	70.2	65.9	69.5	51.8	7.8	49.0
1986	71.4	70.3	67.8	70.5	51.8	6.5	49.6
1988	72.2	71.3	70.9	70.6	52.7	6.6	51.0
1989	73.7	75.1	72.0	72.2	54.3	7.6	52.6
1997	–	69.4[1]	77	77.2	54.4	–	72.0

1 16–24

Source: Central Statistical Office, *Social Trends*, no.21, 1991, Table 4.6, p.68

Update Source: Office of National Statistics, Labour Force Survey

Ethnic minority women often fare even worse than white women, at the bottom of the employment pyramid, where racial discrimination pushes them into unskilled and low-paid jobs. Black women are concentrated particularly in textiles, in the health service and in the hotel and catering industries. They are often left with backstage roles, in places such as kitchens and laundries, since racial prejudice can mean that white women obtain the more visible jobs (receptionists, bank cashiers) which exploit female glamour. The invisibility of black women, which serves to conceal the social benefits which the community gains from their work, is epitomized by South Asian home workers. Cultural reasons may propel them into home working (their husbands' unwillingness for them to be exposed to contact with white men) but often no other work is available to them. In home work women may earn less than fifty pence an hour for unpleasant work in difficult conditions.

The increase in part-time work for women can be linked to the current stress on 'flexibility' [. . .]. Using part-time women workers is one major strategy for employers seeking 'numerical flexibility'. Retailing provides a classic example. In supermarkets a small core of permanent staff can be supplemented by teams of part-timers employed to cater for peak periods of demand such as Friday evenings and Saturdays. Since part-timers can be paid lower wages and are ineligible for fringe benefits, this system of flexibility is highly beneficial to employers. But it has clear disadvantages for women, confirming their use as a secondary labour force. Historically, they have been especially vulnerable to casualized employment conditions. They are unlikely to benefit from other aspects such as 'functional' flexibility, since many employers' reluctance to provide training for women may well debar them from acquiring the range of skills associated with the 'polyvalent' or 'flexible worker'.

Gender divisions at work have been explained in many ways. Economists utilize the framework of supply and demand, in particular the idea of human capital, that is the assets (qualifications, training, skills, experience) accumulated by each individual. Jobs requiring workers to have invested more human capital in themselves through long periods of training are most highly rewarded. Women's domestic role means they characteristically possess less human capital and are forced to take the lowest-paid unskilled jobs. It then becomes economically rational for the wife to stay at home to care for children, because the husband's greater earning capacity makes him the more effective breadwinner.

These arguments seem reasonable, especially since women are less likely to gain access to training. However, research suggests that, even with equivalent training and qualifications, women do less well than men. [An earlier] study found that women persistently received lower rewards for comparable skills (Rubery *et al.*, 1989). Single women with no domestic responsibilities are still found in stereotypical 'women's' jobs. While more women now possess graduate qualifications, the structure of segregation has been largely undented. The economic framework suggests reasons for some aspects of gender differentiation, but does not adequately acknowledge the sex-typing of jobs. Moreover, human capital theory has an uncritical approach to the notion of skill. Phillips and Taylor (1980) point out that skill is to a considerable extent socially constructed. Gender is a key factor in that construction: what men do is 'skilled' simply by virtue of being done by men, while what women do tends to be undervalued.

Other explanations consider the motives of employers. Marxists point to the way capitalists employ women as cheap labour. Beechey (1977) has suggested that women's labour power is actually of lower value than men's, in the sense that it costs less to supply a woman's subsistence needs (the value of labour for Marxists being determined by its costs of production as is the value of any commodity). Because women are subsidized by men within the family, employers can get away paying them less than a subsistence wage (Beechey, 1977). Beechey also suggests that women's bodily needs are less than those of men. This idea is interesting, but does not explain why capitalist employers choose to employ cheaper female labour only in certain jobs, reserving others for men.

Marxists have also conceptualized women as a labour reserve, drawn into the economy at times of labour shortage and expelled back into the home in periods of recession. This idea fits well with the use made of women to cover jobs vacated by men during the two World Wars. But it does not explain why jobs are segregated. When women are drawn into the workforce, it is normally to fill 'women's jobs', not to substitute for men, and if jobs are 'feminized' (for example, clerical work), women subsequently retain them. Rather than being in the same market, in most cases men and women are in two separate non-competing markets.

According to the dual labour market thesis, [. . .] women are seen as concentrated in the 'secondary' segment of the labour market, which is the segment characterized by low pay, poor conditions, insecurity and limited career prospects. Black workers and young people may be used as secondary labour, but women are especially suitable as they can resume their domestic role if made redundant. In other words, the construction of segmented labour markets helps employers achieve numerical flexibility.

Segmented labour market theory fits well with many of the facts about women's employment which we have reviewed and it takes on board the issue of segregation, but it does not altogether cope with all the complexities of the sexual division of labour. Not all 'women's work' is of the casualized secondary kind; there are some women's careers (nursing, teaching, textiles) and in these areas there have been persistent shortages of skilled women. There are also secondary-type jobs for men, in the construction industry for example, but even in these men habitually earn more than average female wages. Like the Marxist approaches, segmented labour market theory offers important insights into some of the ways in which employers exploit female labour, but does not sufficiently acknowledge the way in which gender segregation also benefits men. Some kind of dual systems theory is needed which would supplement an account of capitalist objectives with an understanding of how gender segregation at work is influenced by the domestic division of labour, and how it helps maintain male dominance.

Such a theory would take into account the disadvantages faced by married women because of the pressure of domestic duties. This pressure is compounded by the inadequate provision in Britain of childcare facilities and may be increased by the current policy of 'community care' which pushes more of the efforts and costs of social reproduction onto the shoulders of women. However, single and childless women also face disadvantage in the labour market. Gender inequality is more than simply a reflection of family relations. Paid work, as the preceding discussion has suggested, is a site of patriarchy, arranged on terms which favour male dominance.

The work of Cynthia Cockburn is particularly useful in demonstrating the centrality of gender at work. Cockburn's case studies of printing, tailoring, mail-order retailing and radiography revealed the importance of social attitudes about suitable work for each sex. Her study of the printing industry highlighted the longstanding efforts of male printers to keep women out of their jobs. She argues that jobs and workplaces must be understood as *gendered*. Jobs are characterized as male or female, on the base of particular assumptions about skill and technology. Men portray women as technologically incompetent, and ensure they are so by barring them from technological training. In Cockburn's words 'the appropriation of muscle, capability, tools and machinery by men is an important source of women's subordination, indeed it is part of the process by which females are constituted as women' (Cockburn, 1990, p.88). Technological competence is seen as a sign of superior male intellect and used to justify women's exclusion from top jobs.

Workplace groups are also often segregated, especially in manufacturing industry. Both men and women seem to prefer to work with their own sex. Workplace cultures develop from these segregated friendship groups, women's cultures focusing on domestic activities, families and romances, male cultures on sport and banter about drink and sex. Intruders of the opposite sex are often resented as they disturb the cosy atmosphere of the workgroups. Exclusionary tactics, sometimes quite vicious, may be adopted to freeze them out. In all these ways sexual divisions are actively developed within the workplace. [. . .]

Table 12.6 Theories of the labour market

Human capital theory	Neo-classical economics	Women's lower levels of training etc. confine them to lower-paid jobs	Rational choices made by couples on the basis of family needs and resources
Reserve army theory	Marxist	Women used as labour reserve	Serves capitalists' needs for cheap disposable labour
Segmented labour market theory	Weberian framework, also used by Marxists	Women clustered in secondary labour market sectors	Employers use labour market to 'divide and rule' and to secure flexibility
Dual systems theory	Marxist feminist	Gender segregation of jobs	Serves capitalists' interests (cheap labour) and helps secure continued male social dominance

RACE AND CHANGE

Theorizing race

Class and gender divisions have deep historical roots in Britain. A third dimension of inequality, race, has assumed increasing significance in the post-war period, with the entry into Britain of considerable numbers of immigrants from the West Indies, Africa and the Indian subcontinent. These groups, who have been officially categorized as 'of New Commonwealth ethnic origin', make up the core of what we might call the black British. In 1951 there were some 200,000 New Commonwealth (NC) born immigrants in Britain. By 1981 numbers had increased to over one and a quarter million born overseas, along with over a million children born in Britain into NC families.

Immigration into Britain is hardly new. There has been a black minority presence here since colonial development started, fostered particularly by the slave trade. Many Irish, Jewish and Polish immigrants, among others, entered Britain during the nineteenth and early twentieth centuries. Such groups have often been viewed with suspicion and hostility by the native-born population. However, in the post-war period race relations in Britain took a new orientation with colour in particular becoming the basis of hostility and conflict.

It is essential to see post-war immigration in a long-term context. In his notorious *Rivers of Blood* speech in 1968, Enoch Powell raised the spectre of black immigrants 'swamping' the country, draining economic resources from the indigenous population and diluting British culture, a theme which became central to the discourse of racism. But immigration only took place because the immigrants' home countries had at an earlier date been 'swamped' by thousands of white settlers who took political control, reconstructed the native economies and imposed aspects of British culture in countries where children still study Shakespeare and Dickens in schools and play cricket and football outside them.

Since the onset of colonialism, countries around the world have been intricately linked by chains of economic development. Wallerstein (1974) argues that colonialism brought into being an integrated world economy, in which the 'core' Western industrializing societies exploited the labour and resources of the 'peripheral' societies we now know as the Third World. Whether or not these processes fatally blocked Third World societies from developing is not an issue we have time to explore here, but economists like Barratt-Brown (1974) have suggested that British industrialization was founded upon the exploitation of slave labour in the West Indian and American colonies. Since then there has been a constant process of labour transference to and fro across the globe, with certain types of worker moving from the 'core' nations to the Third World, others moving from Third World nations to the industrialized West. The wholesale transportation of Africans to the West Indies and Americas is only the dramatic example of this vast migrational network. Globally, race relations have developed on the basis of colonialism and labour mobility which set black populations in a disadvantaged and subordinate situation and emphasized the superiority of the more technologically advanced Western 'races'.

Race is in itself a problematic concept; as many have argued, it is doubtful whether it has any scientific base. In the discussion which follows I shall use the terminology suggested by Cashmore and Troyna (1983). They argue that race must be seen as real on the grounds that it has real effects on people's attitudes and behaviour. They distinguish between race as a label or stigmatized identity forced on one group by another and ethnicity as a self-defined and freely chosen cultural identity. Thus, in Britain, the assertion of ethnicity by black groups can be seen as a response to the experience of race. I use the term 'black', as they do, as the most acceptable term available to cover the various NC groups (South Asians, West Indians, Africans) and to distinguish them from other 'white' immigrant groups, such as Cypriots and Irish. The latter, while suffering some of the disadvantages of 'race', are not discriminated against to the same extent, as they are spared the visibility of 'colour'. We must remember, however, that black is a crude umbrella term covering numerous ethnic and regional groups, each of which has its own special position within the British social formation.

As in the case of gender, there is debate as to whether racial inequality can be explained within the framework of class or whether a separate framework, analagous to that of patriarchy, is necessary to understand the specificity of racial disadvantage. For Marxists, class is seen as primary, with race having secondary effects. They suggest that much racial disadvantage arises from the fact that most black British are members of the working class. A slightly different line is taken by Phizacklea and Miles (1980), who argue that black workers are a racialized fraction of the working class, whose economic position is significantly worse than that of white workers because of racist ideologies. The notion of fraction works better here (in the case of race) than in the case of gender. It is indeed true that black minority members are crowded into the lower occupational groupings. Recent research into 'black underachievement' at school suggests that the lower achievement of black students, previously explained as partly the result of cultural handicaps, more or less disappears when results are controlled for class (Asians do better than Afro-Caribbeans since they are more likely to have parents with educational qualifications). However, this approach underplays the role of racism among the white population, which makes the experience of minority groups different at *every* level of the class structure. Growing numbers of ethnic minority members have, as we shall see, moved out of manual jobs.

Something of the same objection can be raised to the application of the Weberian concept of the underclass to blacks in Britain. Black Britons cannot, in the main, be seen as permanently trapped in poverty in the same way as are the blacks in the ghettoes of many

American cities, although this could happen in the future. At the moment, the position of racial minorities in the British class structure is rather more complex, and allows for considerable mobility.

Another concept used by Marxists has been that of migrant labour. [. . .] Castles and Kosack (1973) linked the black presence in Britain to international labour migration, conceiving migrant workers as part of a vast 'international reserve army of labour'. However, this works better for groups like the 'guestworkers' in Germany and Switzerland, whose stay in Europe is only temporary. It fits less well with British minorities who, despite the stress given by some commentators on the prevalence of the 'myth of return', are now widely accepted as being permanently settled. Indeed, in his later work (1984) Castles concedes that orthodox Marxist class theory is insufficient to explain the position of black people in Britain, which arises both from class situation and from ethnic minority status.

Here, Castles appears to be moving closer to a Weberian position, such as that of Rex, who conceptualizes race as a form of negative ascribed status. Rex also points to the importance of different consumption patterns, particularly with regard to housing (Rex and Tomlinson, 1979). For both Castles and Rex, economic and status divisions jointly lead to racial inequalities. Even more stress on status appears in the work of Parkin (1979), who adopts Weber's notion of social closure which refers to the strategies of exclusion used by specific groups against other rival groups. Parkin's explanation gives more weight than any previously discussed to the role of the white populace as a whole, rather than capitalists alone, in sustaining racial divisions.

Clearly, economic considerations, capitalist interests and the class positions in which black Britons are concentrated account for some of the disadvantages they face, but, in my opinion, racial differences cannot be reduced to class or to purely economic factors. We have to consider the important role of white racism in maintaining racial inequality and segregation. Racism is not itself a product of capitalist interests, although capitalists may well take advantage of racial divisions. The ideas of Castles and Parkin point the way towards examining race as a dimension of equality in its own right, although neither go far enough. As yet the idea of a separate racial dynamic is not as developed as the analysis of patriarchy. Such an analysis might proceed by showing how divisions backed by racist ideologies arose from the colonial process, slavery and white imperialism. Despite the decay of colonialism, racist ideas and power disparities between the ex-colonial Western nations and Third World nations have ensured that race divisions remain deep.

The changing patterns of racial inequality

In the 1950s, NC immigrants were induced to come to Britain to offset the labour shortages which accompanied post-war economic reconstruction and expansion. Black immigrants took jobs that whites rejected, for example, in London Transport and the National Health Service. Such 'dirty jobs' were characterized by low pay, poor conditions and unsocial hours (black Britons are still concentrated in shiftwork). Decades later, black workers are still clustered in many of the same industries: textiles, transport, the NHS, hotels and catering. Although some black male workers gained access to better-paid skilled work in engineering and car factories, these are the areas of British manufacturing which have been particularly hit by recession, leading to high unemployment among black groups. Black women as we saw [earlier in the chapter], often perform low-status service work.

When the first NC immigrants arrived, they found themselves openly excluded from access to better quality housing by estate agents and landlords. It was quite common to see notices displayed reading 'No coloureds here'. Rules and procedures governing council house allocation also discriminated against immigrants. This drove the newcomers to purchase cheap housing in decaying inner-city areas which had been vacated by affluent whites as they moved into the suburbs. Later immigrants moved into the same areas, either to be near relatives or friends, or to rent accommodation from their compatriots. Inexorably, black ghetto areas began to form. Not only was the housing in these areas of poor condition, but other resources and facilities, such as schools, were poor and rundown. Crime and unemployment made the ghettoes into 'problem areas', and problems were exacerbated when the remaining white residents vented their frustrations for their own deprivations in hostility towards their black neighbours.

Tension between blacks and whites exploded in the riots which took place in Notting Hill and Nottingham in 1958, and these events consolidated the view of race relations as a problem. The riots led to the passing of the 1962 Immigration Act, followed by several others enacted in the next two decades. The Acts limited rights of entry to black immigrants by various voucher, work permit and quota systems and by confining automatic rights to citizenship to 'patrials', that is those with British parents or grandparents. This latter move was seen as an attempt to cut down on black immigrants without restricting the movement of white ex-Commonwealth members such as Australians and Canadians.

Immigration controls were meant to reassure the white population that there would be no swamping, but arguably they only served to confirm the view that black immigrants were second-class citizens and a threat to the British nation. Race Relations Acts passed in 1965, 1968 and 1976 were designed to make discrimination illegal. They established a series of public bodies (the latest being the Commission for Racial Equality) which were supposed to work actively to promote good race relations. The race relations legislation did help to remove the blatantly discriminatory practices we noted when discussing housing, but did little to prevent the more subtle forms of discrimination, which are particularly widespread in employment.

Tests carried out as part of the Political and Economic Planning survey in the 1960s involved actors playing matched pairs of black and white applicants for jobs and revealed substantial discrimination in up to fifty per cent of cases. The tests have since been replicated a number of times and show that discrimination continues. It is particularly strong in manual work (Smith's report, published in 1977, found that white applicants were ten times more likely to be accepted). In the service sector black men are more likely to be rejected than black women. This kind of discrimination is hard to prove (except by these carefully staged sociological tests). Legislation appears fairly ineffective against it and also against 'institutional racism', that is, racist discrimination which is built into the practices and procedures of institutions such as schools and firms. One good example of institutional racism is exhibited through the widespread practice of obtaining jobs through personal recommendation, which becomes especially important in recession; it is said that 'who you know is more important than what you know' in getting a job. Wrench and Lee (1978) observed this happening in their study of Birmingham school leavers. White boys were more successful than black boys with similar qualifications in getting apprenticeships, and personal connections proved an important factor.

These processes of discrimination have led to the concentration of some minority group in less skilled manual work, [. . .] [and the] under-representation of black minority males in the professional and managerial sector. The table demonstrates that each group has its own distinctive labour market position. For example, West Indians fail to get into service jobs but dominate in skilled manual work. African Asians are the most successful in reaching top jobs, reflecting the fact that many were highly qualified professionals when they were forced to flee from Africa. The table indicates that the pattern of differentiation is less sharp between white and black females, although black women workers are more heavily concentrated in manual work. We should remember, though, that segregation is more marked at job level than sectoral level and this will be true for race as well as gender.

[. . .]

Despite this picture of discrimination, small numbers of black Britons are moving into professional and managerial jobs. Another significant development is the rise in self-employment among some Asian communities. Self-employment, as we noted earlier, has been growing for all groups, but is especially marked among Asians. In 1985, 23.7 per cent of Indian males in the British workforce, and 21.4 per cent of Pakistani and Bangladeshi, were self-employed, as opposed to 17.7 per cent of whites (Afro-Caribbeans are least likely to be self-employed at 8 per cent). The figures are much lower for women, but even here Indian women lead at 9.4 per cent.

This trend has been linked to the growth of an Asian entrepreneurial culture and seen as a sign of successful adaptation to a new environment and evidence of a new prosperity among the Asian communities. It has also been linked to a tradition of successful business enterprise within Indian cultures, displayed earlier, for example, in East Africa. High value placed on hard work and self-sufficiency leads Asian families into this type of investment. However, reviewing the research on Asian businesses in Britain, Cashmore and Troyna conclude that entrepreneurialism may be forced on Asians because they face restricted opportunities elsewhere. Moreover, most of the businesses remain small and rely heavily on family labour, which can be experienced as highly self-exploitative. (One of the reasons for the failure of Afro-Caribbeans to develop a comparable community-centred enterprise sector may be the lack of tightly integrated family and kin networks to provide labour.) Some clothing businesses may be no more than a disguised form of homeworking. However, Asian enterprises do provide a basis of independence and may be seen as part of the assertion of ethnicity as a response to white racism. In class terms, it means that around one fifth of the Asian minority are moving out of the working class into the petite bourgeoisie which would provide a strong challenge to either the underclass theory or the Marxist contention that race disadvantage can be reduced to class. Rather it provides support for an approach showing how class and race interact together. Cashmore and Troyna suggest that Asian entrepreneurs have moved from a disadvantaged position as workers to a disadvantaged position as businessmen, on the basis of race.

Annie Phizacklea links the growth of Asian businesses to the recession of the 1970s (in 1971 only 6 per cent of Indian men were self-employed). [Many studies] show the vulnerability of minority groups to unemployment. This is especially marked for Afro-Caribbeans and for the younger age groups.

[. . .]

Stuart Hall in Hall et al. (1978) has argued that economic recession the 1970s led to the scapegoating of black minorities by British governments wishing to draw attention away from the failures of their own economic policies. Recessions led to increased inner-city decline, with overburdened social services unable to provide funding for improvements. Unemployment among inner-city youths can be linked to rising problems of crime and vandalism. All this led to targeting of Afro-Caribbean youths as a problem group; increased intensity of policing in black areas helped exacerbate racial hostility and resentment. Racist attacks, particularly on Asian families, were on the increase throughout the 1980s (in 1987 there were 2,179 reported in the Metropolitan police area alone, including 47 cases of arson). In 1981, another wave of riots wracked inner-city ghettoized areas around the country. The Gifford Report on race relations in Liverpool (1989) exposed the extent to which race divisions had become rooted in the more highly depressed areas of the country, finding a systematic denial of jobs to black people, particularly in the city centre commercial and retailing enterprises, extensive black unemployment, and a failure of Liverpool City Council to implement its own equal opportunities policies: only 490 out of 30,410 council employees were black.

It is important to stress that racial disadvantage is not confined to the economic sphere. As is the case with gender, the experience of race and racism spreads itself across every area of life. For example, black groups are still concentrated in the least desirable sectors of the housing market. It was believed that young blacks 'underachieved' at school, although, as stated earlier, recent research has suggested that most of this could be accounted for in terms of class differences. However, research into patterns of interaction in schools has revealed that black students are subject to persistent racial harassment from white pupils and that many teachers operate with racist stereotypes which make school an unhappy experience for many minority youngsters (Mac an Ghaill, 1988: Fleming, 1990).

[. . .]

Minority groups have responded to these experiences in various ways. Some have tried to work for equal opportunities through existing bodies like the political parties or trade unions, though arguably white-dominated political organizations have done little to promote racial equality. Others have joined community groups or anti-racist campaigns. Young blacks seem to have responded to the discrimination they know they will face by putting more effort than white youngsters into education. Asian students out-perform whites at school and higher proportions of Asians and Afro-Caribbeans than of whites are currently in higher education. But perhaps most important has been the assertion of ethnicity. This takes differing forms. Afro-Caribbean youths have developed their own 'streetwise' culture and rastafarian creed. The consolidation of Asian community businesses can be read in this way; and the late 1980s have seen a more aggressive response from Muslim Asians with the growing popularity of militant Islamic fundamentalism. All these assertions of independent identity may do much to raise the self-esteem of minority groups (and incidentally add to the richness of cultural life in Britain). But an unfortunate side-effect is the consolidation of segregated lifestyles, which may heighten racial hostility.

This chapter has only begun to explore the many dimensions of racial segmentation in Britain, ignoring, for example, the differentiated experiences of many other ethnic groups (for example Cypriots, Jews and Irish), who also face discriminatory practices and prejudice. Racial diversity is an important feature of modem Britain.

This racial diversity adds to the difficulty of developing a theoretical understanding of race and ethnicity. In this chapter, I have argued that attempts to reduce race to class are insufficient. Racial disadvantage is not confined to economics, but is experienced in every area of life; in particular, notions of white supremacy and superiority are very deeply embedded in all the cultural discourses developed by 'Western' thought. Although the patterns of disadvantage experienced by some black groups are similar to those experienced by the working class as a whole (low educational achievement, poor health, poor housing), racism adds an extra dimension; and racism is not just experienced by working-class blacks. At all levels of the class structure, minority groups experience discrimination and exclusion. Although race is sharply linked to class and although capitalism has benefited from using minority workers as cheap labour (especially women), race, like gender, must be seen as an autonomous source of division.

NOTE

* This chapter has been adapted from, Bradley, H. (1992) 'Changing Social Divisions', in Bocock, R. and Thompson, K. (eds) *Social and Cultural Forms of Modernity*, Polity Press in association with The Open University, pp. 13–29, 35–50.

REFERENCES

Barratt-Brown, M. (1974) *The Economics of Imperialism*, Harmondsworth, Penguin.
Barrett. M, (1987) 'The concept of difference', *Feminist Review* 26, pp.29–41.

Beechey, V. (1977) 'Some notes on female wage labour in capitalist production', *Capital and Class*, 3, pp.45–66.

Bell, D. (1974) *The Coming of Post-industrial Society*, Harmondsworth, Penguin.

Braverman, H. (1974) *Labor and Monopoly Capital*, New York, Monthly Review Press.

Cashmore, E. and Troyna, B. (1983) *Introduction to Race Relations*, London, Routledge and Kegan Paul.

Castles, S. and Kosack, G. (1973) *Immigrant Workers and Class Structure in Western Europe*, Oxford, Oxford University Press.

Castles, S. (1984) *Here For Good*, London, Pluto.

Central Statistical Office (1986, 1990 and 1991) *Social Trends*, nos. 16, 20 and 21, London, HMSO.

Cockburn, C. (1990) 'The material of male power', in Lovell, T. (ed.) *British Feminist Thought*, Oxford, Blackwell.

Crompton, R. and Jones, G. (1984) *White-Collar Proletariat*, London, Macmillan.

Dahrendorf, R. (1959) *Class and Class Conflict in Industrial Societies*, London, Routledge.

Dahrendorf, R. (1987) 'The erosion of citizenship and its consequences for us all', *New Statesman*, 12 June, pp.12–15.

Delphy, C. (1977) *The Main Enemy*, London, Women's Research and Resources Centre.

Fleming, S. (1990) 'Sport and social divisions', presented at 1990 British Sociological Conference.

Gifford Report (1989) 'Loosen the shackles', Liverpool 8 Law Centre.

Glucksmann, M. (1990) *Women Assemble*, London, Routledge.

Goldthorpe, J., Lockwood, D., Bechhofer, F. and Platt, J. (1969) *The Affluent Worker in the Class Structure*, Cambridge, Cambridge University Press.

Gorz, A. (1982) *Farewell to the Working Class*, London, Pluto.

Hakim, C. (1979) 'Occupational segregation by sex', Department of Employment Research Paper No.9, London, Department of Employment.

Hall, S., Critcher, C., Jefferson, T., Clarke, J. and Roberts, B. (1978) *Policing the Crisis*, London, Macmillan.

Hartmann, H. (1981) 'The unhappy marriage of Marxism and Feminism: towards a more progressive union' in Sargent, L. (ed.).

Lewis, J. (1988) 'Women clerical workers in the late nineteenth and early twentieth centuries' in Anderson, G. (ed.) *The White Blouse Revolution*, Manchester, Manchester University Press.

Lockwood, B. (1958) *The Blackcoated Worker*, London, Unwin.

Lockwood, D. (1966) 'Sources of variation in working-class images of society' *Sociological Review* 14, 2, pp.249–67.

Lockwood, D. (1981) 'The weakest link in the chain? Some comments on the Marxist theory of action' *Research in the Sociology of Work* 1, pp.435–81.

Mac an Ghaill, M. (1988) *Young, Gifted and Black*, Milton Keynes, The Open University Press.

Marshall, G., Rose, B., Newby, H. and Vogler, C. (1988) *Social Class in Modern Britain*, London, Unwin Hyman.

Parkin, F. (1979) *Marxism and Class Theory*, London, Tavistock.

Phillips, A. and Taylor, B. (1980) 'Sex and skill: notes towards a feminist economics', *Feminist Review*, 6, pp.70–83.

Phizacklea, A. and Miles, R. (1980) *Labour and Racism*, London, Routledge.

Rex, J. and Tomlinson, S. (1979) *Colonial Immigrants in a British City*, London, Routledge.

Rogers, B. (1988) *Men Only*, London, Pandora.

Rowbotham, S. (1981) 'The trouble with "patriarchy" ', in Feminist Anthology Collective (eds) *No Turning Back*, London, Women's Press.

Rubery, J., Horrell, S., and Burrell, B. (1989) 'Unequal jobs or unequal pay?' *Industrial Relations Journal*, 20, 3, pp.176–91.

Sargent, L. (ed.) (1981) *Women in Revolution*, London, Pluto.

Saunders, P. (1990) *Social Class and Stratification*, London, Routledge.

Scott, J. (1979) *Corporations, Classes and Capitalism*, London, Hutchinson.

Scott, J. (1982) *The Upper Classes*, London, Macmillan.

Smith, D. (1977) *Racial Disadvantage in Britain*, Harmondsworth, Penguin.

Spender, D. (1980) *Man-made Language*, London, Routledge.

Walby, S. (1986) *Patriarchy at Work*, Cambridge, Polity Press.

Wallerstein, I. (1974) *The Modern World System*, New York, Academic Press.

Wrench, J. and Lee, G. (1978) 'A subtle hammering – young black people and the labour market' in Troyna, B. and Smith, D. (eds) (1983) *Racism, School and the Labour Market*, Leicester, National Youth Bureau.

Young, I. (1981) 'Beyond the unhappy marriage: a critique of the dual systems theory' in Sargent, L. (ed.) (1981).

13

WHY INEQUALITY DOESN'T WORK*

Will Hutton

INEQUALITY HURTS US ALL

Inequality, it is said, is the price that has to be paid for economic efficiency. The argument is that attempts to divide the pie more equally simply shrink it – and conversely, the more unequally the pie is divided the bigger it will grow. A capitalist society is by its nature unequal and so faces a trade-off: the more unequal it is, the more economically efficient it becomes.

Without the incentives offered by inequality, either as a reward or punishment, a capitalist economy simply loses its dynamism. Unless there is a hierarchy of profit, capital cannot flow to the areas with highest returns; unless there is a penalty for being out of work, workers will not seek employment. There needs to be fear and greed in the system in order to make it tick.

Attempts to change this are self-defeating. Even if the tax system were so penal that millionaires were eliminated, the improvement in the circumstances of the rest would be minimal; a million pounds spread between 60 million people is worth only a couple of pence per person – but at the same time the system has lost the capacity to reward enterprising individuals by offering them the prospect of becoming millionaires. Everybody is poorer by their loss.

But worse, as neo-liberal social theorists in the US have argued, attempting to narrow inequality by redistributing income from the rich to the poor creates a dependency culture. The poor, instead of trying to improve their position by their own efforts, expect the state to underwrite them. This diminishes them as individuals, making them less responsible; with poor attitudes to parenting, work and wider social obligations. Beyond offering a minimum and targeted safety net, society should make no morally corroding commitment to transfer income from rich to poor.

And attempts to build systems of social solidarity between classes demand the intervention of the state. However effectively equality can be created it is always at the expense of individual liberty. The wealth and freedom of action of the better-off are qualified by state intervention, constraining their liberty in a vain attempt to promote equality. The distribution of income and living standards in society should be left to the market: here as elsewhere there is only trouble in store for those that meddle with market processes.

Although notions like the dependency culture and the need for incentives may seem modern, these are ancient concerns, which have dogged efforts to ameliorate inequality for centuries. It was only in 1948 that the Poor Law, with its distinction between the deserving and undeserving poor, and its system of relief doled out locally on the basis of means-tested household income was formally abolished, to be replaced by what was then called national assistance and is now known as income support. The boards of guardians throughout the nineteenth and early-twentieth centuries were haunted by the conviction that their attempts to provide minimum levels of subsistence would succour fraud and idleness, as the classical economists had predicted. The deserving poor should be helped; but wastrels and indigents should not be subsidised by the better-off.

'Modern' anxiety about the consequences of state action is thus at least a hundred years old. In 1988, Ralph Harris in *Beyond the Welfare State* wrote: 'In Britain, I have no doubt that improved social benefits have increased the incentive for the people to make some kind of a living out of being poor', unconsciously echoing *The Times* in 1902, Reacting to Seebohm Rowntree's revelation in his landmark study that 27.84 per cent of the people in York were living in poverty, the Thunderer insisted that a large proportion of the poor were 'miserable mainly from their own fault'.[1] Herbert Spencer's impassioned accusation in *Man Versus The State* (1884) that liberals were deserting their principles in favour of restrictive legislation would have found equal favour with Harris and other representatives of the New Right a century later. Spencer saw collectivism asserting itself and believed that the concessions already made to state intervention would destroy liberty and ruin the system of *laissez-faire*. Citing the Chimney-Sweepers Act, prescribing the size of chimneys up which sweeps could send young children in an attempt to prevent their maiming or death, and the Acts insisting on compulsory vaccination. Spencer fulminated against such limits on the liberty of contract.

At the end of the nineteenth century, across Europe and the United States, governments legislated to limit the workings of *laissez-faire* – first by inspecting factories and offering minimal standards of education and later by providing subsistence income for the old and out of work. From Bismarck in Germany to the British Liberal government of 1906–14, the state began to put limits against a background of dire warnings from the economic liberals that the market system was being irretrievably endangered – even when it became transparently obvious that it suffered hardly at all and such intervention if anything raised the growth rate. In truth the danger lay in allowing the system to continue without such intervention; and this tension has remained to the present day. Today's New Right do no more than repeat the ancestral warnings of the *laissez faire* economists over the last two centuries: interfere in the operation of the market at your peril; inequality is the price we pay for efficiency; liberty of contract is an indivisible principle; the poor will always be with us: help is self-defeating.

But fifteen years of redesigning the tax and benefit system so that it conforms to such principles has not borne very impressive fruit. Britain has certainly become a more unequal society than it was in 1979 but the pie, rather than expanding more quickly, is if anything expanding more slowly. The collapse of social cohesion that comes when the market is allowed to rip through society has produced a fall in the growth rate; marginalisation, deprivation and exclusion have proved economically irrational.

The social consequences are profound. The virtual stagnation of incomes for people in the bottom third of the population has infected the very marrow of society. Holding families together has become more difficult as the wages and conditions of unskilled adult males has deteriorated. And this has had major implications for public expenditure.

Market rule has recoiled on the state's finances; as the polarisation of society has worsened, public spending on crime, health and specialist education has increased – and social security spending itself, even though rates are meaner in relation to average earnings, has ballooned as poverty drives millions through the drab waiting-rooms of the rump welfare state.

Government efforts to extend the operation of the market in a plethora of areas ranging from housing and pensions to television and sport have not been a notable success, even in their own terms. Instead of extending choice, individual liberty and the general welfare there has been a secular increase in risk, insecurity and cultural impoverishment.

'Marketisation' has seen the growth of private forms of power and the entrenchment of the old class structure that Tory radicals affected to despise. Higher disposable incomes for the top 10 per cent have allowed them to afford ever more expensive private education for their children, with the numbers enrolled at private schools growing substantially over the decade. At the same time state schools have become more discriminating in their intake, in order to maximise exam results and therefore funding. To be born poor means to stay poor and ill-qualified; while to be born rich brings with it educational attainment and career achievement. Class hardens subtly into caste – and economies do not prosper in caste societies.

INEQUALITY AND ECONOMIC PERFORMANCE

The case linking inequality and the economy is simply put. Inequality between classes and regions adversely affects both demand and supply. Demand becomes more volatile and unbalanced while supply is affected by underinvestment and neglect of human capital. Economic cycles are amplified; firms become more like opportunist traders than social organisations committed to production and innovation. As a result, the long-run growth rate tends to fall, unemployment rises and the government's underlying fiscal position deteriorates, and a vicious circle intensifies the volatility of demand and the weakness of supply.

Economic management should be designed to produce a predictable and stable growth in demand over time. This allows firms to budget for returns from new investment that promise to be stable, and encourages them to innovate, train and invest in order to capture these predictable returns. The anticipated rise in demand and the confidence that it will continue attracts the investment in capacity that will both meet the rising demand and is itself part of that demand.

Unfortunately there is a complicating factor – the economic cycle. There is a rhythm in economic life in which the promise of an improving economy leads to more investment, spending and optimism and so causes the economy to surge above its average growth rate. It approaches a peak in which there is so much pressure on capacity, which lags behind the rise in spending, that inflation or interest rates or the trade deficit rise either separately or in combination. This tends to slow down demand, which now starts to fall – the mirror image of the earlier improvement. Because expectations deteriorate, firms cancel or postpone their investments, consumers fearful of redundancy build up their savings and the whole economy slips below its average rate of growth – or even, in a recession, actually contracts.

All capitalist economies experience this rhythm but the less volatile the up and down movements, the more firms are able to sustain the capital accumulation and husband the skilled labour force that lifts the growth rate of a successful economy. The problem with the deliberate encouragement of inequality as a matter of government policy is that it exaggerates the economic cycle in important ways and seriously unbalances the pattern of demand. The events of the 1980s and early 1990s demonstrate the point perfectly.

In the long seven-year upswing from the trough of the 1981 recession to the peak of the Lawson boom in 1988, the distribution of income in Britain became progressively more unequal – a trend that continued into the subsequent downturn. Rising consumption was fuelled in part by the rise in real wages helped by cheap import prices from the increase in sterling; but an important factor was the tax reductions and expectations of more adding to the already rising pre-tax incomes of the top 40 per cent of the population. So if financial deregulation, and the avalanche of credit is unleashed, was one part of the equation, the other was the ability of the richer groups to borrow ever greater amounts. This triggered the housing boom, a key link in the self-reinforcing spiral of credit and spending.

If the inequality of income helped support the housing boom, it also skewed demand towards imports and luxuries. The higher earners paid up for private education, yachts, high-performance cars, race horses, fine arts, and designer clothes. Importers poured in. The boom moved to its climax in 1988, with the reduction in top tax rates to 40 per cent particularly overheating the south-east where most higher rate tax payers lived, emphasising a regional as well as social bias to inequality which had wider malevolent economic consequences.

The consumer boom had its genesis in the south-east because incomes were higher there, as were house prices. The inflation in house prices and property wealth was never matched in the north of England. Scotland and Northern Ireland – yet economic policy had to focus on cooling the south-eastern economic cauldron. It was the uneven geographical nature of the boom, as much as its overall ferocity, that made it so unstable.

The government could not respond with tax increases, still less with tax increases aimed at curbing the spending of the better off in particular regions which would have been in flat contradiction of its doctrine of promoting incentives for the rich. The only policy response that ideology could allow was to raise interest rates, which took a long time to work, and once in operation released powerful deflationary forces that again were intensified by the new inequalities.

With the fall in house prices, the 'feel good' effect that had been supporting consumption was depressed rather sharply. A great deal of evanescent economic activity had been supported by the bubble of housing wealth, and employment in these areas now fell dramatically. But while the south-east might have needed the medicine of 15 per cent interest rates to cool it down, the same rates were fantastically inappropriate to the relatively depressed British industrial regions – as was entry, at around the same time, into the ERM at a rate overvalued to curb inflation. The south-east powered the boom: it now propelled the recession.

The only offsetting measure open to the government as the recession deepened was to allow social security spending to rise automatically. It could not proactively spend its way out of the recession; the doctrine stated that the motor of recovery had to be the private sector and the market – a private sector which, aggressively laying off workers, cutting investment and preserving dividends, found it exceptionally difficult to rekindle economic growth.

Here again the dogmatic commitment to inequality had deleterious economic effects. Firms' employment of part-time and casual labour began to have destabilising effects on overall levels of demand. In the upturn the new 'flexible' labour market allowed employers to suck new workers into the workforce on terms they could quickly break if the economy turned down – and those higher participation rates, especially for women, had increased incomes and hence spending power. But in the downswing the same flexibility saw a sharp rise in unemployment – up 1.5 million over three years – and led to a particularly sharp fall in demand, which reinforced the downturn.

For not only were enormous numbers of people falling out of the labour market, but their loss of income was even more dramatic. With income support worth 7 per cent less in relation to average earnings than during the previous recession in 1979–81, demand fell by some £4 billion or 0.66 per cent of GDP more than it would have done had the old relationship between income support and average earnings held.[2] The government had made a rod for its own back.

The newly unemployed were not the only group to lose their purchasing power over the decade. The failure to index state pensions to wages meant that by 1994 pensioners' spending power was £6 billion a year lower than it would have been. At the same time the relative drop in incomes of the bottom 10 per cent of wage earners by some 7 per cent meant that their spending power had been cut by an additional £3 billion. Rising inequality had robbed the economy of at least £13 billion of spending from those sections of the community whose capacity to save is minimal. They must spend what they receive in income. On the ebbing tide of previous recessions the small boats had been able to float; now they were part of the wreckage.

Free-market theory claims that this should not happen, because in an economy with perfectly functioning markets, losers should be balanced by gainers; in other words, if pensioners and the unemployed receive less benefit, then taxation is lower and those in work should have higher incomes to spend to compensate for the reduced spending by social security recipients. Equally, the growth of low pay should be offset either by higher pay or greater profits, so the level of final demand should be the same.

But those at the bottom of the income scale save less and spend more for every pound of income. Thus redistributing income from the poor to the rich tends to lower effective demand and increase saving. The onus is upon the financial system to ensure that the higher saving from the higher income groups is recycled to maintain the level of final demand.

In reality, of course, markets are not perfect, the economy is not at equilibrium, nor is it closed, and the financial system does not work perfectly. The more unequal the income distribution, as Keynes, Galbraith, Myrdal, Kalecki and Malthus all recognised, the more likely it is that the economy will suffer from periodic crises of underconsumption.

In the 1990–92 recession, the economy had to rely on demand coming from those whose incomes had improved relative to the average; but these were precisely the people who had incurred high levels of debt in the boom. With most mortgages carrying variable interest rates, the same top half of the population that had propelled the boom now found themselves having to retrench severely to meet interest payments that had nearly doubled. Again the south-east was in the vanguard, its income falling back sharply against the national average.

Firms faced a fall in demand more severe than any they had experienced in post-war history. Whilst consumer spending had only stopped growing during the 1979–81 recession, stabilising at around £247 billion (in 1990 prices), in the recession years between 1990 and 1992 consumer spending actually fell by £7.6 billion – the sharpest drop since the war. Industries as disparate as television – dependent upon companies paying handsomely for advertising – and furniture – dependent upon rising consumer spending – found they had made investment decisions upon unrealistic assumptions; and launched into second and third rounds of retrenchment which in turn prolonged the recession. ERM membership prevented the fall in interest rates, which was the only acceptable policy tool available to the government.

But the new inequality, and the attitude towards the welfare state from which it had grown, had other subtle and damaging effects. For example, with the government signalling that public provision of pensions would become progressively meaner and telegraphing its belief in private provision by providing big tax incentives, pension funds mushroomed – but their new size and dividend demands rebounded on company strategies. Business investment fell to a thirty-year low as companies twisted and turned to find the cash to meet the pension funds' demands – and the weaker people in the labour market, the unskilled and non-unionised, were offered worse and worse pay and working conditions.

The dogma of inequality lay behind every gyration of the wild spiral of boom and bust, and the colossal misallocation of resources that it represented. There had been too much investment on the basis of rising consumption and too little on the basis of winning overseas markets. The economy entered the next upswing crippled by a legacy of excessive consumption and underinvestment. Saddled with growing institutional share ownership, firms' investment strategies would be driven by their owners' financial demands; the next boom would be no more sustainable than the previous one. Inequality had not delivered for the economy; and it had pretty disastrous consequences for the state too.

INEQUALITY AND THE STATE

In the 1993–94 financial year Britain's public sector borrowing requirement reached £45.9 billion – the second highest figure as a proportion of national output since the war. Lowering marginal tax rates, while overseeing an explosion of public expenditure driven by the growth of poverty which the state had itself created, proved irrational for the state as well as the larger economy, burdening it with an inbuilt budgetary crisis. Here, as elsewhere, indifference to the growth of inequality has proved counterproductive.

Although comparatively modest plans for public expenditure growth have been continually reined back since the mid-1970s, with some programmes like housing and trade and industry cut to the bone, overall public expenditure in Britain as it emerged from recession was only fractionally lower than in the comparable stage of the economic cycle a decade earlier. For cuts in domestic programmes are instantly cancelled out by the growth of inequality and the demands it makes on the public purse – from sickness benefit to troublesome schools.

At the same time the lower marginal tax rates have not delivered the supply-side goods. The belief was that lower tax rates would, by increasing risk-taking and entrepreneurship, so dynamise economic activity that overall tax revenues would not be impaired. Indeed the famous Laffer curve predicted that tax cuts would raise revenue, partly through the resulting increase in economic growth and partly because people would be less inclined to avoid or evade tax.

This theory always owed more to ideology – and the intrinsic appeal it had for the rich – than to responsible theory or observation. Economic theorists have conventionally claimed that the impact of reduced taxes had two effects. There is an income effect, so that an additional hour of work produces more take-home pay; but there is an offsetting substitution effect, because the same income can be achieved with less work, allowing more leisure. The New Right economists were assuming that there were only dynamising income effects, and no substitution effects. On their theory it could not be possible for a tax cut to persuade an executive to spend more time on the golf course than more time in the office – he or she would want to earn more. And this tallied neatly with the New Right's wider view that the only key to wealth generation is to encourage executives to manage and entrepreneurs to take risks – an idea of stunning banality and naivety. Wealth generation is as much a social as an individual act.

It is therefore no surprise that attempts to measure the impact of lowering marginal tax rates on improving the willingness to work should in general disprove the *laissez faire* case. One study financed by the Treasury concluded in 1986 that the 'changes were small and it is likely that none differ significantly from zero':[3] this so offended the prevailing orthodoxy that the then Chancellor, Nigel Lawson, tried to prevent the report from being published. Atkinson and Mogensen, in a comparison of four countries – UK, Sweden, Germany and Denmark, could barely find discernible effects, with the exception of low-paid women for whom high marginal tax rates did seem to be a deterrent to work. Dilnot and Kell found a 1 per cent increase in the labour supply of the higher paid after the 1985–86 tax cuts – but were unable to work out whether this was because the demand for executives had increased in the run-up to the peak of the boom, or because of an increased willingness to work.

In 1994 the Policy Studies Institute (PSI) in a broad survey of more recently published literature came to the same conclusion, although for the very low paid there did seem to be an increased readiness to work as a result of low taxes, again especially among women. However, as the low paid tended to pay more tax during the 1980s through a combination of direct and indirect tax reforms this is hardly helpful to the New Right case, which is far more concerned with the need to lower marginal rates for the very well-off. Longer and more expensive lunches are not the precondition for entrepreneurship. In any case financial incentives, observed the PSI, were very much less important than social and psychological factors in determining people's working hours.

The claim that the Laffer effect has worked out in practice, with tax cuts paying for themselves because the revenue from higher rate tax payers has greatly increased, is also spurious.[4] What has happened is that the incomes of top earners have exploded, so that even lower tax rates produce a similar tax take. But that does not mean that their income has increased because they work harder with lower taxes; their income has gone up for the very different reasons outlined earlier. Skills are at a premium, and in a deregulated labour market insiders do well at the expense of outsiders. The tax regime has a secondary effect, but is not the motor of this process.

What the tax cuts *have* done is greatly to undermine the government's fiscal position, already under pressure from the big increase in social security spending. The interaction of rising current public spending and the drop in current receipts was to produce the largest current deficit since the war (excluding capital items) – around 6 per cent of GDP in the 1993-4 financial year. By contrast the current balance was in surplus in both the 1979-81 and 1973-75 recessions. As a result chancellors Lamont and Clarke had to raise taxes by the equivalent of some 2.7 per cent of GDP in their two budgets in 1993 to remedy the situation – the largest such rise of its type in modern times.

On the revenue side of the equation, the former adviser to ex-Chancellor Norman Lamont, Bill Robinson, reckons that the total loss to the Exchequer from income tax cuts (£9 billion) and the sale of public assets below their full market cost (£13 billion) is some £22 billion at 1994 prices, or 3.4 per cent of nation output compared with the tax regime prevailing in 1986. The cost of switching from domestic rates to the poll tax and back to the council tax is put at 0.5 per cent of GDP or another £3 billion. All in all the government is at least £25 billion poorer from these three policies alone.[5]

In order to find some savings, the government has continually cut capital investment in the public sector. In relation to the total stock of public assets investment is barely sufficient to stop them wasting away. Investment in the railways per capita runs at a third of the European average; road investment per capita is 70 per cent of the European average.[6] By 1995 the public sector's net worth will be the lowest since the war.

The government has insisted that meeting its pre-announced public expenditure planning totals is a test of its credibility with the financial markets; but as a result it is trapped in a vicious circle. It is forced to cut other important programmes to accommodate the relentless rise in social security outlays. As Bill Robinson observes 'social security is at the heart of [Britain's] budget difficulties'. He tells us that in the autumn of 1992, for example, an unplanned increase of £3 billion in the social security budget demanded equivalent savings elsewhere. 'The inexorable growth of social security is a prime reason', he writes, 'why the government has continually to choose between making swinging cuts in important programmes and failing to control spending.'

Social security spending, Maurice Mullard computes has increased from 9.5 per cent of GDP in 1979 to 12.2 per cent in 1992 and has been the principal reason why fifteen years of restraint have still not delivered decisively lower public spending as a proportion of national output.'[7] Defence spending has shrunk from 4.6 per cent of GDP in 1979 to 4.0 per cent in 1992; housing from 2.3 per cent of GDP to 0.5 per cent; trade and industry from 1.3 per cent of GDP to 0.8 per cent; capital investment in all central government programmes from 2.2 per cent of GDP to 1.4 per cent. It is true that education spending has risen from 4.0 per cent of GDP to 4.7 per cent, and health from 4.5 per cent to 5.8 per cent – but in both cases most of the rise was in 1991 and 1992 in the run-up to the 1992 election and is projected to fall below the 1979 levels by the middle of the 1990s.

The phenomenal rise in social security spending has not come about because benefits have increased in real terms; it is because the economy has been run in such a way that the numbers living in poverty and eligible for benefit have increased dramatically. There used to be 7 million claimants of income support in 1979; in 1993 there were 11 million.

It is mainly men who are the cause of the problem. Not only are there 1.7 million officially unemployed and dependent upon income support – there are another 2 million who are no longer even seeking employment because they know there is none. Around a half are classified as 'longterm sick' and thus eligible for sickness and invalidity benefit. Since 1979 the number of supposed invalids has increased by nearly a million – and these people fall outside the government's net of make-work schemes and support systems for the unemployed – such as they are. Over 70 per cent of them are completely unskilled – exactly the category in which the demand for labour has fallen. Others have taken early retirement and qualify for other forms of income support. With each unemployed or non-employed man costing £9,000 a year in lost tax and income support, the transformation in the male labour market is costing the Exchequer over £36 billion a year.

The government sprang its own trap. It had a two-fold aim. It wanted to cut public spending in order to cut borrowing and lower marginal tax rates; and it wanted to encourage workers to become more mobile in order to improve the workings of the labour market. But the paradox is that the number of unskilled, jobless, male social security claimants has so increased under the impact of policies, that the expenditure increases more than offset any of the savings. Nor, as the terminally demoralised stop looking for work, has there been any significant impact of the unemployed wage-setting in the wider economy. The promotion of inequality has become self-defeating.

The approach pervades the public domain. The aims of housing policy, for example, was to raise public rents to market levels – but those who live in public housing are usually living on at most average incomes. As a result many of them are entitled to housing benefit to help pay their rents. Two-thirds of any increase in rents, estimates the Joseph Rowntree Foundation, are claimed back as housing benefit, and because rents inflate the retail price index they also inflate general social security spending which is linked to the RPI. Rent increases end up reducing GDP, and increasing unemployment and inflation.

For the way public money is spent has profound inter-relationships with the wider economy. In the US, for example, the failure to check rampant inequality has created a mutually reinforcing system of ghetto housing, racial discrimination and deep concentrations of poverty, with heavy implications for public spending. The growth of drug-taking and crime forces up prison populations while people in the deprived areas depend on state support – making social security spending structural rather than cyclical, a permanent overhead rather than a response to crisis.[8]

Any remedial programme becomes massively expensive, involving huge spending on education, housing and a corrective social infrastructure. Given that the economic gains from equality are so poor and the costs so heavy, the most prudent course is simply not to allow such no-go areas of self-sustaining and deepening squalor to develop. But the intoxication with *laissez-faire* economics in both the US and UK has permitted just that: laying up vast problems for the future in return for negligible advantages in the present.

INEQUALITY AND TRAINING

The British approach to training typifies the weaknesses of the neoliberal approach. The government has become aware that there are substantial returns from training, both to the individuals concerned and the wider economy, but has never felt that its own financial position could be so improved by raising skill levels that the investment could be self-financing. From the early abolition of the Industrial Training Boards through to the scrapping of the Manpower Services Commission its instinct has been to reduce state involvement. Nigel Lawson, for example, says in his memoirs that he always argued strongly in cabinet that training should be the responsibility of the private sector and that his contribution was to raise profits so that industry could afford it. Neither he nor any of his successors saw public money spent on training as a form of investment that might ultimately reduce the burden of social security – and indeed in his 1,086 page volume the subject of training merits no more than a few lines. A means of lowering the official unemployment claimant count, yes; an investment, no.

The aim, here as elsewhere, was to allow the market to do the job – even though decisions on training are more exposed to market failure than almost any other. British companies, David Finegold and David Soskice reported in a seminal article in 1988,[9] spent 0.15 per cent of their turnover on training compared with 1 to 2 per cent in Japan, France and West Germany – and the amount has not significantly changed since then.

Government efforts are equally lamentable. More British students finish their education at eighteen than in any other industrialised country;[10] fewer have formal educational qualifications;[11] and their mathematical ability is poor.[12] By international standards, there are fewer places for them on vocational training schemes and the levels of technical competence demanded to achieve any given qualification are at the lower end of the spectrum. Germany, for example, does not consider British NVQ Level 1 demanding enough to merit comparison with its own comparable qualification and insists on a better standard as the first building block in any common European norm.

Britain also ranks poorly in terms of institutional structures that support training. The failures in this area exemplify the malfunctions of the whole system described in this [Hutton, 1995] book. The political structures that might support properly independent public/private partnerships, so meeting local labour market requirements, simply don't exist; there are no incentives in the unchecked market-based system for individuals or firms to invest in the acquisition of skills; and the pressures from the financial system reinforce this trend by emphasising the gains from financial engineering, rather than investment in human capital. There is little political demand to invest in vocational training, because the middle class has its own inside track – public forms of education and training are seen as inferior and irrelevant compared to prestige private school and university education. Because there is no tradition of state initiative to develop the economy, there is consequently little willingness by employers to accept levies to pay for training. Permanently short of funds, training is the economic policy Cinderella to which ritual obeisance is paid but about which nothing effective is ever done.

The story of Training and Enterprise Councils – TECs – is a lamentable fable of the entire failure. Established in 1990, TECs were to be the means of establishing a market-led system of world-class training. They would be constituted as essentially private organisations with a majority of businessmen on their boards and were to take control of government spending on training and develop schemes for unemployment relief in their areas. With a businessman as chief executive, they would be closely in touch with local business needs. They would be free to establish local priorities, design programmes to meet them, place contracts with private training suppliers and cajole local firms into undertaking training they would not otherwise carry out.

At first there was considerable enthusiasm and businessmen rallied to the cause of what appeared to be a private-sector-led programme to develop UK plc. In keeping with the *laissez-faire* approach, there was no national plan or blueprint; TECs were simply established where local consortia wanted to establish them – some were too small and others too big – but no intervention to rationalise their scale was deemed ideologically justifiable.

Although some TECs have done a doughty job in improving levels of training, the experiment has failed to meet initial expectations. The British constitution does not admit the degree of local independence that the TECs were promised. Ministers were not prepared to insist that membership of TECs was compulsory, instead preserving the longstanding doctrine of voluntarism, relying on appeals to social responsibility and civic duty wrapped up with covert promises of honours for those who co-operated.

Without an element of compulsion, every TEC is exposed to the risk that firms who are not members and don't contribute at all poach trained workers from those who are more civically minded. Without constitutional independence from the state and no independent revenue-raising powers they cannot budget with their providers for any longer than the year ahead, which is the Treasury's only permitted time-horizon. Not only this, as Robert Bennett and his colleagues document in their extensive interviews,[13] the Treasury system of controlling spending by annual reviews means that budgets are allocated late and are frequently adjusted downwards after the financial year has already begun. Establishing the longterm relationships with suppliers that firms like Marks and Spencer have pioneered in the private sector is thus impossible for TECs and their training providers; they cannot expect more than non-renewable one-year contracts.

The government's avowed aim to privatise training spending as much as possible, with the Treasury taking the line that if firms want more trained workers they can pay for them is another systemic weakness. As a result, the lion's share of TEC budgets is eaten up by the programmes offered for the unemployed, which are generally poorly funded mechanisms for keeping them off the official register. There have been few additional resources for the much-heralded 'world-class' training programmes, with the Treasury instead constantly looking for efficiency gains from TEC spending on private trainers and always paring back spending levels. What little capacity there was to move money between programmes has been eliminated.

The entire structure of TECs is infected by the British disease. It is a short-term remedy. There is no independent power conferred on the local agents. There is no compulsion. There is no democratic legitimacy. The ideology says that public expenditure on it should be minimised. There is no national blueprint, so standards vary incredibly. TECs have no regulatory competence to ensure that qualifications are uniform throughout the country. They have no autonomy or revenue-raising power. The system is biased against those who are most in need, John Banham, then director-general of the CBI, warned in 1989 that there was a real risk that the TECs might wind up as reconstituted area manpower boards of the Manpower Services Commission simply administering centrally directed initiatives and, if so, the chance of keeping directors 'in the room committed for more than about 50 seconds are very slight'.[14] It was a prescient remark, for in the British context nothing else could happen. The constitutional structure allowed no other outcome and already businessmen are drifting away disillusioned by the whole exercise.

In short, training is in a mess, and highly inequitable in its distribution. Those without educational qualifications on low incomes and from unskilled families need training most. Yet it is precisely these workers who are least likely to receive training.[15]

The trouble is that for any teenager at sixteen who has no educational qualification, it is perfectly rational to get a job – if he (or she) can – rather than forego wages in order to train, because it is only by gaining NVQ at Level 3 that total lifetime earnings start to exceed those of the unskilled worker – and even then the break-even age is not until thirty-five.[16] But NVQ 3 demands intellectual skills equivalent to those needed to gain a GCSE and that is precisely the level of attainment at present beyond the unskilled. It is because they cannot obtain GCSEs that they are looking for unskilled work at sixteen.

Here the poor educational levels reached by most children in the state education sector intersects with the training system. If educational levels were higher, with better achievement in numeracy and literacy, then the system of vocational education would start from a higher base. But it does not, hence the hiatus in which the unskilled find themselves.

There is a mutual and self-destructive compact between the unskilled worker and the firm, in which it makes sense neither for the individual to invest time in training nor for the firm to offer it. As with so much else in the British system, the blind lead the blind. A teenager has to be very long-sighted indeed to want to undertake training that will raise his or her lifetime earnings only after the age of thirty-five and which, although it might help reduce the likelihood of unemployment, is for any individual an impossible risk to assess. At the same time firms are under pressure to maximise short-term profits, and incurring immediate costs for uncertain future benefits is equally irrational. In any case there is no certainty that the trained workers will stay with the firm that shoulders the costs. The rational approach, in terms of the system, is to minimise training and poach the skilled when market conditions demand it.

Yet there are strong positive returns from training and education if the *proper* levels of skill are attained. Vocational training provides a significant return for those who undertake it relative to those who have no qualifications at all. Men and women who succeed in getting at least one A level have higher lifetime earnings than if they had worked during that extra period of study and invested their surplus earnings in the stock market.[17] The pity is that the market-place does not and cannot signal clearly enough that this is the case.

If returns for individuals can be high, then the wider social returns on good education are high too, even if they are notoriously difficult to measure. If it has more skills available to it, the economy can grow more rapidly without reaching inflationary bottlenecks. With lower unemployment and a skilled labour force, social security spending is reduced, thus allowing a compensating increase in investment spending for any given level of public expenditure. Above all, productivity levels are raised as the human capital stock improves. The World Bank reports that the social returns from educational investment and training in underdeveloped countries are as high as 20 or 30 per cent; while some British estimates for post-school training have produced similar figures.[18]

The British government makes no serious attempt to compute what these social returns might be and therefore what the appropriate level of investment in human capital – people's knowledge and capacity – should be. As with so much public expenditure, the Treasury actively resists the very idea of such calculations, preferring instead to downgrade the existence of 'public goods' and 'social returns' and rely as far as possible on market judgements and individual incentives. In consequence the economy is dug further into the pit of a low skills, low wage equilibrium.

Economic efficiency is believed to arise only from individual responses to market signals; the relationship between social cohesion and wealth generation is consistently denied. But the urge to marketise every aspect of the way we live in the name of efficiency has eroded the fabric of our social life, which in its turn has weakened the economy.

NOTES

* This chapter has been adapted from, W. Hutton, *The State We're In*, Jonathan Cape, 1995, pp. 169–192.

1 Both quoted in David Vincent's *Poor Citizens* – see References.

2 Author's estimates.

3 C.V. Brown *et al.*, *Taxation and Family Labour Supply in the UK*, Department of Economics, University of Stirling.

4 *Sunday Times*, 10 July 1993.

5 Bill Robinson, 'Britain's Borrowing Problem', Social Market Foundation.

6 *Transport 2000, Myths and Facts*, Transport 2000, July 1994.

7 Maurice Mullard, *The Politics of Public Expenditure*, Routledge 1993, and calculations for the *Guardian*.

8 John Hagan in 'Paying for Equity', IPPR.

9 *Oxford Review of Economic Policy*, vol. 4, no. 3, 1988.

10 OECD Employment Outlook 1994, op. cit., p. 28.

11 S.J. Prais and Elaine Beadle, 'Pre-vocational schooling in Europe today', NIESR, 1991, p. 36.

12 ibid.

13 Robert Bennett, Peter Wicks and Andrew McCoshan, *Local Empowerment and Business Services*, UCL Press, 1994.

14 ibid.

15 Francis Greene, 'Training: Inequality and Inefficiency' in *Paying for Inequality*, see Glynn and Miliband in References.

16 Bennett, Wicks and McCoshan, op cit., pp. 139–41.

17 R. Bennett, H. Glennerster and Nevison 'Investing in Skills: To stay or not to stay on', *Oxford Review of Economic Policy*, vol. 8, no. 2, pp. 130–45.

18 G. Psacharopoulus and R. Layard (see References), pp. 485–503.

REFERENCES

R. Bennett, H. Glennerster and D. Nevison, 'Investing in Skill; To stay on or not to stay on', in *Oxford Review of Economic Policy*, vol. 8, no. 2, 1992.

Robert Bennett, Peter Wicks and Andrew McCoshan, *Local Empowerment and Business Services*, UCL Press, 1994.

C.V. Brown *et al.*, *Taxation and Family Labour Supply in Great Britain*, University of Stirling, 1986.

David Finegold and David Soskice, 'The Failure of Training in Great Britain: Analysis and Prescription' in *Oxford Review of Economic Policy*, vol. 4, no. 3, 1988.

Andrew Glyn and David Miliband, *Paying for Inequality*, IPPR/Rivers Oram Press, 1994.

John Hagan, 'Crime Inequality and efficiency' in 'Paying for Inequality' pp. 80–99.

Will Hutton, *The State We're In*, Jonathan Cape, 1995.

Maurice Mullard, *The Politics of Public Expenditure*, Routledge, 1993.

G. Psacharopoulus and R. Layard, 'Human Capital and Earnings; British evidence and a critique', in *Review of Economic Studies*, vol. 46, 1979, pp. 485–503.

Bill Robinson, 'Britain's Borrowing Problem', Social Market Foundation Report, no. 4, 1993.

David Vincent, *Poor Citizens; the state and the poor in twentieth-century Britain*, Longman, 1991.

14

A NEW INTERNATIONAL DIVISION OF LABOUR?*

Peter Braham

As a rule, the discussion of employment prospects for migrant labour in the metropolis has been conducted in domestic terms. Most attention has been paid to questions of racial discrimination on the one hand, and labour market segmentation on the other. Conversely, little attention has been devoted to the connections between international migration of labour and international movements of capital. Yet, as suggested in the previous section, changing attitudes towards the recruitment of foreign workers are strongly related to mobility of capital in general and to the operations of multinational corporations (MNCs) in particular.

As their name suggests, MNCs can operate 'geocentrically', planning the location of their production and the pattern of their investment according to the balance of advantage across the whole capitalist world economy. For example, in the short-term these geocentric MNCs have the ability to increase the level of production in one country at the expense of another and in the longer term they could even shift the entire balance of their production between countries. The importance of MNCs can be illustrated by the fact that something like two-fifths of international trade occurs *within* firms, a proportion that becomes even higher if we take into account the flows between companies and their partners in subcontracting agreements. This and other considerations causes some observers to visualize national economies as mere organic elements within an all-embracing world system (e.g. Fröbel *et al.*, 1980, p.8).

In this chapter our interest is not, however, in the pursuit of comparative advantage in general but in the way in which production is located to take advantage of differential wage rates (and by implication of the social and economic conditions which influence these wage rates). We shall explore this further by examining the idea of a 'new international division of labour' (NIDL) developed by Fröbel *et al.* (1980). NIDL draws attention to the impact of MNCs, but its specific purpose is to point to the development of a world market in which manufacturing production (services are not addressed in their thesis) can be divided up into fragments and located in any industrialized or *less developed* part of the world, depending on where the most profitable combination of labour and capital can be obtained. Though this analysis is strong on contemporary empirical detail, it also presents a historical contrast between (i) a 'classical' international division of labour, in which a minority of industrialized countries produced manufactured goods and less developed countries were integrated into the world economy solely as producers of food and raw materials, and (ii) NIDL, in which the traditional 'bisection' of the world economy is undermined (Fröbel *et al.* 1980, pp.44–5).

In brief, what NIDL entails is the shutting down of certain types of manufacturing operations in industrially advanced countries (IACs), and the subsequent opening up of these same operations in the foreign subsidiaries of the same company. In Fröbel *et al.*'s view, the Federal German garment and textile industries represent one of the best examplars of this process (though these industries in other IACs too have, in most cases, drastically cut production at traditional sites of manufacture as output became less competitive in world markets), and an archetypal instance of it is that 'Trousers for the Federal German market are no longer produced for example in Mönchengladbach, but in the Tunisian subsidiary of the same Federal German company' (Fröbel *et al.*, 1980, p.9).

The extent to which for manufacturing the most profitable combination of labour and capital is no longer to be found in the IACs is frequently explained with reference to a supposed crisis of Fordist production at the 'centre' [. . .]. However we should not underestimate the extent to which the optimum location for production shifts away from the centre in response to the erosion of the *initial* advantages derived by IACs from the employment of imported labour. Thus, as action by trade unions on behalf of immigrant workers, action by immigrant workers on their own behalf, or the beneficial effects of health and safety legislation combine to improve the pay and conditions of immigrant labour, so the advantages of decamping to areas of lowcost labour – particularly for firms in labour-intensive spheres – become ever more appealing. It is therefore not surprising to discover that the industries that once expanded by using immigrant workers, or those industries which forestalled decline by the same means, were in the forefront of the drive to relocate production, often to the same countries from which their imported workers originated.

[. . .]

Fröbel *et al.* refer to the creation of a virtually inexhaustible and easily exploitable supply of labour in developing countries, and elsewhere in their book they specify the characteristics of this labour force and the conditions under which these workers are employed. According to Lipietz, most of the jobs that are created in the developing countries involve 'Taylorism' rather than 'Fordism' – and 'primitive Taylorism' at that. [. . .] What he means by this is that the sort of jobs that are relocated – mostly in textiles and electronics – are not linked by any automatic machine system, yet they are fragmented and repetitive and thus labour-intensive in the strictest sense of the term (Lipietz, 1987, p.74).

It is no wonder then that the preferred labour force in this environment is invariably female: this is not simply because in developing countries, as in the IACs, the price of female labour-power is lower, and often very much lower, than that of male labour-power: it also reflects beliefs about the intensity with which women may work when sitting at a sewing machine in textile production or in an electronics factory. The ideological character of these beliefs can be gauged from a variety of sources. For example, an article in the *Far Eastern Economic Review* stated that:

> Most manufacturers prefer female workers because they have a longer attention span than males and can adjust more easily to long hours on the assembly line. In addition they are willing to accept lower pay and are said to have more agile hands, which is especially important in electronics.

> (2 July 1976: quoted in Fröbel *et al.*, 1980, p.348)

And in a feature on Mauritius in the *Financial Times* it was stated that:

There has been some criticism of the fact that most zone industries, especially in the textile and electronic factories, employ mainly women. Some 85 per cent are women, and efforts are being made to switch the trend . . . [This] is not necessarily due to the fact that women in Mauritius receive lower wages than men, but rather because industrialists have found that women are more adaptable than men to most of the skills required.

(18 June 1976: quoted in Fröbel et al., 1980. p.348]

The role of female labour in what Fröbel et al. call 'world market factories', and in particular the way in which the domestic division of labour is seen to prepare them for this role (women are referred to in another Malaysian investment brochure as being qualified 'by both nature and tradition' for work on the assembly line requiring great manual dexterity) is further clarified by this impression gained on a visit to a British-owned Malaysian factory which assembled integrated circuit boards:

. . . well qualified young women who, whilst awaiting their parent-chosen bridegroom, work on flow lines doing minutely routinized assembly tasks under the supervision of generally less or equally qualified males. The latter have what they regard as a career in a 'high tech' industry: the former seem well aware of their subjugation to market, domestic and religiously sanctified hierarchy.

(Loveridge, 1987, p.185)

Though Fröbel et al. emphasize the contrast between the old international division of labour and the new, they see the latter as deepening rather than reversing the historical underdevelopment of lesser developed countries (LDCs): what applied to their agriculture and to mining is now replicated in the industrial sector. In their view there is no discernible transfer of technology. In part, this is because the technology being employed is generally simple (and in any case is dependent on the expertise of foreigners), but it is also because the skills acquired by the workforce in world market factories are seen as minimal because training rarely lasts for more than a few weeks. For these and other reasons, no significant improvement is envisaged in either the material conditions of the population or in its level of skill: only a fraction of the population is employed – at very low wage levels – while the remainder forms a permanent reserve army. In addition to this, Fröbel et al. see world market factories remaining as industrial enclaves, unconnected to the local economy except in so far as the latter provides new labour to be freshly trained when the existing labour force is discarded (Fröbel et al., 1980, p.6).

There are, nevertheless, a number of criticisms to be made of this general thesis. First, Phizacklea contends that the German pattern of relocating the production of garments in the way described by Fröbel et al. was not replicated on the same scale in the UK: in Britain, similar ends were often achieved by subcontracting production to inner-city, secondary sector firms. However, though this strategy was indeed widely adopted in the UK, it should be noted that the structure of the UK garment industry is diverse: textile MNCs exist alongside inner-city sweatshops. And if we examine the conduct of British MNCs such as Coats Patons we see that, just like their German counterparts, their response to being undercut by imports from developing countries was to move much of their own production to such countries in order to take advantage of lower labour costs. (According to a report in the *Financial Times*, in 1981 comparative labour costs for Coats Patons were as low as 10 per cent of British levels in the Phillipines and 6 per cent in Indonesia (*Financial Times*, 29 June 1981)).

A second criticism is that NIDL theorists have exaggerated the scale of the relocation of production, for expressed as a proportion of world-wide industrial output, that of the Third World remains small. There is some truth in this, but what may be of more significance for

NIDL theorists is that in the 1970s and 1980s the employment forces of MNCs in their home countries fell quite markedly as world-wide economic activity slackened, whereas their employment levels fell much less or even expanded in LDCs (Thrift, 1988, p.34).

Thirdly, some commentators (e.g. Jenkins, 1984, and Lipietz, 1987) have argued that where MNCs do relocate production they are as likely, if not more likely, to do so to establish a market position in the economy in question as to be in pursuit of cheap labour.

Though these are powerful criticisms, advocates of NIDL were generally well aware that the amount of direct foreign investment in LDCs was limited. What they sought to draw attention to was the likelihood that, given the three preconditions identified by Fröbel *et al.*, future flows of such investment would escalate, attracted in particular by the prospect of cheap labour. Thus, the path established by the relocation of garment and textile production would be followed by other industries, notably the car component industry. The logic of this argument is that MNCs have in their operations transcended national boundaries. But what this logic overlooks is that reducing direct labour costs – whether by relocation or otherwise – is only one route to competitive advantage, and perhaps one of diminishing importance. An alternative approach is to increase labour productivity by means of technical innovation. And in achieving this objective, as Porter argues, the role of the national environment is profoundly important: 'It shapes the way opportunities are perceived, how specialized skills and resources are developed, and the pressures on firms to mobilize resources in rapid and efficient ways . . . Globalization makes nations more, not less, important' (Porter, 1990, p.736).

[. . .]

NOTE

* This chapter has been adapted from, Braham, P. (1992) 'A new international division of labour', *Political and Economic Forms of Modernity*, Polity Press in association with The Open University.

REFERENCES

Fröbel, F., Heinrichs, J. and Drey, O. (1980) *The New International Division of Labour*, New York, Cambridge University Press.

Jenkins, R. (1984) 'Divisions over the international division of labour', *Capital and Class*, no. 22, pp.28-57.

Lipietz, A. (1987) *Mirages and Miracles: The Crisis of Global Capitalism*, London, Verso.

Loveridge, R. (1987) 'Social accommodations and technological transformations: the case of gender', in Lee, G. and Loveridge, R. (eds) *The Manufacture of Disadvantage*, Milton Keynes, Open University Press.

Porter, M. (1990) *The Competitive Advantage of Nations*, London, Macmillan.

Thrift, N. (1988) 'The geography of international economic disorder', in Massey, D. and Allen, J. (eds) (1988).

15

CULTURE AND MANAGEMENT*

Rosalind Armson, John Martin, Susan Carr, Roger Spear and Tony Walsh

CULTURAL DIFFERENCES IN ATTITUDES AND VALUES

Clearly, [. . .] cultural differences are important and need to be considered when operating in organizations in different cultures. [. . .]

The major systematic study of work-related attitudes described here was carried out by Dr Geert Hofstede, a Dutch social psychologist (Hofstede, 1980). It was based on two questionnaire surveys which produced a total of over 116,000 responses from 40 countries, making it by far the largest organizationally-based study ever carried out. The respondents were all employees of a multinational corporation, IBM, which operates in over a hundred countries in the world. For greater comparability, only the sales and service employees of IBM were considered. The data were collected in thirty-nine countries, in each of which the IBM subsidiary was staffed entirely by indigenous employees. All types of employee in the sales and service departments were surveyed (unskilled workers, professional scientists, top managers, etc.). In each country, the local language was used; the questionnaire was translated into twenty different languages. A Yugoslav self-managed organization was also included in the survey. (At this stage, Yugoslavia was a communist economy with state enterprises, participative self-managed enterprises and small private businesses.) Although not a subsidiary of IBM, this self-managed organization marketed and serviced IBM products.

The survey design enabled several factors to be controlled. All the respondent organizations were doing the same tasks (selling and servicing IBM products) within the same general overall framework. Thus the technology and task content, and some of the formal procedures, were the same. Age categories and gender composition were similar; only the nationalities differed. The differences in attitudes and values could therefore be said to be related to cultural differences rather than organizational ones. The survey was repeated, with stable results, underlining the cultural nature of the differences found.

Hofstede identified four basic dimensions of the differences between national cultures. Each of the forty national cultures studied could be rated from high to low on each of the four *cultural dimensions*, and could thus be given a distinctive classification.

The four dimensions are shown in Table 15.1.

Table 15.1 Hofstede's four dimensions

Rating	High	Low
power–distance	distant	close
uncertainty–avoidance	risk-avoiders	risk-takers
individualism	individualist	collectivist
masculinity–femininity	masculine	feminine

Some typical survey questions are shown in Insert 1.

INSERT 1 SAMPLE QUESTIONS FOR HOFSTEDE'S CULTURAL DIMENSIONS

A Power–distance

(i) How frequently in your experience, does the following problem occur: Employees being afraid to express disagreement with their manager:

- very frequently
- frequently
- sometimes
- seldom
- very seldom

(ii) Which type of manager would you prefer to work for:

- one who makes decisions and then tells staff
- one who makes decisions and explains reasons fully to staff
- one who consults with staff before making decisions

B Uncertainty–avoidance

(i) Company rules should not be broken – even when employees think it is in the company's best interests:

- strongly agree
- agree
- undecided
- disagree
- strongly disagree

(ii) How long do you think you will continue working for this company?

- till I retire
- more than five years
- 2–5 years
- up to two years

C Individualism

(i) How important is it to you to have a job which leaves you sufficient time for your personal or family life?

- of utmost importance
- very important
- of moderate importance
- little importance
- very little or no importance

(ii) How important to you are training opportunities to improve your skills or to learn new skills?

- very little or no importance
- little importance
- moderate importance
- very important
- utmost importance

D Masculinity–femininity

(i) How important is it to you to have an opportunity for high earnings?

- utmost importance
- very important
- moderate importance
- little importance
- very little or no importance

(ii) How important is it to you to work with people who cooperate well with one another?

- very little or no importance
- little importance
- moderate importance
- very important
- utmost importance

The power–distance dimension

The power–distance dimension is concerned with how far the culture encourages superiors to exercise power. In high power–distance cultures such as the Philippines or India, the exercise of power is what being a boss means. Inequality is accepted: 'a place for everyone and everyone in his or her place'. Subordinates consider superiors to be different kinds of people; indeed, it is felt that those in power should try to *look* as powerful as possible. In addition there is latent conflict between the powerful and the powerless. Other people can rarely be trusted because they pose potential threats to one's power; having power over someone, or being dependent on someone, are the bases for working relationships.

In low power–distance cultures such as Austria or Israel, superiors and subordinates consider each other to be colleagues and have values that mean that inequality in society should be minimized. So in low power–distance cultures, those in power have to try to look *less* powerful than they are and, since a latent harmony exists, trust is possible. Superiors are accessible because organization members are interdependent.

In high power–distance cultures, employees are frequently afraid to express disagreement, and prefer to work for managers who take decisions (and responsibility) and tell them what to do. In low power–distance cultures employees are seldom afraid to disagree, and expect to be consulted before decisions are made.

The uncertainty–avoidance dimension

This dimension concerns the degree to which the culture encourages risk-taking. All organizations, in all countries, face environmental change and uncertainty and try to adapt to them. Hofstede found that there was a considerable range across cultures in peoples' attitudes to risk and their ability to tolerate uncertainty.

In strong uncertainty-avoidance cultures like Greece and Portugal, people feel threatened by uncertain situations, and experience greater anxiety and stress under these circumstances. This is countered by hard work, career stability and intolerance of deviancy. There is a search for ultimate values and a great respect for age. In a weak uncertainty–avoidance culture like Denmark and Singapore, life's inherent uncertainty is more easily accepted. Each day is taken as it comes so people experience less stress. There is less need for rules and people take a very pragmatic view of keeping or changing the existing rules. In strong uncertainty–avoidance cultures, employees agree that rules should not be broken and look forward to staying with the firm until they retire.

The individualism–collectivism dimension

This dimension concerns the degree to which the culture encourages individual, as opposed to collectivist or group, concerns. In an individualist culture such as the USA or Britain, identity is based on the individual. The emphasis is on individual initiative or achievement and everyone is supposed to take care of themselves plus only their immediate family. Everybody has the right to a private life and opinion, and may well have only a calculated involvement with the work organization. A collectivist culture such as Pakistan or Peru is characterized by a much tighter social framework, where people are members of extended families or clans which protect them and which, in return, expect loyalty from them. The emphasis is on belonging and the aim is to be a good member. This is in striking contrast to the individualist culture where the ideal is to be a good leader. The collectivist involvement with the work organization is a willingly accepted duty, and there is a belief in the value of group decisions. The value standards applied to members of one's own group, clan or organization can differ considerably from those applied to others.

In the individualist culture it is very important to have time for personal and family life. Job training carries much less value, since it increases commitment to the company. In a collectivist culture the opposite views hold and employees value good physical working conditions, while personal challenge in work is of little importance.

The masculinity–femininity dimension

The final dimension of differentiation between cultures is based on gender stereotypes. Hofstede calls one end 'masculinity' to contrast with 'femininity' at the other. In 'masculine' cultures like Australia and Italy, performance is what counts; money and material standards are important; ambition is the driving force. Big and fast are beautiful, 'machismo' is admired. In 'feminine' cultures like the Netherlands and Sweden, it is the quality of life that matters, people and the environment are important, service provides motivation, small is beautiful and unisex is attractive. As might be expected, a major difference between the cultures at the two ends of this dimension is the behaviours expected of men and women.

In 'masculine' cultures the sex roles are clearly differentiated. Men are expected to be assertive and dominating; women are expected to be caring and nurturing. A dominant woman in a 'masculine' culture is regarded as unfeminine – although she is allowed to be manipulative in the background. In 'feminine' cultures the sex roles in society are more flexible, and there is a belief in equality between the sexes. It is not considered 'unmasculine' for a man to take a caring role.

It is very important in a masculine culture to have the opportunity to achieve high earnings, but of little importance to work with a cooperative group, while in the feminine culture the reverse is the case on both these issues. In addition, feminine cultures value living in a pleasant area, and put little value on gaining recognition for a good job done.

Interpreting the dimensions

Equipped with measurements which locate the forty cultures along the four dimensions, Hofstede produced a set of cultural maps of the world. Two points have to be emphasized in interpreting Hofstede's results. The first is that the descriptions given in the previous section refer to the extremes of the dimensions, to make the concepts clearer. But in practice the cultures are spread out along the scales. So in interpreting the results you should not think in terms of dichotomies. Cultures should not be thought of as *only* 'masculine like Italy' or 'feminine like Sweden'. There are many countries in between: Belgium exactly in the centre; Britain on the masculine side, France on the feminine side. Similarly with uncertainty–avoidance: Japan is very high on this dimension and Singapore is very low, but Thailand is in between, as are West Germany, Greece (moderately high) and Denmark (moderately low).

The second point to remember is that the values given for the various dimensions are averages for all respondents in a particular country. Characterizing a national culture does not mean that *everyone* in that country has *all* the characteristics ascribed to that culture. There are bound to be many individual variations: there are many Japanese risk-takers and many Singaporeans who avoid uncertainty; many Filipinos with low power–distance values and many Israelis with high power–distance attitudes. What the scales do is to describe the common values of the central core of the culture. These common values come about through the socialization of people who are conditioned by similar life experiences and similar education. Although these factors do not make everybody the same, a country's nationals do share a cultural character – which is more clearly visible to foreigners than to themselves.

Classifying cultures by the dimensions

Table 15.2 shows a classification of cultures arranged according to Hofstede's forty dimensions. The forty cultures have been categorized into one of eight 'clusters', by means of a statistical technique known as 'cluster analysis'. This identifies clusters of cultures which are as alike each other as possible while being as different as possible from the cultures assigned to other groups. The clusters were formed entirely on the basis of the answers to the questions on the four work values and the scores on the four dimensions calculated from them. The area names were given *after* the clusters had emerged from the analysis.

The first thing that strikes me about this classification is that it groups cultures which seem to belong together in geographical, linguistic and historical terms. The two exceptions to this are Italy (put in the Germanic group) and the former Yugoslavia (put in the less-developed Latin cluster). The reasons for this need further exploration, but in general the relationship to historical development is most impressive. This gives the whole exercise credibility, since it is from these characteristics that we would expect work attitudes to

Table 15.2 Hofstede's country clusters and their characteristics

	Power-distance	Uncertainty-avoidance	Individualism-collectivism	Masculinity-femininity	
I: More developed Latin	high	high	high	medium	Argentina, Belgium, Brazil, France, Spain
II: Less developed Latin	high	high	low	a range	Chile, Columbia, Mexico, Peru, Portugal, Venezuela, Yugoslavia
III: More developed Asian	medium	high	medium	high	Japan
IV: Less developed Asian	high	low	low	medium	Hong Kong, India, Pakistan, Philippines, Singapore, Taiwan, Thailand
V: Near Eastern	high	high	low	medium	Greece, Iran, Turkey
VI: Germanic	low	high	medium	high	Austria, Germany, Israel, Italy, Switzerland, South Africa
VII: Anglo	low	low/medium	low	high	Australia, Canada, Ireland, New Zealand, United Kingdom, USA
VIII: Nordic	low	low/medium	medium	low	Denmark, Finland, Netherlands, Norway, Sweden

Notes: The scores on the last two characteristics (individualism–collectivism and masculinity–feminism) are based on the first polarity. For example, high = high individualism and low = low individualism and low = high collectivism.

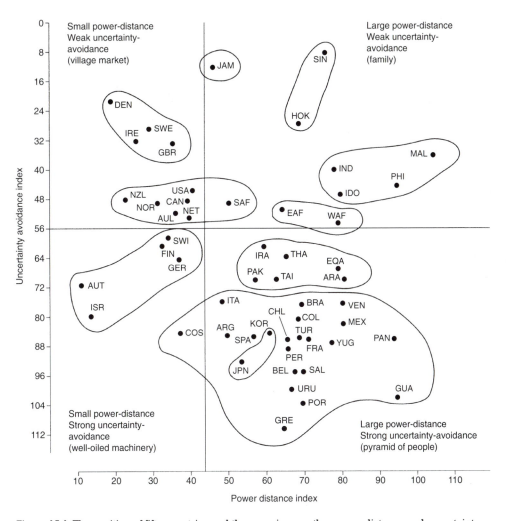

Figure 15.1 The position of fifty countries and three regions on the power-distance and uncertainty-avoidance dimensions

Key: ARA Arab World, ARG Argentina, AUL Australia, AUT Austria, BEL Belgium, BRA Brazil, CAN Canada, CHL Chile, COL Colombia, COS Costa Rica, DEN Denmark, EAT East Africa, EQA Equador, FIN Finland, FRA France, GBR Great Britain, GER Germany, GRE Greece, GUA Guyana, HOK Hong Kong, IDO Indonesia, IND India, IRA Iraq, IRE Ireland, ISR Israel, ITA Italy, JAM Jamaica, JPN Japan, KOR Korea, MAL Malaya, MEX Mexico, NET Netherlands, NOR Norway, NZL New Zealand, PAK Pakistan, PAN Panama, PER Iran, PHI Philippines, POR Portugal, SAF South Africa, SAL San Salvador, SIN Singapore, SPA Spain, SWE Sweden, SWI Switzerland, TAI Taiwan, THA Thailand, TUR Turkey, URU Uruguay, USA United States of America, VEN Venezuela, WAF West Africa, YUG Yugoslavia.

Source: Hofstede, 1994

derive. The results suggest that culture really does matter in relation to work attitudes, since the differences show up so clearly and systematically.

The reasons underlying the patterns are complex, but a couple of plausible explanations include:

- The way that low power–distance seems to be characteristic of the 'protestant' Germanic, Anglo and Nordic countries, whereas most of the rest have high power–distance.
- The tendency for developing countries to have lower individualism than the more developed countries probably reflects their more collective orientation.

Since a culture's work-related values are so distinctive and different, it might be expected that their processes and behaviour would be distinctive too. Hofstede argues very strongly that we should not expect the same conceptions and prescriptions about management, for example, to be appropriate in all these culture areas. Management needs to be culture-specific, since each group would have its own implicit model of organizational functioning. If you consider organizing and managing anything – a jumble sale, a football club for young people, a new project at work, Hofstede suggests that you need to determine the answer to two fundamental questions:

- Who has the power to decide what?
- What rules or procedures will be allowed to attain the desired end?

The dimension of power–distance influences the answer to the first question, and the uncertainty–avoidance dimension, the second. If different countries are mapped onto a graph of these two dimensions, the four quadrants represent different forms of organization (see Figure 15.1).

The less developed Asian group, for example, with its high power–distance and low uncertainty–avoidance, would tend to cope with problems by turning for help to a powerful leader or father figure, and to subscribe implicitly to a metaphor of the organization as a family. By contrast, in the Germanic group (low power–distance, high uncertainty–avoidance) organization members would look for ways of coping by designing rules and procedures which, if carried out, would avoid the need for personal exercise of power, the implicit metaphor here being one of a well-oiled machine. In the Anglo group (low power–distance, low to medium uncertainty–avoidance) the implicit metaphor might be a village market in which coping is achieved flexibly by continuous bargaining among members. In the high power–distance, high uncertainty–avoidance culture of the Latin and Near Eastern groups, both the power relationships and the work processes will tend to be prescribed, and the implicit organizational metaphor will be a hierarchy or pyramid of people.

Hofstede concludes that we should not expect convergence of leadership styles or management practices across different cultural forms, since they are dependent on the implicit model of organizational functioning prevailing in the particular culture. The implicit metaphor is the result of the socialization and mental conditioning to which we are exposed from birth. Changes in culture are, therefore, inevitably very slow.

NOTE

* This chapter has been adapted from, The Open University (1995) T245 *Managing in Organizations*, Block 4 *Interorganizational Relations*, Unit 13 'Environmental Influences', Milton Keynes, The Open University.

REFERENCES

Hofstede, G. (1980) *Culture's Consequences: International Differences in Work Related Values*, Sage Publications.

Hofstede, G. (1994) *Cultures and Organizations*, Harper Collins, Glasgow.

SECTION 3: THE STATE

INTRODUCTION

You should already be aware from previous sections of this book that the role of the state with regard to business has been subject to much scrutiny and interpretation over many centuries. Recent debates about globalisation have thrown up some apparently rather extraordinary arguments that we are witnessing the 'end of the nation-state'. Great caution is needed when approaching these arguments as they in turn unearth other debates about what we mean by both the nation and the state and whether the two are intrinsically linked. I have deliberately avoided using this linked phrase in order to concentrate on what most business decision-makers would consider to be the essence of their relationship with the state – the legislative rules within which they must operate. In chapter 16, Howells provides an overview of both the creation and the operation of the law and the institutions involved in those processes. Although her focus is the English legal system, she makes some interesting comparisons with Scotland and clearly explains the influence of the European Union system over all its member 'states'. The point here is that the state, as a group of institutions and a body of law, is constantly evolving, simply because of the very dynamic nature of the law.

Businesses are one of a number of stakeholder groups within a state who are clearly affected by the law, and who consequently may seek to influence it. Whilst the government of a state is nominally open to influence by all these stakeholder groups, the degree of influence depends on the power held by the group. Businesses, because of the links between their performance and economic performance (and consequently a government's popularity!), clearly hold considerable power. Chapter 17 by Coates examines the concept of power and chapter 18 by McGrew looks at the ways in which power is structured within states. The balance of power and influence which emerges between governments and business interests within a state is dependent on a number of factors. These are explored in chapters 19 and 20. In chapter 19 Min Chen compares the development of government-business relations in two states which until very recently were considered economically successful – Japan and Korea. In chapter 20 on the other hand Bennett outlines the more formal structuring of influence within the European Union.

In the final chapter of this section, McGrew summarises and evaluates the argument that globalisation is a significant threat to the legitimacy of the state. Given the growing economic power of multi-national and 'global' corporations, in terms of the relative influence of their investments and employment potential on an economy, there can be little doubt that government attitudes must be influenced by this. However this may not necessarily constitute the end of the state, merely the redrawing of its boundaries.

16

AN OVERVIEW OF THE ENGLISH LEGAL SYSTEM*

Carol Howells

Law is a constantly changing and evolving subject that has a daily effect on both individual and business relationships. Providing an overview of such a dynamic subject is therefore not an easy task as the detailed provisions are constantly developing and changing. The overview that follows therefore concentrates on the creation, enforcement and nature of law. A few specific examples have been used to illustrate these areas. The aim is to provide a framework and working knowledge of the law-making institutions and raise awareness of the context in which legal rules affect both personal and business activities.

THE NATURE OF LAW

Before considering the sources and systems of law enforcement, it is necessary to consider what the term law itself means. Modern society requires legal rules to function smoothly; individuals and businesses require legal rules for certainty and democratic government requires legal rules to enable it to function effectively. As society has become more complex there has been an increase in both the number of laws made (especially through statutory instruments and directives) and their detail.

Originally many laws developed from a moral code (which in turn had developed to regulate society) but as society has advanced, rules have developed as a result of political decisions. Laws now exist for a mixture of reasons. What then sets the idea of law apart from a set of rules? Law is effectively a set of rules governing human behaviour enforced using a system of recognised control. In most countries the system of recognised control is the court system. The court system will both oversee the development of the law, change and enforce it. This need for enforcement of existing laws has though of course to be balanced by the need to achieve justice.

What are the aims of the law? These are, of course, many and varied and will depend upon the legal jurisdiction under discussion. In a democratic society the aims might include protection, punishment, codification, resolution, arbitration, development, reform and justice. The list however is endless and it is interesting to compare the reasons for the existence of laws and the aims of those laws.

Since 1802 various statutes have been passed in England and Wales to establish standards for specific work places. Originally the aims of such legislation related to the employment of young children in the mills and mines. As society moved through the industrial revolution these aims changed and more statutes were introduced to cover specific industries with the focus moving towards the safety of the workplace. The 1974 Health and Safety at Work etc. Act contains a series of general duties, which apply to workplaces (with some exceptions). The Act was based on recommendations contained in a report on health and safety at work. The report found that the pre-1974 system was too complex and fragmented. Specific workplaces were covered so many did not have the benefit of statutory protection. General duties are now imposed on employers, employees and the self employed which are concerned with accident prevention.

CLASSIFICATION OF LAW

There are many ways in which law can be classified: common law; civil law; public law; private law; domestic law; criminal law; international law, to name a few. Here the differences between the common law and civil law systems will be considered and the specific distinction between English civil and criminal law (English law here is used to describe the laws of England and Wales) will be explored.

It is important to be aware of the context in which the expressions "civil law" and "common law" are used as they can mean different things in different contexts. Civil law, for example, may mean a system of law based on Roman law, any part of a country's laws that are not criminal or any law that is not military law. Common law, for example, may mean the whole system of English law, may be used to refer to case law or the law developed by English judges in the early English common law courts. Always be aware of the context in which the expressions are used.

The civil and common law systems place Scotland in an interesting position. Scotland through its historical alliances with France and the Netherlands has a civil law system. As a result of the 1707 Act of Union however, that system became increasingly influenced by the common law system and the UK Parliament. Many statutes enacted by the UK Parliament prior to devolution applied indiscriminately throughout the UK. The Scottish civil law system could therefore be said to have been adulterated. Each country has however borrowed quite liberally from the law of the other. Certain principles of Scottish law are identical to those of English law and the leading case in English law on establishing liability for negligence is in fact a Scottish case.

Common law and civil law

Two of the major systems of law that have evolved are the Roman law system and the English law system. These systems form the basis of many legal jurisdictions. Jurisdictions basing their system on Roman law are said to have a civil law system and those basing their systems on English law are said to have a common law system.

It is important to distinguish between these two systems because of the differing ways in which law is made and implemented. Each system has a fundamentally different approach to the creation and interpretation of statutes for example. Civil law creates statutory law (usually called codes) by laying down a series of broad principles and leaving the judges to interpret what they mean. In this the judges may seek assistance from previously decided cases involving similar issues and from the opinions of eminent commentators. The method of interpretation looks at the purpose of the provision and interprets the words in such a way as to give effect to the purpose. This is often called the purposive approach. The aim is to apply the spirit rather than the letter of the law.

Common law was originally used to refer to law that was common to the whole country in contrast to law that could vary with local customs. Common law originally consisted mainly of principles established by judges in cases brought before them which judges then applied to similar cases arising in the future. Statutory law also forms part of the common law system and has become increasingly important. Where an English court is required to interpret a statute (Act of Parliament) it will refer to rules of statutory interpretation that have been developed by judges. There are three rules: the literal, golden and mischief rules. The literal rule is used to give the word its ordinary natural meaning. The golden rule is used where the literal rule would produce an absurdity or inconsistency and the mischief rule looks at the defect that the statute was intended to correct. The court will also consider the use of other sources, for example, dictionaries, some government publications and Hansard.

The 1964 case of Adler v. George illustrates the use of the golden rule. Under the 1920 Official Secrets Act it was an offence to obstruct HM Forces "in the vicinity of" a prohibited place. The defendants had obstructed HM Forces in the prohibited place. The Court held that they were guilty of the offence.

European Community law, is drawn from the precepts of the continental civil system. Where a specific area is affected by EC law (for example employment law) legislation of the European Community is the supreme source of law. This leads to some tension in the English legal system as for domestic law (all those laws which are not affected by EC law) the English rules on statutory interpretation are used. For statutes, which have been passed in accordance with European Treaty obligations, the purposive approach must be used. The English courts have therefore had to adjust to using a new and unfamiliar method of interpretation. As the English courts have become used to using the purposive approach they have been more willing to use it for the interpretation of domestic legislation.

The 1981 Transfer of Undertaking Regulations were passed to give effect to EEC Directive 77/187. These were aimed at protecting the employment of persons who are employed in a business that is transferred to another business. The regulations provided that the contract of those persons employed by the transferring business immediately before the transfer should transfer to the new owner. In a 1986 Court of Appeal decision the words "immediately before" were given their literal meaning and it was held that employees dismissed three hours before the transfer took place were not employed immediately before. In a later case, the House of Lords adopted the purposive approach and held that the words "immediately before" should be interpreted in a manner which enabled the regulations effectively to fulfil the purpose for which they were made, i.e. that of giving effect to the aims of EEC Directive 77/187.

English civil and criminal law

One of the main classifications of law used in the English legal system is civil and criminal law. Criminal law consists of crimes which may be defined as "a legal wrong for which the offender is liable to be prosecuted and if convicted punished by the State". Examples of crimes include murder (the killing of another human being with malice aforethought – a common law crime) and theft (a person is guilty of theft if he dishonestly appropriates property belonging to another, with the intention of permanently depriving the other of it – section 1 1968 Theft Act – a statutory crime). Civil law is the greater part of English law but is more difficult to define. It can be seen as that part of the law that is not criminal. Examples of civil law include the law of contract and torts, employment law, and land law. Some areas of law may encompass both civil and criminal law for example, company law (the creation of a company being governed by civil law whereas failing to file the company accounts is an aspect of criminal law).

Table 16.1

	Criminal law	*Civil law*
The laws deal with	Preservation of society and upholding law and order	Creation of rights and obligations
	Relationship of the individual and the state	Relationship between individuals
Breach of the laws leads to	Prosecution	An action
Punishment or Remedy	Various including imprisonment, fines, community sentence, penalty points	Various including damages and injunctions
Burden of Proof	Beyond reasonable doubt	On the balance of probabilities
Terminology	Prosecute, defend, punishment	Sue, claimant, defendant
Title of the case	R v. Defendant (Year) DPP v. Defendant (Year) AG's Reference	Claimant v. Defendant (Year)
Court system	Criminal Court System. Magistrate's Court, Crown Court, Divisional Court of the High Court, Court of Appeal, Criminal Division, House of Lords, European Court of Human Rights	Civil Court System. Magistrate's Court, County Court, High Court, Court of Appeal, Civil Division, House of Lords, European Court of Justice, European Court of Human Rights

SOURCES OF ENGLISH LAW

Since the passing of the European Communities Act 1972 by the UK Parliament there have been three sources of law within the UK.

1 EC law (since 1 January 1973)
2 Statute law (and delegated legislation)
3 Judicial Precedent

The English legal system has been developing over the past 700 years although it was not until 120 years ago that a countrywide court system was introduced. During this development the different sources of law have played different roles in legal development.

EC law

The UK acceded to the European Union on 1 January 1973. The European Communities Act 1972 incorporated Union law into the English domestic legal system from that date.

The accession to the European Union made a fundamental constitutional change in relation to the sources of English law. Previously the UK Parliament had been the supreme law maker: the legislative organs of the European Union now perform that role. European law affects a growing area of activity but at the moment is mainly concerned with consumer protection, restrictive trade practices, employment, agriculture and fisheries, the environment and the free movement of labour, capital and services.

The principle behind EC law is that each Member State (currently 15) shall incorporate into domestic law the principles laid down in EC law. Should the Member State fail to do so (or should the domestic legislation prove defective), the European Commission may bring infringement proceedings in the European Court of Justice. If those are successful the Member State concerned must take steps to remedy the domestic legislation.

Article 119 of the Treaty of Rome lays down the principle of equal pay for equal work. The UK interpreted this as meaning that equal pay must be given for similar work. It enacted the 1970 Equal Pay Act to give effect to this principle. A Directive was then issued in 1975 which made it clear that the principle of equal pay was wider than the UK perception: it covered not just equal pay for similar work but also equal pay for work of equal value. In 1982 the European Commission brought infringement proceedings against the UK in the European Court of Justice, alleging that the Equal Pay Act was defective in that it failed to cover work of equal value. The European Court of Justice found in the Commission's favour. As a result the UK introduced regulations in 1983 to amend the Equal Pay Act (as from 1 January 1984) so that it allowed a woman (or man, where appropriate) to claim their work was of equal value.

The main institutions of the European Union are the Council, the Commission, the European Parliament and the European Court of Justice. The Council is made up of one representative from the Government of each of the member states. Meetings may be general (when they are attended by foreign ministers) or specialised (when they are attended by ministers who are responsible for a particular area, for example agriculture). General policy decisions and community legislation are enacted (although the legislation is based upon proposals made by the Commission). The Commission consists of 15 Commissioners who are appointed by agreement amongst the governments of the member states. The

Commissioners act independently in the interests of the community and each is entrusted with a separate area of policy. The Commission is the guardian of the community treaties and also proposes new policies and laws. The Commission also has the power to initiate action against a member state for violation of a treaty article and to take proceedings against a member state before the European Court of Justice. The European Parliament represents the peoples of the member states. It was originally an advisory and supervisory body but now plays an increasingly important role in both budgetary and legislative issues. This role is likely to increase. The European Parliament may also pass a motion for censure against the Commission, which may result in the resignation of the Commissioners and the appointing of a new Commission. The European Court of Justice may hear an action which has been brought against a member state or make a ruling on the interpretation of an EC treaty or legislation made thereunder where an interlocutory reference has been made from a domestic court of a member state. In hearing the case the court is not bound by its own previous decisions although it has developed a body of consistent case law. The legal system of the European Union is, of course, based on the civil law system.

The sources of European Community law consist of primary legislation and secondary legislation. The primary legislation consists of the three Treaties, which established the communities. Those treaties are European Coal and Steel Community Treaty, the Euratom Treaty and the European Community Treaty together with the single European Act, the Treaty on European Union (1992) (Maastricht Treaty) and the Treaty on European Union 1997 (Treaty of Amsterdam). The provisions of these treaties are directly applicable in the member states without the need for further implementing legislation.

The secondary legislation consists of Regulations, Directives, decisions of the European Court of Justice and recommendations and opinions made or given by the Council or Commission. Regulations are directly applicable in the member states whereas directives have to be given legal effect by the member states themselves. In the UK a statute or statutory instrument are commonly used to implement a directive. A decision of the European Court of Justice will be binding on the member state against which the Court has found. Recommendations and opinions are not directly applicable in member states but may be given legal effect by the member state.

Directives, whilst generally not applicable in a member state can sometimes produce a direct legal effect and create legal rights without having been implemented by domestic legislation of the member state. Strict criteria have been created so this may occur only where the terms of the directive are clear, unconditional and sufficiently precise. They may also be used only in proceedings against a member state and an individual must have taken those proceedings. In order to prevent a member state from taking advantage of their failure to implement a directive there are also certain circumstances where that member state may be liable to compensate an individual who has suffered loss as a result of the non-implementation. In this situation three conditions must be fulfilled. First the purpose of the directive must be to confer rights on individuals. Secondly the nature of those rights must be identifiable from the provisions of the directive and finally there must be a direct causal link between the breach of the member state's obligation and the damage suffered.

In the 1996 case of Dillenkofer the German Federal Republic was held to be liable to compensate holidaymakers who had suffered loss that resulted from Germany's failure to implement a 1990 Council Directive on package travel holidays and tours. The Directive was intended to confer rights on individuals and clearly conferred upon purchasers of package travel a right to the reimbursement of sums already paid and repatriation costs where the travel organiser had become insolvent.

A member state that breaches a community treaty must also compensate an individual who suffers loss as a result.

Statute law

Statutes contain the main laws made by Parliament. To become law a Statute must pass through various stages in the House of Commons and House of Lords and receive Royal Assent.

The ideas for new legislation in the form of a Statute may occur for a number of reasons and may come from a number of sources. A loophole may exist in current legislation, there may be a need for codification of existing legislation, new areas of activity may need regulation, an EC directive may need implementation or a sudden emergency might occur. A new government will have made manifesto commitments, government departments will have a programme of legislation that they would like to introduce. A committee of inquiry, a Royal Commission or the Law Commission may suggest new laws. Pressure groups (interest or lobby groups) may also influence the legislative process. Individual politicians may introduce private members bills. This mix of reasons for and sources of legislation produces a variety of statutes in each parliamentary year.

A statute will begin life as a bill. The bill will have been carefully drafted by Parliamentary Counsel clause by clause. In their drafting of the Bill they need to take account of the lack of precision in language, reconciliation of conflicting demands, all possible scenarios which may occur and time pressures. Many bills are therefore significantly re-drafted before being enacted. Bills fall into one of three categories: public bills (introduced by the government and comprising the majority of legislation); private bills (for example one promoted by a local authority to meet its specific needs); and private member bills (where an MP has introduced proposals for change).

There is a formal procedure that must be followed before a bill can be enacted. This procedure takes place in both the House of Commons and the House of Lords. All bills (except money bills) may be introduced in either House. When a bill is introduced it will have its first reading. Often the bill is presented in dummy form at the table of the House and the title is read out. The bill is then deemed to have been read for the first time. The bill is then printed and published. At its second reading there is often a parliamentary debate on the principles of the bill. The debate concentrates on the principle and not the detailed content. A vote is then taken and the bill accepted or rejected. If the bill is not lost then the committee stage takes place. The committee will vary in size (and can be the whole House) but is usually a standing committee of between sixteen to fifty members (chosen to reflect the relative strength of the political parties in the House). The bill is examined in detail and proposed amendments are also considered. The bill is then reported back to the House (the report stage) and any changes introduced during the committee stage are introduced. A third reading of the bill then takes place (usually this takes place immediately after the report stage) and the debate will culminate in a vote. If the bill is not lost it then undergoes the same procedure in the other House. Once the bill passes all its stages in both Houses it receives Royal Assent (now done by a committee) and becomes a Statute. The Statute will take effect from the date of Royal Assent, from the dates of commencement set out in the statute itself or on a date to be fixed. A Statute may come partially into force so it is always important to check whether the Statute is in fact in force. The Statute will remain in force until it has expressly been repealed.

The House of Commons consists of elected members of Parliament and the House of Lords of hereditary peers (although the number has now been restricted as a result of recent reforms), life peers, judicial peers and Lords spiritual. The House of Lords is an unelected body. Until the early part of this century both Houses held an equal balance of power and this on occasion led to conflict between them. There was a convention that financial matters fell under the authority of the House of Commons but in 1909 the House of Lords rejected the Budget (Finance Bill) in breach of this convention. This lead to the Parliament Acts of 1911 and 1949. A detailed procedure was established. The Acts altered the balance of power by allowing the House of Lords a power of delay (as opposed to veto).

The Parliamentary Acts procedure is not invoked as often as might be thought. The House of Lords will only use its delaying power with caution and many of the amendments suggested to Bills are realistic and thus accepted by the House of Commons. In recent times the 1991 War Crimes Act was passed using the procedure (previously only the 1914 Government of Ireland Act and 1914 Welsh Church Act had been so passed) although the 1998 Crime and Disorder Bill was very nearly affected by the procedure. The House of Commons and House of Lords disagreed over the provision covering the age of consent for sexual intercourse between males. The House of Lords being opposed to the provision. The government removed the provision from the Bill as the Parliamentary session was near to its end. Had the provision not been removed then the whole bill would have been lost (outstanding matters cannot be transferred from one parliamentary session to another but must start afresh in the next session).

Delegated legislation is made by bodies other than Parliament. Those bodies have been given delegated power of legislation by Parliament. Common examples of such legislation include, Order in Council, Statutory Instruments and Local Byelaws. Such legislation can be produced quickly and will often cover detailed and highly complex subjects. The benefits include freeing up Parliamentary time for discussion of principles of new legislation and the use of expertise in producing detailed rules (which many Members of Parliament will lack). An increasing amount of detailed legislation is being produced but controls exist through both Parliament and the courts.

Judicial precedent

The role of the courts in the law making process has already been touched upon in the earlier discussion on statutory interpretation. Statutory interpretation occurs where there is a dispute over the true meaning of a word or section in an Act of Parliament. What happens though in an area such as contract law that is mainly governed by case law? Here the doctrine of judicial precedent must be considered.

The doctrine of judicial precedent means that a judge in deciding a case is bound to follow a ruling of law that was laid down by a higher court on a previous occasion. (The court hierarchy is not considered here but it should be noted that the House of Lords is the most senior UK appeal court and since 1966 has been able to depart from its own previous decisions.) The judge is required to find both on the facts of the particular case and the law that applies to those facts. It is the decision as to the law which forms part of the doctrine of judicial precedent. The decision on the law will contain both the ratio decidendi (the reason for the decision) and obiter dicta (things said by the way). The ratio is the ruling of law, which must be followed in subsequent cases the obiter providing persuasive authority. This persuasive authority is often used to distinguish cases. Lawyers will attempt to distinguish a case from a previous one where they do not wish the ratio to be applied.

In the 1919 case of Balfour v. Balfour a husband and wife entered into an agreement whereby the husband would pay the wife £50 every month whilst he was working abroad. They separated and the court refused to enforce the agreement. By contrast in the 1970 case of Merritt v. Merritt the court enforced a similar agreement. Here the husband and wife had separated before making the agreement.

Whilst Parliamentary legislation is supreme, considerable importance is attached to judicial precedent. Judicial precedent does give an individual judge scope to develop, extend and change the law. Judges constantly apply existing precedents to new fact situations to create new laws. Precedent creates certainty whilst also giving flexibility and can be used to serve the interests of justice. Conversely it has disadvantages as where a judge reaches an incorrect or unjust decision it must be appealed to a higher court. This can be both costly and time consuming.

In the 1992 case of R v. R the court abolished a husband's immunity from criminal liability for raping his wife (this immunity had existed for 250 years). The court had developed the common law by looking at the changes, which had taken place in society. Parliament then placed this change on a statutory footing in the 1994 Criminal Justice and Public Order Act.

LEGAL PERSONALITY

Before looking briefly at some specific areas of English law it is important to consider who may become involved in an action or prosecution within the English legal system. Rules have been developed as to whom the law will recognise as a person and specific legal consequences flow from these rules. The concept of legal personality deals with the question as to who may be entitled to claim rights and duties and creates the ideas of natural and artificial persons.

A natural person includes human beings. There are guidelines that have been developed as to when life begins and ends. However it is worth noting that a dead person may have some limited legal rights (for example the right to have their possessions disposed of according to the wishes expressed in their will). Not all natural persons have the same rights and duties. A minor (someone who is under 18 years of age) is treated differently in law and, for example, cannot own land and may only enter into certain types of contract (necessaries or contracts of employment for their benefit). A person who has been made bankrupt under the Insolvency Acts cannot act as a company director (unless they have permission of the court). A minor can pursue an action in a civil court but will act through their "next friend" or "guardian ad litem" (this will depend on whether they are the claimant or defendant). In certain circumstances (such as an action in the tort of negligence) they may wait until they reach the age of eighteen to pursue the action. The action can in effect be put on hold until they reach the age of majority. (In English law certain actions must be started within a specific time limit for example in the law of contracts within six years from the alleged breach and in the law of tort within three years of the time at which the claimant becomes aware of the damage).

There are two types of artificial person. The first is known as the corporation sole. These are rare but include the Crown and Bishops of the Church of England. When a natural person dies their belongings are transferred and are subject to certain legal rules and regulations (such as the payment of tax). When the holder of an office recognised as a corporation sole dies the office continues to exist and the belongings of the office are not transferred but they continue unchanged. The corporation aggregate is better known. They can be created by Royal Charter (e.g. the BBC), by Statute (e.g. a local authority) or under the Companies Acts (e.g. ICI, Marks and Spencer or the Body Shop). The majority are created under the Companies Acts. A corporation aggregate has limited legal liability. This means, for example, that the members of a company are only liable for the amount of money that they have invested in the company. The company has a separate legal identity (and is a separate legal entity) from its members and it is the company that is liable without limit for its own debt.

The importance of legal personality is clearly shown in the differences between a company and a partnership. Each will consist of several members but their legal liabilities are very different. The company has a separate legal personality so its members have limited liability and the company unlimited legal liability. The partnership has no separate legal personality and each individual member is liable for the acts of the partnership and the other members. This is known as joint and several liability. The consequences that follow are illustrated in the table below.

Table 16.2

	Company	*Partnership*
Separate legal Personality	Yes	No
Limited liability	Company – No Members – Yes	Partnership – No Members – No
Perpetual succession	Yes	No
Ability to act in own name	Yes	Legal Regulations on use of a Trading Name
Own land	Yes	Partners jointly own partnership property
Membership	Liability is limited to the amount invested in the company	Liability is unlimited with each partner personally responsible for the debts of the partnership in full
Formation	Formation requirements under the Companies Act	Easy to Form Partnership Act 1890 defines a partnership as a relationship between two or more people carrying on business in common with a view to making a profit

THE ENGLISH LAW OF CONTRACT

The English law of contract is based upon the doctrine of freedom to contract. The parties to a contract can choose to bind themselves to whatever terms they wish. The laws governing contract have evolved through case law although major pieces of legislation have radically altered some of the rules (e.g. Unfair Contract Terms Act 1977). A business will be involved in making contracts on a daily basis and these can range from the simpler forms of contract (purchasing a business lunch) to the more complicated (sub-contracts for supply or insurance). All these contracts will comply with the general principles of formation (although they may also have to comply with additional legal rules as in the case of employment contracts, consumer contracts or contracts for the sale of land etc.).

A contract is an agreement between two or more parties. The agreement being binding upon the parties. Most contracts do not have to be written (contracts for the sale of land or consumer credit being two of the exceptions) and can be quite easily formed. Of the many contracts formed each day few end up in court. Most are performed to the parties' satisfaction. Where a breach does occur often a compromise or settlement is reached and the cost and delay caused by a court trial avoided.

When looking at the law of contract there are several elements that need to be considered. First is the question of formation of the contract, secondly the question of the contractual terms, thirdly whether there is anything which may make the contract invalid, fourthly how the contract can be ended and finally what remedies are available should something go wrong.

The area of formation of the contract is an important one. If the contract has not been properly formed it will not exist. To be properly formed there must be an intention to create legal relations, an offer and acceptance of that offer. The offer and acceptance must be backed by consideration. Consideration is important as this fulfils the idea of the contract being a bargain between two or more parties. Consideration can be many things and must be adequate although not always of true value. The offer to contract can be made in many forms (verbally, through an advertisement, in writing or by conduct). It can also be made to different parties (an individual, a group of people or the world at large). The terms of the offer must be clear and unconditional. Those terms must have been accepted as they stand and consideration provided.

The 1893 case of Carlill v. Carbolic Smokeball Company concerned an advertisement. The Carbolic Smokeball Company manufactured a patent medicine – a "smokeball". An advertisement was placed offering £100 to any person who caught influenza after having sniffed the smokeball three times a day for two weeks. The advertisement stated that £1000 had been deposited at the Alliance Bank to show their sincerity. Mrs Carlill used the smokeball as advertised and contracted influenza. She claimed her £100 and the company refused to pay. The court held that it was possible to make an offer to the whole world and the deposit of £1000 was an indication of an intention to create legal relations. Consideration had been provided by the actual sniffing of the smokeball (the purchase price was not consideration as that supported the contract with the seller of the smokeball). A contract existed and Mrs Carlill was entitled to the £100 reward.

Once it has been established that there is a contractual agreement in existence, the terms of that contract may need to be considered. Through the terms the precise obligations of the parties can be established. Terms of the contract may be express or implied. Express terms will be those that have been specifically agreed between the parties. Implied terms often originate from a Statute such as the term satisfactory quality that is implied into contracts for the sale of goods to consumers under the 1979 Sale of Goods Act. On occasion the courts may imply a contractual term to give "business efficacy" to the agreement made between the parties.

Not all the terms of the contract will have equal importance so the courts have tended to place a term into one of three categories. A condition is a term which is said to be of the essence, that goes to the core of the contract. A warranty is a term that can be regarded as collateral to the contract. An innominate term is one that cannot be classified until the results of the breach of the terms are known. If a condition is breached the innocent party is entitled to end the contract and claim damages, if a warranty is breached only damages can be claimed. The court will decide upon the remedy where an innominate term is breached.

A contract may contain an exclusion or limitation clause. An exclusion clause is an attempt to exclude liability for a specific event. These are commonly found in contracts (e.g.

in car parks excluding liability for loss or damage). There are strict rules on the operation and validity of exclusion clauses. Limitation clauses are also common but here there is an attempt to limit liability (such as in the development of films where damage is limited to the replacement of the film). Again just because one exists does not mean that it is automatically valid. These areas are covered by both common law and statutory rules (Unfair Contract Terms Act 1979).

Once the contract and its terms have been established any element that may make the contract invalid needs to be considered. Was there a false representation that induced one of the parties to enter into the contract? Was one or even both of the parties operating under a mistaken belief? Was there undue pressure (duress) such that the contract was not entered into voluntarily, or are the purposes of the contract illegal? Any of these considerations may invalidate the contract and have to be considered carefully.

A contract may be ended in several ways. The most common is the full and proper performance of the contract. Other methods include frustration (for example where the parties contract for the hire of a hall which subsequently burns down before the planned event) or breach (where one party fails to fulfil their obligations under the contract). Damages are available where there has been breach of a contract although the courts have developed guidelines to assess the level of damages. Damages will be awarded for the loss arising from the breach of the contract and for any additional loss that was in the contemplation of the parties when the contract was made.

This is a very brief overview of the English law of contract. It is a detailed and developing subject but the examples used here clearly illustrate the role of both statute law and judicial precedent.

THE ENGLISH LAW OF TORTS

The law of torts covers a very wide area and much of the law of torts, like the law of contract, has been developed through case law. The word tort is French in origin and means a wrong. So the law of torts deals with civil (as opposed to criminal) wrongs. The rules of the law of torts have been developed to determine when one party can be compensated for the behaviour of another. It is a developing area of law but there will not automatically be a legal remedy for every wrong suffered. A claimant will only succeed if it can be shown that the defendant's action falls into a category established by the law of torts. Areas of the law of torts include occupiers' liability, trespass, nuisance, and negligence.

Occupiers' liability is governed by the Occupiers' Liability Acts of 1957 and 1984. These statutes clearly lay down the circumstances in which an occupier may be held liable if a person is injured on their property. The 1957 Act states that the occupier must take such care as is reasonable in all the circumstances to see that a visitor will be reasonably safe in using the premises for the purposes for which he is invited or permitted to be there. Merely warning of the danger will not be enough unless it is sufficient to make the visitor reasonably safe. If an occupier puts up a notice stating that liability under the Occupiers' Liability Acts is excluded that notice can be tested. The Unfair Contract Terms Act 1979 covers both contractual and tortious liability. A notice seeking to exclude liability for death or personal injury caused by negligence is void. One which seeks to exclude liability for other loss or damage caused by negligence must satisfy the requirements of reasonableness. Negligence under the Unfair Contract Terms Act 1979 will cover breach of the duty of care under the Occupiers' Liability Acts.

The 1984 Act covers the occupiers' liability to trespassers. Here the duty of common humanity is imposed. This is a lower standard than that of the 1957 Act and reflects the fact that the trespasser has not been expressly or impliedly invited onto the property.

The law of trespass covers trespass to land, persons or goods (and equivalent criminal offences exist). Trespass to the person will take place where force is directly and intentionally inflicted on another person. Force covers any physical contact from touching someone's arm to punching him or her. There is no need to prove any damage (although if there is no damage any compensation awarded will be nominal). If consent has been given to the force no action can be pursued (for example agreement to a medical operation or to shake a person's hand). Trespass to goods is an intentional and direct act of interference with goods that are in someone else's possession. An act of conversion may also take place where the goods are taken but not damaged. Trespass to land is the most commonly known example and consists of an unjustifiable interference with the possession of land.

The area of nuisance, like that of trespass, is in three categories: public nuisance; private nuisance; and statutory nuisance. Public nuisance is in effect a crime as it consists of generating harm to members of the public. Much of the behaviour amounting to a public nuisance will also be governed by criminal law (for example an obstruction of the highway or pollution of a public water supply) but where an individual pursues an action in tort they may, if certain conditions are met, be awarded damages (or obtain an injunction). A private nuisance will be committed where an individual interferes with another's use or enjoyment of land. Here conflicting interests need to be reconciled as an individual is free to do what he wishes on his land as long as he does not affect his neighbour's enjoyment of his land. A private nuisance may consist of many things (noise, dust, vibrations or the encroachment of tree roots). The duration of the nuisance must be taken into account as will the locality in which it occurred. An example of a statutory nuisance may be found in the 1990 Environmental Protection Act and may amount to a state of affairs or action that is prejudicial to health or a nuisance. (Examples include emissions of smoke and gas, premises in a state that is prejudicial to health or accumulations of animals.)

The tort of negligence is a changing and ever-growing area. All claims in tort will involve the same basic elements but some (such as psychiatric damage or pure economic loss) have additional and complex rules. To establish a claim in negligence three things must be proved: First that the defendant owed the claimant a duty of care; secondly that the duty of care had been breached; and finally that the claimant has suffered damage as a result of that breach.

To establish a duty of care: forseeability, proximity and reasonableness must be considered. The law will not impose a duty in every situation. Some situations establish a clear-cut duty (for example driver and road users, doctor and patient) whilst others need careful consideration. Mere carelessness may not be enough.

The 1932 case of Donaghue v. Stevenson established the general principles for liability in negligence. Here two friends went to a café in Paisley where one bought the other a bottle of ginger beer. Some of the ginger beer was poured and drunk. When the remaining ginger beer was poured from the bottle a decomposed snail floated into the glass. The lady suffered shock and became ill as a result. She could not take any action against the café owner, as she had not bought the drinks so she sued the manufacturers instead. The court decided that a manufacturer selling products to consumers that are not examined after manufacture owes a duty to take reasonable care to see that the consumer is not injured.

It must be established that a reasonable person in the position of the defendant could reasonably have foreseen that the other might be injured. That the defendant and the person injured were either physically close (such as a person injured in a car accident) or had a close relationship (such as a parent and child or manufacturer and consumer). That it was just and fair to impose liability (in certain circumstances where a large number of individuals may pursue an action the courts may be reluctant to impose liability).

Various factors will be considered in establishing whether the duty of care has been breached. A person will be regarded as negligent where they fail to reach the standard of conduct that a reasonable person would reach. Factors that are taken into account include the likelihood of the harm, the risk of serious injury and the actual cost of preventing the harm.

In the 1951 case of Bolton v. Stone a batsman struck a cricket ball out of a cricket ground (hitting it 100 yards over a 17 foot high fence). The ball hit Ms Stone who was standing by a bus stop. It was established that cricket balls had only been hit out of the cricket ground six times in thirty years. The chances of being hit were foreseeable but were therefore very small. The cricket club did owe a duty to people outside the cricket ground but as the chance of being hit was minimal they were not liable for it.

Finally the damage must have been suffered as a result of the breach. The legal rules create a distinction between causation in fact and causation in law. To determine causation in fact the court will see whether the damage would have been suffered "but for" the defendant's negligence. Causation in law on the other hand considers whether the damage is too remote from the negligent act. The defendant must also take their victim as they find them. This simply means that if the person who suffers as a result of the breach has some special sensitivity and suffers more damage than an average person as a result of the negligent act, the defendant is liable for that damage (this is sometimes known as the eggshell skull rule).

In the 1974 case of Robinson v. Post Office a workman slipped on an oily ladder at work and cut his shin. As part of the accident procedure he was given an anti-tetanus injection. He suffered an allergic reaction and brain damage resulted. It was shown that even if he had been given an allergy test the allergic reaction would not have shown. The court held that the defendants were liable. They had to take their victim as they found them and it was reasonably foreseeable that an anti-tetanus injection would be needed following a cut shin.

Finally it is worth noting that where a claimant has in some way contributed to the damage suffered the court may reduce the amount of compensation awarded (for example the amount of compensation may be reduced by up to 25% in a road traffic accident where the claimant was not wearing a seat belt).

As can be seen from the above the law of torts is both interesting and challenging as it covers such a wide variety of behaviour and events. The aim is to provide compensation for the person who has been affected by the wrong (or provide an injunction to put a stop to the wrong).

ENFORCEMENT

Laws are enforced and grievances addressed by a variety of systems and bodies. It is important to have an effective method to enable disputes to be settled in a clear, certain and consistent way. Different types of disputes however will require different methods of enforcement.

Criminal matters will be dealt with by the criminal court system. Crimes regarded as serious are tried in the Crown Court and those with less serious consequences by the Magistrate's Court. The Crown Prosecution Service prosecutes most criminal cases (although bodies such as the Health and Safety Executive or Local Trading Standards departments may also bring cases). The magistrate's courts initially hear all cases but will refer the more serious to the Crown Court. This helps to ensure that the cases are tried in the appropriate court and that there is sufficient evidence against the accused person to proceed to trial. Trials in the Crown Court will be heard by a judge and jury (which will consist of twelve adults selected at random from the local electoral register). The judge will make a decision based on the law and the jury on the facts. In the magistrate's court the case may be heard by a single magistrate or a bench of magistrates (usually three). Their decision will be based on both the law and the facts.

Civil matters are dealt with by the appropriate civil court. Factors which will be taken into account in determining the appropriate court include the amount of the claim and the complexity of the legal issues involved. Some matters have to be heard in a specific court (for example some matters involving consumer credit may only be heard in the county court). Matters will usually be heard by a single judge alone (with the exception of libel cases). Their decision will be based on both the law and facts. Recent reforms of the civil system (the Access to Justice Act) have attempted to speed up procedures and reduce costs but the civil system remains an expensive way in which to settle a dispute.

As an alternative to a court hearing some matters may be heard by a tribunal. Since the introduction of the welfare state there has been a rapid increase in the number of tribunals. A tribunal, like a court, has rules on procedure and reasons for a decision will generally be given. Legal representation is available although a tribunal hearing is intended to be an informal affair. They provide a quick and cheap alternative to the costs and delays which exist in the court system. Examples of matters which are deemed suitable for tribunals include employment disputes or compulsory purchase orders for land.

Arbitration is a further alternative to using the court or tribunal systems. This may take many forms but is commonly found in commercial contracts when waiting for resolution in the court system may simply be impractical. Various Statutes (such as the 1996 Arbitration Act) regulate the law relating to arbitration. The parties can agree as to the method of resolving their dispute and the Statutes provide safeguards. The arbitrator should be impartial with the necessary expertise in the relevant area. Using the method of dispute resolution may see the matter resolved in a matter of weeks (or months). Agreements to go to arbitration need to be clear and precise however as often there is no route for an appeal into the court system.

Alternative Dispute Resolution is an expanding area of practice. Here the parties will reach an agreement over the resolution of their dispute. An agreement to use this method of dispute resolution does not prevent the parties taking court action should they fail to reach such an agreement. Again this can be a useful method of quickly resolving a dispute.

There are many other bodies that may be able to advise or assist with a claim and many regulatory bodies exist to regulate specific industries. Insurance may also cover specific events (for example a car accident, or accident at work) and the use of legal insurance to cover the costs of a court action is becoming increasingly common. Some insurance companies offer free legal advice lines.

Advice may be sought from the Citizens Advice Bureau (this may be on any matter but trained advisors exist for more specialised areas such as immigration or benefit claims) or a local law centre. Some lawyers will undertake pro bono work (for example a barrister may give up to three days' work free where a person is unable to pay for legal advice). The local Trading Standards officer or the Environmental Health Department will provide specific advice on matters such as a misleading description or an unclean restaurant (and they may also initiate criminal prosecutions where appropriate). The Health and Safety Executive exist to investigate complaints relating to safety in the workplace. Professional bodies will have their own complaints system (such as the Office for Supervision of Solicitors). The Race Relations Board and Equal Opportunities Commission will investigate allegations of discrimination. Certain industries may have an Ombudsman (for example the banking or insurance industry): an independent person who will investigate complaints relating to the exercise of administrative functions. Regulation of public services also exists through bodies such as OFFER (Office for Electricity Regulation) or OFWAT (Office of Water Supply).

The Legal Services Commission is responsible for both the Community Legal Services and Criminal Defence Service. The Community Legal Service replaces the legal aid scheme in civil and family cases. It will cover advice, assistance and representation by lawyers and non-lawyers. The Criminal Defence Service replaces the legal aid scheme in criminal cases. It will ensure that an individual accused or suspected of a crime will have representation. These recent changes have attracted much criticism but the intention is to secure better value for money and flexibility to meet changing priorities and needs in the provision of legal services.

Many individuals still seek advice from a lawyer but an increasing range of alternative advice is now available. One of the difficulties may, however, be locating the source of the most appropriate advice. With increased regulation, the new Legal Services Commission and the widening of access to justice this may be increasingly difficult.

FUTURE ISSUES

The United Kingdom was instrumental in the drafting of the European Convention on Human Rights and Fundamental Freedoms that came into force in 1953. The aim was to establish human rights and fundamental freedoms that applied uniformly across Europe. It was not until 1965 however that UK citizens were given the right to petition under the convention. The European Court of Human Rights (ECHR) is often confused with the European Court of Justice (ECJ) but the two have entirely different functions. The ECHR will hear cases where a violation of the convention is alleged whereas the ECJ is the court of the European Union and will hear cases that involve the member states.

Even though UK citizens have had the right to petition under the convention since 1965 it has not (until now) been incorporated into English law. The convention contains such rights as the right to life (Article 2), not to be subjected to degrading punishment (Article 3), to liberty and security of person (Article 5), to a fair and public hearing (Article 6), to respect for privacy and family life (Article 8), to freedom of thought and considerence (Article 9), to freedom of expression (Article 10) to peaceful assembly (Article 11) and to marry (Article 12). To take a case to the ECHR is not an easy process and the UK is one of the few countries that has no constitutional bill of rights. Many other European countries have either a bill of rights or have enshrined the Convention into law. This has changed as a result of the 1998 Human Rights Act. This Statute requires legislation to be read in conjunction with the Convention to ensure that convention rights are protected. Parliament has however retained its supremacy over the courts as a judge may only make a declaration of incompatibility where domestic law conflicts with a Convention right. Parliament will then use a fast track legislative procedure to make any corrections to domestic legislation that are deemed necessary. The Statute will only allow an individual who has been a victim of an alleged violation to bring proceedings, so to a certain extent the effectiveness of the Statute depends upon the willingness of individuals to bring an action (and bear the costs involved) and the role which the judiciary are prepared to play in defending an individual's fundamental rights as set out in the Convention. The Statute should have far reaching consequences in all aspects of individual and business activities.

Summary

Whilst this has provided a brief overview of the creation, enforcement and nature of law, its all-pervasive nature should be clear and its effect on both individual and business activities noted. It is an area undergoing rapid change but is an area of which all businesses must be aware as it is the backdrop to their activities. It can act as both a limitation and development tool and cannot be ignored.

NOTE

* This chapter has been commissioned by the Course Team, 2000.

17

POWER AND THE STATE*

David Coates

INTRODUCTION

- Power is a difficult concept to define; and many definitions exist. They share a sense of power as the ability to shape action.
- Individuals exercise power. So too do institutions. Much of the power exercised by individuals derives from the roles they play within key social institutions.
- Both public and private institutions exercise power by making and enforcing rules. Patterns of private power are affected by the extent and the nature of public regulation.

THE MEASUREMENT OF POWER

It is with this relationship of private power to public power that this [chapter is] concerned. Our focus will be on public power – on the power of governments. But our concern will not be so much with the procedures through which governments make and pass laws as with the interplay of governments with the societies they govern. We want to know *how powerful governments are, or can be, in their dealings with key centres of private power; and we want to know to how easy or difficult it is for those without private power to use government to redress their private grievances.* [. . .]

The question of how to recognize and measure power has preoccupied many political scientists in the post-war period and part of the debate between them surveyed [was] by Steven Lukes (1974). Lukes refers to a much-cited study of local politics in the United States – a study of New Haven in Connecticut by Robert Dahl, called *Who Governs?* – and to an equally cited critique of Dahl's work by two other American political scientists, Peter Bachrach and Morton Baratz. The exchange between them, and Lukes's comments upon it, will help to extend our understanding of contemporary power relationships in the UK.

The Dahl method emphasized in the 'one-dimensional view' section of the article is available for use by us too. We can begin to decide how powerful the government is by looking at the way government policy is formulated and implemented – at the way issues are resolved in the political arena. According to this approach to the recognition and measurement of power, we need to look at government policy on one day (to see what ministers intend to do) and then look again on another (to see what they have achieved).

In some cases, ministers will have formulated legislative proposals, successfully steered these proposals through Parliament unamended, and seen them implemented without difficulty. In those cases we can say that the power of ministers is high. But on other issues, where the degree of resistance is greater, ministers will have had more difficulty steering their legislation through or seeing it successfully implemented. Then we can say that their power is limited. But either way, the charting of the effectiveness of government initiatives will give us one measure of the degree of power enjoyed by the senior politicians and administrators who formally control the state.

This approach to the recognition and measurement of power is what Steven Lukes calls 'a one-dimensional view of power'. It is a way into the complexities of political power which focuses on the surface detail of political life. It even offers us a way of assessing the relative power of key interest groups, and not just the government itself. If, for example, the CBI wants government policy to include wage restraint, and the TUC wants wage restraint eased, then we can draw a model of their interaction with the government – by treating government policy as a ball, as shown in Figure 17.1, and the CBI and TUC as pressures operating upon it. If government policy rolls to the right, rather than to the left, then the power of the TUC on this issue seems larger than that of the CBI. If it rolls to the left, then the CBI seems ahead of the TUC in influence; and so on.

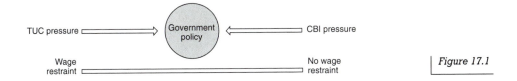

Figure 17.1

I say 'seems larger' and 'seems ahead' because in reality this measure of power only touches the surface of the relationships we are seeking to measure. The detail of political life is important, but it is only the top layer of the phenomenon we need to examine. The example we have just cited could have used the analogy of a hockey or football match to measure movement on the 'playing pitch' of wage restraint. But we need to know too why it was that pitch on which the game was being played. Why weren't the CBI, the TUC and the government discussing and contesting public ownership, levels of investment, industrial democracy, maternity and paternity leave, job sharing, equal opportunities and so on? For the distribution of political power affects not only the *outcomes* of political debate, but also the *agenda* around which that debate is organized.

[. . .] For example the biggest problem with equal opportunities legislation [in the 1970s] was not getting the laws passed and implemented. That was (and remains) difficult enough. The real problem was one of having the issue of equal opportunities discussed seriously at all in political circles. For years such discussion was effectively blocked out of politics; and this blocking is a second face of power. To measure power in this second sense, we need to know how easy it is for the government to fix its own agenda. We need to know the ability of key interest groups to get their concerns considered by the government, and have them considered on their own terms. We need to know about the ability of politicians and private groups to keep items out of public life, or to set very restricted terms for their public discussion. The fixing of the political agenda is a dimension of power which the measurement of surface effects never touches. A full analysis of the distribution of power requires us to know, that is, where the match is being played as well as who is winning. We need to have a clear sense of *where the football or hockey pitch is*, and who or what put it there, as well as knowing to which end of the pitch the ball is actually being hit.

Finally there is a 'third dimension of power', a dimension that touches the question of social process. Stay with the image of the hockey pitch and the TUC–CBI struggle for influence upon it. We can draw this as shown in Figure 17.2.

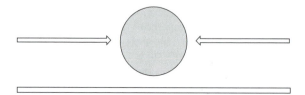

Figure 17.2

But actually we need to know the gradient of the ground as well. Perhaps it ought to be drawn as shown in Figure 17.3.

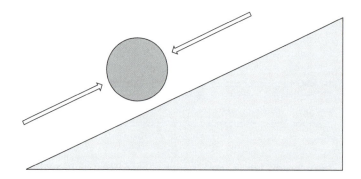

Figure 17.3

Various factors seem to fix the gradient on which power relationships around the government are played out: factors such as property rights, market forces, economic conditions, legal systems, patterns of social division, general cultural variables. These factors are easier to illustrate than to quantify. So, for example, it is more difficult to obtain better maternity rights if economic competition is tight and sexist attitudes are unchallenged than it is if neither of these conditions apply. It is easier for the TUC to influence the government when employment is high than when it is low, when the culture favours collective over individual goals, and when the legal constraints on picketing and striking are easier. It is more difficult for private industry to obtain state aid if the ruling orthodoxies of economic life are monetarist rather than Keynesian, and so on.

Lukes talks of 'the bias of the system' being sustained by what he calls 'socially structured and culturally patterned . . . practices of institutions'. This is a very important notion, but also one which is particularly hard to grasp. Again an example might help. In 1977 the Labour government was running a wage policy, with an income norm of 10 per cent. That wage policy was challenged by an official strike of firemen – firemen who were seeking a 30 per cent pay rise (some £900 a year) to supplement their basic annual salary of £3,000. The firemen had to strike for eleven weeks to win a better offer, one that still fell far short of the £900 they sought. Yet, at the same time, the Labour government implemented the recommendations of its review body on the salaries of senior officials in the public sector, awarding the head of the then publicly owned British Steel an extra 10 per cent in line with the policy. Sir Charles Villier's salary then rose by £3,000, to £33,000, and did so without industrial action by him (he didn't have to go on strike). His pay rise came easily, and did so in response to the logic of market forces which might otherwise draw senior figures out of the public sector into the private. One man got as a pre-tax rise what others had as their total pre-tax salary; and did so because of the particular constellation of salary structures, market forces and general cultural attitudes surrounding the making of state policy. The gradient ran with Sir Charles, and ran against the firemen.

This is just an example of power relationships in Lukes's third sense. Perhaps there are other very different examples that spring to mind. But let's stay with trade unionism for a minute, because it will help to take us into the discussion of the general distribution of power in a complex industrial society like the UK. The *visibility* of union strike action often creates the impression of trade union power. Thus, on the first dimension of power, trade union action suggests potency. Unions strike, wage settlements rise, the 'ball' shifts in the direction that the trade unions require. But think a while. Why strike if things are going your way? Trade unions strike because (and when) the agenda of decision making (in the state sector, or in industry generally) goes against them. They strike because they cannot fix the agenda: they are relatively powerless at the second level of power – and, beneath that, at the third. Strikes, if successful, can then recapture part of the ground lost by the slope of the hill: but they touch neither the placing of the pitch nor the slope of the hill on which it sits.

We can illustrate that by drawing our gradient picture again, and by listing the things that tilt the gradient either for or against easy wage settlements; see Figure 17.4.

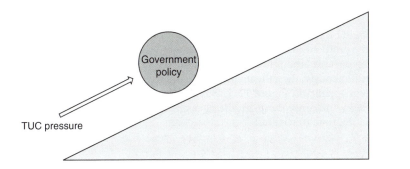

Figure 17.4

I would put it this way. The basic asymmetry in the distribution of power in an industrial society like the UK dominates both unions and their members. The individual worker faces an employer who is armed with immensely superior sanctions (that is why unionism arose in the first place) and that asymmetry of power does not go away because of the union's presence. Without unionism, workers are vulnerable to dismissal and loss of wages, sanctions that are necessarily traumatic for them but are only marginal to the costs of the employer. Even when unionized, work groups still face an authority structure in industry that is mainly in private hands, in which managerial policy is implemented automatically unless unions act quickly to stop it. So even at the level of the individual firm, union power is often necessarily negative and reactive, no matter how easy the conditions of bargaining happen to be; and in the broader social context, union power is still frequently of that kind. That is, it is still engaged in attempting to shape and reverse policies initiated elsewhere, ones that are carried through quite automatically by market forces and private managerial structures unless the unions are strong enough to block them.

So as far as I can tell the forces stacking the gradient against effective union power seem to include such things as: (1) the private ownership of industry and commerce, and the right to manage which that ownership brings; (2) the pressure of market forces in a competitively-exposed economy; (3) the general framework of laws which limit trade union activity and the disposition of senior civil servants to work more closely with management than with unions; and (4) the general political climate of ideas – those that treat unionism as a problem and undesirable. It is these which ensure that unions are invariably obliged to push the ball up a hill down which, left to itself, it would roll automatically. The tide of power runs with the gradient of market forces. That of the unions does not; and as a result unions have to work very hard indeed to move government policy in their direction, and to keep it there, once moved; see Figure 17.5.

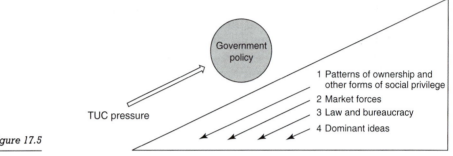

Figure 17.5

Now to stop there would be to give a very one-sided view of union power. Clearly there are factors which ease the gradient, or even tip it in the unions' favour. The gradient eases with full employment, favourable labour law, the spread of radical ideas, and so on. If they appear, and appear simultaneously, then the incline of the hill would have to be drawn very differently from the way it appears in Figure 17.5. But Figure 17.5 seems the right way to draw it now – to me at least – because these 'gradient-easing' factors are largely absent [in the view of the author at the time of writing].

NOTE

*   This chapter has been adapted from, The Open University (1991, 1995) D103 *Society and Social Science*, Block 4 *Politics and Power*, Unit 15 'Power and the State', Milton Keynes, The Open University.

REFERENCES

S. Lukes, *Power: A Radical View*, 1974, Macmillan.

18

PUTTING THE ADVANCED CAPITALIST STATE IN PERSPECTIVE*

Anthony McGrew

The post-war period witnessed a massive expansion of the state apparatus and state activity in all Western societies. This raises a series of intriguing questions: Does this expansion represent an accretion of power by the state in capitalist societies? Or is it a sign of a weak state unable to resist societal demands? In whose interests does the ACS 'rule'? Is the state best conceived as a 'capitalist' state or an 'autonomous' state? These are somewhat intimidating questions. Perhaps by engaging with some of the existing literature which has analysed these issues we can begin to sketch in the outlines of some 'answers'. Not only will this involve confronting different theoretical approaches to the state but also focusing upon '. . . the state's authoritative actions and inactions, the public policies that are and are not adopted' (Nordlinger, 1981, p.2): what the state does or fails to do.

[. . .]

Political controversy within society over the proper role of the ACS has had the effect of rejuvenating the study of the state within sociology and associated disciplines. A 'state debate' has emerged delivering some new insights into the ACS. Within this debate, two distinct approaches can be identified to the key questions of state power and the relationship between state and civil society. 'Society-centred' approaches, which embrace a variety of theoretical traditions, view the ACS as tightly constrained by the structure of power within society and heavily reliant, for the most part, upon the political support and economic resources generated by powerful private actors. In effect, the tendency is for state action or inaction to reflect the interests of the dominant groups within society, whether dominant classes or elites. Thus Nordlinger writes that the ACS in such approaches '. . . is commonly seen as a permeable, vulnerable, and malleable entity, not necessarily in the hands of most individuals and groups, but in those of the most powerful' (Nordlinger, 1981, p.3). In comparison 'state-centred approaches' stress the power of the ACS in relation to societal forces and its ability to act '. . . contrary to the demands of the politically best endowed private actors, whether these are voters, well organized 'special interest' groups, the managers of huge corporations, or any other set of societal actor' (Nordlinger, 1981, p.2).

Within each of these two general approaches can be located a heterogeneous grouping of theoretical accounts of the ACS. These are given more exposure in the two subsequent sections.

SOCIETY-CENTRED APPROACHES

Paul Lewis (1992) has identified the emergence of liberal democracy with both the extension of the franchise and the consolidation of social and political pluralism. Representative government in all ACSs is supplemented by the existence of a universe of diverse social and political groupings within civil society. In addition to the 'vote', citizens thus have the ability to channel their demands on the state through those social groups, organizations, or movements with which they are associated. Accordingly, liberal democracy, as the previous chapter implied, is commonly equated with polyarchy: a system in which power and political resources are largely fragmented. Within this classical pluralist tradition, the state's role is primarily conceived as processing political issues and securing a societal consensus by delivering policy outcomes that do not diverge substantially from the status quo and which reflect the demands of the public. Such a conception implies an essentially neutral or broker model of the state, and a correspondingly wide dispersion of power throughout society such that no one group or set of interests systematically dominates the political process.

Few political scientists or sociologists would accept that classical pluralism offers even a remotely accurate account of the state or policy making in ACSs. Even its original proponents, Robert Dahl and Charles Lindblom, no longer argue that it provides a fair representation of American liberal democracy at work, let alone democracy in other ACSs (Dahl, 1985; Lindblom, 1977). Coming to terms with the structural changes in capitalist societies in the 1960s and 1970s, particularly the growth of state bureaucracy and state interventionism within the economy, has forced advocates of classical pluralism to review their assumptions and adapt their account accordingly. In virtually all capitalist societies, the growth of corporate power and state bureaucracy has 'distorted' the political process. Nordlinger even refers to the ACS as the 'distorted liberal state' (Nordlinger, 1981, p.157). Moreover, the increasing specialization, technical nature and overwhelming volume of policy issues has encouraged the formation of functionally differentiated 'policy communities' e.g., health, social security, energy, defence, education etc. Within these 'policy communities' officials and experts from the responsible state agencies concerned, together with representatives of the most influential or knowledgeable private organized interests, formulate public policy often with only very limited participation by elected politicians.

Health policy in most ACSs is formulated in this manner. In the UK, for instance, Department of Health officials, representatives of the professional medical associations (BMA etc.) and other major interests (i.e. pharmaceutical companies) jointly determine much health policy. Moreover, in most key policy sectors such consultative machinery or policy networks are institutionalized through formal or informal committee structures. Japan is a principal example of such institutionalization, since in almost every policy sector government departments have spawned considerable numbers of consultative committees through which the major organized interests and experts are co-opted into the policy formulation process (Eccleston, 1989). This 'privileging' of the most powerful organized interests within the policy process limits effective democratic participation, since it excludes the less influential and specifically those critical of the status quo who become relegated to 'outsiders'. It also reinforces executive domination of the policy process since Parliaments or legislatures are substantially by-passed. Accordingly, neo-pluralists paint a picture of the democratic process in most ACSs as one of unequal and restricted group competition in which there exists a 'privileging' within the policy process of the more powerful organized interests within civil society. In the case of business and corporate interests, neo-pluralists

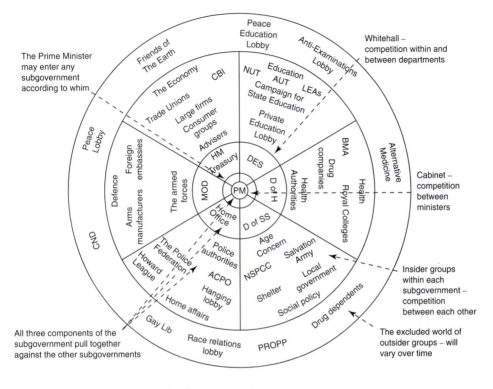

The Prime Minister may enter any subgovernment according to whim

Whitehall – competition within and between departments

Cabinet – competition between ministers

Insider groups within each subgovernment – competition between each other

The excluded world of outsider groups – will vary over time

All three components of the subgovernment pull together against the other subgovernments

Figure 18.1 Pressure groups and policy communities
Source: Kingdom, 1991, p. 421

argue that such 'privileging' is a structural necessity rather than a consciously articulated choice made by state managers or politicians. For, as Lindblom acknowledges: 'Because public functions in the market system rest in the hands of business, it follows that jobs, prices, production, growth, the standard of living, and the economic security of everyone all rest in their hands. Consequently government officials cannot be indifferent to how well business performs its functions' (Lindblom, 1977, p.122). The consequence of this is that:

> It becomes a major task of government to design and maintain an inducement system for businessmen, to be solicitous of business interests, and to grant them, for its value as an incentive, intimacy of participation in government itself. In all these respects the relation between government and business is unlike the relation between government and any other interest group in society.
>
> (Dahl and Lindblom, 1976, p.xxxvii)

Neo-pluralism delivers an account of the ACS that is significantly removed from that of classical pluralism. Power in capitalist societies is argued to be highly concentrated whilst corporate interests and economic issues dominate the political agenda. The existence of such inequalities in the distribution of power resources and in access to government decision makers undermines the classical pluralist notion of a highly competitive political process which no single set of interests can systematically dominate. Furthermore, since the state in a capitalist society has to be constantly attentive to the needs of corporate capital, the pluralist fiction of a neutral arbiter between competing interests is replaced with the notion of a 'distorted liberal state'.

Evidence of a further kind of 'distortion' of the liberal democratic state is to be found in the numerous studies of social and political 'elites' which some argue exercise extensive power within capitalist society (Mills, 1956). Elite theories stress the natural tendency for power within all social institutions and organizations to become centralized within the hands of a dominant group or *elite*. This is particularly the case in capitalist societies where mass politics, the centrality of huge organizations in social life, the growth of bureaucracy, reliance upon expertise etc., encourage the formation of elites. Several recent studies of British and American society point to the domination of key social institutions, such as the military, civil service, church, business, finance, the press, the judiciary and on, by elites whose members share similar social backgrounds and often similar political outlooks (Scott, 1991; Domhoff, 1978). In Britain the key elites are remarkable in the degree to which they share common social origins. Corresponding studies of Japanese society suggest equivalent conclusions (Eccleston, 1989). Some elite theorists therefore argue that, because elites tend to be recruited from the same social strata, they function as a socially cohesive political group. Many decades ago, C. Wright Mills argued that American society was ruled by a power elite and this remains a 'popularized' explanation of the American political process (Mills, 1956). As Lukes acknowledges, political influence rarely has to be exerted openly but rather operates more 'informally' within elite networks. Accordingly, it is through their ability to shape the political agenda, so avoiding open confrontation where their interests may be under threat, linked with a societal attachment to consensus decision making, that enables elites to 'control' the political process. But the existence of elites, however defined, does not convincingly demonstrate that the political process is directed or even considerably influenced by their activities. Elitist accounts share in common a view of the ACS as permeated at key levels by dominant social elites such that the state apparatus is perceived as functioning substantially in the interests of a (powerful) minority of its citizens.

If elite theorists point to the existence of a 'ruling elite' within ACSs, Marxism, at least its classical brands, points to a 'ruling class' (Scott, 1991). This distinction is critical, for within traditional Marxist accounts it is the class nature of capitalist society and the consequent class nature of the state itself that is fundamental to an understanding of power and the state in western societies. A classical Marxist account of the state is to be found in Ralph Miliband's *The State in Capitalist Society* (Miliband, 1969). Miliband argued that power within capitalist society resides within a fairly cohesive capitalist class. In effect, the state substantially expresses and acts to secure 'bourgeois' dominance within capitalist society. This is achieved because, within Britain, the US, France and other capitalist societies, state managers, those in senior positions in business, the military, the judiciary and so on are largely recruited from the ranks of the dominant capitalist class. In addition, the 'ruling class' can exploit its social networks to gain access to the key decision making sites within state and civil society. The state is also constrained by the need to ensure continued capital accumulation. Taken together Miliband therefore constructed what is broadly regarded as an 'instrumentalist' account – in the sense that the state is conceived as an instrument of capital – of the ACS (Held, 1987, p.207–8).

This account attracted considerable criticism, mostly from within Marxist or *marxisant* circles. Poulantzas argued that an 'instrumentalist' account was insensitive to the structural factors which conditioned state action, namely its need to secure the conditions for the continued reproduction of capitalist society even when the necessary action conflicted with the short-term interests of the capitalist class. For Poulantzas, the ACS often acted 'relatively autonomously' from the capitalist class where such action was functional to the long term stability of the capitalist order. Evidence for this, Poulantzas argued, was to be found in the institutionalization of the welfare state which appeared to conflict with the core interests of the capitalist class. These two polarized positions of 'instrumentalism' and 'structuralism' have shaped an on-going debate within neo-Marxism on the role of the state in advanced capitalist societies.

Despite their origins in rather different theoretical traditions, the various accounts of the ACS which have been elaborated in the last few pages all share a common preoccupation with the societal constraints upon and the social basis of state power. They represent the central core of 'society-based approaches' to the ACS. For they consider that the autonomous power of the ACS is severely compromised by its dependence upon dominant socio-economic groups for the political and economic resources essential to its continued survival. Whether exaggerated or not, this claim requires critical scrutiny.

STATE-CENTRED APPROACHES

When President Truman initiated the Marshall Aid Plan to provide direct financial assistance for the post-war reconstruction of Europe he did so in the knowledge that powerful corporate, labour, and political elites at home openly opposed the policy.

Despite overwhelming opposition from industrialists, labour unions, and a significant section of its own party, the first Thatcher government in Britain pursued a severely deflationary economic strategy at the peak of an economic recession in which unemployment had reached well over 3 million. Japanese rice farmers face the 1990s with the gloomy prospect of mass bankruptcies following their government's decision to liberalize the rice trade – so allowing imports of cheaper US rice to flood the domestic market – even though farmers remain a powerful force within the governing LDP party. What each of these vignettes appears to illustrate is the autonomous power of the state; its ability to articulate and pursue actions and policies which can run counter to the interests of the most dominant or powerful groups (classes) in society.

Nordlinger, in his extensive study of the autonomy of the liberal democratic state, delivers a powerful critique of 'society-centred approaches' to the ACS precisely because they '. . . strenuously [deny] the possibility of the state translating its preferences into authoritative actions when opposed by societal actors who control the weightiest political resources' (Nordlinger, 1981, p.3). Attempts to understand the autonomous power of the state have generated a range of 'state-centred approaches' to the study of the ACS.

A very influential strand of theorizing has been that of the 'New Right' which, as noted earlier, launched a sustained attack on the welfare state in the 1980s. Underlying 'new right' accounts of the ACS is an unusual juxtaposition of neo-conservative and neo-liberal political philosophies. The result is an interesting diversity of theoretical interpretations. Yet within this broad 'school' there is a shared set of assumptions that the state is not subordinate to societal forces but can and does act quite autonomously. Focusing upon the massive post-war expansion of the welfare state in capitalist societies, 'new right' accounts lay stress on the internal political and bureaucratic imperatives of the state rather than on a massive upsurge in societal demand for welfare provision. Governments and politicians are conceived as having a rational, institutionally based interest in expanding state welfare programmes and expenditure since this helps win votes and consolidates their own power bases. Moreover, competition between parties for political office encourages politicians to '. . . create unrealizable citizen expectations of what the government can deliver . . .' (Dunleavy and O'Leary, 1987, p.102), and so to increase citizen demands upon the state. State bureaucracy also has a rational incentive to expand since this enhances the budgets, career prospects and bureaucratic power of state managers. Since welfare programmes are labour-intensive, there are additional pressures from public-sector unions to sustain or increase spending levels. This suggests the conclusion that: 'Under liberal democratic and adversarial political arrangements, and without some sort of constitutional constraint upon the action (and spending) of governments, politicians, bureaucrats and voters acting rationally will tend to generate welfare state policies which are . . . in the long run unsustainable' (Pierson, 1991, p.47). As the Alber reading highlighted, during the late 1970s and throughout the 1980s, this analysis of the state captured the political imagination of many conservative politicians throughout the industrialized world since it appeared to offer a convincing account of the 'crisis of the welfare state'. Both in Britain and the US it strongly informed the political agenda of radical conservative administrations which sought to 'roll back the state'.

Central to 'new right' thinking is a conception of the ACS as a powerful and 'despotic' bureaucratic apparatus which has its own institutional momentum. Rather than the highly responsive and responsible state envisaged in pluralism, many 'new right' accounts proffer an image of the ACS as a quasi-autonomous set of governing institutions with enormous resources and administrative power at its disposal.

This portrait of an extremely powerful state apparatus would not be rejected totally by all state theorists. Indeed, throughout the 1970s and 1980s there was a general awareness that, within all capitalist societies, the state had acquired a more directive role with respect to the economy and civil society. This was predicated on studies of the policy-making process which demonstrated a growing tendency towards the 'institutionalization' of powerful organized interests – e.g. trade unions, professional associations, employers' organizations, corporate capital – within the state decision making apparatus (Schmitter, 1974). Since trade unions and business interests could potentially disrupt or undermine state policy, the obvious solution was to 'incorporate' them into the policy-making arena. In the environment of economic crisis which pervaded the 1970s, this appeared a highly effective political strategy for governments to adopt since it provided a formal framework within which the state could attempt to hold together the post-war consensus on 'managed capitalism': a consensus increasingly threatened by rising unemployment and surging inflation. Accordingly, the 1970s witnessed an intensification of this process of incorporation as well as its regularization through formal institutional mechanisms. In Britain, the CBI and TUC participated in many 'tripartite' structures whilst in Sweden and other Scandinavian democracies such forums played a critical role in the formulation of national economic strategy. But in return for institutionalized access to government, so providing these groups with a privileged position in the policy process, the state acquired expanded control over these 'private' associations. As a result, rather than limiting its scope for autonomous action such 'corporatist' strategies enhanced the autonomous power of the state (Nordlinger, 1981, p.171). Thus, in the mid-1970s the TUC and CBI in Britain found themselves locked into a 'social contract' arrangement with the state in which, for few immediate tangible benefits, both agreed to contain national wage demands and price rises respectively. Despite the 'social contract' operating against the direct material interests of their own members, both these associations 'policed' its operation on behalf of the state.

'Corporatism' (which describes this process of incorporation) is much more than a state strategy for dealing with the inherent crisis tendencies within advanced capitalist societies. Several writers have suggested that it is a novel institutional form of the ACS – a particular kind of state structure – which is evident to varying degrees in Sweden, Norway, Austria, Finland and the Netherlands (Schmitter, 1974). Panitch, for instance, considers corporatism as '. . . a political structure within advanced capitalism which integrates organized socio-economic producer groups through a system of representation and co-operative mutual interaction at the leadership level and mobilization and social control at the mass level' (Panitch, 1980, p.173). Others have pointed to a more limited conception of corporatism as a mode of public policy making, restricted to a delimited set of policy sectors in almost all ACSs. This is often referred to as *sectoral corporatism*. In this regard Japan is particularly interesting since the incorporation of the major organized interests into government is distinguished by its sectoral nature and by the exclusion of labour interests (Eccleston, 1989). Whilst it is no longer as evident in the UK, Schmitter argues that corporatism none the less remains a visible feature of the political economy of most European nations (Schmitter, 1989) (see Table 18.1).

Table 18.1 **A cumulative scale of corporatism**

1 Pluralism
    United States, Canada, Australia, New Zealand;

2 Weak corporatism
    United Kingdom, Italy;

3 Medium corporatism
    Ireland, Belgium, West Germany, Denmark, Finland, Switzerland (borderline case);

4 Strong corporatism
    Austria, Sweden, Norway, the Netherlands;

Not covered by the scale are cases of

5 'Concertation without labour'
    Japan, France.

Source: Lehmbruch, 1984, p.66

Corporatist theoreticians accept that although corporatism may no longer reflect the political reality in all capitalist societies, nevertheless where they do exist corporatist modes or forms of policy making articulate the autonomous power of the state. This is so because:

> State officials have the greatest agenda setting capacity . . . since they decide who is to participate in consultations and invariably they chair the relevant committees. Hence their policy influence seems bound to be considerable. Administrative elites in the Scandinavian countries are disproportionately represented on all the commissions and boards and committees engaged in corporatist policy making. If the policy making area is technical and complex, public officials have a decided advantage. . . . Finally if the relevant interests in the corporatist process are conflicting and balanced, then the opportunities for state elites to act autonomously are immensely enhanced.
>
> (Dunleavy and O'Leary, 1987, p.195–6)

Contemporary neo-Marxist accounts of the ACS share some of the same conceptual terrain with corporatist and 'new right' theorizing. One significant area of overlap is in the primacy given to politics and the corresponding emphasis upon the state as '. . . an actor in its own right pursuing particular interests . . . different from those of societal agents' (Bertramsen *et al*, 1991, p.98). There is also a shared recognition that there can be no effective differentiation between the state and civil society. However, what distinguishes recent neo-Marxist accounts is a concentration upon the 'capitalist' nature of the contemporary Western state. According to such accounts, the state in advanced societies is essentially 'capitalist' not because it acts in the interests of a dominant capitalist class, nor because it is constrained to do so by structural forces which prevent the prosecution of alternative anti-capitalist policies. Rather it is a 'capitalist state' because, in the process of sustaining and reproducing its own programmes, state managers must sustain and create the conditions for private capital accumulation. Since the state itself is heavily dependent upon the revenues derived from the taxation of profits and wages to maintain its programmes, failure to facilitate capital accumulation is likely to have politically destabilizing consequences (Carnoy, 1984, pp. 133–4). How state managers formulate strategies for encouraging private accumulation, and precisely what policies are followed, remain complex and indeterminate processes suffused by politics since '. . . there can be no single, unambiguous reference point for state managers how the state should serve the needs and interests of capital' (Jessop, 1990, p.357). In this respect the state in advanced capitalist societies is accorded extensive autonomy from capital, yet still remains essentially a 'capitalist state'. This is underwritten too by the state's need to secure the legitimacy of its actions within the context of a liberal-democratic polity.

Offe points to the apparent contradiction between the state's need to sustain its legitimacy and the need to sustain the conditions for private accumulation. By contradiction Offe is referring to the fact that both are essential to the survival of the state but each can pull it in opposing directions. Since the state's power derives in part from the legitimacy accorded it through the political process, it cannot afford to be perceived as acting partially, by systematically privileging corporate capital, without endangering its political support. Yet, to sustain mass support, it requires substantial revenues to finance welfare and other programmes. However, revenues derive largely from the taxes on profits and wages so that the state is obliged to assist the process of capital accumulation and thus act partially. As a consequence, the state in advanced capitalist society is caught between the contradictory imperatives of accumulation and legitimation, i.e. between 'capitalism' and 'democracy'. Reconciling this contradiction prises open a political space for the state to formulate and pursue strategies and policies which reflect '. . . the institutional self-interest of the actors in the state apparatus' (Offe, 1976, p.6). This 'autonomy' is enhanced further by the fact that there are diverse and conflicting interests between different sectors of capital, e.g. industrial, financial, national as against international etc., and within civil society more generally. Accordingly, the precise strategies and policies adopted by the state to reconcile the conflicting demands of capitalist accumulation and legitimation are a product of political negotiation and the outcome of a rather indeterminate political process within which '. . . the personnel of the state try to ensure their own jobs and hence ensure the continued existence of the State apparatuses' (Carnoy, 1984, p.136).

Alber (1988) emphasized the diverse responses amongst advanced states to the economic crises of the late 1970s and 1980s. In the UK and the US, this was the era of 'Thatcherism' and 'Reaganomics' respectively. Both articulated strategies for rejuvenating and re-structuring the domestic economy to make it more competitive with new centres of economic power such as Japan and Germany. 'Thatcherism', in particular, articulated a break with post-war orthodoxy by pursuing an economic strategy, involving 'rolling back the state', encouraging competition, privatization, and reforming the welfare state. This was accompanied by a distinctively 'populist' political strategy designed to sustain essential support for and legitimation of these radical policy initiatives. Even so, many 'unpopular' policy measures were adopted and implemented against the back drop of considerable resistance. In other advanced countries, rather different, although equally unpopular and resisted, economic and political strategies were adopted to deal with the crisis. In France, a socialist government abandoned nationalization and in Sweden the social democratic government jettisoned the long standing commitment to full employment (Gourevitch, 1986).

Recent scholarship has focused upon the critical role of the state in organizing the appropriate political and economic conditions for the successful accumulation of capital. Jessop, in his analysis of the 'Thatcher era' in the UK, suggests that the state adopted a highly proactive role throughout the 1980s (Jessop *et al.*, 1988). Rather than simply reacting to the economic crisis, it sought to pursue a determined transformation of the British economy and society through a radical agenda of reform, marketization, industrial restructuring and economic rationalization. Through the active assertion of an ideological programme – 'Thatcherism' – the state sought '. . . the mobilization and reproduction of active consent through the exercise of political, intellectual and moral leadership' (Jessop quoted in Bertramsen *et al.*, 1991, p. 110). This was achieved by the state consciously building, manipulating and consolidating its own 'power base': a dynamic coalition of quite different social groups and political actors e.g. the skilled working class, the City, 'new right' groups, moral crusaders etc., as well as appealing to more 'populist' sentiments within British society (Jessop *et al.*, 1988). In this regard the state is conceived more as a kind of 'power broker' constructing and sustaining the political coalitions vital to the success of its strategy for enhancing corporate profitability whilst simultaneously marginalizing societal resistance to its policies. There exists here a trace of, what some would identify as 'Marxist–pluralism'.

STATE AUTONOMY AND STATE POWER

This short excursion into theories of the ACS has offered a variety of accounts concerning the functions of the state in advanced capitalist societies (see Table 18.2) and the issue of in whose interests the state 'rules'. But equally it appears it has left us with a nagging question: which of these two sets of approaches to the ACS – the society-centred or the state-centred – is the more convincing?

Table 18.2 Theoretical accounts of the ACS

	Neo-Marxist	Weberian/pluralist
Society-centred	structural and instrumental accounts (Miliband, Poulantz)	elitist (Mills) neo-pluralism (Lindblom, Dahl)
State-centred	post-Marxist (Offe, Jessop)	(neo-) corporatism (Lehmbruch) new right (neo-institutionalism)

One way in which these two distinctive approaches can be reconciled is by acknowledging the significant differences between ACSs in terms of the resources (administrative, political, coercive, financial, ideological, knowledge), capacities and instruments of state power. Mann refers to these resources and capacities as embodying the 'infrastructural power' of the state by which he means the ability '. . . to penetrate civil society and implement decisions throughout the realm' (Mann, 1988, p.4). Some ACSs have considerable 'infrastructural power' and others relatively less so. The greater the infrastructural power of the state, the greater is its influence over civil society. Accordingly it is possible to differentiate, as do both Krasner and Skocpol, between 'strong' states and 'weak' states (Krasner, 1978; Skocpol, 1985). A 'strong state' is one which is able to implement its decisions against societal resistance and/or can resist societal demands from even the most powerful private groups (Nordlinger, 1981, p.22). By comparison a 'weak state' can do neither of these things '. . . owing to societal resistance and lack of resources' (Bertramsen *et al.*, 1991, p.99). Studies which have exploited this typology tend to classify ACSs such as Japan and France as 'strong states' whilst the US and Canada are classified as 'weak states' (Atkinson and Coleman, 1990).

NOTE

* This chapter has been adapted from, McGrew, A. (1992) 'Putting the Advanced Capitalist State in Perspective' in Allen, J., Braham, P. and Lewis, P. (eds) *Political and Economic Forms of Modernity*, pp. 93–105. Polity Press in association with The Open University.

REFERENCES

Alber, J. (1988) 'Continuities and changes in the idea of the welfare state', *Politics and Society*, vol.16, no.4, pp.451–68.

Atkinson, M.M. and Coleman, W.D. (1990) 'Strong states and weak states; sectoral policy networks in advanced capitalist economies', *British Journal of Political Science*, vol.19, pp.47–67.

Bertramsen, R.B., Thomsen, J.P.F., and Torfing, J. (1991) *State, Economy and Society*, London, Unwin Hyman.

Carnoy, M. (1984) *The State and Political Theory*, Princeton NT, Princeton University Press.

Dahl, R.A. (1985) *A Preface to Economic Democracy*, Cambridge, Polity Press.

Dahl, R.A. and Lindblom, C. (1976) *Politics, Economics and Welfare*, 2nd Edition, Chicago, Chicago University Press.

Domhoff, G. (1978) *Who Really Rules?*, Santa Monica, Calif., Goodyear Publishing.

Dunleavy, P. and O'Leary, B. (1987) *Theories of the State: the Politics of Liberal Democracy*, London, Macmillan.

Eccleston, B. (1989) *State and Society in post-War Japan*, Cambridge, Polity Press.

Gourevitch, P. (1986) *Politics in Hard Times*, Ithaca, Cornell University Press.

Held, D. (1987) *Models of Democracy*, Polity Press, Cambridge.

Jessop, B. (1990) *State Theory*, Cambridge, Polity Press.

Jessop, B., Bonnett, K., Bromley, S. and Ling, T.(1988) *Thatcherism*, Cambridge, Polity Press.

Kingdom, P. (1991) *Government and Politics in the UK*, Polity Press, Cambridge.

Krasner, S. (1978) *Defending the National Interest*, Princeton NJ, Princeton University Press.

Lehmbruch, G. (1984) 'Consertation and the structure of corporatist networks', in Goldthorpe, J. (ed.) (1984).

Lewis, P.G. (1992) 'Democracy in Modern Societies', in *Political and Economic Forms of Modernity*, UK.

Lindblom, C. (1977) *Politics and Markets*, New York, Basic Books.

Mann, M. (1988) *States, War and Capitalism*, Oxford, Basil Blackwell.

Miliband, R. (1969) *The State in Capitalist Society*, London, Quartet Books.

Mills, C. Wright (1956) *The Power Elite*, Oxford, Oxford University Press.

Nordlinger, E. (1981) *On the Autonomy of the Democratic State*, Harvard, Mass., Harvard University Press.

Offe, C. (1976) 'Laws of motion of reformist state policies', mimeo.

Panitch, L. (1980) 'Recent theorizations on corporatism', *British Journal of Sociology*, vol.31, no.2, pp.159–87.

Pierson, C. (1991) *Beyond the Welfare State?*, Cambridge, Polity Press.

Schmitter, P. (1974) 'Still the century of corporatism?', *Review of Politics*, vol.36, pt.1, pp.85–131.

Schmitter, P. (1989) 'Corporatism is dead! Long live corporatism', *Government and Opposition*, vol.24, no.1, pp.54–73.

Scott, J. (1991) *Who Rules Britain?*, Cambridge, Polity Press.

Skocpol, T. (1985) 'Bringing the state back in', in Evans, P.R., Rueschemeyer, D. and Skocpol, T. (eds) *Bringing the State Back In*. Cambridge, Cambridge University Press.

19

GOVERNMENT–BUSINESS RELATIONS IN JAPAN AND KOREA*

Min Chen

INTRODUCTION

The rapid industrialization process in Japan and Korea was not only spectacular but also unprecedented in modern history. The active role that the Japanese and Korean governments played in bringing about such dynamic economic growth has often been cited as one of their major sources of strength. Both governments were involved in the process by developing industrial policies and fostering close relationships with priority industries and related big businesses. Their interventions were justified on the grounds that they wanted to catch up with advanced industrialized nations within the shortest possible time.

However, the existence of intimate government–industry relations in Japan and Korea does not testify to a "Japan Inc." or "Korea Inc." conspiracy. Japanese and Korean businessmen are not motivated much differently from their Western counterparts, despite their differing interests. Their willingness to collaborate with government is not because they are exceptionally patriotic, or culturally devoted. Rather, it is because they have known through their experience that such collaboration can bring material benefit. It is also true that industrial policy is not unique to these two countries. Close governmental relationships with priority industries and related big businesses are also quite commonly seen elsewhere in the world. For many developing countries, these phenomena are more sources of trouble than of strength. This is because they contribute to widespread favoritism, corruption, and the suffocation of competition. Nevertheless, in Japan and Korea the result seems to have been quite remarkable and the channel seems to have been fairly effective.

By the late 1980s, pressure to change these government–business relationships had developed. More criticisms were heard about the defects of heavy governmental involvement in industries and there was a growing voice among the industries to restrict governmental roles. This chapter will focus on the study of governmental relations with business in both Japan and Korea. It will include discussions of their historical legacies, the outstanding features of such relationships, and an analysis of their strengths and weaknesses, as well as their trends of development.

HISTORICAL PERSPECTIVE OF GOVERNMENT–BUSINESS RELATIONS

Japan

The Meiji Restoration in 1868 marked a turning point in Japanese history, when the new government took upon itself the responsibility to industrialize the nation within the shortest possible time. The situation was critical: after the arrival of the American fleet in 1853, Japan's doors were forced open and the threat that she would become another colony of the West was very real. The imposition of unequal commercial treaties in 1858 and 1866 stripped Japan of tariff protection and introduced a flood of imports that amounted to 71 per cent of Japan's foreign trade by 1871.

The only viable option open to the Japanese government seemed to be a rapid political and economic transformation so that Japan could match Western development and thereby deal with the West on equal terms. This option was reflected in the popular slogan of "*fukoku kyohei*" (rich country – strong army). The lack of private capital, modern commercial skills and techniques, a modern economic infrastructure, as well as a modern liberal merchant class meant that if Japan was to catch up with the West progress would have to be initiated by the government or not at all.

The existing channels of economic control, which were established from the Tokugawa period (1603–1868), facilitated governmental involvement in transforming the Japanese economy (Lockwood 1955). The reform measure in the Meiji period further strengthened the role of the government by allowing the state to borrow private capital and invest it in the development of strategic industries such as mining, shipbuilding, communications, armaments and textiles. When these enterprises became mature, the state transferred them at extremely low prices to selected private hands. The large-scale transfer of major state-owned enterprises in 1880, the first attempt to privatize, paved the way for the formation of the large industrial and financial combines called *zaibatsu*.

The government intervention in business had not only benefitted emerging modern industrial firms, especially *zaibatsus*, but also brought the active support of big business to the government. Time and again, *zaibatsus* loyally supported many important international and domestic policies of the successive governments. The armed revolt at Satsuma in 1877, for example, was suppressed by government troops paid by Mitsui Bank and transported by Mitsubushi's ships. The government's expansionist policies during the First and Second World Wars received vigorous support from *zaibatsus*, which in return benefitted from the government's war efforts (Morikawa, 1992).

The defeat of the Japanese Empire at the end of the Second World War, and the ensuing democratic reform instituted by General Douglas MacArthur, did not fundamentally change the relationship between the government and big business. Although the family-dominated and vertically-linked *zaibatsu* were dismantled under the charge of war crimes, they were quickly replaced by large horizontally-linked *keiretsus*. These new groups were not strict monopolies because they competed against each other, but they together formed an oligopoly. Some used the old *zaibatsu* names, such as Mitsubishi, Mitsui and Sumitomo (Yanaga 1968: 30–62). While the militarists were tried and disgraced, the old theme of catching up with the West was further reinforced. It was generally agreed that Japan's defeat resulted from its backward economy and technology. The focus shifted from military expansion to economic revival.

Big business was once again endowed with the historical mission of reconstructing the war-shattered Japanese economy (Johnson 1982: 308). A strong link between the government and big business was reestablished in Japan. The government bureaucracy, the ruling political party (LDP), and the private sector combined to form a powerful intertwined triangle in which the government implemented a system of "administrative guidance." Key governmental departments, such as the Ministry of International Trade and Industry (MITI) and the Ministry of Finance (MOF), have been actively involved in business by giving favors to and subsidizing those businesses whose activities conformed to national priority. On the other hand, big business has exerted tremendous influence on the political process through informal communication links with the LDP leadership. Money has been channeled from big business to those political candidates who strongly support the interests of big business.

Korea

Korea's industrialization took place at a much later time. More than one-half of the industrial base that was left behind by Japanese colonial rule in 1945 was destroyed during the Korean War, which lasted from 1950 to 1953. In the 1950s the Korean economy lived on American military and economic aid. While some import substitution projects, such as sugar refining and textiles, were introduced during the 1950s, the US-educated President Syngman Rhee was more interested in introducing free market principles than in heavy governmental intervention.

The few earliest *chaebols*, such as Sambo, Samsung, Kaepoong, Lucky (later Lucky-Goldstar), Taehan, and Tongyang, experienced relatively rapid development in the 1950s. As Rhee's government dispensed with favorable concessions in the form of import licenses, foreign exchanges at favorable rates and governmental properties expropriated from the Japanese, these early starters became a ready target of the civil revolution in 1960 that led to the collapse of Rhee's government. In August 1960, twenty-four companies were required to pay a total fine of $65 million for tax evasion and unfair profiteering.. The military government of Park Chung Hee, which replaced the civilian government in a coup in 1961, continued the campaign against the corrupt *chaebol* owners (Park 1982).

These events had a number of effects on the developments that followed later. First, the Korean government established its superior position *vis-à-vis* big business. This later allowed the government a relatively free hand to push big business into the priority industries. The Korean counterpart of Japan's MITI is the Ministry of Trade and Industry (MITI), which helped the government to create and implement its industrial policies. Second, the government took over some commercial banks previously dominated by private business-men. This laid the foundation for the governmental control of bank credit. Third, the badly tarnished *chaebols* learned the importance of developing good relations with the government and also established their own organization, the Federation of Korean Industries.

In the 1960s and 1970s, Korea experienced an unprecedented economic boom, in which the government and business firms formed a team. The government made five-year economic plans and set economic targets. Business firms that had developed a close relationship with the government received strong support in developing their businesses according to the government plans. As a former general trained in Japan, President Park was impressed with the Japanese governmental involvement in business. With the support of the government, large *chaebols* had achieved rapid development and were able to survive on their own by the mid-1970s.

The dramatic ascendence of *chaebols* did cause concern for the government. Beginning from 1974, President Park adopted a series of measures to limit the excessive growth of *chaebols*. Some private firms were pushed to list their stocks on the open capital market. The tax payments and bank credits to big businesses were closely monitored. These were followed by compulsory sales of real estate not used for business purposes, forced divestment of many subsidiaries of the top twenty business groups, and the revocation of some large trade associations. Ultimately, however, these measures were not strongly enforced and the share of the ten largest *chaebols* in the manufacturing sector consequently grew from 21.8 per cent in 1975 to 24.2 per cent in 1982 (Song 1990: 115).

By the early 1980s the Korean economy became so heavily dependent on *chaebols* that it was almost impossible to curtail their activities without hurting the growth of the economy. The decade of 1975–1985 witnessed a new trend in which *chaebols* intensified competition between each other and began to focus their attention on advancing their specific skills by investing in technology, marketing, and managerial know-how. Meanwhile, the *chaebols'* social status had also been remarkably improved. In the economic downturn of the late 1970s and the early 1980s, the government was forced to openly acknowledge that its interventionist attitude could be very harmful to economic development, and began to allow the private sector to take more initiatives. The *chaebols* had also come to realize that in spite of major advantages there could be some undesirable and severe consequences. For instance, ICC-Kykje, then Korea's seventh largest, was severely punished by the government and lost its credit line almost overnight for not paying the donations expected by two quasi-governmental organizations that had ties with the then President Chun Doo-Huan (Kearney 1991: 41–42).

In short, Japan and Korea shared a similar historical legacy of heavy governmental involvement in business which was justified on the ground that, in order to catch up with the advanced nations, the government should assume the responsibility for defining industrial policies and for using whatever means were available to achieve identified goals. Although the Korean government was heavily influenced by the Japanese government's relationship with its industry, the government–business relationship was developed much later than in Japan and in a much more volatile way, with one major difference being that the partnership between the government and business in Japan had been institutionalized ever since the Meiji Restoration.

GOVERNMENT–BUSINESS RELATIONS IN JAPAN

The major players

The three major players in Japan – bureaucracy, business, and the LDP – have developed extensive channels of communication in their triangular relationship.

Bureaucracy

The Ministry of International Trade and Industry (MITI), formed in 1949, is the most important institution in Japan's industrial policy-making process. The Ministry is responsible for: (1) constructing the structure of industry and adjusting dislocations; (2) guiding the development of industries and their distribution activities; (3) coordinating Japan's foreign trade and commercial ties; (4) managing specific areas such as raw material and energy to supply industries, small businesses, etc. The Ministry of Finance (MOF), a major rival of MITI, controls important tools to implement industrial policies, ranging from the budgetary process and cheap government loans to selective tax measures (Magaziner and Hout 1980: 40–43).

Business

Zaikai, which translates as "business world," represents the peak associations of big business, including the Federation of Economic Organizations (*keidanren*), the Federation of Employers' Associations (*nikkeiren*), the Committee for Economic Development (*keizai-doyukai*), and the Japan Chamber of Commerce and Industry. *Keidanren* has a membership of more than 100 industry-wide associations and around 800 large corporations. *Keidanren* has had a powerful influence on government, with the most notable example being the merger of the Democratic Party and the Liberal Party to form the LDP in 1955. The power of *keidanren* is derived from massive financial contributions to the LDP.

The large industrial groups, or *keiretsus*, embrace various industrial sectors and account for nearly one-third of the total economy. The biggest are Mitsubishi, Mitsui, Sumitomo, Fuji, Dai-Ichi Kangyo, and Sanwa ("the Big Six"). The presidents of the member firms participate in presidents' clubs, which serve as an important channel for policy coordination, collaboration, and conflict resolution among members. At a lower level, the inter-firm group member is itself the center of a group of small and medium-sized companies (subcontractors and parts suppliers). Ninety-eight per cent of the manufacturing companies in Japan have less than a hundred employees. The importance of *keiretsus* in the government–business relationship is manifested in *keiretsu* dependence on the "in-house" bank, which is influenced by the Bank of Japan (BOJ) in terms of monetary policy, credit, and loans rationing.

The LDP

The LDP has been until most recently very successful in winning elections. A simple majority (256 of the 511 seats in the House of Representatives) was regarded as a Party disaster, which could lead to the resignation of the incumbent prime minister. Its uninterrupted tenure of office for the past few decades was a necessary guarantee of the government–industry relationship in Japan (Reading 1992: 230–243). The vote is obtained by chains of personal connections that reach all the way to local influential figures. Traditionally, gift-giving is expected as a reward to those who can mobilize voters, thereby resulting in many scandals and vote-buying.

The Party is a coalition of various factions that are seeking higher representation and more seats in the Cabinet. The Japanese single, multi-member non-transferable electoral vote system gives the factions their chance. Factional competition is most heated in the biennial contest for presidency of the LDP, which virtually guarantees access to the premiership due to the LDP's majority in the Diet. As money plays an important role in getting votes, a successful LDP leader should be someone who is capable of raising the necessary funding. This ability is the single most important precondition for promotion as opposed to possessing a legislative track record. Big business is the main source of funding for both the Party and individual politicians.

The dynamics of the triangular relationships

There is frequent formal and informal consultation among the three players. Their communication is made easier by the fact that the majority of the elite members are recruited from Tokyo University. Policy clubs and advisory councils gather together officials, business tycoons and politicians on a regular basis. Trade and industry associations constitute another channel in the communication chain. *Keiretsu* groups embody the industrial constituency and channel ideas to and from key bureaucratic institutions. The LDP assumes a central position between the bureaucracy and business, coordinating their interests and playing the role of referee. It serves to hold the triangle together.

The bureaucracy maintains good access to the communication networks by practicing *amakudari* (descending from heaven), which moves retired bureaucrats from MITI, MOF, and other key institutions into the LDP, where some may become ministers, or into the Bank of Japan, public corporations, commercial banks, trade and industry associations, and private corporations. As bureaucracy is a major player in policy-making, private businesses are eager to employ the retired bureaucrats in order to benefit from the personal bonds these people have built up in their former ministries. In addition, key policy-deliberating councils, such as the Economic Council, the Industrial Structure Council, and the Foreign Capital Council, are set up by the Economic Planning Agency, MITI, and MOF, respectively, to communicate with business.

The relationship between these key players is characterized by interdependence (see Figure 19.1). The bureaucracy needs the approval of the Diet for its policies and is thereby compelled to maintain good ties with the LDP, which dominates the Diet. The business privileges that are distributed by the bureaucracy can help LDP politicians take care of the interests of certain businesses in return for electoral constituency and contributions from industries. The LDP politicians have to guarantee a closer fit between bureaucratic actions and popular expectations; getting involved in this triangle, the business reaps huge benefits but becomes heavily dependent.

Such a triangular relationship seems to benefit each party and is justified by the hundred-year-old imperative of catching up with the West, which has contributed to a sense of national mission and during the postwar period has protected successive governments from public supervision. Nevertheless, it would be simplistic to assume that such cooperation is always harmonious, as each side has its own interests. The United States' increasingly harsh demands for reducing the trade surplus, for example, have sharpened conflicts of interest among the three players and have increased the tensions on their traditional relationship. It is also a triangle of corruption, breeding one scandal after another. A recent National Tax Administration Agency survey revealed that $400 million in spending by the construction industry is unaccounted for each year. It has become common knowledge that most of this money goes into the pockets of politicians (TBT 1993: 28).

Industrial policy instruments

Industrial policy has received a consistently high priority in the postwar period in Japan, but the objectives and the instruments have changed. During the first period of reconstruction, which ran from the end of the Second World War to the mid-1960s, the government–industry relationship could be characterized as the "government industrial guidance model," in which the government controlled extensive subsidization, preferential capital, and license allocation. This was the prime period of MITI. The first period was replaced by a new "private sector industrial guidance model," in which MITI's role began to erode seriously (Johnson 1982). Pressures were building up for the liberalization of capital, the internationalization of Japan's economy, environmental protection, and the reduction of MITI's role in the economy. Mitsubishi's decision to form a joint venture with Chrysler against MITI's arrangement of a Mitsubishi–Isuzu venture was a milestone event demonstrating MITI's weakening position.

The government controlled a wide range of policy instruments. Once identified as being strategic, an industry became the candidate of both protective and nurturing instruments. The protective instruments mainly comprised trade tariffs, the restriction of imports and foreign capital, and a commodity tax system favoring home-produced goods. Nurturing policies covered below-market interest rates on loans from public and private financial institutions, special depreciation status and tax exemptions, subsidy grants, authorization of foreign currency to import necessary foreign technology, and exemptions from import duties on necessary machinery and equipment.

Public procurement has also been effectively used to enforce industrial policies. Although MITI itself does not have public procurement budgets, several governmental organs, such as the Defense Agency, the Ministry of Construction, and the Ministry of Transport have

Recruitment
from Tokyo
University

Liberal Democratic Party

Interdependance of the LDP
and the Bureaucracy

Interdependence of the LDP
and *Zaikal*

TRUST
Many ministers are retired civil
servants
DEPENDENCE
Dependence on micro-budgetary
favours. Technical advice given the
weight and complexity of legislation.
Assistance at Question Time.
Minister s short tenure of office.

TRUST
Tradition of government–industry
collaboration.
Close informal associations
(policy clubs).
DEPENDENCE
Finance: Elevated costs of general
elections.
Factional competition for
LDP presidency

Constitutional dependence
of Bureaucracy on the Diet.
Amakudari
Prospect of retirement into
political office on retirement.
Political representation
in inter-ministerial conflicts
over jurisdiction, etc.

BUT
Electoral costs of the negative
consequences of economic growth.
Need to accommodate USA criticism
of trade surplus, etc.

Policy
Demand for special treatment
for big business.
BUT
Difficulty of sustaining image
of 'social responsibility' given
close association with
scandal and faction-riven LDP.

INTERDEPENDENCE OF BUREAUCRACY
AND *ZAIKAI*

BUREAUCRACY

ZAIKAI

Advisory councils
Amakudari
Personal associations
Temporary exchange of
officials (e.g. MITI to
keidanren)

(The peak associations
of big business:
*keidanren, nikkeiren,
keizai doyukai*, Japan
Chambers of Commerce
and Industry)

Recruitment
from Tokyo
University

Recruitment
from Tokyo
University

Figure 19.1 Triangular relationships among the leading players in government–industry relations
Source: Boyd, 1987, p. 69

significant procurement budgets. Many public corporations, such as Nippon Telephone and Telegraph, also have substantial procurement capabilities. The procurement decisions of these organizations are heavily influenced by the governmental procurement policies based on the priorities of the governmental industrial policies.

Various cartels were also organized by MITI to control Japan's industrial output, market share, and investment (Magaziner and Hout 1980–36). The industry associations collaborate closely with MITI in the organization of such cartels, which are designed to achieve a number of goals such as rationalization of production, promotion of vertical integration, short-term production allocation, reduction of excessive production, and export price floors during trade crises. Under growing public pressure to reduce the monopoly of cartels, the Fair Trade Commission passed a series of measures to limit the role and number of cartels. The number of cartels has decreased by half in a decade from 1,000 in the early 1970s down to about 500 in the early 1980s (Boyd 1987: 82). Moreover, the policy objectives have also changed in the remaining cartels, with more than 400 of them being designed to promote environmental protection or protect small and medium-sized enterprises from the *keiretsus*.

GOVERNMENT–BUSINESS RELATIONS IN SOUTH KOREA

Government domination

Business and government in Korea interact in diverse ways. The government plays a combination of roles, such as a competitor and customer, caretaker and regulator, and supporter and money extractor of business; the most prominent roles are of regulator and supporter. The Korean government has been heavily involved in business activities in the market-place.

The government not only makes strategic plans to identify priority industries, but also places a substantial portion of investment funds under its budget to achieve the goals set by the plans. By controlling commercial banks and manipulating interest rates, the government also controls credit. The Korean government has also maintained a strong tax administration. Moreover, the government owns a large number of enterprises (when the government owns more than 50 per cent of an enterprise, it is called a government enterprise) (Song 1990: 117), including the Korean Development Bank, the Korean Highway Corp., the Korean Trade Promotion Corp., the Korean Broadcasting Corp., the Korean Tourism Corp., the Korean Land Promotion Corp., the Korean Electric Power Corp., the Pohang Steel Corp., and the Korean Telecommunications Authority.

The Korean government also has considerable power in determining which company should enter specific sectors of the economy. In many industries, private companies need the approval of the government before they can start a new business. Meanwhile, the government also has the power to force some companies out of specific industrial sectors. The governmental power to manipulate entry or exit of private companies has been one of the most powerful instruments that it wields to influence private business. At the micro-level, the government's role has also been evident where, for example, it exercised strict control on labor movements prior to the mid-1980s. Product prices and wages in private firms were heavily regulated until the early 1980s.

For a long time the Korean government would choose a select group of companies in targeted industries and support those businesses by providing them with financial and tax incentives, plus information services. The "chosen" companies were typically large, export-orientated corporations and were awarded many privileges. Government favoritism toward these companies led to questionable business dealings and monopolistic tendencies. The government didn't try to end these practices until the early 1980s, when the Law of Monopoly Regulation and Fair Trade was finally passed.

In comparison to Japan, Korean government intervention seems to be widespread. Unlike the triangular structure of the Japanese bureaucracy, LDP and business, the Korean government has clearly played a dominant role in its relations with business. Since the Korean government had until most recently been very authoritarian, the role of the parliament and leading parties had been minimal. Korean businesses had to be much more subservient to the government. The history of Korean shipbuilding illustrates this point. Hyundai was virtually compelled by the Park government to venture into shipbuilding, even though it did not have the necessary skill or experience. By following the advice of the government, Hyundai successfully constructed supertankers within the shortest possible time and became one of the leading shipbuilders in the world.

Government and the birth of *chaebols*

From the end of the Korean War up until the mid-1970s, the Korean government helped *chaebols* reap huge profits in a number of ways. Based on chronology, *chaebols* can be classified into three groups: (1) the late 1950s; (2) the 1960s; (3) the 1970s (Lee and Yoo 1987: 96). *Chaebols* of the late 1950s, such as Hyundai, Samsung, and Lucky-Goldstar, were created by self-made founders who benefitted from the sale of government properties, preference in taxation, and the preferential allotment of grants. The governmental sale of "enemy property," i.e. the factories left behind by the Japanese in 1945, was particularly significant for some *chaebols* formed in this period. *Chaebols* of the 1960s, such as Hanjin, Korea Explosive, Hyosung, Sangyong, and Dong-A, took shape with the help of foreign loans induced to implement five-year plans. *Chaebols* of the 1970s developed by taking advantage of the rapid growth in exports and domestic demand; these *chaebols* include Daewoo, Sunkyong, Lotte, Kolon and Doosan.

In short, the role played by the government was significant in the development of *chaebols*. This can be clearly illustrated by the government's control of commercial bank credit, where the government controlled both the price and quantity. Interest rates were kept very low, with real interest rates (bank's general loan rates minus inflation rates) averaging a negative number in the 1950s and 1970s; this has led to chronic excess demand for bank credit. *Chaebols*, the government-favored locomotives of rapid industrialization, naturally benefitted the most from subsidized bank credit as well as the government's own development funds. *Chaebols* can afford to lower their cost of capital by using the external source of capital made available by the government policies. Even in the late 1980s, when the Korean government began to push *chaebols* to lower their indebtedness, the debt-to-equity ratio averaged 5.1:1, with the seventh largest *chaebol*, Hanjin's, reaching a staggering 14:1 ratio (Kearney 1991: 51). Since *chaebols* have virtually been allowed by the government to indulge in over-dependence on these external sources of funds, *chaebol* owners have good reason to discount the risk of bankruptcy significantly.

It was estimated that the profit received by the *chaebols* from the distorted money market amounted to some $5.2 billion, which was more than half of the estimated total net value of the top fifty *chaebols* in 1980 (Jung 1989: 21).In addition, other types of government subsidies in the forms of tariff barriers, tax incentives, and wage/labor movement controls were also available. Although this estimate may be subject to a wide range of variations, the government did play a crucial role in the rapid expansion period of *chaebols*. As will be shown in the following section, *chaebols* have also contributed to the government's drive for rapid industrialization by venturing into many large and risky projects with relatively insufficient technological and financial capabilities.

The role of *chaebols*

While the Korean government's role in the development of the Korean economy is significant, the role played by *chaebol* founders should not be ignored. They consisted of a group of men with outstanding leadership, sharp vision, great determination, and unfailing devotion. The market distortions discussed earlier were not initially created by the Korean government solely for the sake of those *chaebol* founders, but the government's development strategies have resulted in generating new opportunities that the *chaebol* founders took quick and full advantage of.

The rapid industrialization and fast-changing industrial structure has forced *chaebols* to continuously look for new opportunities. If they do not constantly form new businesses they will suffer from lower growth rates and lose their relative share in the market. Therefore, *chaebols* tend to diversify into products and markets that are not related to their current lines of business: *Chaebols* include almost all large private corporations, and *chaebol* affiliates have grown faster than non-*chaebol* companies. Major *chaebols* are among the fastest-growing conglomerates in the world.

Chaebols have been widely criticized for their monopolistic power and also for their control of economic wealth. In that early 1980s, for example, 80 per cent of major commodities were controlled at one point by a very limited number of *chaebols* (Kearney 1991: 39). Nevertheless, *chaebol* business structure also has positive effects on the Korean economy. It is much easier for these well-diversified and large business groups to undertake risky projects that normally require substantial investment. In comparison with large state enterprises, *chaebols* are much less bureaucratic and more dynamic. Large and diversified business groups can match up with the power of foreign MNCs in both the world and domestic markets. Also, they are in a better position to move into highly technological capital-intensive industries. *Chaebols* have indeed championed Korean industrialization within a short period of time.

Summary/Conclusion

This chapter has reviewed and analyzed the historical evolution of government–business relationships in Japan and Korea. As discussed earlier, this relationship in both Japan and Korea has been distinguished by heavy governmental involvement. Encouraged by a catch-up mentality, both the Japanese and Korean governments felt obligated to take the lead in economic development, concentrating national resources and pushing the private sector to develop in targeted areas. Nevertheless, there are various differences in the ways and degrees in which they were involved in this development. For the Japanese, the three major players (i.e. the government, LDP, and business) deal with each other in a triangular framework, in which none would survive well without the others. In the case of Korea, government bureaucracy took charge in its relations with business, while the Korean parliament, until just recently, had very little power. In comparison with the Japanese government, the Korean government intervenes much more directly and extensively in the economy. In other words, "Japan Inc." symbolizes a government–business partnership in which the policy represents a consensus between equals. "Korea Inc.," meanwhile, connotes an unequal partnership in which the government sets the policies and businessmen tend to follow (Lee and Yoo 1987: 104).

By the 1980s, this kind of government–business relationship had been under growing pressure, both domestically and internationally. Various problems from heavy governmental involvement, such as built-in corruption, low efficiency, and a distorted market, had become better known to both government and business. Among the basic measures taken by both governments since the early 1980s are efforts to open the domestic market to foreign competition, more reliance on price and market mechanisms, and the promotion of small and medium-sized companies. On the other hand, many large business groups that had already accumulated substantial strength and experience by the 1980s and had been good at dealing with foreign competition, also began to realize the advantage of less governmental intervention, thereby pushing for less of it in the economy. The defeat of LDP in the 1993 election in Japan temporarily broke down the so-called golden triangle, while the current democratic reform in Korea has greatly weakened the government's ability to manipulate businesses. Nevertheless, in spite of these policy changes, big business groups in the two countries still have countless links to their respective governments; therefore, the process of disengaging government from business will be slow and involved.

NOTE

* This chapter has been adapted from, Chen, Min (1995) *Asian Management Systems*, Thomson, ch. 11, pp. 151–165.

REFERENCES

Boyd, Richard (1987) "Government–Industry Relations in Japan: Access, Communication, and Competitive Collaboration," in Stephen Wilks and Maurice Wright (eds), *Comparative Government–Industry Relations: Western Europe, the United States and Japan*, New York: Oxford University Press, pp. 61–89.

Johnson, Chalmers (1982) *MITI and the Japanese Miracle*, Stanford, Calif.: Stanford University Press.

Jung, Ku Hyuan (1989) "Business–Government Relations in Korea," in Kae H. Chung and Hak Chong Lee (eds), *Korean Managerial Dynamics*, New York: Praeger, pp. 11–27.

Kearney, Robert P. (1991) *The Warrior Worker: The History and Challenge of South Korea's Economic Miracle*, New York: Henry Holt & Co.

Lee, S.M. and S.J. Yoo (1987) "Management Style and Practice of Korean *Chaebols*," *California Management Review* 95: 95–110.

Lockwood, William (1955) *The Economic Development of Japan*, New York: Oxford University Press.

Magaziner, Ira C. and Thomas M. Hout (1980) *Japanese Industrial Policy*, Berkeley, Calif.: University of California Press.

Morikawa, Hidemasa (1992) *Zaibatsu: The Rise and Fall of Family Enterprise Groups in Japan*, Tokyo: University of Tokyo Press.

Park, Byung-yoon (1982) *Chaebol and Politics*, Seoul, Hankook Yangseo.

Reading, Brian (1992) *Japan: The Coming Collapse*, New York: HarperCollins.

Song, Byung Nak (1990) *The Rise of the Korean Economy*, New York: Oxford University Press.

TBT (1993) "A Bad Case of the Japanese," *Tokyo Business Today* (January/February): 26–34.

Yanaga, Chitoshi (1968) *Big Business in Japanese Politics*, New Haven, Conn., Yale University Press.

20

BUSINESS ROUTES OF INFLUENCE IN BRUSSELS: EXPLORING THE CHOICE OF DIRECT REPRESENTATION*

Robert J. Bennett

ROUTES OF INFLUENCE

There are generally three main routes by which businesses seek to influence European regulations. First (i) a *direct route* developing their own 'Brussels Strategy' is an option for some companies. For example Greenwood *et al.*, Mazey and Richardson and Pedler and van Schendelen[1] have demonstrated the increasing role of direct lobbying by individual companies in Brussels. In addition, many companies and organizations make use of the facilities of other bodies, such as the CBI Brussels office or Brussels-based British Business Bureau or launch 'missions', briefing sessions or other initiatives in Brussels whilst not actually maintaining an office there. Indeed, Mazey and Richardson[2] claim that a European strategy is now 'essential' to big businesses.

Previous assessments suggest that it is only large, particularly transnational companies (which may include ones that are not based in the EU) that seek to negotiate directly with European institutions.[3] More commonly associations have to be the chosen vehicle since most firms cannot individually afford, or cannot gain, direct and effective access to national governments or the EC. This process can occur through: (ii) a *national association route*, whereby national business associations either lobby European institutions directly as a 'Brussels strategy'[4] or lobby their national governments in order to influence the response within European technical committees by national civil service officials and ministers. The use of nationally-based associations to lobby in Brussels is recognized as common where a sector has little internationalization, where domestic protections play a major role, where an industry is more concentrated in one country than other parts of Europe, or where there are clear 'national interests' (e.g. fisheries). It is also favoured as a supplementary route to others in many other cases, because regulations have to have member state support in the Council of Ministers, have to be implemented 'at home', and influence on national bodies has been argued to secure the best access to the Council. Hence winning a case is unlikely without domestic support.[5]

A third possible approach, (iii) the *European association route*, exists where businesses either join European business associations directly (which is uncommon), or national business associations work with each other, merge to form 'Euro-groups', or join European federations of associations (which is by far the most common European phenomenon). The use of European associations draws on some of the formal consultation machinery of the EU, such as the Economic and Social Committee, which is organized through a set of technical committees and subcommittees which seek explicitly to draw on technical advice from businesses and their associations in often quite specifically defined subsectors.[6] This process has been seen as compensating for the lack of direct contact between citizens and EU institutions.[7] A single European association or federation can present to the Commission a single agreed point of view from a whole sector which can overcome legitimacy and cost constraints for both parties. The Commission officials can then negotiate with only one body, which reduces 'bureaucratic overload', staff time and costs,[8] whilst the association will also offer cost economies to its members, although there may be considerable costs in agreeing a single view with its members or member associations. It is also argued that European associations allow 'symbiotic, power-dependence relations' to be developed with the Commission that can lead to its bureaucratic advocacy for a sector (as within specific DGs) or more generally for industrial interests as a whole (especially within DGIII),[9] i.e. European Associations may provide a means to work from the inside of the Commission.

The three routes overlap, and it has been recognized that there are multiple and overlapping routes for influence in European affairs by direct lobbying through national institutions and through European bodies. However, in the choice between these routes, the importance of some form of direct Brussels strategy has rapidly increased.

HYPOTHESES UNDERLYING THE CHOICE OF ROUTES OF INFLUENCE

To explain the use of direct representation over either national or European associations requires assessment of how businesses interrelate with their sectors, and how business associations differ between sectors.

It is clear from most previous discussions, that company size is a key determining characteristic of the *capacity* to follow a direct route, since only large companies have the potential resources required. Hence we include company size as a major feature in the following analysis. The extent of influence of company size becomes one of our key hypotheses examined. But many (perhaps most) large companies do not directly lobby, so that other features must also be important in influencing the choice of a direct route.

The sector of a business is a feature of importance identified in previous case studies. Greenwood,[11] for example, suggests that the 'prestige' of a sector is important: for example, the Commission is keen to encourage high technology sectors that may affect future economic growth, so this opens up more opportunities for direct influence. An overlapping feature, argued by McLaughlin *et al.*,[12] is the 'clout' of the sector: some companies and sectors have more political weight and leverage than others for national or EU-wide reasons of their employment or contribution to GNP, for instance the car industry or pharmaceuticals. This again opens up more opportunities for direct influence. Greenwood[13] extends this idea by also noting the political power of some sectors, despite their low economic weight, for instance farming. Hence, whilst the size and resources of a company determine whether it has the capacity to exert direct influence, other features about the company's sector tend to determine whether or not the Commission and other European bodies are more receptive to influence.

Whilst the importance of the sector is recognized as important, there is no way easily to measure objectively such features as 'clout' or 'prestige'. We adopt a different approach below based on assessing a sector's level of concentration and organization as means to address the extent of its 'weight' in Brussels. This is supported by the wide range of analyses[14] which show that it is not the distinction of standard sectoral classifications (such as the SIC), but the sectoral market conditions that most affects sector 'clout'. For example, the level of competition in the sector is important: low profit margin or over-capacity stimulates co-operation and greater lobbying of government.[15] Also important is the degree of market dominance, organization or the concentration of the sector within relatively few firms, since high levels of organization and concentration stimulate cooperation, which permits monitoring between firms, reduces opting out and again stimulates lobbying because such sectors have clout.[16] The relative value of the sector is also important since, in general, more valuable sectors have more clout with government and this in turn encourages their cooperative organization.[17] The extent of localization within one area or country encourages deeper social and political networks to develop.[18] And the level of cross border operations can be important since this stimulates the need for a European or international approach, as opposed to a national view, and the resources this demands.[19] The level of government or Commission intervention and co-ordination in the sector is also important since this stimulates the need for a greater level of sectoral organization.[20]

The sector also strongly influences the extent of development of business associations. The extent of association development is likely to be a major influence on direct lobbying. If there is a large and effective association then this may provide a preferred alternative to direct representation. The extent of development of associations depends on how far businesses can act collectively rather than individually. This collective action problem (CAP), originally elaborated by Olson,[21] creates particular difficulties for influence and lobbying since associations that influence Brussels are providing something to members the benefits of which cannot be excluded from non-member businesses. As a result businesses will lack incentives to become members since they can free ride on the benefits provided by members. The free rider problem means that the greater the extent to which associations encompass all businesses the greater will be the advantage gained by an individual business from opting out and free riding on the rest. Olson suggests that this results in endemic fragmentation and smallness of influence associations since the search, bargaining and monitoring costs between businesses in such associations to check on cheating or opting out can only be kept low and effective, or solidarity can remain high, where the association is small in membership. This is a result confirmed in empirical assessments.[22] As a consequence association size is both an outcome of, and an explanatory factor lying behind, the density of membership of an influence-orientated association. We thus would expect to include the influence of size and density of associations as explanatory variables in any systematic assessment of the extent of direct lobbying.

However, at a European level, it is argued by Greenwood[23] that 'it is almost impossible to use Olson's topology, . . . because of the difficulty of ascertaining who precisely has influence with federated associations'. This complexity, he argues, 'makes it extremely difficult to apply some of the traditional theories of collective action to the European level (since) . . . a range of selective incentives may not be necessary in Euro groups as a supplement to the goal-oriented role to entice membership'.[24] However, we argue here that part of Olson's ideas *can* be used to explain key aspects of the choice of using direct representation in Europe. But this depends on extending the arguments about what is expected from the dynamics of associations for their different *types* of members.

A key aspect of association dynamics is argued by Hirschman[25] to result from the interplay of exit, voice, loyalty and involvement. A high rate of *exit* (or low density of membership) will be indicative of an association that offers few individual or collective benefits to members. Direct lobbying is an indicator of exit or opting out strategies by a business from its sector association. We would thus expect more direct lobbying where associations are smaller and less effective. However, this will also be influenced by *voice*, which is an alternative to exit that allows a member to influence decision making within the association, including its influence strategy. However, voice takes time and effort and is usually more costly than exit so that it is usually on option only for the most capable or larger and more influential members. Hence, we might expect that whilst sectors with the smallest associations have more direct lobbying, where these sectors also have a strong presence of larger companies there may also be a strong participation in their associations. This will also draw on the concept of *loyalty*, which creates a threshold to exit and hence makes voice more likely: individuals stay as members because they feel they have to, for personal reasons, in order to gain benefits for their businesses, which may be more possible for the largest businesses, or as a commitment to a level of collective solidarity. This fits with the argument that there is a potential cost of 'non-membership' of an association: that businesses miss out on 'legitimacy' or 'status' by not being members of an association.[26] However, loyalty alone, Hirschman argues, is usually insufficient without *involvement*,[27] where a member receives some specific rewards or benefits; for example by being given status, or access to some more exclusive benefits. It seems likely that a large business might therefore choose to stay as a member of an association for European lobbying purposes because it can strongly influence the association's strategy, although it may also directly lobby, thus giving it the chance of two routes of influence. This hypothesis is suggested also by Useem[28] who has argued that large companies may be able to exercise a disproportionate control over associations as a result of their power, using threats of exit to gain stronger voice and involvement and hence influence over their association.

The Hirschman/Useem view of the dynamics of associations will clearly have different effects for different businesses in different sectors and different types or sizes of association. Where the sector is highly concentrated a very small influence-oriented association will often be able to encompass a very high density of members. In such a situation monitoring, scrutiny, and peer pressure between businesses is clearly possible in a way that would be impossible for large associations. This can reduce free riding and opting out and increase the use of the association for lobbying. Very small associations should also be more able to agree a single collective view. In addition, very small associations are likely to be strongly managed by their members rather than giving extensive executive authority to a council or director/chief executive. This should mean that member businesses will be more likely to use the association for influence purposes, rather than direct lobbying, since they should be in closer agreement with, or have more direct control over, its views and objectives. Hence we would generally expect more direct lobbying by businesses in small and densely membered associations than in large associations with low density of membership.

The dynamics of associations, their sectors and individual business size characteristics are thus each important but *interrelated* variables that must be assessed jointly, which is how they are treated in the analysis which follows. We attempt to assess the interrelations of the key features, underlying the level of association development between businesses as influences on choice of direct lobbying. Important features are the size of a sector's businesses, the sector's level of competition, the extent of organization between firms, the degree of market concentration across different size classes of business, the spread of size classes, overall sector value, degree of localization, extent of internationalization and cross border trade, and the level of government intervention. These features interact with each other and many are difficult to measure.

NOTES

* This chapter has been adapted from, R. J. Bennett (1999) *Political Studies*, XLVII, pp. 241–246.

1 Greenwood, J., R. Grote and K. Ronit, *Organised Interests and the European Community*, (London, Sage, 1992); S. Mazey and J. Richardson (eds), *Lobbying in the European Community* (Oxford, Oxford University Press, 1993); R. H. Pedler and M. P. C. M. van Schendelen (eds), *Lobbying in the European Union: Companies, Trade Associations and Issue Groups* (Aldershot, Darmouth, 1994).

2 Mazey and Richardson, *Lobbying in the European Community*.

3 See e.g. J. Greenwood and K. Ronit, 'Interest groups in the European Community', *West European Politics*, 71, 1 (1994, 31–52: J. Greenwood (ed.), *European Casebook on Business Alliances* (London, Prentice Hall, 1995): Pedler and van Schendelen, *Lobbying in the European Union*: W. Grant, 'Pressure Groups and the European Community: an Overview', in Mazey and Richardson, *Lobbying in the European Community*, pp. 27–46.

4 Greenwood and Ronit, 'Interest groups in the European Community'.

5 M. P. C. M. van Schendelen (ed.), *National, Public and Private EC Lobbying* (Aldershot, Dartmouth, 1993): Greenwood and Ronit, 'Interest groups in the European Community'.

6 See Economic and Social Committee, *Community Advisory Committee for the Representation of Socio-economic Interests* (Farnborough, Saxon House, 1980): Commission of the European Communities, *An Open and Structured Dialogue*.

7 Greenwood and Ronit, 'Interest groups in the European Community'.

8 Mazey and Richardson, 'Interest groups in the European Community.

9 Greenwood and Ronit, 'Interest groups in the European Community', p. 43, J. McLaughlin, A. G. Jordan and W. Maloney, 'Corporate lobbying in the European Community', *Journal of Common Market Studies*, 31, 2, (1993), 192–211: Grant, 'Pressure Groups in the European Community'.

10 van Schendelen, *National, Public and Private EC Lobbying*: Mazey and Richardson, *Lobbying in the European Community*: Greenwood, *European Casebook*.

11 Greenwood, *European Casebook*, p. 6.

12 McLaughlin *et al.*, 'Corporate lobbying in the European Community'.

13 Greenwood, *European Casebook*.

14 W. Streeck and P. C. Schmitter (eds), *Private Interest Government: Beyond Market and State* (London, Sage, 1985): J. R. Bowman, *Capitalist Collective Action: Competition, Co-operation and Conflict in the Coal Industry* (Cambridge, Cambridge University Press, 1989): M. S. Mizruchi, *The Structure of Corporate Political Action: Interfirm Relations and their Consequences* (Cambridge MA, Harvard University Press, 1992): B. Unger and F. van Waarden, *Convergence or Diversity: Internationalisation and Economic Policy Response* (Aldershot, Avebury, 1995): Greenwood and Ronit, 'Interest groups in the European Community': Mazey and Richardson, *Lobbying in the European Community*: C. Crouch and F. Traxler, *Organised Industrial Relations in Europe: What Future?* (Aldershot, Avebury, 1995): R. J. Bennett, 'The Impact of European economic integration on business associations: the UK case', *West European Politics*, 20, 3 (1997), 61–90.

15 Bowman, *Capitalist Collective Action*.

16 Mizruchi, *The Structure of Corporate Political Action*.

17 Streeck and Schmitter, *Private Interest Government*: J. McLaughlin *et al.*, 'Corporate lobbying in the EC': Greenwood and Ronit, 'Interest groups in the European Community'.

18 See e.g. E. H. Lorenz, 'Flexible production systems and the social construction of trust', *Politics and Society*, 21, 3, (1993), 307–24.

19 S. Bowen, 'Companies, Trade Associations and Information Exchange', in R. J. Bennett (ed.), *Trade Associations in Britain and Germany* (London and Bonn, Anglo-German Foundation, 1997), pp. 35–39.

20 Streeck and Schmitter, *Private Interest Government*; F. van Waarden, 'Two Logics of Collective

Action? Business Associations as Distinct from Trade Unions: the Problem of Associations of Organizations', in D. Sadowski and O. Jacobi (eds), *Employers' Associations in Europe: Policy and Organization* (Baden-Baden, Nomos, 1991), pp. 51–84; B. Unger and F. van Waarden, *Convergence or Diversity*; Crouch and Traxler, *Organised Industrial Relations in Europe*.

21 M. Olson, *The Logic of Collective Action: Public Goods and the Theory of Groups* (Cambridge MA, Harvard University Press, 2nd ed., 1971).

22 See e.g. Streeck and Schmitter, *Private Interest Government*; W. Grant (ed.), *Business Interests, Organisational Development and Private Interest Government* (Berlin, Walter de Gruyter, 1987); van Schendelen, *National, Public and Private Lobbying*; Sadowski and Jacobi, *Employer's Association in Europe*; L. Lanzalaco, 'Coping with Heterogeneity: Peak Associations of Business within and across Western European Nations', in Greenwood *et al.*, *Organized Interests and the European Community*, pp. 173–92.

23 Greenwood, *European Casebook*, p. 9.

24 Greenwood, *European Casebook*, p. 293.

25 A. O. Hirschman, *Exit, Voice and Loyalty* (Cambridge MA, Harvard University Press, 1970); A. O. Hirschman, *Shifting Involvements: Private Interest and Public Action* (Oxford, Basil Blackwell, 1982).

26 See Greenwood, *European Casebook*, who cites 'Interest groups and public policy: the insider/outsider model revised', *Journal of Public Policy*, 14 (1995), 17–38.

27 A. O. Hirschman, *Shifting Involvements*.

28 M. Useem, *The Inner Circle: Large Corporations and the Rise of the Business Political Activity in the US and UK* (Oxford, Oxford University Press, 1984).

21

GLOBALIZATION AND THE ADVANCED CAPITALIST STATE[*]

Anthony McGrew

No contemporary analysis of the ACS can afford to ignore the stresses to which it is subject because of its strategic location at the intersection of international and domestic processes. As the earlier discussion has made clear, both the formation and the nature of the ACS can only be properly understood by reference to both endogenous and exogenous forces of social change. Moreover, as patterns of global interconnectedness appear to be intensifying, the distinctions between the internal and the external, the foreign and the domestic, seem increasingly anachronistic. A moment's reflection on some of the critical social issues which confront the ACS, such as drug abuse or the environment, would confirm that each has a global or transnational dimension. Few issues can now be defined as purely 'domestic' or specifically 'international'. On the contrary, it is more accurate to view states as confronted by 'intermestic' problems. However we choose to recognize the erosion of this traditional distinction, the central point is that all ACSs are increasingly subject to globalizing forces which impose powerful constraints on state sovereignty and press heavily upon the everyday lives of its citizens.

Globalization '. . . should be understood as the re-ordering of time and distance in our lives. Our lives, in other words, are increasingly influenced by activities and events happening well away from the social context in which we carry on our day-to-day activities' (Giddens, 1989, p.520). To talk of globalization is to recognize that there are dynamic processes at work constructing and weaving networks of interaction and interconnectedness across the states and societies which make up the modern world system. Globalization has two distinct dimensions: scope (or stretching) and intensity (or deepening). On the one hand it defines a process or set of processes which embrace most of the globe or which operate worldwide: the concept therefore has a spatial connotation. Politics and other social activities are becoming 'stretched' across the globe. On the other hand it also implies an intensification in the levels of interaction, interconnectedness, or interdependence between the states and societies which constitute the world community. Accordingly alongside the 'stretching' goes a 'deepening' of the impact of global processes on national and local communities.

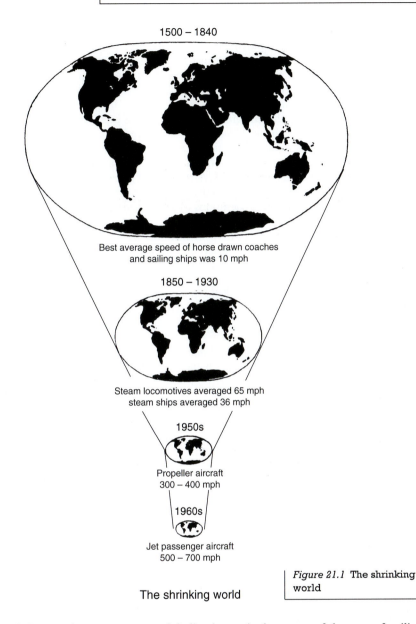

1500 – 1840

Best average speed of horse drawn coaches
and sailing ships was 10 mph

1850 – 1930

Steam locomotives averaged 65 mph
steam ships averaged 36 mph

1950s

Propeller aircraft
300 – 400 mph

1960s

Jet passenger aircraft
500 – 700 mph

The shrinking world

Figure 21.1 The shrinking world

Far from being an abstract concept, globalization articulates one of the more familiar features of modern existence. A single moment's reflection on the contents of our own kitchen cupboards or fridges would underline the fact that, simply as passive consumers, we are very much part of a global network of production and exchange.

In his analysis of the welfare state, Alber (1988) stresses the significance of global forces – the economic crisis of the 1970s and early 1980s - in stimulating a restructuring of welfare provision within all capitalist societies. A combination of factors made it increasingly difficult for governments, of whatever political persuasion, to sustain the growth in welfare programmes which had occurred in the 1960s or to protect workers from the consequences of growing international competition. The kind of 'managed capitalism' which had emerged in the post-war period no longer meshed with an increasingly globally integrated economic and financial system. Full employment or extensive welfare provision which require high levels of taxation, are difficult to sustain when capital is so readily mobile and foreign competition so intense. Underlying this erosion of 'managed capitalism' in the 1980s has been an acceleration in processes of economic globalization and the consequent break-up of the post-war global order.

As Keohane observed, 'the European welfare state was built on foundations provided by American hegemony' (Keohane, 1984, p.22). 'Managed capitalism' did not simply reflect a domestic political settlement but rather was constructed upon the post-war global settlement of a liberal (free trade) world economic order underwritten by US military and economic power. Within this world order, structures of global economic management, such as the International Monetary Fund (IMF) and General Agreement on Tariffs and Trade (GATT), nurtured the economic conditions which helped sustain the rapid post-war growth of Western economies and enabled the massive expansion of welfare provision. Both 'managed capitalism' and a regulated world economy were mutually reinforcing. However, by the mid-1980s the combined effects of economic recession, the resultant global economic restructuring, the intensification of the financial and economic integration of Western economies, and the emergence of new centres of economic power such as Japan and Germany, had seriously undermined the post-war global capitalist order. As the 1990s dawned, the conditions essential to the survival of the welfare state in its conventional form had been transformed:

> . . . the reconstruction of the international political economy has definitively altered the circumstances in which welfare states have to operate. Exposing national economies and national corporatist arrangements to the unregulated world economy has transformed the circumstances under which any government might seek, for example, to pursue a policy of full employment . . .
>
> The deregulation of international markets and of financial institutions, in particular, have tended to weaken the capacities of the interventionist state, to render all economies more open and to make national capital and more especially national labour movements much more subject to the terms and conditions of international competition.
>
> (Pierson, 1991, pp.177, 188)

For some, this process of 'reconstruction' signals an even more profound shift in the nature of global capitalism. Lash and Urry, for instance, argue that organized or 'managed capitalism' is giving way to a form of 'disorganized capitalism' in which national economies are becoming increasingly beyond the control of national governments, partly as a consequence of the accelerating globalization of production and exchange (Lash and Urry, 1987, p.308; Offe, 1984). But it is not simply the capacity of the capitalist state to control its own economy that is at issue.

Writing in the early 1970s, Morse pointed to the ways in which the global movement of goods, money, ideas, images, knowledge, technology, etc., challenged the ability of the ACS to govern effectively within its own territory (Morse, 1976). Morse argued that growing international interdependence diminished the effectiveness of national governments and thereby encouraged a corresponding attachment to international forms of regulation or co-operation. Over the last three decades there has been a startling expansion in levels of international co-operation. Through a myriad of international institutions, such as the IMF, GATT, International Civil Aviation Organization, International Telecommunications Union, Organization of Economic Cooperation and Development etc., informal arrangements such as the G7, and international networks of key policy makers, advanced capitalist states have created a vast array of *international regimes*: sets of international rules, norms, procedures, modes of decision making and organizations. These embrace those issue-areas in which states have become increasingly interdependent or where transnational activities create common problems. Such regimes seek to regulate high policy domains, such as defence and global finance, as well as welfare policy domains such as the trade in narcotics, environmental issues and AIDS.

International regimes, in effect, express the growing internationalization of the advanced capitalist state and the internationalization of state elites. Within Europe, this internationalization has culminated in the evolution of the European Communities from a common market into a quasi-supranational political structure which can take decisions binding upon member governments: a contemporary illustration of this legislative power being the implementation across the EC of the Social Charter. Advanced capitalist states are enmeshed in an extensive array of formal and informal international regimes which make them simultaneously both the determinants as well as the objects of an expanding field of international regulatory practices. In some domains, the sovereignty of the ACS is severely compromised by its participation in these regimes whilst in others it is sometimes enhanced. Clearly ACSs have always operated under external constraints of all kinds. However, it is frequently argued that international co-operation restricts the exercise of state autonomy - the capacity to act independently, within circumscribed parameters, in the articulation and pursuit of domestic and international policy objectives - across a range of policy domains. Yet, in a more interconnected world, international co-operation has become increasingly vital to the achievement of a host of domestic policy objectives. For instance dealing with drug addiction requires international co-operation to combat the global trade in narcotics, whilst domestic economic management demands co-operation on interest rates and currency fluctuations. The ACS thus confronts a major dilemma as it attempts to balance effectiveness against a potential loss of autonomy.

For some, such a choice merely reinforces growing evidence of the decline of the nation-state and calls into question its continued viability.

NOTE

* This chapter has been adapted from, McGrew, A. (1992) 'Globalisation and the advanced capitalist state', in Allen, J., Braham, P. and Lewis, P. (eds) *Political and Economic Forms of Modernity*, Polity Press in association with The Open University, ch. 2, pp. 106–110.

REFERENCES

Alber, J. (1988) 'Continuities and changes in the idea of the welfare state', *Politics and Society*, vol.16, no.4, pp.451–68.

Giddens, A. (1989) *Sociology*, Cambridge, Polity Press.

Keohane, R.O. (1984) 'The world political economy and the crisis of embedded liberalism', in Goldthorpe, J. (ed.) *Order and Conflict in Contemporary Capitalism*, Oxford, Clarendon Press.

Lash, S. and Urry, J. (1987) *The End of Organized Capitalism*, Cambridge, Polity Press.

Morse, E. (1976) *Modernization and the Transformation of International Relations*, New York, Free Press.

Offe, C. (1984) *Contradictions of the Welfare State*, London, Hutchinson.

Pierson, C. (1991) *Beyond the Welfare State?*, Cambridge, Polity Press.

SECTION 4: THE SYSTEM? TECHNOLOGY, ECOLOGY AND GLOBALISATION

INTRODUCTION

In this last section we return to our opening concern of how we conceptualise the environment. Our examination of each of the three previous 'environments' – the economy, society and the state – was informed by an associated academic discipline. The method of examination used on each of these environments is termed analysis. It is supported by accepted models of how each of them works and concepts which are central to understanding the role of businesses in them. This method sheds some light on the nature of the relationships between businesses and the separate environments. However, I hope it has also become apparent that separating the world in such a way, while facilitating understanding of it at a simple level, cannot hope to reflect fully the complex phenomena which we observe in it. Three phenomena in particular have challenged established methods of analysis – the rapid development of information and communication technologies (ICTs), the developing debate over the treatment of our physical environment and, of course, globalisation. We have already seen that globalisation is an issue to which there are several aspects and on which there are several perspectives. However, the other two phenomena, which are equally complex, require further consideration. The word 'system' is commonly incorporated into businesses' descriptions of the environments on which these phenomena directly impact – information and/or communication system and 'eco-system'. As we shall see, however, 'system' can also be used as an overarching phrase to describe the world of business encompassing the three previously examined environments.

The emergence and application of ICTs to many areas of our lives since the 1960s spawned the development of a new discipline based on a different method of examination – systems. The sheer breadth of consequences of the application of new technologies needed to be understood, for forecasting purposes if nothing else. This was why an alternative method was adopted to try to model 'the whole picture'. In chapter 22, Ackoff describes the philosophical development of the systems approach within business organisations. He compares the 'holistic synthesis' of systems thinkers to the 'reductionist analysis' of scientific thinkers. However one of the dangers of this becomes apparent in chapter 23 by McKay *et al*. Their appraisal of Bell's 'Information Society' thesis, which could be considered holistic in its approach, uncovered its narrow determinism. This was partly the result of the values underlying Bell's conception of the system and partly the result of a lack of depth in his understanding of the components involved in the system, which, ironically, may have been developed through analysis. This optimistic determinism is very typical of the liberal approach to technology. Chapter 24 by Hudson provides us with a further example, though she is more cautious in her conclusions. This also shows how systems are in the 'eye of the beholder'. Hudson's system is concerned with the structure of information and communication technologies and its impact on the economy. Manders and Brenner provide a more critical view of how businesses use technology in chapter 25. Their system is more to do with the interaction of social structures and technologies. While accepting the nature and rapidity of change in information technology, they place it within the traditional marxist framework of a capitalist production system. We can begin to see here how systems, like other models, can be constructed differently depending on the values held by the constructor.

This is also evident in the construction of 'eco-system' models which contribute to the debate about business' relationship with the natural environment. Chapter 26 by Lovins *et al.* urges businesses to extend current business practices to take account of the environmental costs of decisions and to build environmental sustainability into their operations in the next wave of strategic change. Their argument is premised on a model of the natural environment as a resource system. Boehmer-Christiansen questions this premise very directly in chapter 27. She views the environment as more a political system, in which businesses and the connected activities of science and innovation hold considerable power to influence public perceptions of ecological issues.

22

CREATING THE CORPORATE FUTURE*

Russell L. Ackoff

ANALYSIS

Children given something they [do] not understand – a radio, a clock, or a toy – are almost certain to try to take it apart to see how it works. From an understanding of how the parts work they try to extract an understanding of the whole. This three-stage process – (1) taking apart the thing to be understood, (2) trying to understand the behavior of the parts taken separately, and (3) trying to assemble this understanding into an understanding of the whole – became the basic method of inquiry of the age initiated by the Renaissance. It is called *analysis*. No wonder that today we use *analysis* and *inquiry* synonymously. For example, we speak of 'analyzing a problem' and 'trying to solve a problem' interchangeably. Most of us would be hard pressed if asked to identify an alternative to the analytical method.

Commitment to the analytical method induces observation and experimentation, which, in fact, brought about what we think of today as modern science. Over time, the use of this method led to a series of questions about the nature of reality, the answers to which formed [the] world view of the Machine Age.

REDUCTIONISM

According to the viewpoint of the Machine Age, in order to understand something it has to be taken apart conceptually or physically. Then how does one come to understand its parts? The answer to this question is obvious: by taking the parts apart. But this answer obviously leads to another question: Is there any end to such a process? The answer to this question is not obvious. It depends on whether one believes that the world as a whole is understandable in principle, if not in practice. In the age initiated by the Renaissance it was generally believed that complete understanding of the world was possible. In fact, by the mid-nineteenth century many leading scientists believed that such understanding was within their grasp. If one believes this, then the answer to the second question must be yes. Given the commitment to the analytical method, unless there are ultimate parts, *elements*, complete understanding of the universe would not be possible. If there are such indivisible parts and we come to understand them and their behavior, then complete understanding of the world is possible, at least in principle. Therefore, the belief in elements is a fundamental underpinning of the Machine-Age view of the world. The doctrine that asserts this belief is called *reductionism*: all reality and our experience of it can be reduced to ultimate indivisible elements.

Formulated so abstractly, this doctrine may not appear to be familiar; but it is very familiar to most of us in its specific manifestations. In physics, for example, with the work of the nineteenth century English chemist John Dalton people generally came to accept a speculation of Democritus and other ancient Greek philosopher[s] as well as the seventeenth century French philosopher Descartes: all physical objects are reducible to indivisible particles of matter, or *atoms*. These elements were believed to have only two intrinsic properties: mass and energy. Physicists tried to build their understanding of nature on a foundation of an understanding of these elements.

Chemistry, like physics, had its elements. They appeared in the familiar Periodic Table. Biologists believed that all life was reducible to a single element, the *cell*. [. . .] Linguists tried to reduce language to indivisible elements of sound called *phonemes*; and so on and on.

In every domain of inquiry men sought to gain understanding by looking for elements. In a sense, Machine-Age science was a crusade whose Holy Grail was the element.

DETERMINISM

Once the elements of a thing had been identified and were themselves understood it was necessary to assemble such understanding into an understanding of the whole. This required an explanation of the *relationships* between the parts, or how they interacted. It is not surprising that in an age in which it was widely believed that all things were reducible to elements it was also believed that one simple relationship, *cause–effect*, was sufficient to explain all interactions.

Cause–effect is such a familiar concept that many of us have forgotten what it means. It may be helpful, therefore, to review its meaning. One thing is said to be the cause of another, its effect, if the cause is both *necessary* and *sufficient* for its effect. One thing is necessary for another if the other cannot occur unless the first does. One thing is sufficient for another if the occurrence of the first assures the occurrence of the second. The program directed at explaining all natural phenomena by using only the cause–effect relationship led to a series of questions whose answers provided the remaining foundations for the Machine-Age view of the world.

First, the following question arose: Is everything in the universe the effect of some cause? The answer to this question was dictated by the prevailing belief in the possibility of understanding the universe completely. For this to be possible, everything had to be taken as the effect of some cause, otherwise they could not be related or understood. This doctrine was called *determinism*. It precluded anything occurring by either chance or choice.

Now, if everything in the universe is caused, then each cause is itself the effect of a previous cause. If we start tracing back through the chain of causes do we come to a beginning of the process? The answer to this question was also dictated by the belief in the complete understandability of the universe. It was yes. Therefore, a *first cause* was postulated and taken to be God. This line of reasoning was called the 'cosmological proof of the existence of God.' It is significant that this proof derived from the commitment to the cause–effect relationship and the belief in the complete understandability of the universe.

Because God was conceptualized as the first cause, He was taken to be the *creator*. As we will see, not all concepts of God attribute this function to Him, or even attribute individuality or 'Himness' to Him.

The doctrine of determinism gave rise to yet another critical question to which philosophers of the Machine Age devoted much of their time. How can we explain free will, choice, and purpose in a deterministic universe? There was no generally accepted answer to this question, but this did not create a problem because there was widespread agreement on this much: the concept of free will or choice was not needed to explain any natural phenomenon, including the behavior of man.

Some held that free will was an illusion granted to us by a merciful God who realized how dull life would be without it. Man was thought to be like a fly who, riding on the trunk of an elephant, believes he is steering it. This belief makes the ride more interesting and the elephant does not mind.

Another important consequence of the commitment to causal thinking derives from the acceptance of a cause as sufficient for its effect. Because of this a cause was taken to explain its effect *completely*. Nothing else was required to explain it, *not even the environment*. Therefore, Machine-Age thinking was, to a large extent, *environment-free*; it tried to develop understanding of natural phenomena without using the concept of environment. For example, what does the word 'freely' in the familiar 'Law of Freely Falling Bodies' mean? It means a body falling in the absence of any environmental influences. The apparent universality of such laws (and there were many) does not derive from their applicability to every environment for, strictly speaking, they apply to none; it derives from the fact that they apply *approximately* to most environments that we experience.

Perhaps even more revealing of the environment-free orientation of Machine-Age science is the nature of the place in which its inquiry was usually conducted, the *laboratory*. A laboratory is a place so constructed as to facilitate exclusion of the environment. It is a place in which the effect of one variable on another can be studied without the intervention of the environment.

MECHANISM

The concept of the universe that derives from the exclusive use of analysis and the doctrines of reductionism and determinism is *mechanistic*. The world was viewed as a machine, not merely like one. The universe was frequently compared to a hermetically sealed clock. This is a very revealing comparison, implying that it had no environment. Like a clock, its behavior was thought to be determined by its internal structure and the causal laws of nature.

THE INDUSTRIAL REVOLUTION

This revolution had to do with the replacement of man by man-made machines as a source of work. Its two central concepts were *work* and *machine*. Whatever was thought of work, it was believed to be *real*, particularly after the Reformation. Because all real things were believed to be reducible to atoms and atoms had only two intrinsic properties, mass (matter) and energy, work was conceptualized as the application of energy to matter so as to change its properties. For example, the movement of coal and its transformation into heat (energy) were considered to be work. Thought, however, was not taken to be work because it did not involve the application of energy to matter.

A machine was considered any object that could be used to apply energy to matter. Not surprisingly, it was believed that all machines were reducible to elementary machines: the lever, pulley, wheel and axle, and inclined plane (of which the wedge and screw are modifications).

The mechanization of work was greatly facilitated by reducing it to a set of simple tasks. Therefore, work was *analyzed* to reduce it to its *elements*. These elements were tasks so simple that they could only be done by one person – for example, tightening a screw or driving a nail. Then many of the work elements were mechanized. Not all were because either the technology required was not available or, although available, it was more costly than the use of human labor. Therefore, people and machines, each doing elementary tasks, were aggregated to do the whole job. The result was the industrialized production and assembly line that forms the spine of the modern factory.

The benefits of the Industrial Revolution are too obvious to dwell on here. They were many and significant. The same can be said of its costs. However, there is one cost which we have only recently become aware of, derived from what might be called the irony of the Industrial Revolution. In our effort to replace ourselves with machines as a source of energy, we reduced our work to elementary tasks designed to be simple enough to be done by machines, eventually if not immediately. In this way *we were reduced to behaving like machines*, doing very simple repetitive tasks. Our work became dehumanized. This is the source of one of the most critical problems facing us today, our alienation from work.

The nature of the workplace developed during the Industrial Revolution was dictated by the application of the analytical method to work. If there were another way of thinking about work, it would be possible to conceive of another kind of workplace, one very different from the kind that we know today. This possibility is one that recently has been given much thought. I will return to it after we have seen what the alternative way of thinking is.
[. . .]

THE SYSTEMS AGE

No age has a starting point; it emerges imperceptibly in bits and pieces that eventually combine, first to produce an awareness that something fundamental is happening, then to provide a new world view.

Doubts about a prevailing world view usually begin with the appearances of *dilemmas*. A dilemma is a problem or question that cannot be solved or answered within the prevailing world view and therefore calls it into question. We have already considered one such question: how can we account for free will in a mechanistic universe? In physics, Heisenberg's *Uncertainty Principle* presented another such dilemma. He showed that within the prevailing paradigm in physics two critical properties of point particles could not be determined simultaneously; as the accuracy of the determination of one increases, the accuracy of the other decreases. This called into question the belief that the world is completely understandable, even in principle.

Then there was the dilemma that arose as all the king's men tried and failed to put Humpty Dumpty together again. Some things, once disassembled, could not be reassembled. The essential properties of other things could not be inferred from either the properties of their parts or their interactions, as for example, the personality or intelligence of a human being. More recently, in their studies of servomechanisms, machines that control other machines, Arturo Rosenblueth and Norbert Wiener argued that such machines could only be understood if they were assumed to display choice and goal-seeking behavior. Choice and mechanism, however, are incompatible concepts. This dilemma had a special significance which is discussed later in this chapter.

In the latter part of the last century and the early part of this one, dilemmas arose with increasing frequency in every field of inquiry. Investigators confronted with dilemmas in one field gradually became aware of those arising in other fields and the similarities among them. They also became aware of the fact that the prevailing mechanistic view of the world and the beliefs on which it was based were increasingly being brought into question. This awareness was intensified by events that took place just before, during, and immediately after World War II.

This war took science and scientists out of their laboratories and into the 'real world' in an effort to solve important problems arising in large, complex organizations – military, governmental, and corporate. Scientists discovered that the problems they faced could not be disassembled into any one discipline and that the interactions of the solutions of disassembled parts were of greater importance than the solutions considered separately. This in turn led to the formation of interdisciplinary efforts. In the late 1930s, Operational Research, an interdisciplinary activity, emerged out of the British military establishment to deal with the management and control of its complex operations.

By the 1950s interdisciplinary scientific activities proliferated. These included the management sciences, decision sciences, computer sciences, information sciences, cybernetics, policy sciences, peace science, and many others. The overlap of interest among them and the similarities in their practices led to a search for a theme common to all of them.

By the mid-1950s it was generally recognized that the source of similarities of the interdisciplines was their shared preoccupation with the behavior of *systems*. This concept gradually came to be recognized as one that could be used to organize an increasingly varied set of intellectual pursuits. Of greater importance, however, was the fact that it revealed the fundamental dilemma of the Machine Age and suggested how its world view might be modified to escape the horns of that dilemma. It is for this reason that I refer to the emerging era as the *Systems Age*.

THE NATURE OF A SYSTEM

Before we can begin to understand the change in world view that the focus on systems is bringing about, we must first understand the concept of systems itself.

A system is a set of two or more elements that satisfies the following three conditions.

1 *The behavior of each element has an effect on the behavior of the whole.* Consider, for example, that system which is, perhaps, the most familiar to us: the human body. Each of its parts – the heart, lungs, stomach, and so on – has an effect on the performance of the whole. However, one part of the body, the appendix, is not known to have any such effect. It is not surprising, therefore, that it is called the appendix which means 'attached to,' not 'a part of.' If a function is found for the appendix, its name would probably be changed.
2 *The behavior of the elements and their effects on the whole are interdependent.* This condition implies that the way each element behaves and the way it affects the whole depends on how at least one other element behaves. No element has an independent effect on the system as a whole. In the human body, for example, the way the heart behaves and the way it affects the body as a whole depends on the behavior of the brain, lungs, and other parts of the body. The same is true for the brain and lungs.
3 *However subgroups of the elements are formed, each has an effect on the behavior of the whole and none has an independent effect on it.* To put it another way, the elements of a system are so connected that independent subgroups of them cannot be formed.

A system, therefore, is a whole that cannot be divided into independent parts. From this, two of its most important properties derive: every part of a system has properties that it loses when separated from the system, and every system has some properties – its essential ones – that none of its parts do. An organ or part of the body, for example, if removed from the body does not continue to operate as it did before removal. The eye detached from the body cannot see. On the other hand, people can run, play piano, read, write, and do many other things that none of their parts can do by themselves. No part of a human being is human; only the whole is.

The essential properties of a system taken as a whole derive from the *interactions* of its parts, not their actions taken separately. Therefore, *when a system is taken apart it loses its essential properties.* Because of this – and this is the critical point – *a system is a whole that cannot be understood by analysis.*

Realization of this fact is the primary source of the intellectual revolution that is bringing about a change of age. It has become clear that a method other than analysis is required for understanding the behavior and properties of systems.

SYSTEMS THINKING

Synthesis, or putting things together, is the key to systems thinking just as analysis, or taking them apart, was the key to Machine-Age thinking. Synthesis, of course, is as old as analysis – Aristotle dealt with both – but it is taking on a new meaning and significance in a new context just as analysis did with the emergence of the Machine Age. Synthesis and analysis are complementary processes. Like the head and tail of a coin, they can be considered separately, but they cannot be separated. Therefore, the differences between Systems-Age and Machine-Age thinking derives not from the fact that one synthesizes and the other analyzes, but from the fact that systems thinking combines the two in a new way.

Systems thinking reverses the three-stage order of Machine-Age thinking: (1) decomposition of that which is to be explained, (2) explanation of the behavior or properties of the parts taken separately, and (3) aggregating these explanations into an explanation of the whole. This third step, of course, is synthesis. In the systems approach there are also three steps:

1   Identify a containing whole (system) of which the thing to be explained is a part.
2   Explain the behavior or properties of the containing whole.
3   Then explain the behavior or properties of the thing to be explained in terms of its *role(s)* or *function(s)* within its containing whole.

Note that in this sequence, synthesis precedes analysis.

In analytical thinking the thing to be explained is treated as a whole to be taken apart. In synthetic thinking the thing to be explained is treated as a part of a containing whole. The former *reduces* the focus of the investigator; the latter *expands* it.

An example might help clarify the difference. A Machine-Age thinker, confronted with the need to explain a university, would begin by disassembling it until he reached its elements; for example, from university to college, from college to department, and from department to faculty, students, and subject matter. Then he would define faculty, student, and subject matter. Finally, he would aggregate these into a definition of a department, thence to college, and conclude with a definition of a university.

A systems thinker confronted with the same task would begin by identifying a system containing the university; for example, the educational system. Then such a thinker would define the objectives and functions of the educational system and do so with respect to the still larger social system that contains it. Finally, he or she would explain or define the university in terms of its roles and functions in the educational system.

These two approaches should not (but often do) yield contradictory or conflicting results: they are complementary. Development of this complementarity is a major task of systems thinking. Analysis focuses on *structure*; it reveals *how things work*. Synthesis focuses on *function*; it reveals *why things operate as they do*. Therefore, analysis yields *knowledge*; synthesis yields *understanding*. The former enables us to *describe*; the latter, to *explain*.

Analysis looks *into* things; synthesis looks *out* of things. Machine-Age thinking was concerned only with the interactions of the parts of the thing to be explained; systems thinking is similarly concerned, but it is additionally occupied with the interactions of that thing with other things in its environment and with its environment itself. It is also concerned with the *functional* interaction of the parts of a system. This orientation derives from the preoccupation of systems thinking with the *design* and *redesign* of systems. In systems design, parts identified by analysis of the function(s) to be performed by the whole are not put together like unchangeable pieces of a jigsaw puzzle; they are designed to fit each other so as to work together *harmoniously* as well as efficiently and effectively.

Harmony has to do not only with the effect of the interactions of the parts on the whole, but also with the effects of the functioning of the whole and the interactions of the parts on the parts themselves. It is also concerned with the effects of the functioning of the parts and the whole on the containing system and other systems in its environment. This concern with harmony has important implications in the management of systems – implications that are explored below.

There are considerable differences between what might be called analytical and synthetic management. [. . .] One such difference is worth noting here. It is based on the following systems principle:

> If each part of a system, considered separately, is made to operate as efficiently as possible, the system as a whole will *not* operate as effectively as possible.

Although the general validity of this principle is not apparent, its validity in specific instances is. For example, consider the large number of types of automobile that are available. Suppose we bring one of each of these into a large garage and then employ a number of outstanding automotive engineers to determine which one has the best carburetor. When they have done so, we record the result and ask them to do the same for engines. We continue this process until we have covered all the parts required for an automobile. Then we ask the engineers to remove and assemble these parts. Would we obtain the best possible automobile? Of course not. We would not even obtain an automobile because *the parts would not fit together*; even if they did, *they would not work well together. The performance of a system depends more on how its parts interact than on how they act independently of each other.*

Similarly, an all-star baseball or football team is seldom if ever the best team available, although one might argue that it would be if its members were allowed to play together for a year or so. True, but if they became the best team it is very unlikely that all of its members would be on the new all-star team.

The current methodology of management is predominantly based on Machine-Age thinking. When managers are confronted with large complex problem or tasks, they almost always break them down into solvable or manageable parts; they 'cut them down to size.' Then they arrange to have each part solved or performed as well as possible. The outputs of these separate efforts are then assembled into a 'solution' of the whole. Yet we can be sure that the sum of the best solutions obtained from the parts taken separately is *not* the best solution to the whole. Fortunately, it is seldom the worst.

Awareness of this conflict between parts and the whole is reflected in the widespread recognition of the need for *coordinating* the behavior of the parts of a system. At the same time, however, measures of performance are set for the parts that bring them into conflict. Formulation of these measures is commonly based on the assumption that the best performance of the whole can be reduced to the sum of the best performances of its parts taken separately. The systems principle, however, asserts that this is not possible. Therefore, another and more effective way of organizing and managing the parts is required. One is considered below.

The application of systems thinking, whether to management or the world, like the application of Machine-Age thinking, raises a number of fundamental questions. The answers to these questions provide the doctrines from which a systems view of the world derives. Let us see how.

EXPANSIONISM

In systems thinking, increases in understanding are believed to be obtainable by expanding the systems to be understood, not by reducing them to their elements. Understanding proceeds from the whole to its parts, not from the parts to the whole as knowledge does.

If the behavior of a system is to be explained by referring to its containing system (the suprasystem), how is the behavior of the suprasystem to be explained? The answer is obvious: by reference to a more inclusive system, one that contains the suprasystem. Then the fundamental question – Is there any end to this process of expansion? Recall that when the corresponding question arose in the Machine Age – Is there any end to the process of reduction? – the answer was dictated by the belief that, at least in principle, complete understanding of the universe was possible. In the early part of this century, however, this belief was shattered by such dilemmas as that formulated by Heisenberg. As a result, we have come to believe that complete understanding of anything, let alone everything, is an *ideal* that can be approached continuously but *can never be attained*. Therefore, there is no need to assume the existence of an ultimate whole which if understood would yield the ultimate answer.

This means that we are free to believe or not in an all-containing whole. Since our understanding will never embrace such a whole, even if it exists, it makes no practical difference if we assume it to exist. Nevertheless, many individuals find comfort in assuming existence of such a unifying whole. Not surprisingly, they call it God. This God however, is very different from the Machine-Age God who was conceptualized as an individual who had created the universe. God-as-the-whole cannot be individualized or personified, and cannot be thought of as the creator. To do so would make no more sense than to speak of man as creator of his organs. In this holistic view of things man is taken as a part of God just as his heart is taken as a part of man.

Many will recognize that this holistic concept of God is precisely the one embraced by many Eastern religions which conceptualize God as a system, not as an element. It is not surprising, therefore, that in the past two decades many of the young people in the West – products of the emerging Systems Age – turned to religions of the East.

The East has used the concept of a system to organize its thinking about the universe for centuries, but it has not thought about systems scientifically. There is some hope, therefore, that in the creation of systems sciences the cultures of the East and West can be synthesized. The twain may yet meet in the Systems Age.

The doctrine of expansionism has a major effect on the way we go about trying to solve problems. In the Machine Age, when something did not work satisfactorily, we looked for improvement by manipulating the behavior of its parts; we looked for solutions from within and worked our way out from the interior only when we failed there. In the Systems Age we look for solutions from without and work our way in when we fail there.

[. . .]

PRODUCER–PRODUCT

The Machine Age's commitment to cause and effect was the source of many dilemmas, including the one involving free will. At the turn of the century the American philosopher E. A. Singer, Jr., showed that science had, in effect, been cheating. It was using two different relationships but calling both cause and effect. He pointed out, for example, that acorns do not cause oaks because they are *not* sufficient, even though they are necessary, for oaks. An acorn thrown into the ocean, or planted in the desert or an Arctic ice cap does not yield an oak. To call the relationship between an acorn and an oak 'probabilistic' or 'non deterministic causality,' as many scientists did, was cheating because it is not possible to have a probability other than 1.0 associated with a cause; a cause completely determines its effect. Therefore, Singer chose to call this relationship 'producer–product' and to differentiate it from cause–effect.

Singer went on to ask what the universe would look like if producer–product is applied to it rather than cause–effect. One might think of Singer's question in this way: an orange, when sliced vertically, yields a cross-sectional view that is very different from the view revealed when it is sliced horizontally. Yet both are views of the same thing. The more views we have of a thing, the better we can understand it. Singer argued similarly about the universe.

As Singer and Ackoff and Emery have shown, the view of the universe revealed by viewing it in terms of producer–product is quite different from that yielded by viewing it in terms of cause–effect. Because a producer is only necessary and not sufficient for its product, it cannot provide a complete explanation of it. There are always other necessary conditions, coproducers of its product. For example, moisture is a coproducer of an oak along with an acorn. These other necessary conditions taken collectively constitute the acorn's environment. Therefore, the use of the producer–product relationship requires the environment to explain everything whereas use of cause–effect requires the environment to explain nothing. Science based on the producer–product relationship is environment-*full*, not environment-*free*.

A law based on the producer–product relationship must specify the environment(s) under which it applies. No such law can apply in every environment, because if it did no environmental conditions would be necessary. Thus there are no universal laws in this view of the universe. For example, we have learned more recently that the law that everything that goes up must come down is not universally true. (Unfortunately, some things that we have put up with the intention that they do not come down, nevertheless have done so.) Environmentally relative laws can use probabilistic concepts in a consistent and meaningful way. In an environment in which all the necessary coproducing conditions are not specified – hence may or may not be present – it is not only meaningful but it is useful to speak of the probability of production. For example, we can determine the probability of an acorn producing an oak in a specified environment in which some of the relevant properties are not known. Therefore, the probability determined is the probability that the unspecified but necessary environmental conditions are present.

TELEOLOGY

Singer showed by reasoning that is too complicated to reproduce here that in the producer-product-based view of the world, such concepts as choice, purpose, and free will could be made operationally and objectively meaningful. A system's ends – *goals, objectives, and ideals* – could be established as objectively as the number of elements it contained. This made it possible to look at systems *teleologically*, in an output-oriented way, rather than deterministically, in an input-oriented way.

Objective teleology does not replace determinism, [. . .] it complements it. These are different views of the same thing, but the teleological approach is more fruitful when applied to systems.

Centuries ago Aristotle invoked teleological concepts to explain why things, inanimate as well as animate, behaved as they did; but he employed a *subjective* teleology. Among those who carry on in his spirit are some psychologists who try to explain human behavior by invoking such (unobservable, they claim) intervening variables as beliefs, feelings, attitudes, and drives which at best are only observable by those who have them. In an objective teleology, beliefs, feelings, attitudes, and the like are attributable to human beings because of *what they do*; hence are observable. These properties are derived from observed regularities of behavior under varied conditions. Such concepts do not lie behind behavior, but in it; hence are observable. In an objective teleology functional characteristics of systems are not treated as metaphysical forces, but as observable properties of the systems' behavior. [. . .]

Systems-oriented investigators focus on teleological (goal seeking and purposeful) systems. In the Machine Age, even human beings were thought of as machines. In the Systems Age, even machines are thought of as parts of purposeful systems. We now believe that a machine cannot be understood except by reference to the purpose for which it is used by the purposeful system of which it is a part. For example, we cannot understand why an automobile is like it is without understanding the purposes for which it is used. Moreover, some machines, teleogical mechanisms, are seen to have goals, if not purposes, of their own.

Ordinary machines serve the purposes of others but have no purposes of their own. *Organisms* and *organizations* are systems that usually have purposes of their own. However, the parts of an organism (i.e. heart, lungs, brain) do not have purposes of their own, but the parts of an organization do. Therefore, when we focus on organizations we are concerned with three levels of purpose: the purposes of the system, of its parts, and of the system of which it is part, the suprasystem.

There is a functional division of labor among the parts of all types of systems. A set of elements or parts, all of which do the same thing, does not constitute a system; it is an aggregation. For example, a collection of people waiting for a bus does not constitute a system, nor does a collection of clocks all ticking away on the same shelf. Each part of a system has a function in the system, and some of these must differ. To organize a system, as we will see, is to divide its labor functionally among its parts and to arrange for their coordination.

THE POSTINDUSTRIAL REVOLUTION

To complete this account of the change of age that we are in, we should consider the effect of systems thinking on the Industrial Revolution.

The conversion of the Industrial Revolution into what has come to be called the *Postindustrial Revolution* has its origins in the last century. Scientists who explore the use of electricity as a source of energy found that it could not be observed easily. Therefore, they developed such *instruments* as the ammeter, ohmeter, and voltmeter to observe it for them. The development of instruments exploded in this century, particularly after the advent of electronics and sonar and radar. Look at the dashboard of a large commercial airplane, or even one in an automobile. These instruments *generate symbols* that represent the properties of objects or events. Such symbols are called *data*. Instruments, therefore, are observing devices, but they are not machines in the Machine-Age sense because they do not apply energy to matter in order to transform it. The technology of instrumentation is fundamentally different from that of mechanization.

Another technology with this same characteristic emerged when the telegraph was invented in the last century. It was followed by the telephone, wireless, radio, television, and so on. This technology, like that of instrumentation, has nothing to do with mechanization; it has to do with the *transmission of symbols*, or *communication*.

The technologies of observation and communication formed the two sides of a technological arch that could not carry any weight until a keystone was dropped into place. This did not occur until the 1940s when the *computer* was developed. It too did no work in the Machine-Age sense; *it manipulated symbols logically*, which, as John Dewey pointed out, is the nature of *thought*. It is for this reason that the computer is often referred to as a thinking machine.

Because the computer appeared at a time when we had begun to put things back together again, and because the technologies of observation, communication, and computation all involve the manipulation of symbols, people began to consider systems that combine these three functions. They found that such systems could be used to *control* other systems, to *automate*. Automation is fundamentally different from mechanization. Mechanization has to do with the replacement of *muscle*; automation with the replacement of *mind*. Automation is to the Postindustrial Revolution what mechanization was to the Industrial Revolution.

Automatons are certainly not machines in the Machine-Age sense, and they need not be purposeless. It was for this reason that they came to be called teleological mechanisms. However, automation is no more an essential ingredient of the systems approach than is high technology in general. Both come with the Systems Age and are among its producers as well as its products. The technology of the Postindustrial Revolution is neither a panacea nor a plague; it is what we make of it. It generates a host of problems and possibilities that systems thinking must address. The problems it generates are highly infectious, particularly to less-technologically developed cultures. The systems approach provides a more effective way than previously has been available for dealing with both the problems and the possibilities generated by the Postindustrial Revolution, but is by no means limited to this special set of either or both.

NOTE

* This chapter has been adapted from, Ackoff, R. L. (1981) *Creating the Corporate Future*, John Wiley and Sons Inc.

23

DANIEL BELL AND THE
INFORMATION SOCIETY*

Hugh Mackay, Nick Heap and
Ray Thomas

The idea that we are moving towards an information society took root in the USA in the 1960s, in the context of rising prosperity, the automation of the workplace, an age of economic plenty and an assumption that the demise of repetitive, unsatisfying work was imminent. Daniel Bell, writing on *The Coming of Post-Industrial Society* in 1973 identified three stages of economic progress: the pre-industrial (dominated by agriculture), the industrial (dominated by manufacturing) and the post industrial (dominated by the service sector). Bell suggests that there is a historical progression through the three, with advanced Western economies then entering the third stage. Bell contrasts key elements of each of these stages in Table 23.1

Although Bell was referring to 'postindustrial society', he identifies 'the information society' as one element of this; his later work is concerned explicitly with 'the information society', and the distinction seems to matter little. A quotation from Bell gives an outline of his argument:

> In the coming century, the emergence of a new social framework based on telecommunications may be decisive for the way in which economic and social exchanges are conducted, the way knowledge is created and retrieved, and the character of work and occupations in which men engage. This revolution in the organisation and processing of information and knowledge, in which the computer plays a central role, has as its context the development of what I have called the postindustrial society. Three dimensions of the postindustrial society are relevant to the discussion of telecommunications:
>
> 1 The change from a good-producing to a service society.
> 2 The centrality of the codification of theoretical knowledge for innovation in technology.
> 3 The creation of new 'intellectual technology' as a key tool of systems analysis and decision theory.
>
> (Bell (1980) *The Coming of Post-Industrial Society*, pp. 500–1)

Table 23.1

Mode of production	Preindustrial extractive	Industrial-Fabrication	Postindustrial-Processing; recycling		
		Secondary	Tertiary	Quaternary	Quinary
Economic sector	Primary Agriculture Mining Fishing Timber Oil and gas	Goods-producing Manufacturing Durables Nondurables Heavy construction	Transportation Utilities	Trade Finance Insurance Real estate	Health Education Research Government Recreation
Transforming resource	Natural power Wind, water, draught animal, human muscle	Created energy Electricity – oil, gas, coal, nuclear power	Information Computer and data transmission systems		
Strategic resource	Raw materials	Financial capital	Knowledge		
Technology	Craft	Machine technology	Intellectual technology		
Skill base	Artisan, manual worker, farmer	Engineer, semiskilled worker	Scientist, technical and professional occupations		
Methodology	Common sense trial and error; experience	Empiricism, experimentation	Abstract theory, models, simulations, decision theory, systems analysis		
Time perspective	Orientation to the past	Ad hoc adaptiveness, experimentation	Future orientation; forecasting and planning		
Design	Game against nature	Game against fabricated nature	Game between persons		
Axial principle	Traditionalism	Economic growth	Codification of theoretical knowledge		

Source: From Bell (1973) The Coming of Post-Industrial Society, pp. 504–5

In short, Bell accords considerable significance to the developments he describes as under way; and attributes their basis to the technology. One common element of all work on the information society is the acceptance of the increasing centrality of information, IT and IT workers. Zorkoczy and Heap (1995) in Chapter 1 of *Information Technology – an Introduction*, discuss definitions of 'information' and the implications of these. [. . .]

Arguing that we are witnessing a shift to the third sector, Bell cites evidence of the significant and growing proportion of the workforce which is engaged in service sector work – over 50% in the USA, Japan and Western Europe; and refers to studies (e.g. Porat, 1976) which show a similar proportion of the workforce to be engaged in what can be defined as 'information activity'. There can be little doubt that in advanced industrial societies, in employment terms, of the three sectors – primary (agriculture and extractive), secondary (manufacturing or industrial) and tertiary (service) – the primary has been in long-term decline (for nearly 200 years), the secondary has been declining for a couple of decades (this is the process often referred to as deindustrialisation), and the tertiary is the only growing sector. [. . .]

Bell's argument is not only, however, of a march through the sectors. Bell argues that each has its 'axial principles', or driving force: in the case of industrial society, these included production and profit, and the rational pursuit of economic growth through the application of energy and machinery. By contrast he sees knowledge and information as the dynamic features of post industrial society. These are the features that stimulate economic growth, are the source of innovation in the organisation and management of the economy, and are the final product. Bell's analysis of a shift to the service sector includes:

1 the kind of work which people do;
2 changes in the occupational structure (the decline of blue and rise of white collar workers); and
3 a focus on who controls the new key resources (entrepreneurs give way to knowledge élites).

In his later work on 'the information society' (1980), Bell refers to knowledge having replaced labour as the source of value; information has become more than merely a resource, it is a commodity which can be bought and sold; and the information-processing occupations are becoming increasingly central. In the same way as the steam engine was the prime innovative technology at the core of the Industrial Revolution, computer technology will be the innovational technology in the Information Society. Computer-based information systems will replace the factory as the societal symbol; codified theoretical knowledge plays an increasingly central role in informing technological innovation: and the intellectual and knowledge industries will replace machinery and chemicals as the leading industries. Bell forecasts the emergence of a new social framework based on telecommunications which, in Bell's words which I have quoted, will have profound implications for work, the economy and society.

In sum, Bell – though he does not argue that the post industrial society means the end of capitalism – is talking about the emergence of a new socio-economic system. Although I have focused on one author's work, there are many others who take a similar line, including Alvin Toffler.

Other proponents of the thesis come from an entirely different political position from Bell; I shall introduce briefly some of the key ideas of two of these. Alain Touraine (1974) and Andre Gorz (1980). Touraine, like Bell, stresses the centrality of knowledge and the control of information, the importance of information and of the 'technocracy'. He differs from Bell, however, in that he identifies and focuses on social conflict, specifically between, on the one hand, technocrats and bureaucrats and, on the other, a range of social groupings including students and consumers. He identifies a principal opposition between social classes, though he sees this deriving not from ownership or control of resources but from access to information: class, in other words, comes to be replaced by new social movements.

Gorz, too, develops arguments about the changing role of work in post industrial economies. New technology, he argues, leads to an aristocracy of secure, well-paid workers, and a growing mass of unemployed, with the majority of the population in between belonging to the post industrial working class – to whom work no longer represents a source of identity or a meaningful activity. Work, he argues, becomes instrumental, to earn a wage. Gorz argues that increasing numbers of unemployed and deskilled cannot be sustained at the ideological level. In other words, he argues that, through new technology, the work ethic – and, with it, capitalism, becomes undermined. He sees the emerging social order as going beyond capitalism, in that technology is abolishing work, in two senses: first, the quantity of labour required for material production becomes marginal: and, secondly, work no longer involves direct contact between worker and matter. He cites surveys which purport to show that people are less satisfied with work than they were, and that work is less central to their lives – which, he argues, is undermining the moral and ideological foundations of industrialism.

CRITICISMS OF THE INFORMATION SOCIETY

So what, then, are the criticisms which are made of the 'information society thesis'? First, is IT as central to contemporary society as is suggested? The claims which were made for earlier technologies should cause us to err on the side of caution: television and radio, when they arrived, were seen as media which would expose all Americans, especially children, to the correctly spoken word, to great literature and drama, and so on – the same euphoric dream as has been presented by some in relation to IT (say, in the form of home computers). It is probably two decades since a computer scientist claimed the following for home computer terminals:

> [they] have potential for catalogue ordering, activity planning, home library and education, and family health, including histories, diagnoses, doctors' speciality lists, and emergency procedures; family recreation, including music selection and games; career guidance, tax records and returns: home safety and property maintenance, including house plan retrieval, maintenance schedules, electrical and other physical facility layouts, and energy management; and budgeting and banking
>
> (cited by Weizenbaum, 1985 p. 553)

You can judge for yourself the extent to which these far-reaching claims have been realised in practice.

And, apart from the technology, what about the growth of information workers? How, precisely, are these defined? For example, teachers and judges can be categorised as information workers – which, in one sense, may be appropriate; but is the growth of the category of 'information workers' thus more a process of *re-labelling* jobs, rather than any more substantive change?

Second is the criticism that it is not a march of progress from the primary, through the secondary to the tertiary sector. Rather, much of the service (tertiary) sector has grown *because* of a growth in manufacturing, rather than as a replacement for it. Information, Gershuny (1983) argues, is not a separate sector: rather, all sectors are becoming more information intensive: information activities take place throughout the economy. The information economy is still a manufacturing one. Others have argued that the relationship between the service or information sectors and economic growth varies between states, depending, in particular, on their level of industrialisation.

Third is the empirical evidence about us moving towards a leisure society – with automated manufacturing, political participation and an emphasis on the quality of life [. . .] Whilst the automation of work has made a few jobs *more* skilled, many routine, semi-skilled and unskilled, jobs remain – indeed, they are found in abundance in the burgeoning service sector – for example, fast food outlets. Various commentators, notably Piore and Sabel (1984), have pointed to the development of a (shrinking) core and (growing) periphery to the labour market. The former enjoy such benefits as private health insurance, private pensions, generous sick pay, more generous maternity benefits and private education; whilst the latter depend on diminishing unemployment and social benefits, the growing amount of part-time and fixed contract work, deteriorating state education, health and pension provision. The title of Piore and Sabel's book is *The Second Industrial Divide*. It is important not to confuse unemployment and underemployment with leisure – which, by conventional definition, is something which is enjoyed alongside a full-time, paid job in the household, rather than instead of this. It is hard to see political participation increasing, and, if it were, I should have thought the availability of suitable technology unlikely to be a key cause. Finally, my view is that we can see materialism as at least as powerful a force as hitherto, with little discernible shift to the more idealistic, humanistic claims of the information society theorists. In short, a leisure society simply does not seem to have materialised – at least for the vast majority of the population.

Fourth is the status of IT workers. Are these the new enlightened élite referred to by information society theorists? Clearly, there has been a huge growth in employment in the computer and telecommunications industries. Most hi-tech work, however, involves relatively little skill. Whilst the use of IT perhaps (more likely in the past, in my view) carries glamorous connotations for some, the experience of many is that such work is tedious and undemanding – with a similar division of labour and form of control as experienced in older industries. At the professional end of the spectrum – those to whom the argument is meant to apply – the pattern is less clear-cut. It is important to consider whether systems analysts, for example, are mere technicians, or whether they enjoy some new-found strategic significance within organisations. We have only to look at the centrality of the engineer in the USSR or the cost accountant in the post-war Western world to see that it is feasible for an occupational group to usurp such power. Any answer, however, has to be tentative at this stage. Certainly the British Computer Society (BCS) and other professional organisations are working actively to enhance the professional status of information systems (IS) personnel. As yet, however, we can see little prominence for IT managers on the boards of corporations – with some interesting exceptions.

Fifth, has the information society led to greater equality – between social classes, men and women, the industrialised and less developed worlds, the able-bodied and the disabled? Or has it made the rich richer and those in power more powerful?

Clearly the relationship of IT to equality is an enormously complex question, since there are many other factors which intervene in any direct relationship between IT and inequality. However, in broad terms, both global inequality (between rich and poor nations) and national inequality (within the UK) are increasing significantly. Thomas argues that IT, rather than creating an information society, is likely to be economically and socially divisive – both within industrialised societies and between these and the rest of the world. IT, in short, *fragments* society, [even though it] does offer some exciting possibilities for overcoming disadvantage. [. . .]

Finally, does the information society have any features which are not adequately explained by notions of industrial capitalism? Dealing with information does not in itself confer power. Marx argued long ago that science and technology have always been used to find substitutes for human labour, and that capital has always sought to reduce costs and maintain competitive advantage through the development and deployment of new technologies; and

Weber pointed to the increasing rationalisation of all areas of the social. The market, perhaps, explains the developments which we are experiencing. Rather than something new, what we are experiencing is simply more of the same: 'business as usual'.

At the same time, they and others argue that the information-society thesis is *ideological*, in that it seeks to create truths which obscure the vested interests involved in IT. IT relates to power, yet the analysis of power in the information society thesis is limited or non-existent. Rather, it encourages our unquestioning acceptance of IT.

Finally, of course, the thesis contains strong hints of technological determinism. Not far beneath the surface of much discussion of the information society is that it is natural, logical, exciting and positive; that it is inevitable, and that we have to adapt to the technology. In this way it can be seen as masking the social relations which lie behind technology, rather than increasing our understanding of the links between technology and society, how the technology is political and how it is socially shaped – as opposed to being inevitable. In short, it denies, or ignores, the social shaping of technology.

Having outlined the arguments and the criticisms which are made of these, my own view is that there is something new – on two counts. First, in cultural terms: in advanced industrial societies, technology now enjoys a status, and absorbs our time, in a way which is entirely unprecedented. Technology is thus mediating and shaping our daily lives, our identities and our culture as never before. It is important to note that to many people elsewhere in the world this is not applicable, and hence, if this significance constitutes a revolution, then it is one which affects particular societies, but not others.

Second is the issue of state surveillance. Another thing which, to me, is new and vitally significant, is the extended capacity of the state to exercise surveillance over its population. IT is double-edged: at the same time as providing (some of) us with greater access to information, it also empowers organisations to gather information on *all* individuals. The state, in particular, enjoys an unprecendented capacity to know about its citizens – through telephone bugging, telephone call logging, the recording of credit-card transactions, video cameras in public places and the associated digitisation of graphical images, laser listening devices, not to mention the huge range of increasingly inter-linked government databases and the commercial databases which support credit-checking and marketing profiling. I would argue that this capacity of the state to know so much about the lives, activities and thoughts of its citizenry constitutes a threat to democracy, or a shift to a new form of democracy, in that it discourages the expression of deviant thought or opinion.

The Information Society is here, in advanced industrial societies – whether we like it or not, or agree with it or not – in that IT is undoubtedly pervasive and important in our daily lives; and increasingly so. At the same time, it has not changed the fundamentals of life – for most of us. Yet it offers – tantalisingly – the prospect of a very different world; you may see this in optimistic terms – or pessimistically. At the very least, it is important for providing us with a framework for understanding IT in contemporary society.

NOTE

* This chapter has been adapted from, The Open University (1997) THD204 *Information Technology and Society*, Block 1 *Differing Perspectives*, Milton Keynes, The Open University.

REFERENCES

D. Bell (1973) *The Coming of Post-Industrial Society*, Basic Books, New York.

D. Bell (1980) 'The Social framework of the Information Society', In T. Forester (ed.) *The Microelectronics Revolution*, Blackwell, Oxford.

J. Gershuny (1983) *Social Innovation and the Division of Labour*, Oxford University Press.

A. Gorz (1980) *Farewell to the Working Class*, Pluto, London.

M. Piore and C. Sabel (1984) *The Second Industrial Divide: Possibilities for Prosperity*, Basic Books, New York.

M. Porat (1976) *The Information Economy*. PhD thesis, Stanford University.

A. Toffler (1980) *The Third Wave*, Morrow, New York.

A. Touraine (1974) *The Postindustrial Society*, Wildwood House, London.

J. Weizenbaum (1985) 'Once more, the computer revolution'. In T. Forester (ed.) *The Microelectronics Revolution*, Blackwell, Oxford.

P. Zorkoczy and N. Heap (1995) *Information technology: an Introduction*, Pitman.

24

GLOBAL INFORMATION INFRASTRUCTURE: ELIMINATING THE DISTANCE BARRIER†

Heather E. Hudson[*]

We are in the midst of a global information revolution driven by the convergence and proliferation of information and communication technologies. The telecommunicators sector is changing at warp speed, driven by technological innovation that results in new equipment services, and also by new entrants and alliances between companies with experience in a wide range of information industries from telecommunication to broadcasting to computer hardware and software to publishing. Three major trends are carving these changes: the rapid introduction of new technologies and services; the restructuring of the telecommunications sector; and globalization of economies and of communications. Together these developments are not only changing the world of telecommunications, but the ways people work, learn, and interact.

> The death of distance as a determination of the cost of communications will probably be the single most important economic force shaping society in the first half of the next century.[1]

The death of distance could have profound implications for both individuals and organizations. The ability to work "anytime, anywhere" allows "road warriors" to work without offices on planes, in hotels, and at client sites, and enables information workers to telecommute from their homes rather than traveling to work. This flexibility can be two-edged for individuals, who can work wherever they choose but may never escape the "virtual workplace." Organizations may reduce their overhead costs and improve their productivity, but they must also learn how to manage their decentralized workforce.

One-major technological trend is the extension of "information superhighways" in the form of broadband networks; another is the increasing ubiquity of communications using wireless technologies (that will, however, initially provide access to squirts rather than floods of information).[2] Personal communications networks using microcellular technology will allow people in urban areas not only to talk on pocket-sized telephones, but to transmit and receive data using wireless modems. In rural and developing areas, these services may be available from low earth-orbiting (LEO) satellite systems.

On an international level, the death of distance has profound implications for the globalization of industries and national economies. Rural regions in Europe and North America may lure businesses with their pleasant environment and lower labor costs; however, they are no longer competing only with cities in their own countries. Companies may hire information workers in developing countries where labor is far cheaper not only for data entry and word processing, but for writing computer programs. Conversely, developing countries now find themselves competing in global markets, where quality and suitability of products may be as important as price.

GLOBAL NETWORKING: CHANGING THE GEOGRAPHY OF BUSINESS

Telecommunications networks now link manufacturers with assembly plants, designers with factories, software engineers with hardware vendors, suppliers with retailers, retailers with customers. No longer is it necessary to have all the expertise in-house. Software engineers in Silicon Valley complain that they are laid off while contractors transmit code from Russia and India. Freelance designers can now send clothing patterns directly to an automated garment factory. Customers can order anything from airline tickets to winter clothing online and do their own banking and bill paying electronically.

These trends open opportunities for innovative entrepreneurs around the world. For consumers, they offer more choice and lower prices because there is no overhead cost for sales clerks and order takers. Yet these changes pose threats to traditional businesses as well as to employees. Increasingly, companies that want to compete on price will have to "work smarter" to reduce costs and respond to market changes, while others will have to rethink how to add value to attract customers. High levels of customer service and individualized attention are likely to become more important. As Wells Fargo found, a bank that offers assistance from a human twenty-four hours a day in addition to online electronic banking can attract new customers. And computer vendors that offer free and easy-to-reach customer support may be able to charge a premium, or at least not lose customers to commodity discounters.

More than half the computers in US offices are linked to local area networks (LANs). Increasingly, businesses are also linking into the Internet to reach counterparts in other organizations, specialized databases, and potential customers. Each month, some 2,000 businesses join the more than 20,000 that have already set up "virtual shop" on the Internet.[3] Federal Express's 30,000 employees around the world are linked via the Internet to "internet" sites within the company's Memphis headquarters; some 12,000 customers a day track their own packages using Federal Express's Internet Web site, rather than calling a human operator. Ford Motor Company engineers in Asia, Europe and the United States worked together electronically to design the Taurus automobile. Pharmaceutical company Eli Lilly uses information compiled on its intranet sites to schedule clinical trials and submissions for approval of new drugs in countries around the world. Visa International provides an information service called Visa Vue for its 19,000 member banks on an internal Web site.[4] As electronic security improves, in the form of "firewalls" to prevent unauthorized access to private networks and encryption to protect the privacy of personal and financial data, more companies will use the Internet to sell products and services as well as to link their employees.

The Internet opens a global market to the small business and lets low budget nonprofit organizations reach interested parties across the country or the world. While Reuters and

Dow Jones are repackaging financial information for electronic subscribers, a startup company in Silicon Valley called QuoteCom is selling financial information over the Internet for as little as $10 per month. The Future Fantasy Bookstore in Palo Alto, California, put its catalog on the Internet and suddenly became a global firm.[5] Small businesses with computer expertise can also set up shop as gateways to the Internet for their communities. In eastern Washington state, the Palouse Economic Development Council has established Palouse Net, a World Wide Web server and Internet aggregator for farmers and small businesses in rural Washington and Idaho.[6]

Telecommunications networks are creating a global information workforce, as employers seek the cheapest labor, ranging from clerical work, such as data entry, to software programming and research and development. American Airlines uses key punch operators in Barbados to enter data from its flight coupons, which are then fed by satellite and telephone lines back to American's central computers in Tulsa, Oklahoma. American reportedly saved $3.5 million on data processing in its first year.[7] Mead Data Central, a provider of data base services, hires overseas workers primarily in Ireland, the Philippines, and South Korea to enter documents in its data bases. There are now at least seventy US data processing firms with overseas facilities.[8]

In the short run, these clerical jobs offer attractive employment opportunities for developing countries, particularly those such as the Commonwealth Caribbean countries and the Philippines with relatively high literacy rates and an English-speaking work force. However, not only do these jobs have the same disadvantages as similar jobs in industrialized countries (low pay, boredom, little chance of advancement, stress from the pressure to reach productivity targets or from computerized monitoring), but they also may be made obsolete by optical scanners and voice recognition technology that can transform hard copy and spoken words into digitized text.

Some countries and enterprises may together be able to use telecommunications to create a competitive advantage at the other end of the information work continuum. India has built software development parks equipped with satellite uplinks, so that foreign high tech companies can hire Indian engineers and programmers at a fraction of the cost of expanding its professional workforce in the United States, and India can retain professionals who might otherwise join its massive brain drain. Just as North American and European laborers complained in the 1980s about the growth of offshore manufacturing, highly skilled information workers in Silicon Valley now fear losing their jobs to lower paid offshore professionals.

As demand for these services grows, users will need access to more bandwidth, to speed searches, to download software, and transmit videos and graphics. Some telecommunications companies, such as AT&T and MCI, are becoming Internet service providers, concluding that the Internet must be viewed as an opportunity rather than a threat. Others fear that the Internet will steal traffic, as users opt for flat rate voice and video transmissions rather than paying for time or bits. Traditional telephone companies will have to respond to the demand for new and cheaper services as an opportunity rather than a threat if they are to survive. Rather than local monopolies providing telephone services over copper wires, in many countries we may find cable television companies, electric utilities and wireless operators competing with telephone companies to reach the end user, offering a combination of voice, data, and video services.

TOWARD GLOBAL INFORMATION INFRASTRUCTURE (GII)

These technological and economic trends have led policy makers to call for the construction of "information highways" linking communities and nations. The phenomenal growth of the Internet as an information resource, communications tool, and electronic marketplace has focused attention on the need for national and global "information infrastructure" (NII and GII) to bring the Internet and other forms of electronic communications within reach of people around the world.

The Clinton Administration announced the National Information Infrastructure Initiative (NII) in 1993, calling for joint industry and government efforts to create a seamless and interoperable national broadband infrastructure, an "Information Superhighway" to link all Americans. Vice President Al Gore challenged US Industry to connect all of the country's schools, libraries, hospitals and clinics to the information highway by the year 2000. The Telecommunications Act of 1996 requires discounts for the provision of "advanced services" to schools, health care facilities, and libraries.

Federal and state governments are funding research and pilot projects to spur innovative applications. The High Performance Computing and Communications Program is supporting university research. The National Telecommunications and Information Administration (NTIA) provides funds for telecommunications applications in distance education and health care delivery. The Rural Utilities Service (formerly the Rural Electrification Administration) funds educational and health care projects providing advanced telecommunications technology and services for rural Americans. Many states are offering inducements to the carriers to accelerate the upgrading of their facilities and to provide access to schools and other community locations. State governments are also providing seed money to communities and economic development agencies to help them to plan and initiate projects using telecommunications as a development tool.

The European Commission published a White Paper in 1993 on "Growth, Competitiveness and Employment" that emphasized an urgent need to develop a European-wide information infrastructure to help restore economic growth and competitiveness, open up new markets and create jobs.[9] Acting on the White Paper's recommendations, the European Commission called on a high-level group of information industry representatives to produce a report recommending practical measures for implementation. This report, entitled "Europe and the Global information Society" urged the European Union to trust market forces and private sector initiatives, but noted that spending on education, health and research may have to be retargeted toward new priorities, and a new form of public/private sector partnership would be needed to implement the group's recommended action plan. It recommended:

1 Accelerated liberalization of the telecommunications industry;
2 Identification of the degree of regulation required;
3 Interconnection of networks and interoperability of services to avoid fragmentation of information infrastructure;
4 Reduction in tariffs, to bring them in line with those of other advanced industrialized regions;
5 Review of the standardization process to increase its speed and responsiveness to the market.[10]

In response, the European Commission has set out a detailed work program in four key areas: regulation, applications, social and societal aspects, and the promotion of the information society. The European Union has taken a major step toward liberalization by opening the telecommunications markets of member countries to competition as of January 1998. It also approved $3.8 billion under its Fourth Framework Program to support research and development in communications technologies and development of applications in distance education, health care and other social services.

Canada also has plans to build a network of networks linking Canadian communities, businesses, government agencies and institutions. The Canadian government sees the information highway as a catalyst to help Canadians share information, and to gain an edge in productivity and information industries in global markets. It has identified three key objectives for the Canadian information highway:

1 To create jobs through innovation and investment;
2 To reinforce Canadian sovereignty and identity;
3 To ensure universal access at reasonable cost.[11]

These objectives emphasize cultural as well as economic priorities. Canada's information Highway Advisory Council, composed of representatives of communications industries, business users, academics performers and consumers, takes a distinctively cultural perspective:

> The Information Highway, in our view, is not so much about information as it is about communication in both its narrowest and broadest senses. It is not a cold and barren highway with exits and entrances that carry traffic, but a series of culturally rich and dynamic intersecting communities. . . . Rather than a highway, it is a personalized village square where people eliminate the barriers of time and distance and interact in a kaleidoscope of different ways.[12]

In Japan, the Nippon Telegraph and Telephone Corporation (NTT) has announced its intent to wire every school, home and office with fiber optic cable by the year 2010. Japan's Ministry of Posts and Telecommunications (MPT) estimates the cost of building this network to be between $150 billion and $230 billion. The Japanese are also investing in projects and trials to ensure that users will be able to access a wide variety of services. For example, in 1994, the MPT launched a $50 million three-year pilot project to assess the feasibility of integrating telecommunications and broadcast services, such as video on demand, high definition television, videoconferencing, teleshopping and telemedicine through fiber-to-the-home networks.[13]

In 1995, the G-7[14] nations together embraced the goal of global information infrastructure, and initiated a series of demonstrations and pilot projects using high capacity networks and switching. The APEC (Asia Pacific Economic Conference) nations are also sponsoring projects using telecommunications networks for distance education and training, health care delivery, and economic development. Yet there are still areas in the industrialized G-7 countries with very limited access to telecommunications. APEC members include not only the industrialized Economies of Japan, Singapore, the United States, and Canada, but also countries with much greater gaps in their infrastructure, such as China, Thailand, and the Philippines.

GII: PROMISE OR HYPE?

Against this background, why all the hyperbole about electronic superhighways? Several themes recur in these information infrastructure initiatives. There are dual assumptions that converging technologies will result in information services with both social and economic benefits, and that both public and private sectors must be engaged to ensure the installation of national broadband networks. Yet these assumptions need to be carefully examined. Each new communication technology has been heralded as offering numerous benefits. Satellites and cable television were to provide the courses taught by the best instructors to students in schools, homes and workplaces. Videoconferencing was to largely eliminate business travel. Telemedicine was to replace referral of patients to specialists. Computers were to replace traditional teaching with more personalized and interactive instruction.

To some extent all of the prophesies have been fulfilled, yet the potential of the technologies is far from fully realized. In many cases, it took institutional change and incentives to innovate in order for these technologies to have much effect. In North America, the more remarkable change is in these incentives rather than the technologies. As school districts face shrinking budgets and new curricular requirements, as spiraling health care budgets are targeted by governments and insurance companies, and as business realizes that people must "work smarter" to compete in a global economy, they find new and compelling reasons to turn to telecommunications and information technologies.

Thus, investment in technology alone will not likely result in major social benefits. Policymakers in these countries appear aware that public sector stimulus is needed to foster new educational and social service applications; there is widespread belief in the need to fund trials and demonstration projects. Yet seed money for pilot projects may not ensure longterm implementation. Schools with International Services Digital Network (ISDN) access will benefit if the services they can access turn out to be cost-effective means of achieving their educational priorities. If the services are perceived as frills, or if there is no budget allocation to buy computers or pay monthly usage charges, connection to the information highway will mean little. Similarly, if insurers will not authorize payment for teleconsultations, or physicians are not authorized to practice beyond their borders, telemedical applications will remain limited. And if prices for connection and usage are beyond the reach of low income and rural residents, small businesses and nonprofit organizations, the much-heralded information society will be very narrowly based.

The US communications industry has adopted the banner of the "information superhighway," with the assumption that there is an enormous new market in information services. While these applications are generally viewed in the United States strictly in business terms, in other countries cultural impact is also a major concern. Both Canada and the European Union stress the need to use these networks to strengthen their own cultures. Yet, the proliferation of cable- and satellite-delivered channels in Canada and western Europe tells a different story: the demand for content is so great that operators turn to inexpensive sources of content to fill them, and this content is overwhelmingly American.

Another recurring theme is the "we will be left behind" argument. In the late 1980s, US telephone companies sought to convince American policymakers that the United States was at a disadvantage because its citizens did not have Minitels, small computer terminals provided to French households by France Telecom. Yet Americans had much of the functionality of the Minitel through widely available facilities, including telephone access to audiotex services and growing access to personal computers equipped with modems. Today, Canada, the European Union and Japan are all concerned that they will be left behind the United States if they do not implement their own information infrastructures. Notably the report to the European Union states:. "The first countries to enter the information era will be in a position to dictate the course of future developments to the latecomers."[15] But is this really so? It may be that their technology companies will have an advantage if they have a ready market for fast packet technologies, such as Asynchronous Transfer Mode (ATM) servers, set-top boxes, and multiplexers that can also be exported. But the real payoff for users will be from the application of these technologies to access and share information that can contribute to the development of their own societies and the competitiveness of their economies.

PROMISES AND PARADOXES

New technologies and services are alluring, but they also present challenges and paradoxes for the telecommunications industry, users and policymakers. Consider the following:

Technological Trojan horses

New technologies are introducing changes faster than policymakers can respond:

- "Callback" services (where calls between countries with which international tariffs are actually reoriginated from a third country with much lower rates such as the United States) are undermining the traditional strategy of monopoly carriers in many developing countries that use high international rates to cross-subsidize domestic rates and generate income that can be invested in domestic infrastructure.
- Satellite broadcasting has introduced foreign and commercialized programs in western Europe and in much of Asia, forcing domestic broadcasters to innovate to hold on to their audiences.
- The Internet, seen by many policymakers as an important tool for their industries to remain competitive, opens the door to unfiltered information that may be considered inappropriate or illegal in their countries.

Competition and consolidation

While telecommunications services are increasingly being liberalized to attract competitive providers, there is also a growing tendency to consolidate. The result may be only a few major players or consortia in the international environment, as well as a few providers in major domestic markets. These new oligopolies will be able to offer a greater range of services than their predecessors and may make it easier for users looking for "one-stop shopping" to meet their telecommunications needs. The danger, however, is that they will form cartels that will prevent significant competition in price, service, or innovation.

Access and control

Some governments that see information technology as critical to their economic development strategy are at the same time concerned about the socio-political implications of access. One of the most ironic examples of the simultaneously held goals of modernization and control is Singapore, which is staking its economic future on becoming an "intelligent island." The Singapore One venture intends to extend optical fiber optics throughout the island, to connect every business, home and school.[16] Yet Singapore has retained tight control over individual access to information. The government applies broadcast contest regulations to the Internet, holding Internet service providers accountable for content accessible to their customers. Also, it is illegal for individuals to install satellite antennas, so that Singaporeans cannot watch satellite-transmitted programs from regional satellites, including those uplinked from Singapore's own industrial parks.

Cable television networks offer the advantage of controlling access so that network operators can charge for reception. In Singapore and China, another perceived advantage of cable is that information its citizens receive can be monitored. Another technology with paradoxical capabilities to expand and control choice is video compression. Using video compression, programmers can pack many television signals on a single satellite transponder, enabling television viewers to choose from hundreds of digitally compressed channels. Yet video compression also provides a cost-effective means for program distributors to precensor programs by editing different versions for different countries, then compressing and encrypting them for distribution on regional satellites. Viewers in each country will be able to see only the programs their governments have approved.

Universal service as a moving target

New technologies and services are forcing policymakers to rethink their goals of universality. In both industrialized and developing regions, 'universal service has become a moving target, as policymakers must adjust their goals to make new services more accessible. For example, the US Telecommunications Act of 1996 redefines universal service to include access to schools, libraries and health care facilities, and to include not only "basic" telephone service but also "advanced services," a term whose definition will evolve over time.

CLOSING THE GAP

The World Bank estimates that investment in telecommunications in the developing world must double to meet the growing demand for telecommunications services.[17] In spite of accelerated investment in many developing regions during the past decade, the vast majority of people living in developing countries still lack access to basic telecommunications. Yet there is cause for optimism. New technologies offer the possibility of technological leapfrogging, e.g., to reach end users through wireless local loops or small satellite terminals rather than stringing wire and cable. Digital transmission and switching are increasing reliability and lowering cost, as well as making it possible for subscribers in developing countries to use electronic mail and voice messaging, and to access the Internet.

The newly industrializing economies of eastern Europe, Asia, and Latin America are starting to close the gap. Their growing economies appear promising to the telecommunications industry and to investors who are looking for new markets. Most of these countries are also taking steps to encourage investment by privatizing their operators, providing investment incentives, and/or introducing competition.

Information gaps show least signs of shrinking in the poorest countries, two-thirds of which have less than one telephone line per 100 inhabitants. Telecommunications is not a panacea for countries with populations near the subsistence level as well as urgent demands on foreign exchange for food, fuel and medicine. Yet, as these countries develop market economies and seek to take maximum advantage of scarce expertise, they will need to invest in telecommunications. Of course, these regions are less attractive to investors than more prosperous economies; in general, they have also been the most reluctant to reduce their governments' role as a monopoly operator. Their networks are also the least efficient, in terms of reliability and the number of lines per telecommunications employee. Restructuring their telecommunications sectors to improve productivity and encourage investment will be necessary if they are to begin to close the gap.

NEW GAPS?

As investment in telecommunications infrastructure increases, the gap between information haves and have nots may become based on price and choice rather than technology. Countries that continue to favor telecommunications monopolies, or seek to control access to information, may limit user access even where technology is available. In most of Europe, access to the Internet is much more expensive than in North America. As one commentator states: "Digital Europe has many medieval features: road tolls and extortion-like taxes, witch hunts, an oppressed citizenry, and powers-that-be in feudal towers."[18] Access is much less affordable in many developing countries. Even professionals in many African countries cannot afford to use telecommunications services.

China may be the world's largest market for telecommunications, but the government is reluctant to allow access to information from abroad. Although credited with introducing market reforms in the Chinese economy, Deng Xiaoping voiced his ambivalence about opening China's doors to the world: "When the door opens, some flies are bound to come in."[19] Government attempts to control access include banning satellite antennas, blocking access to Internet sites, and impeding access to the Internet itself and to other means of electronic communication.

Clever users will inevitably find means to bypass these roadblocks, as shown by dissidents' use of facsimile and electronic mail during the Tiananmen Square uprising in China, the proliferation of satellite antennas in countries where they are officially banned and the widespread availability of supposedly illegal callback services that undercut international tariffs. Yet these strategies are likely to be limited to an elite few with the technical know-how or political connections to end-run the regulations. Only where governments recognize that suffocation is worse than a few flies will the gaps really disappear.

REMAINING BARRIERS

New technologies have eliminated distance for the international finance industry, which trades not only around the world but around the clock; for employees who collaborate on projects across time zones; for "footloose" businesses that operate from rural communities; and for students and researchers who can search libraries and databases beyond their borders. Yet in many parts of the world, to paraphrase Mark Twain, "the news of its death has been greatly exaggerated." Some people may live hours or days from the nearest telephone. Others have facilities available but cannot afford to use them. Still others may not know how to use these new tools to find the information they need, or how to reorganize their work to take advantage of the information available to them. These barriers must also be eliminated if distance is truly to disappear.

NOTES

† This chapter has been adapted from, Hudson, Heather E., "Global information infrastructure: eliminating the distance barrier," *Business Economics*, April, 1998, p. 25.

* Heather E. Hudson is Professor and Director of the Telecommunications Management and Policy Program of the McLaren School of Business at the University of San Francisco, CA.

1 "The Death of Distance," *The Economist*, September 30, 1995.

2 Hudson, Heather E., "The Internet Wake-Up Call," *Asian Telecommunications*, December 1997.

3 Browning, John, "Joys of the Express Lane," *Globe and Mail Report on Business Magazine*, January 1995, p. 103.

4 Cortese, Amy, "Here Comes the Intranet," *Business Week*, February 26, 1996, pp. 76–84.

5 Browning, p. 103.

6 Parker, Edwin B. and Heather E. Hudson, *Electronic Byways. State Policies for Rural Development through Telecommunications*, second edition. Washington, DC: Aspen Institute, 1995.

7 Stokes, Bruce, "Beaming Jobs Overseas," *National Journal*, July 27, 1985, p. 1727.

8 Stokes, p. 1729.

9 Commission of the European Communities, *Growth, Competitiveness, Employment: The Challenges and Ways Forward into the 21st Century*, (White Paper). Brussels: European Commission, 1993.

10 Commission of the European Communities, *Europe and the Global information Society*, Brussels: European Commission, 1994.

11 Industry Canada, *The Canadian Information Highway*, Ottawa: Industry Canada, April 1994.

12 Information Highway Advisory Council, *Canada's Information Highway: Providing New Dimensions for Learning, Creativity and Entrepreneurship*, Ottawa: Industry Canada, November 1994.

13 Industry Canada, 1994.

14 The G-7 is an association of seven major industrialized world powers: Canada, France, Germany, Japan, Russia, the United Kingdom, and the United States.

15 Commission of the European Communities, 1994.

16 Hudson, Heather E., *Global Connections: International Telecommunications Infrastructure and Policy*, New York: Wiley, 1997, pp. 279–60.

17 Cane, Alan, "Transforming the Way We Live and Work,", "International Telecommunications: Financial Times Survey," *Financial Times*, October 3, 1995, pp. 1–2.

18 Gregston, Brent, "Power and Privilege," *Internet World*, November 1995, p. 96.

19 Schwankert, Steven, "Dragons at the Gates," *Internet World*, November 1995, p. 112.

25

GLOBALIZATION, NEW PRODUCTION CONCEPTS AND INCOME DISTRIBUTION*

A.J.C. Manders and Y.S. Brenner

[. . .]

The development and introduction of [. . .] new production concepts or principles of organization of production began with a major technological change. Until the 1960s the production concepts were based on electro-mechanics. Dosi characterized this technological paradigm as follows: "Within the electro-mechanical paradigm, higher efficiency of production (stemming from standardization, economies of scale etc.), generally associated with 'Taylorist' and 'Fordist' principles of organization of production, is also correlated with very high degrees of inflexibility - in terms of acceptable variance in production runs and mixes. Fundamental dimensions of technical progress along the old technological trajectory and the increasing economies of scale and economies of standardization" (Dosi, 1988).

In the 1970s there was a change to an electronic paradigm. One of its visible manifestations was the introduction of the computer into the realm of machine control of which the most important feature was the far greater flexibility it brought into the organization of production. Aspects of the organization of the production process were taken to include the conscious and structured consideration for flows of material and information, and the logical consequences thereof in an industrial environment, i.e. in sub-contracting, product design and design changes, marketing, distribution, sales and after-sales service.

The power of monster conglomerates is well-known and needs here no elaboration.[1] But while there is little new in the tendency towards monopoly the stimulus it received in the 1980s from technological developments made it different. The new type of globalized monopoly exorcised the odium of malpractice and illegality from a great many monopolistic and oligopolistic practices. In fact, corporations manufacturing production technology but not they alone, ushered in a new market structure.[2] Together with changes in the world economy, for example the change from a sellers' to a buyers' market, the introduction of Computer Integrated Manufacturing (CIM), Design for Assembly, Co-makership and Just-in-Time - in short all elements of new international production concepts - caused a revision of large corporations' market strategy. From being companies in many countries, important multinationals became global or transnational concerns which is something different. Such a company consists of a network of production centres all over the world. The term here is globalization. Globalization in this context must be defined as a strategy of worldwide sourcing, leading to a search for ever cheaper labour, a flexibilisation of labour and the adoption of new international production technology and production organization-concepts.[3] The most obvious reasons for this change were the growing capital-intensity of manufacture; the accelerating momentum of technologies; the emergence of a growing body of universal users; and the spreading of neoprotectionist pressures. Since the late 1980s the pursuit of economies of scale was inordinately increasing the capital-intensity of manufacturing. This was, and will probably continue to be, a major source of "globalization" in spite of the fact that new production concepts (known as Lean Production, Batch-Size-One, Toyotism or whatever) opened up the opportunity to produce on order with short but efficient production runs (economies of scope).

The accelerating pace at which new technologies are discovered and applied causes the costs of research and development (R&D) to soar, while the diffusion of new technology through the industrialized countries is so rapidly advancing that it has become difficult to sustain technological advantage. This forces companies planning to penetrate Japanese, American and European markets with new products to invade the entire zone simultaneously rather than gradually country by country, as they used to do. Finally the emergence of an unprecedented massive body of universal users is pushing companies in this direction.

Coalition-forming is the specific type of cooperation which accompanies globalization together with co-makership and just-in-time deliverance. Coalitions differ from mergers and takeovers because they allow participants to retain relative independence. Their *raison d'être* is that they provide the opportunity for establishing positions in strategic markets. They have a "synergistic" effect by recruiting partners to fill gaps in each other's operations and to increase the possibility for exploiting economies of scale. They lead to cost and risk spreading and help to arrive at new standards.[5] Instead of keeping the results of R&D activities secret for as long as possible, nowadays in an early stage these results are a matter of bargaining with others' competitors to prevent too much difference in product standards from making it impossible to connect the products of various producers with each other. The dramatic development with regard to different standards in the software for videos was the main cause for this shift in strategy with electronics companies. These types of alliances and coalitions, especially favoured by capital-intensive industries with high R&D costs and a broad technological basis, practically dominate production in aviation, electronics and increasingly also motor vehicles. Even the largest enterprises feel that they can no longer afford the independence which previously they were jealously protecting. To maintain international standards large enterprises need to specialize in order to reduce the cost associated with the increasing complexity of their operations. They must avoid the risk of destroying competency by diversification, or from engaging prematurely in activities outside the technological and market paradigms with which they are familiar. Last but not least, the new form of subcontracting known as co-makership is an important shift in management strategy. This method which was introduced long ago by large Japanese firms, partly to circumvent the traditional life-long job-security of their employees, simply meant that labour-intensive work was relegated to small, often family firms. In the Western World the term refers to a strategy by which more and more large enterprises try to reduce costs, limit risks and increase profits by building up a network of stringently-vetted suppliers. As (parts of the) production became simplified, a subcontractor was able to perform certain tasks with great efficiency. Such a co-makers network generally consists of small firms located within a radius of 100 kilometres from the major enterprise which can deliver the required sub-assemblies at extremely short notice. This phenomenon is particularly widespread in the automobile industry but other enterprises are rapidly adopting it. An idea about the working of such a network can be gained from the working of the policy at the Renault/PSA combination, where since 1988, between 300 and 400 sub-contractors are vetted each year. The number of vendors on the approved list has since grown to 250, and the suppliers on it are audited at two-year intervals. Other examples are Boeing and Nike. With the exception of a small number of core activities the Boeing 777 is designed and produced completely by co-makers from all over the world. They are interconnected by a computernetwork consisting of seven mainframe computers which connect 2,800 workstations. This production concept reduces total development cost up to 20 per cent. Nike no longer produces sports shoes. It concentrates activities on research, product design and the organization of production.

Closely related to the concept of co-makership is the "Just-in-time" concept (JIT) which also originated in Japan. For production based on a flow concept, with minimal changeover times, a flexible organization, a weak functional-orientation and the capability for small-batch profitability, the vital factors are high quality and the arrival of sub-assemblies at the factory gate at exactly the right time. This is what is meant by the Just-in-time philosophy, and the slogan "zero defects, zero delay, zero stock". The idea is that the production and assembly cycles of both the main producer and the co-maker will eventually harmonize as though they were parts of a single system (encycling). A recent example is the new production centre of Volkswagen in Resende, Brazil. Co-makers are producing the car while Volkswagen is responsible for the design, the cabin, the final control and sales. However, in reality co-makership means a shift of the burden of maintaining stocks to the small co-maker firms, which are in severe competition one with the other. The advantage of this strategy for the huge company is that it not only relieves the large industries from their culturally ingrained responsibilities to workers, but affords them the opportunity to be more flexible in the reactions to changes in demand and technological innovations. The so-called co-makership enables them to order the part-products precisely in the quantities required and to shift the maintenance of stocks to the small firms. Moreover, owing to the competition between these small producers it tends to reduce the prices they have to pay for their output to a bare minimum. Again, the small producers' income is driven down towards subsistence levels, while the large enterprises concentrate on the tasks in which due to their capital and time advantage they hold a virtual monopoly.

This concentration on globalization, coalition-forming, core activity and co-makership is the salient feature of new strategic planning. It introduces a new market structure dominated by something close to what used to be known as natural monopolies. The new market structure implies the presence of a near monopoly in certain semi-finished goods and in particular production processes. It facilitates the determination of prices in line with investment plans with little regard for market competition. Consequently variations in the volume of demand do not influence prices but determine the volume of production. Effective demand remains the final arbiter of production, but instead of influencing prices it determines the volume of employment. If in a number of important industries a new investment produces a greater output than an equivalent investment did before, and oligopolistic structures prevent prices from falling, then irrespective of rising or falling interest rates, unemployment will increase. But if sticky producer prices prevent consumer prices from falling, then consumer demand cannot increase in line with rising productivity and profits can no longer be made in the marketplace. The result is that producers turn to process innovation because in an inert or shrinking market the way to preserve or increase profitability is to reduce production costs. With this, competition shifts from markets to process-innovation and to innovation in the organization of production. The most efficient process innovator makes the highest profits. As process innovation usually involves high

R&D expenditure and costly new equipment, the new structure replaces familiar market competition by a scramble for investment funds. And so, since process innovation is normally associated with a reduced demand for labour (and an increased demand for funds) the final outcome is growing unemployment and rising rates of interest. Consequently the whole idea of the self-correcting economic mechanism falls into disarray.

With this becomes questionable the entire theory by which prices, wages and the rates of interest regulate the economic system towards full employment equilibrium. If prices are determined by investment plans, then the latter determine the volume of demand, and income effects thwart price effects.[5] Inflation, rates of interest and economic growth all rise together. but the volume of employment dwindles. In other words, the new market structure allows large enterprises. or practically compels them, not to pass on to consumers in lower prices the advantages of innovation, and with this the entire full employment equilibrium-restoring mechanism at the root of mainstream economic thought becomes a travesty. State intervention to regulate income distribution becomes an unavoidable necessity.

The conclusion from all this is that the latest technological developments and the related new production strategies advance the polarization of society. The distribution of income between consumers and the controllers of capital has been lopsided in favour of the latter. The progress of technology no longer adds to consumer demand but reduces employment. Productivity continues to rise but consumers' real disposable incomes lag behind. The surplus of income which should have become available for the purchase of more services does not materialize. The extra demand for labour in the service sector does not match the loss of jobs in industry, as would have happened if prices had not been prevented from falling and real incomes from rising. The self-regulating mechanism of competition is failing and monopoly is increasingly replacing competition. As in the 1930s, the rich get richer and the poor poorer. If we wish to avoid this predicament the only way to do it is by more government intervention to adjust demand to supply.

NOTES

For example, in the USA the percentage of the working population in this sector rose from 55 per cent in l948 to 67 per cent in 1974; in France it rose from 20 per cent in 1950 to 44 per cent in 1970, and in West Germany from 28 per cent in 1950 to 42 per cent in 1968. This shift was the result of an impressive rise in productivity in the goods producing sectors and did not cause a shortage of agricultural and industrial products. On the contrary, there were indications that the market for goods in the rich countries was approaching saturation.

*   This chapter has been adapted from, Manders, A. J. C. and Brenner, Y. S. (1999) "Globalization, production concepts and income distribution", *International Journal of Social Economies*, vol. 26, pp. 564–568.

1   For example, in the 1970s, five Dutch conglomerates directly employed 18 per cent of the working population, and indirectly many more. These five controlled electronics, metallurgy, food processing, chemicals and oil. In Germany, some 2,000 businesses employed about 50 per cent of the total labour force. In the USA some 2,000 corporations controlled about 80 per cent of all resources used in manufacturing. By 1994, their share in employment had fallen more steeply than the fall in overall employment, but their grip on all other resources had increased. Globalization had added an entirely new dimension to the familiar problem of economic concentration.

2   The process was triggered by three developments in the production sphere: (1) in computer-aided manufacturing (CAM), flexible manufacturing systems (FMS) and robotics; (2) in computer-aided design (CAD) and paperless knowledge work; and (3) in the increased understanding of physical phenomena. The combination of all three provided the basis for computer-integrated manufacturing (CIM).

3   Recently (in the Dutch newspaper, *NRC*, 20 June 1996), A. Kleinknecht presented the results of his research on globalization. His conclusion is that globalization is a mirage for The Netherlands. This is convincingly true for the extent of locating Dutch production activities abroad. We are stressing here the internationalization of production technology and the concepts of production organization and its impact for competition and income distribution.

4   Kenichi Ohmae listed several examples for this type of cooperation. In aero engines: General Electric and Rolls-Royce; Pratt and Whitney-Kawasaki Rolls-Royce. In motor vehicles (components and assembly): GM and Toyota; Chrysler and Mitsubushi; Volkswagen and Nissan; Volvo and Renault. In consumer electronics: Matsushita and Kodak; JVC and Telefunken and Thorn, Philips and Sony. In computers: AT&T and Olivetti, Hitachi and Hewlett & Packard; Fujitsu and Amdahl and Siemens and ICL; IBM and Matsushita.

In The Netherlands, Philips cooperates with Sony in the field of compact-disc players and Matsushita and Yahama in efforts to establish a standard for interactive CD in seeking a standard for CD-video. A detailed study of the technological alliances into which Philips had entered by 1989, and of the multiplicity of relationships with other companies working with it tandem (with five or more cooperation agreements) lists 27 agreements with Siemens, 11 with Thomson, ten with Matsushita, eight with Bull, Olivetti and Sony, seven with AT&T and Bosch, six with DEC and Nixdorf, five with Alcatel (CGE), Hewlett-Packard and STC (+ICL). Of the listed inter-company agreements 43 per cent were finalized between 1986 and 1988. During the same period the proportion of alliances in professional products and in the systems sector (including production automation) rose from 10 per cent prior to 1986, to more than 13 per cent in 1989.

5   Whether this has always been the case because, as Post-Keynesians believe, production antecedes sales, and producers only learn *ex-post* from the movement of prices if their estimations of the markets were correct, or if this is a new phenomenon, is here irrelevant.

REFERENCES

Brenner, Y.S. and Brenner-Golomb, N. (1996), *A Theory of Full Employment*, Kluwer Academic Publishers, Boston/Dordrecht/London.

Dosi, G. (1988), "Sources, procedures and micro-economic effects of innovation", *Journal of Economic Literature*, Vol. 26, pp. 1120–71.

Manders, A.J.C. (1990), *Sturing van Produktie-Technologie (Decision making about Production Technology)*, Kerkebosch, Zeist.

Ohmae, K. (1985), *Triad. De Opkomst van Mondiale Konkurrentie*, Veen, Utrecht/Antwerpen.

26

A ROAD MAP FOR NATURAL CAPITALISM†

Amory B. Lovins, L. Hunter Lovins, and Paul Hawken*

On September 16, 1991, a small group of scientists was sealed inside Biosphere II, a glittering 3.2-acre glass and metal dome in Oracle, Arizona. Two years later, when the radical attempt to replicate the earth's main ecosystems in miniature ended, the engineered environment was dying. The gaunt researchers had survived only because fresh air had been pumped in. Despite $200 million worth of elaborate equipment, Biosphere II had failed to generate breathable air, drinkable water, and adequate food for just eight people. Yet Biosphere I, the planet we all inhabit, effortlessly performs those tasks every day for 6 billion of us.

Disturbingly, Biosphere I is now itself at risk. The earth's ability to sustain life, and therefore economic activity, is threatened by the way we extract, process, transport, and dispose of a vast flow of resources – some 220 billion tons a year, or more than 20 times the average American's body weight every day. With dangerously narrow focus, our industries look only at the exploitable resources of the earth's ecosystems – its oceans, forests, and plains – and not at the larger services that those systems provide for free. Resources and ecosystem services both come from the earth – even from the same biological systems – but they're two different things. Forests, for instance, not only produce the resource of wood fiber but also provide such ecosystem services as water storage, habitat, and regulation of the atmosphere and climate. Yet companies that earn income from harvesting the wood fiber resource often do so in ways that damage the forest's ability to carry out its other vital tasks.

Unfortunately, the cost of destroying ecosystem services becomes apparent only when the services start to break down. In China's Yangtze basin in 1998, for example, deforestation triggered flooding that killed 3,700 people, dislocated 223 million, and inundated 60 million acres of cropland. That $30 billion disaster forced a logging moratorium and a $12 billion crash program of reforestation.

The reason companies (and governments) are so prodigal with ecosystem services is that the value of those services doesn't appear on the business balance sheet. But that's a staggering omission. The economy, after all, is embedded in the environment. Recent calculations published in the journal *Nature* conservatively estimate the value of all the earth's ecosystem services to be at least $33 trillion a year. That's close to the gross world product, and it implies a capitalized book value on the order of half a quadrillion dollars. What's more, for most of these services, there is no known substitute at any price, and we can't live without them.

This article puts forward a new approach not only for protecting the biosphere but also for improving profits and competitiveness. Some very simple changes to the way we run our businesses, built on advanced techniques for making resources more productive, can yield startling benefits both for today's shareholders and for future generations.

This approach is called *natural capitalism* because it's what capitalism might become if its largest category of capital – the "natural capital" of ecosystem services – were properly valued. The journey to natural capitalism involves four major shifts in business practices, all vitally interlinked:

- *Dramatically increase the productivity of natural resources.* Reducing the wasteful and destructive flow of resources from depletion to pollution represents a major business opportunity. Through fundamental changes in both production design and technology, farsighted companies are developing ways to make natural resources – energy, minerals, water, forests – stretch 5, 10, even 100 times further than they do today. These major resource savings often yield higher profits than small resource savings do – or even saving no resources at all would – and not only pay for themselves over time but in many cases reduce initial capital investments.
- *Shift to biologically inspired production models*. Natural capitalism seeks not merely to reduce waste but to eliminate the very concept of waste. In closed-loop production systems, modeled on nature's designs, every output either is returned harmlessly to the ecosystem as a nutrient, like compost, or becomes an input for manufacturing another product. Such systems can often be designed to eliminate the use of toxic materials, which can hamper nature's ability to reprocess materials.
- *Move to a solutions-based business model*. The business model of traditional manufacturing rests on the sale of goods. In the new model, value is instead delivered as a flow of services – providing illumination, for example, rather than selling light-bulbs. This model entails a new perception of value, a move from the acquisition of goods as a measure of affluence to one where well-being is measured by the continuous satisfaction of changing expectations for quality, utility, and performance. The new relationship aligns the interests of providers and customers in ways that reward them for implementing the first two innovations of natural capitalism – resource productivity and closed-loop manufacturing.
- *Reinvest in natural capital*. Ultimately, business must restore, sustain, and expand the planet's ecosystems so that they can produce their vital services and biological resources even more abundantly. Pressures to do so are mounting as human needs expand, the costs engendered by deteriorating ecosystems rise, and the environmental awareness of consumers increases. Fortunately, these pressures all create business value.

Natural capitalism is not motivated by a current scarcity of natural resources. Indeed, although many biological resources, like fish, are becoming scarce, most mined resources, such as copper and oil, seem ever more abundant. Indices of average commodity prices are at 28-year lows, thanks partly to powerful extractive technologies, which are often subsidized and whose damage to natural capital remains unaccounted for. Yet even despite these artificially low prices, using resources manyfold more productively can now be so profitable that pioneering companies – large and small – have already embarked on the journey toward natural capitalism.[1]

Still the question arises – if large resource savings are available and profitable, why haven't they all been captured already? The answer is simple: scores of common practices in both the private and public sectors systematically reward companies for wasting natural resources and penalize them for boosting resource productivity. For example, most companies expense their consumption of raw materials through the income statement but pass resource-saving investment through the balance sheet. That distortion makes it more tax efficient to waste fuel than to invest in improving fuel efficiency. In short, even though the road seems clear, the compass that companies use to direct their journey is broken. Later we'll look in more detail at some of the obstacles to resource productivity – and some of the important business opportunities they reveal. But first, let's map the route toward natural capitalism.

DRAMATICALLY INCREASE THE PRODUCTIVITY OF NATURAL RESOURCES

In the first stage of a company's journey toward natural capitalism, it strives to wring out the waste of energy, water, materials, and other resources throughout its production systems and other operations. There are two main ways companies can do this at a profit. First, they can adopt a fresh approach to design that considers industrial systems as a whole rather than part by part. Second, companies can replace old industrial technologies with new ones, particularly with those based on natural processes and materials.

Implementing whole-system design

Inventor Edwin Land once remarked that "people who seem to have had a new idea have often simply stopped having an old idea." This is particularly true when designing for resource savings. The old idea is one of diminishing returns – the greater the resource saving, the higher the cost. But that old idea is giving way to the new idea that bigger savings can cost less – that saving a large fraction of resources can actually cost less than saving a small fraction of resources. This is the concept of expanding returns, and it governs much of the revolutionary thinking behind whole-system design. Lean manufacturing is an example of whole-system thinking that has helped many companies dramatically reduce such forms of waste as lead times, defect rates, and inventory. Applying whole-system thinking to the productivity of natural resources can achieve even more.

Consider Interface Corporation, a leading maker of materials for commercial interiors. In its new Shanghai carpet factory, a liquid had to be circulated through a standard pumping loop similar to those used in nearly all industries. A top European company designed the system to use pumps requiring a total of 95 horsepower. But before construction began, Interface's engineer, Jan Schilham, realized that two embarrassingly simple design changes would cut that power requirement to only 7 horsepower – a 92% reduction. His redesigned system cost less to build, involved no new technology, and worked better in all respects.

What two design changes achieved this 12-fold saving in pumping power? First, Schilham chose fatter-than-usual pipes, which create much less friction than thin pipes do and therefore need far less pumping energy. The original designer had chosen thin pipes because, according to the textbook method, the extra cost of fatter ones wouldn't be justified by the pumping energy that they would save. This standard design trade-off optimizes the pipes by themselves but "pessimizes" the larger system. Schilham optimized the *whole* system by counting not only the higher capital cost of the fatter pipes but also the *lower capital* cost of the smaller pumping equipment that would be needed. The pumps, motors, motor controls, and electrical components could all be much smaller because there'd be less friction to overcome. Capital cost would fall far more for the smaller equipment than it would rise for the fatter pipe. Choosing big pipes and small pumps – rather than small pipes and big pumps – would therefore make the whole system cost less to build, even before counting its future energy savings.

Schilham's second innovation was to reduce the friction even more by making the pipes short and straight rather than long and crooked. He did this by laying out the pipes first, *then* positioning the various tanks, boilers, and other equipment that they connected. Designers normally locate the production equipment in arbitrary positions and then have a pipe fitter connect everything. Awkward placement forces the pipes to make numerous bends that greatly increase friction. The pipe fitters don't mind: they're paid by the hour, they profit from the extra pipes and fittings, and they don't pay for the oversized pumps or inflated electric bills. In addition to reducing those four kinds of costs, Schilham's short, straight pipes were easier to insulate, saving an extra 70 kilowatts of heat loss and repaying the insulation's cost in three months.

This small example has big implications for two reasons. First, pumping is the largest application of motors, and motors use three-quarters of all industrial electricity. Second, the lessons are very widely relevant. Interface's pumping loop shows how simple changes in design mentality can yield huge resource savings and returns on investment. This isn't rocket science; often it's just a rediscovery of good Victorian engineering principles that have been lost because of specialization.

Whole-system thinking can help managers find small changes that lead to big savings that are cheap, free, or even better than free (because they make the whole system cheaper to build). They can do this because often the right investment in one part of the system can produce multiple benefits throughout the system. For example, companies would gain 18 distinct economic benefits – of which direct energy savings is only one – if they switched from ordinary motors to premium-efficiency motors or from ordinary lighting ballasts (the transformer-like boxes that control fluorescent lamps) to electronic ballasts that automatically dim the lamps to match available daylight. If everyone in America integrated these and other selected technologies into all existing motor and lighting systems in an optimal way, the nation's $220-billion-a-year electric bill would be cut in half. The after-tax return on investing in these changes would in most cases exceed 100% per year.

The profits from saving electricity could be increased even further if companies also incorporated the best off-the-shelf improvements into their building structure and their office, heating, cooling, and other equipment. Overall, such changes could cut national electricity consumption by at least 75% and produce returns of around 100% a year on the investments made. More important, because workers would be more comfortable, better able to see, and less fatigued by noise, their productivity and the quality of their output would rise. Eight recent case studies of people working in well-designed, energy-efficient buildings measured labor productivity gains of 6% to 16%. Since a typical office pays about 100 times as much for people as it does for energy, this increased productivity in people is worth about 6 to 16 times as much as eliminating the entire energy bill.

Energy-saving, productivity-enhancing improvements can often be achieved at even lower cost by piggybacking them onto the periodic renovations that all buildings and factories need. A recent proposal for reallocating the normal 20-year renovation budget for a standard 200,000-square-foot glass-clad office tower near Chicago, Illinois, shows the potential of whole-system design. The proposal suggested replacing the ageing glazing system with a new kind of window that lets in nearly six times more daylight than the old sun-blocking glass units. The new windows would reduce the flow of heat and noise four times better than traditional windows do. So even though the glass costs slightly more, the overall cost of the renovation would be reduced because the windows would let in cool, glare-free daylight that, when combined with more efficient lighting and office equipment, would reduce the need for air-conditioning by 75%. Installing a fourfold more efficient, but fourfold smaller, air-conditioning system would cost $200,000 less than giving the old system its normal 20-year renovation. The $200,000 saved would, in turn, pay for the extra cost of the new windows and other improvements. This whole-system approach to renovation would not only save

75% of the building's total energy use, it would also greatly improve the building's comfort and marketability. Yet it would cost essentially the same as the normal renovation. There are about 100,000 twenty-year-old glass office towers in the United States that are ripe for such improvement.

Major gains in resource productivity require that the right steps be taken in the right order. Small changes made at the downstream end of a process often create far larger savings further upstream. In almost any industry that uses a pumping system, for example, saving one unit of liquid flow or friction in an exit pipe saves about ten units of fuel, cost, and pollution at the power station.

Of course, the original reduction in flow itself can bring direct benefits, which are often the reason changes are made in the first place. In the 1980s, while California's industry grew 30%, for example, its water use was cut by 30%, largely to avoid increased wastewater fees. But the resulting reduction in pumping energy (and the roughly tenfold larger saving in power-plant fuel and pollution) delivered bonus savings that were at the time largely unanticipated.

To see how downstream cuts in resource consumption can create huge savings upstream, consider how reducing the use of wood fiber disproportionately reduces the pressure to cut down forests. In round numbers, half of all harvested wood fiber is used for such structural products as lumber; the other half is used for paper and cardboard. In both cases, the biggest leverage comes from reducing the amount of the retail product used. If it takes, for example, three pounds of harvested trees to produce one pound of product, then saving one pound of product will save three pounds of trees – plus all the environmental damage avoided by not having to cut them down in the first place.

The easiest savings come from not using paper that's unwanted or unneeded. In an experiment at its Swiss headquarters, for example, Dow Europe cut office paper flow by about 30% in six weeks simply by discouraging unneeded information. For instance, mailing lists were eliminated and senders of memos got back receipts indicating whether each recipient had wanted the information. Taking those and other small steps, Dow was also able to increase labor productivity by a similar proportion because people could focus on what they really needed to read. Similarly, Danish hearing-aid maker Oticon saved upwards of 30% of its paper as a by-product of redesigning its business processes to produce better decisions faster. Setting the default on office printers and copiers to double-sided mode reduced AT&T's paper costs by about 15%. Recently developed copiers and printers can even strip off old toner and printer ink, permitting each sheet to be reused about ten times.

Further savings can come from using thinner but stronger and more opaque paper, and from designing packaging more thoughtfully. In a 30-month effort at reducing such waste, Johnson & Johnson saved 2,750 tons of packaging, 1,600 tons of paper, $2.8 million, and at least 330 acres of forest annually. The downstream savings in paper use are multiplied by the savings further upstream, as less need for paper products (or less need for fiber to make each product) translates into less raw paper, less raw paper means less pulp, and less pulp requires fewer trees to be harvested from the forest. Recycling paper and substituting alternative fibers such as wheat straw will save even more.

Comparable savings can be achieved for the wood fiber used in structural products. Pacific Gas and Electric, for example, sponsored an innovative design developed by Davis Energy Group that used engineered wood products to reduce the amount of wood needed in a stud wall for a typical tract house by more than 70%. These walls were stronger, cheaper, more stable, and insulated twice as well. Using them enabled the designers to eliminate heating and cooling equipment in a climate where temperatures range from freezing to 113°F. Eliminating the equipment made the whole house much less expensive both to build and to run while still maintaining high levels of comfort. Taken together, these and many other savings in the paper and construction industries could make our use of wood fiber so much more productive that, in principle, the entire world's present wood fiber needs could probably be met by an intensive tree farm about the size of Iowa.

Adopting innovative technologies

Implementing whole-system design goes hand in hand with introducing alternative, environmentally friendly technologies. Many of these are already available and profitable but not widely known. Some, like the "designer catalysts" that are transforming the chemical industry, are already runaway successes. Others are still making their way to market, delayed by cultural rather than by economic or technical barriers.

The automobile industry is particularly ripe for technological charge. After a century of development, motorcar technology is showing signs of age. Only 1% of the energy consumed by today's cars is actually used to move the driver: only 15% to 20% of the power generated by burning gasoline reaches the wheels (the rest is lost in the engine and drive-train) and 95% of the resulting propulsion moves the car, not the driver. The industry's infrastructure is hugely expensive and inefficient. Its convergent products compete for narrow niches in saturated core markets at commoditylike prices. Auto making is capital intensive, and product cycles are long. It is profitable in good years but subject to large losses in bad years. Like the typewriter industry just before the advent of personal computers, it is vulnerable to displacement by something completely different.

Enter the Hypercar. Since 1993, when Rocky Mountain Institute placed this automotive concept in the public domain, several dozen current and potential auto manufacturers have committed billions of dollars to its development and commercialization. The Hypercar integrates the best existing technologies to reduce the consumption of fuel as much as 85% and the amount of materials used up to 90% by introducing four main innovations.

First, making the vehicle out of advanced polymer composites, chiefly carbon fiber, reduces its weight by two-thirds while maintaining crashworthiness. Second, aerodynamic design and better tires reduce air resistance by as much as 70% and rolling resistance by up to 80%. Together, these innovations save about two-thirds of the fuel. Third, 30% to 50% of the remaining fuel is saved by using a "hybrid-electric" drive. In such a system, the wheels are turned by electric motors whose power is made onboard by a small engine or turbine, or even more efficiently by a fuel cell. The fuel cell generates electricity directly by chemically combining stored hydrogen with oxygen, producing pure hot water as its only by-product. Interactions between the small, clean, efficient power source and the ultralight, low-drag auto body then further reduce the weight, cost, and complexity of both. Fourth, much of the traditional hardware – from transmissions and differentials to gauges and certain parts of the suspension – can be replaced by electronics controlled with highly integrated, customizable, and upgradable software.

These technologies make it feasible to manufacture pollution-free, high-performance cars, sport utilities, pickup trucks, and vans that get 80 to 200 miles per gallon (or its energy equivalent in other fuels). These improvements will not require any compromise in quality or utility. Fuel savings will not come from making the vehicles small, sluggish, unsafe, or unaffordable, nor will they depend on government fuel taxes, mandates, or subsidies. Rather, Hypercars will succeed for the same reason that people buy compact discs instead of phonograph records: the CD is a superior product that redefines market expectations. From the manufacturers' perspective, Hypercars will cut cycle times, capital needs, body part counts, and assembly effort and space by as much as tenfold. Early adopters will have a huge competitive advantage – which is why dozens of corporations, including most automakers, are now racing to bring Hypercar-like products to market.[2]

In the long term, the Hypercar will transform industries other than automobiles. It will displace about an eighth of the steel market directly and most of the rest eventually, as carbon fiber becomes far cheaper. Hypercars and their cousins could ultimately save as much oil as OPEC now sells. Indeed, oil may well become uncompetitive as a fuel long before it becomes scarce and costly. Similar challenges face the coal and electricity industries because the development of the Hypercar is likely to accelerate greatly the commercialization of inexpensive hydrogen fuel cells. These fuel cells will help shift power production from centralized coalfired and nuclear power stations to networks of decentralized, small-scale generators. In fact, fuel-cell-powered Hypercars could themselves be part of these networks. They'd be, in effect, 20-kilowatt power plants on wheels. Given that cars are left parked – that is, unused – more than 95% of the time, these Hypercars could be plugged into a grid and could then sell back enough electricity to repay as much as half the predicted cost of leasing them. A national Hypercar fleet could ultimately have five to ten times the generating capacity of the national electric grid.

As radical as it sounds, the Hypercar is not an isolated case. Similar ideas are emerging in such industries as chemicals, semiconductors, general manufacturing, transportation, water and waste-water treatment, agriculture, forestry, energy, real estate, and urban design. For example, the amount of carbon dioxide released for each microchip manufactured can be reduced almost 100-fold through improvements that are now profitable or soon will be.

Some of the most striking developments come from emulating nature's techniques. In her book, *Biomimicry*, Janine Benyus points out that spiders convert digested crickets and flies into silk that's as strong as Kevlar without the need for boiling sulfuric acid and high-temperature extruders. Using no furnaces, abalone can convert seawater into an inner shell twice as tough as our best ceramics. Trees turn sunlight, water, soil, and air into cellulose, a sugar stronger than nylon but one-fourth as dense. They then bind it into wood, a natural composite with a higher bending strength than concrete, aluminum alloy, or steel. We may never become as skillful as spiders, abalone, or trees, but smart designers are already realizing that nature's environmentally benign chemistry offers attractive alternatives to industrial brute force.

Whether through better design or through new technologies, reducing waste represents a vast business opportunity. The US economy is not even 10% as energy efficient as the laws of physics allow. Just the energy thrown off as waste heat by US power stations equals the total energy use of Japan. Materials efficiency is even worse: only about 1% of all the materials mobilized to serve America is actually made into products and still in use six months after sale. In every sector, there are opportunities for reducing the amount of resources that go into a production process, the steps required to run that process, and the amount of pollution generated and by-products discarded at the end. These all represent avoidable costs and hence profits to be won.

REDESIGN PRODUCTION ACCORDING TO BIOLOGICAL MODELS

In the second stage on the journey to natural capitalism, companies use closed-loop manufacturing to create new products and processes that can totally prevent waste. This plus more efficient production processes could cut companies' long-term materials requirements by more than 90% in most sectors.

The central principle of closed-loop manufacturing, as architect Paul Bierman-Lytle of the engineering firm CH2M Hill puts it, is "waste equals food." Every output of manufacturing should be either composted into natural nutrients or remanufactured into technical nutrients – that is, it should be returned to the ecosystem or recycled for further production. Closed-loop production systems are designed to eliminate any materials that incur disposal costs, especially toxic ones, because the alternative – isolating them to prevent harm to natural systems – tends to be costly and risky. Indeed, meeting EPA and OSHA standards by eliminating harmful materials often makes a manufacturing process cost less than the hazardous process it replaced. Motorola, for example, formerly used chloro-fluorocarbons for cleaning printed circuit boards after soldering. When CFCs were outlawed because they destroy stratospheric ozone, Motorola at first explored such alternatives as orange-peel terpenes. But it turned out to be even cheaper – and to produce a better product – to redesign the whole soldering process so that it needed no cleaning operations or cleaning materials at all.

Closed-loop manufacturing is more than just a theory. The US remanufacturing industry in 1996 reported revenues of $53 billion – more than consumer-durables manufacturing (appliances; furniture; audio, video, farm, and garden equipment). Xerox, whose bottom line has swelled by $700 million from remanufacturing, expects to save another $1 billion just by remanufacturing its new, entirely reusable or recyclable line of "green" photocopiers. What's more, policy makers in some countries are already taking steps to encourage industry to think along these lines. German law, for example, makes many manufacturers responsible for their products forever, and Japan is following suit.

Combining closed-loop manufacturing with resource efficiency is especially powerful. DuPont, for example, gets much of its polyester industrial film back from customers after they use it and recycles it into new film. DuPont also makes its polyester film ever stronger and thinner so it uses less material and costs less to make. Yet because the film performs better, customers are willing to pay more for it. As DuPont chairman Jack Krol noted in 1997, "Our ability to continually improve the inherent properties [of our films] enables this process [of developing more productive materials, at lower cost, and higher profits] to go on indefinitely."

Interface is leading the way to this next frontier of industrial ecology. While its competitors are "down cycling" nylon-and-PVC-based carpet into less valuable carpet backing, Interface has invented a new floorcovering material called Solenium, which can be completely remanufactured into identical new product. This fundamental innovation emerged from a clean-sheet redesign. Executives at Interface didn't ask how they could sell more carpet of the familiar kind: they asked how they could create a dream product that would best meet their customers' needs while protecting and nourishing natural capital.

Solenium lasts four times longer and uses 40% less material than ordinary carpets – an 86% reduction in materials intensity. What's more, Solenium is free of chlorine and other toxic materials, is virtually stainproof, doesn't grow mildew, can easily be cleaned with water, and offers aesthetic advantages over traditional carpets. It's so superior in every respect that Interface doesn't market it as an environmental product – just a better one.

Solenium is only one part of Interface's drive to eliminate every form of waste. Chairman Ray C. Anderson defines waste as "any measurable input that does not produce customer value," and he considers all inputs to be waste until shown otherwise. Between 1994 and 1998, this zero-waste approach led to a systematic treasure hunt that helped to keep resource inputs constant while revenues rose by $200 million. Indeed, $67 million of the revenue increase can be directly attributed to the company's 60% reduction in landfill waste.

Subsequently, president Charlie Eitel expanded the definition of waste to include all fossil fuel inputs, and now many customers are eager to buy products from the company's recently opened solar-powered carpet factory. Interface's green strategy has not only won plaudits from environmentalists, it has also proved a remarkably successful business strategy. Between 1993 and 1998, revenue has more than doubled, profits have more than tripled, and the number of employees has increased by 73%.

CHANGE THE BUSINESS MODEL

In addition to its drive to eliminate waste, Interface has made a fundamental shift in its business model – the third stage on the journey toward natural capitalism. The company has realized that clients want to walk on and look at carpets – but not necessarily to own them. Traditionally, broadloom carpets in office buildings are replaced every decade because some portions look worn out. When that happens, companies suffer the disruption of shutting down their offices and removing their furniture. Billions of pounds of carpets are removed each year and sent to landfills, where they will last up to 20,000 years. To escape this unproductive and wasteful cycle, Interface is transforming itself from a company that sells and fits carpets into one that provides floorcovering services.

Under its Evergreen Lease, Interface no longer sells carpets but rather leases a floor-covering service for a monthly fee, accepting responsibility for keeping the carpet fresh and clean. Monthly inspections detect and replace worn carpet tiles. Since at most 20% of an area typically shows at least 80% of the wear, replacing only the worn parts reduces the consumption of carpeting material by about 80%. It also minimizes the disruption that customers experience – worn tiles are seldom found under furniture. Finally, for the customer, leasing carpets can provide a tax advantage by turning a capital expenditure into a tax-deductible expense. The result: the customer gets cheaper and better services that cost the supplier far less to produce. Indeed, the energy saved from not producing a whole new carpet is in itself enough to produce all the carpeting that the new business model requires. Taken together, the 5-fold savings in carpeting material that Interface achieves through the Evergreen Lease and the 7-fold materials savings achieved through the use of Solenium deliver a stunning 35-fold reduction in the flow of materials needed to sustain a superior floor-covering service. Remanufacturing, and even making carpet initially from renewable materials, can then reduce the extraction of virgin resources essentially to the company's goal of zero.

Interface's shift to a service-leasing business reflects a fundamental change from the basic model of most manufacturing companies, which still look on their businesses as machines for producing and selling products. The more products sold, the better – at least for the company, if not always for the customer or the earth. But any model that wastes natural resources also wastes money. Ultimately, that model will be unable to compete with a service model that emphasizes solving problems and building long-term relationships with customers rather than making and selling products. The shift to what James Womack of the Lean Enterprise Institute calls a "solutions economy" will almost always improve customer value *and* providers' bottom lines because it aligns both parties' interests, offering rewards for doing more and better with less.

Interface is not alone. Elevator giant Schindler, for example, prefers leasing vertical transportation services to selling elevators because leasing lets it capture the savings from its elevators' lower energy and maintenance costs. Dow Chemical and Safety-Kleen prefer leasing dissolving services to selling solvents because they can reuse the same solvent scores of times, reducing costs. United Technologies' Carrier division, the world's largest manufacturer of air conditioners, is shifting its mission from selling air conditioners to leasing comfort. Making its air conditioners more durable and efficient may compromise future equipment sales, but it provides what customers want and will pay for – better comfort at lower cost. But Carrier is going even further. It's starting to team up with other companies to make buildings more efficient so that they need less air-conditioning, or even none at all, to yield the same level of comfort. Carrier will get paid to provide the agreed-upon level of comfort, however that's delivered. Higher profits will come from providing better solutions rather than from selling more equipment. Since comfort with little or no air-conditioning (via better building design) works better and costs less than comfort with copious air-conditioning, Carrier is smart to capture this opportunity itself before its competitors do. As they say at 3M: "We'd rather eat our *own* lunch, thank you."

The shift to a service business model promises benefits not just to participating businesses but to the entire economy as well. Womack points out that by helping customers reduce their need for capital goods such as carpets or elevators, and by rewarding suppliers for extending and maximizing asset values rather than for churning them, adoption of the service model will reduce the volatility in the turnover of capital goods that lies at the heart of the business cycle. That would significantly reduce the overall volatility of the world's economy. At present, the producers of capital goods face feast or famine because the buying decisions of households and corporations are extremely sensitive to fluctuating income. But in a continuous-flow-of-services economy, those swings would be greatly reduced, bringing a welcome stability to businesses. Excess capacity – another form of waste and source of risk – need no longer be retained for meeting peak demand. The result of adopting the new model would be an economy in which we grow and get richer by using less and become stronger by being leaner and more stable.

REINVEST IN NATURAL CAPITAL

The foundation of textbook capitalism is the prudent reinvestment of earnings in productive capital. Natural capitalists who have dramatically raised their resource productivity, closed their loops, and shifted to a solutions-based business model have one key task remaining. They must reinvest in restoring, sustaining, and expanding the most important form of capital – their own natural habitat and biological resource base.

This was not always so important. Until recently, business could ignore damage to the ecosystem because it didn't affect production and didn't increase costs. But that situation is changing. In 1998 alone, violent weather displaced 300 million people and caused upwards of $90 billion worth of damage, representing more weather-related destruction than was reported through the entire decade of the 1980s. The increase in damage is strongly linked to deforestation and climate change, factors that accelerate the frequency and severity of natural disasters and are the consequences of inefficient industrialization. If the flow of services from industrial systems is to be sustained or increased in the future for a growing population, the vital flow of services from living systems will have to be maintained or increased as well. Without reinvestment in natural capital, shortages of ecosystem services are likely to become the limiting factor to prosperity in the next century. When a manufacturer realizes that a supplier of key components is overextended and running behind on deliveries, it takes immediate action lest its own production lines come to a halt. The ecosystem is a supplier of key components for the life of the planet, and it is now falling behind on its orders.

Failure to protect and reinvest in natural capital can also hit a company's revenues indirectly. Many companies are discovering that public perceptions of environmental responsibility, or its lack thereof, affect sales. MacMillan Bloedel, targeted by environmental activists as an emblematic clear-cutter and chlorine user, lost 5% of its sales almost overnight: when dropped as a UK supplier by Scott Paper and Kimberly-Clark. Numerous case studies show that companies leading the way in implementing changes that help protect the environment tend to gain disproportionate advantage, while companies perceived as irresponsible lose their franchise, their legitimacy, and their shirts. Even businesses that claim to be committed to the concept of sustainable development but whose strategy is seen as mistaken, like Monsanto, are encountering stiffening public resistance to their products. Not surprisingly, University of Oregon business professor Michael Russo, along with many other analysts, has found that a strong environmental rating is "a consistent predictor of profitability."

The pioneering corporations that have made reinvestments in natural capital are starting to see some interesting paybacks. The independent power producer AES, for example, has long pursued a policy of planting trees to offset the carbon emissions of its power plants. That ethical stance, once thought quixotic, now looks like a smart investment because a dozen brokers are now starting to create markets in carbon reduction. Similarly, certification by the Forest Stewardship Council of certain sustainably grown and harvested products has given Collins Pine the extra profit margins that enabled its US manufacturing operations to survive brutal competition. Taking an even longer view, Swiss Re and other European reinsurers are seeking to cut their storm-damage losses by pressing for international public policy to protect the climate and by investing in climate-safe technologies that also promise good profits. Yet most companies still do not realize that a vibrant ecological web underpins their survival and their business success. Enriching natural capital is not just a public good – it is vital to every company's longevity.

It turns out that changing industrial processes so that they actually replenish and magnify the stock of natural capital can prove especially profitable because nature does the production; people need just step back and let life flourish. Industries that directly harvest living resources, such as forestry, farming, and fishing, offer the most suggestive examples. Here are three:

- Allan Savory of the Center for Holistic Management in Albuquerque, New Mexico, has redesigned cattle ranching to raise the carrying capacity of rangelands, which have often been degraded not by overgrazing but by undergrazing and grazing the wrong way. Savory's solution is to keep the cattle moving from place to place, grazing intensively but briefly at each site, so that they mimic the dense but constantly moving herds of native grazing animals that coevolved with grasslands. Thousands of ranchers are estimated to be applying this approach, improving both their range and their profits. This "management-intensive rotational grazing" method, long standard in New Zealand, yields such clearly superior returns that over 15% of Wisconsin's dairy farms have adopted it in the past few years.
- The California Rice Industry Association has discovered that letting nature's diversity flourish can be more profitable than forcing it to produce a single product. By flooding 150,000 to 200,000 acres of Sacramento valley rice fields – about 30% of California's rice-growing area – after harvest, farmers are able to create seasonal wetlands that support millions of wildfowl, replenish groundwater, improve fertility, and yield other valuable benefits. In addition, the farmers bale and sell the rice straw, whose high silica content – formerly an air-pollution hazard when the straw was burned – adds insect resistance and hence value as a construction material when it's resold instead.
- John Todd of Living Technologies in Burlington, Vermont, has used biological Living Machines – linked tanks of bacteria, algae, plants, and other organisms – to turn sewage into clean water. That not only yields cleaner water at a reduced cost, with no toxicity or odor, but it also produces commercially valuable flowers and makes the plant compatible with its residential neighborhood. A similar plant at the Ethel M Chocolates factory in Las Vegas, Nevada, not only handles difficult industrial wastes effectively but is showcased in its public tours.

Although such practices are still evolving, the broad lessons they teach are clear. In almost all climates, soils, and societies, working with nature is more productive than working against it. Reinvesting in nature allows farmers, fishermen, and forest managers to match or exceed the high yields and profits sustained by traditional input-intensive, chemically driven practices. Although much of mainstream business is still headed the other way, the profitability of sustainable, nature-emulating practices is already being proven. In the future, many industries that don't now consider themselves dependent on a biological resource base will become more so as they shift their raw materials and production processes more to biological ones. There is evidence that many business leaders are starting to think this way. The consulting firm Arthur D. Little surveyed a group of North American and European business leaders and found that 83% of them already believe that they can derive "real business value [from implementing a] sustainable-development approach to strategy and operations."

A BROKEN COMPASS?

If the road ahead is this clear, why are so many companies straying or falling by the wayside? We believe the reason is that the instruments companies use to set their targets, measure their performance, and hand out rewards are faulty. In other words, the markets are full of distortions and perverse incentives. Of the more than 60 specific forms of misdirection that we have identified,[3] the most obvious involve the ways companies allocate capital and the way governments set policy and impose taxes. Merely correcting these defective practices would uncover huge opportunities for profit.

Consider how companies make purchasing decisions. Decisions to buy small items are typically based on their initial cost rather than their full lifecycle cost, a practice that can add up to major wastage. Distribution transformers that supply electricity to buildings and factories, for example, are a minor item at just $320 apiece, and most companies try to save a quick buck by buying the lowest-price models. Yet nearly all the nation's electricity must flow through transformers, and using the cheaper but less efficient models wastes $1 billion a year. Such examples are legion. Equipping standard new office-lighting circuits with fatter wire that reduces electrical resistance could generate after-tax returns of 193% a year. Instead, wire as thin as the National Electrical Code permits is usually selected because it costs less up-front. But the code is meant only to prevent fires from overheated wiring, not to save money. Ironically, an electrician who chooses fatter wire – thereby reducing long-term electricity bills – doesn't get the job. After paying for the extra copper, he's no longer the low bidder.

Some companies do consider more than just the initial price in their purchasing decisions but still don't go far enough. Most of them use a crude payback estimate rather than more accurate metrics like discounted cash flow. A few years ago, the median simple payback these companies were demanding from energy efficiency was 1.9 years. That's equivalent to requiring an after-tax return of around 71% per year – about six times the marginal cost of capital.

Most companies also miss major opportunities by treating their facilities costs as an overhead to be minimized, typically by laying off engineers, rather than as a profit center to be optimized – by using those engineers to save resources. Deficient measurement and accounting practices also prevent companies from allocating costs – and waste – with any accuracy. For example, only a few semiconductor plants worldwide regularly and accurately measure how much energy they're using to produce a unit of chilled water or clean air for their clean-room production facilities. That makes it hard for them to improve efficiency. In fact, in an effort to save time, semiconductor makers frequently build new plants as exact copies of previous ones – a design method nicknamed "infectious repetitis."

Many executives pay too little attention to saving resources because they are often a small percentage of total costs (energy costs run to about 2% in most industries). But those resource savings drop straight to the bottom line and so represent a far greater percentage of profits. Many executives also think they already "did" efficiency in the 1970s, when the oil shock forced them to rethink old habits. They're forgetting that with today's far better technologies, it's profitable to start all over again. Malden Mills, the Massachusetts maker of such products as Polartec, was already using "efficient" metal-halide lamps in the mid-1990s. But a recent warehouse retrofit reduced the energy used for lighting by another 93%, improved visibility, and paid for itself in 18 months.

The way people are rewarded often creates perverse incentives. Architects and engineers, for example, are traditionally compensated for what they spend, not for what they save. Even the striking economics of the retrofit design for the Chicago office tower described earlier wasn't incentive enough actually to implement it. The property was controlled by a leasing agent who earned a commission every time she leased space, so she didn't want to wait the few extra months needed to refit the building. Her decision to reject the efficiency-quadrupling renovation proved costly for both her and her client. The building was so uncomfortable and expensive to occupy that it didn't lease, so ultimately the owner had to unload it at a firesale price. Moreover, the new owner will for the next 20 years be deprived of the opportunity to save capital cost.

If corporate practices obscure the benefits of natural capitalism, government policy positively undermines it. In nearly every country on the planet, tax laws penalize what we want more of – jobs and income – while subsidizing what we want less of – resource depletion and pollution. In every state but Oregon, regulated utilities are rewarded for selling more energy, water, and other resources, and penalized for selling less, even if increased production would cost more than improved customer efficiency. In most of America's arid western states, use-it-or-lose-it water laws encourage inefficient water consumption. Additionally, in many towns, inefficient use of land is enforced through outdated regulations, such as guidelines for ultrawide suburban streets recommended by 1950s civil-defense planners to accommodate the heavy equipment needed to clear up rubble after a nuclear attack.

The costs of these perverse incentives are staggering: $300 billion in annual energy wasted in the United States, and $1 trillion already misallocated to unnecessary air-conditioning equipment and the power supplies to run it (about 40% of the nation's peak electric load). Across the entire economy, unneeded expenditures to subsidize, encourage, and try to remedy inefficiency and damage that should not have occurred in the first place probably account for most, if not all, of the GDP growth of the past two decades. Indeed, according to former World Bank economist Herman Daly and his colleague John Cobb (along with many other analysts), Americans are hardly better off than they were in 1980. But if the US government and private industry could redirect the dollars currently earmarked for remedial costs toward reinvestment in natural and human capital, they could bring about a genuine improvement in the nation's welfare. Companies, too, are finding that wasting resources also means wasting money and people. These intertwined forms of waste have equally intertwined solutions. Firing the unproductive tons, gallons, and kilowatt-hours often makes it possible to keep the people, who will have more and better work to do.

RECOGNIZING THE SCARCITY SHIFT

In the end, the real trouble with our economic compass is that it points in exactly the wrong direction. Most businesses are behaving as if people were still scarce and nature still abundant – the conditions that helped to fuel the first Industrial Revolution. At that time, people were relatively scarce compared with the present-day population. The rapid mechanization of the textile industries created explosive economic growth that created labor shortages in the factory and the field. The Industrial Revolution, responding to those shortages and mechanizing one industry after another, made people a hundred times more productive than they had ever been.

The logic of economizing on the scarcest resource, because it limits progress, remains correct. But the pattern of scarcity is shifting: now people aren't scarce but nature is. This shows up first in industries that depend directly on ecological health. Here, production is increasingly constrained by fish rather than by boats and nets, by forests rather than by chain saws, by fertile topsoil rather than by plows. Moreover, unlike the traditional factors of industrial production – capital and labor – the biological limiting factors cannot be substituted for one other. In the industrial system, we can easily exchange machinery for labor. But no technology or amount of money can substitute for a stable climate and a productive biosphere. Even proper pricing can't replace the priceless.

Natural capitalism addresses those problems by reintegrating ecological with economic goals. Because it is both necessary and profitable, it will subsume traditional industrialism within a new economy and a new paradigm of production, just as industrialism previously subsumed agrarianism. The companies that first make the changes we have described will have a competitive edge. Those that don't make that effort won't be a problem because ultimately they won't be around. In making that choice, as Henry Ford said, "Whether you believe you can, or whether you believe you can't, you're absolutely right."

NOTES

† This chapter has been adapted from, Lovins, A. B., Lovins, L. H. and Hawken, P. (1999) "A road map for natural capitalism", *Harvard Business Review*, May/June.

* A MacArthur Fellow, Amory B. Lovins is the research director and CFO of Rocky Mountain Institute (RMI). L. Hunter Lovins is the CEO of RMI, the nonprofit resource policy center they cofounded in 1982 in Snowmass, Colorado (http://www.rmi.org). Paul Hawken is the founder of the Smith & Hawken retail and catalog company, cofounder of the knowledge-management software company Datafusion, and author of *Growing a Business* (Simon & Schuster, 1983) and *The Ecology of Commerce* (Harper Collins, 1993). He and the Lovinses consult for businesses worldwide and have coauthored the forthcoming *Natural Capitalism* (Little Brown, September 1999). If you would like to explore the concept of natural capitalism further, join our authors in the HBR Web Forum at http://www.hbr.org/forum.

1 Our book, *Natural capitalism*, provides hundreds of examples of how companies of almost every type and size, often through modest shifts in business logic and practice, have dramatically improved their bottom lines.

2 Nonproprietary details are posted at http://www.hypercar.com.

3 Summarized in the report "Climate: Making Sense *and* Making Money" at http://www.rmi.org/catalog/climate.html.

27

REFLECTIONS ON THE POLITICS LINKING SCIENCE, ENVIRONMENT AND INNOVATION*

Sonja Boehmer-Christiansen

Green technological innovation is the subject of much current research because it is expected to serve 'competitiveness' and 'ecological modernization'. Research needs to be extended to cover institutional innovation and the combined socio-political impacts of the new environmentalism. One entry into this area is to examine the links between science, environmental protection, innovation, and the distribution of political power. It is argued that institutionalized science – or the research-cum-consultancy enterprise - thrives on the claim that it is able to solve 'fashionable' problems, especially future ones, by technological progress. There is little historical reason to reject such claims. However, these claims make science, and especially the environmental sciences, of immediate interest to those seeking new powers or defending existing privileges or markets. Proposed solutions tend to be threats to vested interests and distributions of wealth and influence. But the power of science reaches beyond responding to the concerns of the day, it strives to select those problems for society which create markets for planned research agendas and technologies still on the computer screen. The research enterprise, at the root of much technological and technical innovation, is not likely to succeed in imposing its choices on society without support in the market place or from government. It therefore becomes an important, if neglected, political actor, influencing and persuading not only with appeals to rationality, but also with promises of enhanced security, health and wealth. Having identified and selected problems, these are presented to society with pleas for remedial or preventative action. This chapter reflects on the impact of these pleas on contemporary world politics. It is concluded that political systems must learn to evaluate and judge scientific claims more cautiously because research networks and the informal influence of science entrepreneurs on 'the public' tend to turn environmental change into policy problems. Once technological 'fixes' are offered simultaneously, potential implementors and enforcers form alliances demanding state intervention, to resolve the alleged problems. How real is the global environmental problem

- the allegedly ever-growing 'okologische Problemdruck'? Does the seeking of green competiveness in the 'North' in the name of preventing catastrophe, whilst de facto opposing industrialization and resource developments in the 'South' in the name of 'sustainable development', represent the essence of global politics of the 1990s?

SIGN-POSTS: OBSERVING ENVIRONMENTALISM AND RESEARCH IN THE 'REAL' WORLD

These reflections are drawn from an analysis of environmental politics since the 1960s[1] in relation to concerns raised by students of development.[2] Questions are raised about how science and environmentalism, particularly 'eco-alarmism',[3] have influenced innovation and international investment policies, and how these in turn are, or may be, affecting the inter- and intranational distribution of wealth, well-being, and political power. The very use of the idea of 'environmental protection' or 'okologischer Problemsdruck' in politics needs examination, for the idea is usually used in association with emphatic calls for state action, often at the global level.

From observation, the idea is put most persuasively and disseminated most effectively by the international research enterprise, that sector of the knowledge industry which is not only growing rapidly, but always needs more public or private resources to sustain itself.

Who believes its 'epistemic' or knowledge-based claims about environmental decline and impending disaster, and who uses them for the justification of non-environmental ends?

Innovation is broadly defined to include directed technological and institutional developments. Environment is increasingly impossible to define, for it has become a new label for land, resources, nature or simply the physical, and therefore measurable, universe. Hugely diverse in time, place, and value (as placed on it by political systems) means the word should never be in the singular when applied to large areas. There is no global environment, rather many environments most of which have long ceased to be 'natural'. Environmentalism, especially in its more extreme form, is not science, but an ideology largely constructed from science. It assumes that human activities, especially those of industrial society, are destructive and ultimately pathological. Transformation of society and curtailment of many activities, such as mining, forest clearance, burning coal, and building roads, are allegedly required 'to save the planet'.

Environmentalism thrives on one-world images which in turn tend to be used to rationalize globalization processes, such as free flows of capital, expertise, and technology. While eco-alarmism includes a broad range of analyses about the inter-relationship between societies and their environments, they all point to humanity and prevailing technology as problems not as solutions. With rising fears of planetary survival, modernity turns into risk and enlightenment is distrusted. Beliefs and institutions are conceptualized as barriers and obstacles: mankind has sinned and ought to change.

ENVIRONMENTAL INNOVATION

Environmental innovation is all around us today, and it is difficult not to welcome this when viewed from an environmental perspective. The research community is indeed devising sophisticated methods for measuring sustainability and for carrying out integrated environmental assessment. It offers 'policy-relevant' computer models and equations, as well as indicators to enhance environmental efficiency.[4] Much of this knowledge is gradually incorporated into policy, strategy, and planning. What are the political impacts?

A publication by the Japanese Technology Council was recently summarized for the UK government under the heading 'Fourteen proposals for a new earth: policy triad for the environment, economy and energy'. The proposals argue that:

Global warming and other environmental problems requiring new responses have a serious effect on the global environment, on which the survival of all humankind depends, and call for a re-examination of civilisation as we know it . . . business, consumers, and the government (must) work together continuously and comprehensively to build an environment-friendly socio-economic structure . . . (and there is) the need for technological responses . . . and international initiatives.

(*Ortis News*, Vol. 3, No. 23, 1994, p. 7)

What do such green agendas, which are now disseminated by virtually all established institutions in Europe and the world, increasingly with reference to 'global security', mean in political and social terms? Threats usually benefit specific marketing solutions. Without a solution already being at hand, be these nuclear power, solar cells, energy efficiency or subsidies for farmers growing wood for power stations, problems tend to be ignored by political systems.

. . . AND THE ROLE OF ELITES

Research into how scientific, commercial, and political elites use scientific evidence and promise future findings in the building of international and national environmental regimes raises the question of whether environmentalism, especially eco-alarmism, has become the ideological motor of 'Northern' innovation and accumulation, that is of ecological modernization, while also being used, by others, as a tool of protectionism and 'eco-colonialism' in the 'South' (see North, 1995). Groups that benefit from both developments can be identified as a driving force behind the construction of 'degrading' global environmental threats.

Since the late 1970s, one may observe the emergence of increasingly wealthy and professional, usually US-based, environmental research organizations and consultancies which also act as pressure groups. They practice 'advocacy' and are at home in centres or institutes for international environmental law, environmental science, conservation bodies and, above all, in the US-based Environmental Defense Fund, the World Watch Institute, and the World Resources Institute. These bodies assert serious global dangers with vast amounts of 'scientific' evidence while also opposing large-scale development in the South on environmental grounds and for the sake of indigenous people. They act indeed in the name of the losers in their own societies, urging politicians to act on the basis of their advice; especially at the global level where the US government is often most effective.[5] They also market their own highly expert services. International lobbies of 'independent' experts put pressure on the 'hegemonic' government to open intergovernmental bodies to their expertise and influence, and then to subject them to 'independent' scrutiny and evaluation. While there may or may not be environmental benefits in the end, well-paid markets are created for expertise.[6] Other needs, not selected and evaluated by these experts, may well be ignored.

Environmental consultancies and research bodies are sprouting like mushrooms in 'Northern' soils. Eco-alarmists advise the insurance industry, inviting them to raise premiums on precautionary grounds. Legal firms are expanding into environmental consultancy, litigation, and lobbying. Consultancies and expensive commercial conferences are equally flourishing in the wake of environmental directives, targets, and statutes devised by national and international bureaucracies under pressure from politicians and lobbies. Treasuries are greening so that they may impose taxes on energy and road use without having to ask parliamentary approval. The environment has surely become a product as well as a tool of contemporary policies, of the marketing enterprise and professional regulation. To prevent the demise of the planet, consumers must pay more, and the more 'efficient' producers or service providers are rewarded.

One observation applies to most of the green rhetoric in vogue during the mid-1990s, be it from research funding bodies, industry or government, political parties or universities – it consistently avoids the concepts of the political and social. At most there is reference to the socio-economic dimensions, aspects, or considerations. Attitudes may be measures as providing 'social' knowledge. Knowledge is quickly reduced to science, and science to 'hard' numerical data about physical objects or systems or to 'socio-economic' knowledge that can be measured in monetary terms.[7] Research is marketed as relevant when it supports the economic and commercial goals of prevailing authorities and funding bodies. A false veil of 'objectivity' is created and increasingly incorporated into official environmental debates.

THE POLITICAL UTILITY OF MAINSTREAM ECONOMICS

Reflections of the above kind are clearly tentative and need interpretation in the context of personal maps of reality. To identify my own, an American institutional economist writing in the late 1980s may be quoted:

> Ceremonial incantations (supply side economics) and financial manipulations (corporate mergers) are the contemporary ways and means of getting something for nothing, of exploiting the underlying population and the underlying economy
>
> (Dugger, 1988, p. 244)[8]

What impact is environmentalism, in both its guises of ecological modernization and sustainable development, having on these incantations and manipulations? Have they been absorbed into theory rather painlessly? If so, they would become part of professional advice and, one could argue, have come to serve existing political structures rather than challenging them. Finance can exploit consumers by making them pay more for 'green' products and reap larger rents which in part creates more disposable wealth at the top, in part more investment in 'objective knowledge'. To those watching from below, technological 'determinism' appears to be defining their opportunities.

The attraction of 'mainstream' economic theory, and its recommendations, and hence of allegedly value-free and purely-technical advice, to political elites, lies in the power it promises to bestow on those who manage to apply them effectively. Did monetarism capture ecology by internalization of 'external' costs, in that it justifies rises in taxation or the imposition of levies which increase revenue to governments and income to selected industries?[9] In the context of ageing green parties and the weakening of environmental protests, green rhetoric seems to be spreading through the business community promising more income to lawyers as they seek to replace protest by litigation. Has environmental awareness-raising achieved its goals in the North, or has the radical social potential of environmentalism been transformed? The idea that the welfare/social democratic state is an historical aberration is gaining currency among the Right. The question is whether the green agenda supports or resists this idea in practice. Are we in danger of creating a world in which science and technology will protect the 'environment' of the North so that people there can be better neglected as a useless and inflexible underclass, while the application of science and technology is resisted elsewhere with reference to the same expertise?[10]

WHAT HAS HAPPENED TO THE SOCIAL MOVEMENTS?

Led by natural scientists predicting, at various times, global acidification, cooling, or warming, the death of the oceans, or of the forests, politicians, business leaders, and technological 'fixers' are now advocating sustainability. Authority and industry have converted to green managerialism, apparently ready to conquer the world. This at least, is one view of the world as seen from Britain in 1995. Yet once, environmentalism comprised a faith in social movements and was perceived as a subversive and liberating instrument of civil society. It was directed against the centralizing, hierarchical power of state and the unrestrained capacity of elites to consume resources and services. Are we simply observing a normal process of absorption or social learning, as some American scholars appear to be arguing, or has something sinister happened to the concern for the environment? Gorz (1980) claimed in the mid seventies that 'the ecological movement is not an end in itself, but a stage in a larger struggle'. If it is not, then 'what was unthinkable yesterday becomes taken for granted today, and fundamentally nothing changes'.

Whether the changes brought about by modern industrial society will destroy the Earth cannot be predicted or proven, only believed. The existence of very real environmental problems is not sufficiently addressed, however, because the political process does not pick them up. Understood problems do not require more research (and hence justify delay), often they do not generate, or promise to generate, more wealth. They tend to be site, society, and region specific, rather than global, and hence do not attract global lobbies. As any geographer knows, humankind has always changed the face of the Earth, and this face changes continuously for natural and man-made reasons. Any objective assessment of such change as 'good' or bad', harmless, or harmful is impossible, for every assessment implicitly assumes that change is good or bad for somebody.

Poverty does not generate wealth, nor does it invite technological innovation because the all-important market for new products is lacking. The solution of real environmental problems may not require much transfer of knowledge or technology, but rather the application and implementation of what is already available. This may be resisted on political grounds (for example, see Reis and Marguils, 1991). Environmental regulation can only be a matter or political judgement and not of science; environmental policy-making may become the province of experts seeking efficiency and assuming that there are few political inputs to their choices or political implications from them. In fact, political judgements are entrusted to an interest group, the experts are no longer 'on tap' but 'on top'. I would argue that this should be resisted, if only because professionals cannot in the end do more than make assessments which serve their own pockets and values.

TOWARDS A CONCEPTUAL FRAMEWORK FOR INTERDISCIPLINARY ANALYSIS OF ENVIRONMENTALISM AND ITS IMPACTS

Elites in search of economic miracles and power

If Dugger's description of how elites behave is considered credible, one might theorize that environmentalism cannot but be reinterpreted and captured by commercial and political elites. This was possible because green ideology was so readily incorporated into conventional economic thinking and capitalist objectives.[11]

How was this achieved? Experience here might refer the social and political impacts of the 'Thatcher or Reagan' economic miracles,[12] with the former at least greening considerably towards the end of her career, or to the impact of World Bank/IMF policies (or rather of the conditions under which private capital provides credits) on structural adjustments in many poor societies.[13] Events in the GDR both before it became a part of the world economy and after the political Wende also provide lessons about the interaction of economic theory, politics and environmental policy (Boehmer-Christiansen, 1992).[14] The world-view tentatively attributed to global political elites in the post-communist era is a form of monetarism which reflects the interests of financial elites. This view is combined with a desire for deregulation when this serves to shed inherited welfare responsibilities and enhance productive efficiency, as well as re-regulation and subsidies, especially when this serves the development and transfer of 'clean' technology and environmental capacity to country areas which are not competitors. Vast amounts of private money are currently seeking profitable investments. States are needed to 'insure' their associated risks.[15]

Elites and their professional advisors tend to shape international politics in the context of changing technologies which they themselves have earlier selected and financed, often with public money. Commercial elites tend to use the structures and networks of the modern state (including non- and intergovernmental organizations) to 'greenwash' their expansion and justify financial globalization. Persuasion, regulation, and subsidization are used to create markets for new technologies. Global systems of information exchange, vague commitments under environmental treaties, and small, but influential, policy networks tend to implement the existing expectations and commitments of technical elites in the name of 'global governance' (Sand, 1990). This includes global environment protection as a step towards more expensive energy, from which governments, shareholders, major energy supply companies, and certain technologies stand to benefit. People still continue to die in large numbers from contaminated water and lack of food because here the related environmental damage is not described as global, and there are no commercial benefits.

If political and commercial elites really believed that man-made environmental change was destroying the world, they would surely be less willing to fund natural science research (including space observation and telematics) rather than research into how societies might be transformed into a more sustainable collection. More probing questions need to be asked now and empirical evidence sought. Has environmentalism come to serve the political Right and can global US hegemony threats to the planet be used to justify the globalization of financial and other 'power' systems? Why is 'joint implementation' under the Framework Convention on Climate Change Convention so strongly resisted, while experimentation with renewable energy technologies in the South using taxpayers' money via the Global Environment Facility is approved by environmental lobbies? Is eco-technological modernization in Europe not already assisting in the creation of a social 'underclass', flexible workers, and a highly innovative elite?

Most Northern political elites (as those of the Asian rim) have indeed recognized the innovative potential of environmentalism. This means that they have escaped the influence of the natural science research enterprise and selected from aspects of knowledge available on environmental risks and threats those which appear solvable by technological 'fixes' and hence investment-cum-regulation. It then needs to be asked what the consequences of the above attempts to implement goals defined by global environmentalism are. Do they, under certain conditions, contribute to the weakening or social cohesion and participation (and hence of governability)?

'The environment' has been absorbed into official development rhetoric, mainstream economic theory, and most research agendas. Given the world view of scientific expertise in which the ordinary human being and 'the political' in general are suppressed or ignored in the name of efficiency, the direct benefits of economic growth and innovation cannot but be 'captured' by elites.[16] What is the responsibility of our political institutions, and their encouragement of single-issue lobbying? Restating the fundamental question: has the tendency of environmentalism to ignore politics, and of economics to devalue it (and therefore humanity), led to 'the environment' being 'captured' by Northern elites with right-wing convictions to become a tool of what used to be called 'international capitalism' or now 'casino capitalism' (Strange, 1988)?

SCIENTIFIC INSTITUTIONS AS POLITICAL ACTORS

The production and dissemination of data and knowledge derived from the research enterprise has a growing influence on the global political economy; it justifies this influence increasingly with reference to global environmental threats, in its tacit collusion with eco-alarmism.[17] The scientific research institutions of the 'hard' sciences are important actors in the technological innovation process, but their major aim is improved understanding, not the solving of problems through the application of knowledge. In any case, such knowledge is of little use if the problem is rooted in human institutions and behaviour.

The creation of knowledge as a commodity is also becoming more rather than less dependent on political, corporate, or charitable patronage. By specializing in the production of 'policy-relevant' findings for government, the role of science as a political actor is increased, for it must try to shape policy to serve its own, always threatened, project and create demand for future knowledge. Research has a direct interest in ensuring the adoption of research intensive policies, and hence in uncertainty and the identification of research intensive problems. Scientists and engineers have a stake in uncertain problems that appear solvable, as well as in the development of new technologies that improve their capacity to measure and observe. Research institutions do not, therefore, make independent or value-free policy-advisors (Boehmer-Christiansen, 1993, 1994a, b). We cannot take 'scientific advice' for granted, not because it is 'constructed' by human beings, but because human beings cannot but constitute an interested party.

As one of the first beneficiaries of the information revolution (telematics), the international science community gained influence through its ability to communicate rapidly, use networks and create 'consensus' that could rapidly be disseminated via the media and institutions of learning to a global range of institutions.[18] The global research enterprise captured the environmental regime formation process, with the support of inter-governmental bureaucracies, specific commercial interests offering technological solutions, e.g. CFC substitution for ozone depleting substances, nuclear power, renewables, energy efficiency to replace cheap coal and oil because of their power over information and their acceptance as objective authority.

Scientific institutions are political actors like other institutions in the global game of obtaining rent from economic activity. The declining utility of the physical sciences to contemporary elites (as well as advancing computer and information technology) may have attracted them towards 'eco-alarmism' and the modelling of world futures in order to scare politicians. The natural sciences are eager, and able, to study the planet Earth mathematically as a set of linked (by computer) physical systems. Humankind, if considered at all, is viewed as a biological species and agent of change united by its use of money and tools. Decision-making becomes a technocratic mathematical exercise based on the assumed rational behaviour of individuals. A vast research agenda is awaiting the social sciences, providing that they do not adopt a political perspective.

The limits of (natural) scientific knowledge in 'measuring' a selected environmental problem need to be understood better in order to protect environmental policy and subsequent innovation from excessive professionalization, on the one hand, and political manipulation on the other. Too much science may be bad for innovation because the push for application is missing; but too much innovation may harm society as well. Societies will have to decide through political processes whether they:

- ignore 'the environment' because they have other things to worry about;
- strive to understand an environmental 'problem' to advance the frontiers of pure knowledge;
- regulate environmental consumption by NIMBYism (not in my backyard protests) and taxation policies; or
- rush into precautionary or remedial action and innovate along a broad front.

Some societies may be able to achieve a balance, but this should surely not be decided at the global level for the benefit of an illusionary global benefit which, in practice, means the benefit of elites in charge of global policies.

SCIENCE, INNOVATION, AND ENVIRONMENT
IDENTIFYING LINKAGES

Assuming that environmental politics decide what new types of knowledge are needed and how knowledge is used; that research is an actor in this process; that environmental politics remain primarily a national process with deep roots in culture and tradition; and that the politics of policy formation link scientific research and innovation to the environment, then a number of fairly distinct roles of the 'environment' can be observed:

1 symbolic – preserving the political status quo by diverting public attention to future problems, with reallocation of resources to research but little technological innovation;
2 stimulating technological innovation processes which strengthens political/commercial centres at the expense of peripheries;
3 stimulating technological and institutional innovation to serve political centres and enhance corporate decisions and investments;
4 stimulating innovation to serve a 'common interest' or a 'public good' such as welfare, employment.

Specific forces, geographical factors and historical contexts will decide a particular national outcome. The interaction of all of these and their realizations in practical life have impacts not only on how relatively simple criteria of assessment such as economic efficiency or competitiveness are interpreted, but also on socio-political processes.

Given these assumptions, innovation stimulated by science and environmentalism remains a culture-based activity and not something that is likely to be readily globalized by multi-national companies, irrespective of how globalized the scientific research enterprise may be. Their products, however, are easily sold and hence 'globalized'. While reinforcing links between environmental protection and regulation (or competitive advantage and economic lobby, when marketing its own expertise, it tends to promise wealth and welfare especially to the poor.[19]

It follows that scientific knowledge as an input to the innovation process will continue to serve those national/cultural interests that are able to reap the benefits of technical innovation which remains largely a national activity. Green technological innovation is the subject of much current interest in the OECD and Europe because it is assumed to serve the economy by developing 'clean technology', new materials, biotechnology, telematics, information highways, etc. Steps are under way to reduce certain emissions globally by using 'best' technology. This will involve 'technology transfer' from OECD countries with loans or with grants supported by OECD tax payers.[20] Clean technology research disseminates information between corporate, political interests and regulators, with the latter increasingly aiding the former.[21]

About 95 per cent of global R&D is concentrated in OECD countries and is naturally directed at meeting the needs (or desires) of their elites. Most new technologies and innovations can be presented as more environment-friendly in one way or another because there is no, and can be no, single measure for environment-friendliness. Those researching clean technology find that environment goals at the industrial-cum-commercial level serve only to create competitive advantage. For governments, the environment tends to become a justification for 'forcing' technological change by demanding investment, creating new markets, or pushing competitors out of markets. Economies will indeed become more efficient and cleaner. What do societies gain? Surely very little if there is not institutional change as well, in particular change enabling societies to influence science and technology trajectories.

Institutional innovation may be the underlying condition for technological innovation.[22] Institutions, by changing power, income, and welfare relationships between groups, create new green 'markets' and policies or act to resist their development. Institutional innovation may require a change in the distribution of power in order to improve the availability, distribution, and application of new and existing knowledge. Here too the 'environmental' argument (e.g. sustainability) can be used politically, e.g. to strengthen local government vis-à-vis centralizing governments, as is happening in the UK, or to increase the power of national governments to obtain information from industry, or of one ministry vis-à-vis another.[23] At the global level this raises the question of whether the environmental-cum-innovation mission indeed assists those social forces which, as some of the participants of the UNCED process believe, counter exploitation by a 'global economy' by empowering local communities and implementing 'sustainable' development from the 'bottom-up', rather than becoming greenwash for the neglect of the poor everywhere.

RESEARCH QUESTIONS FOR THE SOCIAL SCIENCES

One task of the social sciences is to study innovation from a sociological and political perspective with a view to ensuring that its benefits become more widely available. This task is difficult to accomplish if research is funded by contracts deliberately seeking apolitical allegedly value-free advice. It needs to be done without conceptually undermining the role of the state and states as decision-takers and enforcers or of scientific research as such. States themselves may need protection because they are the primary and often only instrument societies have evolved to define and protect common and longer-term public interests and values against those of particular groups.

It might be asked whether the attention paid to global and regional environmental destruction since the 1970s was encouraged by governments wishing to draw attention away from the globalization of poverty. Environmental improvements generally benefit the rich, while the more damaging activities and developments take place in areas inhabited by the politically weak. This would appear to be a normal outcome of democratic decision-making in a society where political power remains de facto unevenly distributed. But can the hypothesis that the research enterprise advised political elites that global environmental protection was the task they should fund in the name of stimulating technical innovation be tested? Or did 'public concern' really press political elites into action, with more research simply being the easiest and cheapest response? By whom and how is 'concern' created? Far too much of the environmental policy literature assumes public concern as a starting point of advocacy. Environmental concern is also a tool of political manipulation or governance (Boehmer-Christiansen, 1990).

The major research area must surely be to ask whether observed responses to the threatened environmental disasters have resulted in overall innovative responses and whether these will:

1 create wealth at home and export opportunities abroad, especially to the world's peasants, slum dwellers, and unemployed youths;
2 initiate a new social as well as technological 'paradigm';
3 create more fairness between peoples as well as more benign, less destructive relationships with the biosphere.

The idea that elites use knowledge to serve their own pre-existing ends applies to states as well as corporations and non-governmental organizations. It raises questions which only case studies can hope to answer:

4 how each has used and sponsored science in relation to environmental protection;
5 whether, how and why the 'environment', or the goal of sustainability, have stimulated innovation in a specific society;

6 how environmental protection and innovation relate to the more fundamental functions of governance.

The factors, forces, and processes, including the role of international institutions and agendas, in the emergence of 'the environment' as either a progressive, innovative mission, or as conservative agenda designed to resist or prevent change, even as a tool to maintain ideological hegemony, can then be explored (Kohler-Koch, 1994).

These questions focus on the role of government as a facilitator and ultimate decision-maker in negotiations which must define a public interest rather than produce a mere resultant of single issue lobbying. Such research would teach us a great deal about each other's societies and the rapid changes they are undergoing and lead towards a better evaluation of various complaints about international environmental policies and regimes, going beyond the officially encouraged collection of social statistics for the building of databases and models. It would extend the clean technology project, already of interest to governments but addressing only technological innovation, to questions concerned with:

7 environmental institutional innovation (conceptual, legal, administrative, organizational, educational);
8 assessment of the socio-political impacts of seeking green competitiveness, especially in technologically weak countries;
9 the role of scientific institutions in directing research policy and R&D spending.

How responsive are science and innovation to social needs rather than internally decided trajectories? What type of changes were advocated, for example, by Green Parties, compared to what was implemented? Which proposals were selected by socio-economic–political contexts and transformed into successful innovation? Why has environmentalism been so creative as well as flexible in its political utility to some elites rather than others? A study of languages can help here in unravelling how different cultures have observed 'environmentalism'. If only English is used we tend to think in one way and evaluate in similar fashion.[24] Identifying institutional innovation and assessing the social and political impacts of the ecological modernization of the most industrialized nations will require complex qualitative analysis which must develop from within cultural contexts. The study of innovation must become human, not system or regime-centred. This cannot be achieved by economistic analysis given its reductionist view of the human individual and static view of society. The challenge to the social sciences is profound. Probably the only way to approach the subject of interaction between science, environment, and innovation, and their combined impact on the distribution of power, is through case studies which do not make arbitrary distinctions, such as between national and international activities or decisions, but do take cultural contexts into account. How do the different societies conceptualize the interaction and how do they deal with any political implications?

CONCLUSION

The socio-political utility of eco-alarmism is considerable and ranges from the justification of 'old' political and economic agendas, including 'cultural imperialism', to the promotion of feminist, socialist as well as extreme nationalist programmes. Eco-alarmism has already been astonishingly innovative both technologically and institutionally, creating a new 'paradigm' for economic progress in the North. However, elsewhere it appears to be advocating, rather successfully, a form of 'ecologism' which gains political support in the North because it creates global markets for Northern knowledge while containing competition from the 'South'. No wonder the South (and some 're-industrializing' nations) remains suspicious, especially of green NGOs currently so active in shaping international policies.

The broader political and cultural impacts of green policies therefore need analysis. Democratic political institutions must remain empowered to make and enforce environmental decisions, and the social sciences might be handmaids of such institutions. If we fail, I suspect that the conceptual underpinnings of scientific environmentalism are powerful and elitist enough to achieve little more than commercial globalization serving global elites wherever they may be found geographically. This needs to be resisted in the name of human sovereignty, diversity, and the political sustainability of common interest institutions, surely the ultimate conditions for environmental protection.

Eco-alarmism and its potential for stimulating innovation does more than provide science and technology with new contemporary agendas and pleas for support. The declining usefulness of the physical sciences to the contemporary state and advancing computer and information technology are attracting the natural sciences not only towards complex earth systems, but also towards 'eco-alarmism' and uncertainty as justifications for demanding public resources. This lays the foundation for future technological change with far too little societal debate indeed. Outsiders feel trapped in technological determinism. Politics needs to open the research and development system, and institutional innovations with practical feasibility are needed. Innovative success here would appear to depend on how benign and realistic the conceptions are which the research community and other actors construct and disseminate. The environmental problematique as a political–scientific construct has attracted relatively little funding in the social sciences, and this serves as evidence for the concerns expressed here.[25] Should we suspect that eco-alarmism, as increasingly 'operationalized' by prevailing political structures, may serve to stimulate the dissemination of a politically maligned interpretation of reality, as well as that of 'clean technology'?

To summarize the many issues which arise from the interactions between science, innovation, and environment in society, general research topics have been explored dealing with three fundamental questions:

- what are the impacts of existing environmental policies and measures on the distribution of decision-making power, work, welfare, and income distribution, as well as conflict potential in any society or the European Union;
- how is the society–environment dichotomy dealt with in the conceptual thought of a society;
- how can observed differences be explained, and what is their impact on supra-national policy information?

The designers and implementors of environmental instruments are not asking how their society, or international relations, can be improved but how these can be more effectively manipulated to generate innovation for the sake of gaining competitive advantage, i.e. for the sake of confirming existing structures of economic power. The impacts of eco-alarmism and its potential for both stimulating and repressing innovation also needs examination as a means for making technological change socially responsive and politically sustainable, especially at the global level. A new social theory may be needed which includes nature without setting it up as an ideal of purity defiled by humanity.

The links between science, innovation, and environmental protection are ambivalent and certainly not linear. Combined, they reinforce each other. Uncontrolled, they may turn into a new political force which may push us blindly towards a kind of globalization that, by increasing inequality and poverty, may make the world less governable and more violent. Innovation links problems to solutions, but political processes first have to create an effective need for both, taking into account political as well as economic impacts. Complex processes are at work nationally and globally. They can only be recognized thorough interdisciplinary and comparative research that does not strive to be apolitical.

NOTES

* This chapter has been adapted from, Boehmer-Christiansen, S. (1995), 'Reflections on the politics linking science, environment and innovation', *Innovation*, September, Carfax.

1 I have studied environmental policy formation in relation to: marine pollution control (1972–1981); acid rain (since 1980); and global warming (since 1984). A societal comparison formed the basis of joint books with Skea (Boehmer-Christiansen and Skea, 1991/1993) and with Weidner (Boehmer-Christiansen and Weidner, 1995).

2 For example, by Redclift (1993).

3 For a discussion of eco-alarmism and modernization, see Mol and Spaargarten (1993).

5 The IICR conference was an excellent example of this vigour, though profound political doubts were also raised. At the global level, the IPCC working group summarizes a consensus of climate modelling efforts, while the Human Dimension of Global Change project undertaken under ISSC auspices (but largely an American data collection/modelling effort using the largest available computers and space observation data) hopes to 'integrate' its findings with those of the natural sciences working on the International Geosphere-Biosphere Project. See Boehmer-Christansen (1994a, b).

5 The MacArthur Foundation, for example, is funding research designed for advocacy and dissemination purposes which is directed at 'greening' World Bank credit policies, as well as governance structures in the name or democracy and transparency; de facto this means that 'outsiders', like unelected and unaccountable NGOs, can influence policy directly as well as obtain lucrative consultancies as environmental advisors.

6 For an example, see commentary by Hunter and Udall (1994) on the World Bank's New Inspection Panel.

7 Robert Evans, of the Science Studies Centre at the University of Bath, has concluded from his study of falsification and uncertainty in macro-economic modelling, that 'economic policy based on macroeconomic models is based ultimately on the convictions of the modelling team about how the economy works.' [*Science Policy Support Group News*, November 1994). I have concluded that the same is true for climate change models, though how climate works may be rather better understood than economies. At least it does not change as fast!

8 The author advocates the idea of democratic planning.

9 In Britain, subsidies were withdrawn from the coal industry and given to the nuclear industry with reference to environmental arguments.

10 I should like to thank Hans Dieleman, of Erasmus University for his discussions of this issue while walking through Vienna in November 1994.

11 'State socialism' similarly served an elite which privileged scientists and engineers, but failed to be innovative institutionally and technologically. The amount of 'surplus' produced by an economy, and hence efficiency and competitiveness, are surely politically irrelevant if the 'surplus' is allocated only to the elite.

12 In the UK monetarism combined with single-party conviction politics created more private affluence at the top and much more public squalor and poverty elsewhere. The term 'miracle' was used confidently in the late 1980s on the basis of statistical evidence of fast economic growth. In fact efficiency gains were brought about by 'demanning', that is unemployment and transferring social costs from the economy to a reluctant state committed to cutting expenditure and reducing revenue apart from privatizing public assets without compensation. If one listens to some British politicians today, the miracle is about to be repeated thanks to low cost labour and 'flexibility'.

13 Rich (1994) (Environmental Defense Fund) attacks the institution rather than the sources of its funds, and hence the investment policies of wealthy elites and advocates a degree of

environmental conditionality which would turn recipients of World Bank money into even more dependent 'colonies' of international finance, though undoubtedly greener ones.

14 In the German case, political adjustment was possible because of huge (and unexpected) transfer of public monies from West to East.

15 In the European Union, policy pressures are really re-regulatory. Once national regimes have been weakened, EC regulation can step in to enhance political integration and strengthen the competitiveness of dominant industries, often German industry. Weaker firms are 'merged' or disappear.

16 Proposals to increase indirect taxes in order to internalize externalities as more efficient abound and allow parliaments to be by-passed. The idea is attractive to treasuries which need more 'non-tax' incomes. Privatizing the environment by allowing trade in pollution permits and energy taxes, and giving security of tenure to large landlords (methods that owe much to conventional economic theory), appears to have persuaded many environmentalists that this should be the way forward.

17 The list of exaggerated environmental threats is long: soil erosion in the USA, oil pollution of the ocean in the 1970s, Waldsterben, desertification, radioactivity, global warming, ozone depletion causing cancer.

18 See Tuang (1994). Tuang agrees with Albert Gore that the free flow of ideas will remove outdated rules and institutions and create new ones. The questions of who can join, and who will be excluded from these new forms of instant communications are not raised.

19 See *International Research and Assessment: proposals for better organization and decision making*, USA, Carnegie Commission, 1992. These claims are made on the assumption that there are 'international needs for science advice in the field of environment' (p. 21). The report was written by what might be called the world's most prestigious private research lobby (Sigma Yi, JOC, WWF, Harvard University, US Meteorological Society, the National Research Council, UN, NOOA, MIT, WRI).

20 Maurice Strong may serve as symbol for environmental globalism. He organized the two major environment conferences (Stockholm and Rio) and has direct interests in the oil and nuclear industries.

21 This is the message of the UK Advisory Committee on Business and the Environment, *Fourth Progress Report*, DTI/DoE, London, October 1994. Environmental regulation must not burden industry, but enhance competitiveness. Subsidization of new (green) technologies is strongly advocated.

22 The UK has been worrying for decades about why it has been relatively unsuccessful in transforming new knowledge and inventions into innovations. The answer is likely to be an institutional one, but institutions are much harder to change than policies and ministers.

23 See Boehmer-Christiansen (1995). It was not scientific concern alone which brought global warming to the global political agenda, but the political utility of the issue for a broad range of interests, the most powerful among them were new energy technologies needing markets and subsidies when the price of oil collapsed in 1986.

24 The German 'nachhaltig' or 'dauerhaft' do not mean the same as 'sustainable' ('erhaltbar' may be 'better'). I am not aware of a German equivalent or 'environmentalism', i.e. the ideology of Umweltschutz. Does this mean that in spite of its tendency for abstraction, German culture does not recognize the ideological dimension?

25 Global warming predictions do require 'dehumanized' quantitative socio-economic scenarios (GNP, emission volumes, population, energy prices, and technology 'predictions') and project straight lines many decades into the future. Included into uncertain global climate models to produce dire warnings (and uncertainties), society remains a single, 'rational' but apolitical species divided at the most into equal countries. The German publication of the Wissenschafiliche Beirat der Bundesregierung Globale Umweltveranderung, *Welt im Wandel (Elemente einer Systemanalyse)*, WBGU, Bremerhaven 1993, offers an extreme example which in essence is based on assumptions and trend analysis.

REFERENCES

Boehmer-Christiansen, S. (1990), 'Energy policy and public opinion: manipulation of environmental threats by vested interests', *Energy Policy*, Vol. 18, No. 9.

Boehmer-Christiansen, S. (1992), 'Taken to the cleaners: the fate of the East German energy sector since 1990', *Environmental Politics*, Vol. 1, No. 2.

Boehmer-Christiansen, S. (1993), 'Science policy, the IPCC and the climate convention: the codification of a global research agenda', *Energy and Environment*, Vol. 4, pp. 362–408.

Boehmer-Christiansen, S. (1994a), 'Global climate protection policy: the limits of scientific advice', Parts I and II, *Global Environmental Change*, Vol. 14, Nos 2 and 3.

Boehmer-Christiansen, S. (1994b), 'A scientific agenda for climate policy?', *Nature*, Vol. 372, No. 1.

Boehmer-Christiansen, S. (1995), 'Britain and the intergovernmental panel on climate change: the impacts of scientific advice on global warming', Parts I and II, *Environmental Politics*, Vol. 4, Nos 1 and 2.

Boehmer-Christiansen, S. and Skea, J. F. (1991/1993), *Acid Politics: energy and environmental policies in Britain and Germany*, London, Belhaven.

Boehmer-Christiansen, S. and Weidner, H. (1995), *The Regulation of Vehicle Emission in Britain and Germany: the catalytic conversion*, London, Pinter.

Dugger, N. (1988), 'An institutional theory of economic planning', in Tool, M. R. (ed.), *Evolutionary Economics – Volume II: Institutional theory and policy*, New York, Sharpe.

Gorz, A. (1980), *Ecology as Politics*, London, Pluto Press.

Hunter, D. B. and Udall, L. (1994), 'Overview', *Environment*, Vol. 36, No. 9.

Kohler-Koch, (1994), 'The evolution of organized interests in the EC-driving forces; co-evolution or new type of governance', Paper prepared for the IPSA World Congress, Berlin, 21–25 August.

Mol, A. F. and Spaargarten, G. (1993), 'Environment, modernity and the risk-society: the apocalyptical horizon of environmental reforms', *International Sociology*, Vol. 8, No. 4.

North, R. D. (1995), *Life on a Modern Planet: a manifesto for progress*, Manchester, Manchester University Press.

Redclift, M. R. (1993), 'Development and the environment: managing the contradictions', *Innovation*, Vol. 6, pp. 444–56.

Reis, E. and Marguils, S. (1991), 'Options for slowing Amazon jungle clearing', in Dombush, R. and Potera, J. (eds), *Global Warning Economic Policy Responses*, London, MIT Press, pp. 335–74.

Rich, B. (1994), *Mortgaging the Earth*, London, Earthscan.

Sand, P. H. (1990), *Lessons Learned in Global Governance*, New York, World Resources Institute.

Strange, S. (1988), *States and Markets* (second edition), London, Pinter.

Tuang, P. (1994), 'Institutional instability, governance and telematics', Brighton, SPRU, Paper prepared for the IPSA World Congress, Berlin, 21–25 August.

INDEX